On Interpreting Keynes

A study in reconciliation

Bruce Littleboy

London and New York

First published 1990 by Routledge
11 New Fetter Lane, London EC4P 4EE

Simultaneously published in the USA and Canada
by Routledge
a division of Routledge, Chapman and Hall, Inc.
29 West 35th Street, New York, NY 10001

Typeset by LaserScript Limited, Mitcham, Surrey
Printed in Great Britain

British Library Cataloguing in Publication Data

Littleboy, Bruce, *1956–*
    On interpreting Keynes : a study in reconciliation.
    1. Economics. Theories of Keynes, John Maynard, 1883–1946
    I. Title
    303.156

    ISBN 0-415-04475-8

Library of Congress Cataloging in Publication Data

Littleboy, Bruce, 1956–
    On interpreting Keynes : a study in reconciliation / Bruce Littleboy.
        p.   cm.
    Includes bibliographical references
    ISBN 0-415-04475-8
    1. Keynesian economics. I. Title.
HB99.7.L58   1990
330.15'6—dc20   90-8400
                                                           CIP

Epigraph

If the author has already created something, our historian will set out clearly the past and the probable future course of his development, he will put him with others and compare them, and separate by analysis the choice of his material and his treatment; he will wisely sum up the author and give him general advice for his future path. The most astonishing works may be created; the swarm of historical neuters will always be in their place, ready to consider the author through their long telescopes. The echo is heard at once, but always in the form of 'criticism', though the critic never dreamed of the work's possibility a moment before. It never comes to have an influence, but only a criticism; and the criticism itself has no influence, but only breeds another criticism. ...They put their blotting paper on the blackest writing, and their thick brushes over the most graceful designs; these they call 'corrections' – and that is all. Their critical pens never cease to fly, for they have lost power over them; they are driven by their pens instead of driving them ...

The progress of science has been amazingly rapid in the last decade; but consider the savants, those exhausted hens. They are certainly not 'harmonious' natures; they can merely cackle more than before, because they lay eggs oftener; but the eggs are always smaller though their books are bigger.

Friedrich Nietzsche, *The Use and Abuse of History*, Bobbs-Merrill, New York, 2nd edn, 1957, pp. 33–4 and p. 46.

Contents

Preface

There is discontent about how the textbooks have come to interpret Keynes. Two major schools criticizing the textbook orthodoxy have emerged, the 'fundamentalist' and the Clower–Leijonhufvud (or 'reductionist') factions. There is almost no effective communication between them.

Upon closely examining the texts of the leading representatives of the respective schools, my finding is that there can be, and should be, a reconciliation. Both sides have valid criticisms of the conventional renditions of Keynes. Arguments between them, however, can often be traced to simple misunderstandings and to mere differences of emphasis.

The fundamentalists have been too quick to condemn Clower and Leijonhufvud. Defects in each approach can be repaired by drawing upon the insights of the other. If this is done, Keynesians can more effectively argue their case against new classical economics and legitimize, at least in principle, an activist role in demand management.

The reductionist position is particularly valid in terms of its interpretation of Keynes's views about the short run (dealt with in Part two), but the fundamentalists legitimately point to difficulties about Leijonhufvud's interpretation of long-run aspects in Keynes's writings (discussed in Part three).

Fundamentalism has been associated with a denial of the very existence of a Walrasian equilibrium; expectations can be volatile and many decisions made in historical time are irreversible. The reductionist position points to problems of co-ordination failure. Individual agents cannot reliably grope towards such an equilibrium. I argue (in Part four) that fundamentalism successfully points to the subjective character of economic affairs, but scope can be preserved for the reductionist view that suboptimal behaviour can be explained in part by determinate, objective constraints.

By suggesting that Keynes introduced the notion of a 'conventional equilibrium', I observe that behaviour under Knightian uncertainty need not be wayward and unruly. Conventions can enhance stability. They can form at suboptimal vectors, and no effective excess demand signals need be endogenously generated to disturb the system's state of rest. A long-run unemployment equilibrium is then possible.

Albeit often critical of others, the overall tone of this work is intended to be optimistic and constructive. In any growing branch of knowledge and conjecture, tendencies for the reconciliation of conflict do emerge. Even when an opportunity is grasped, an attempted synthesis none the less sometimes fails to find a proper focus and balance.

No one could sensibly postulate the existence of a smooth, automatic and benign tendency towards convergence. The past is difficult enough to fathom without confidently predicting the future as well. Nevertheless, many do tire of seemingly ceaseless squabbles, especially when patiently accumulated empirical evidence never really fits any simple worldview. Eclecticism can then foreshadow a formal synthesis.

In assessing the current state of any debate, it is never clear who is really winning. Alliances shift. Elites circulate, and after the lions who make the primary breakthroughs come the foxes who cunningly reformulate the questions. Insights of one school can be casually appropriated (after years of bitter dispute) by another and absorbed into its research programme. Macroeconomic theory itself evolves, and so does the consensus over the perceived significance of any phase of its development. Milton Friedman, for example, has become a respectable critic who has persuaded orthodox Keynesians to retreat from their ambitious attempts to use fiscal policy to finetune economies. Similarly, new Keynesians have accepted the rational expectations hypothesis in order to do battle with the new classicists over the issues of price flexibility and market clearing.

In the realm of doctrinal history, developments are likewise difficult to predict, and neither Keynesian fundamentalism nor reductionism has had the impact on economic theory their founders must have hoped for. Clower, Leijonhufvud and Shackle are all cited with respect, but macroeconomics has followed its own agenda. The terrain of the struggle between Keynesians and classicists has changed, and, while the technology of warfare has become more sophisticated, interest in Keynes's insights remains. A substantial group of economists continue to feel instinctively that markets do not function smoothly or reliably, and there is always some sympathy towards attempts to express such beliefs in a convincing, analytical form.

The literature grows, but not necessarily our understanding of Keynes. Interpreters of received doctrine stand on the shoulders of the great, but can their weight be borne? Perhaps Keynes's interpreters are slowly crushing him to death.

Bruce Littleboy

Acknowledgements

Thanks are extended to Ghanshyam Mehta who inspired my research into this area. Athol Fitzgibbons and Dick Staveley have also indirectly influenced this work. Encouragement from Geoff Harcourt, Robert Skidelsky, E. Roy Weintraub, Robert Clower and Axel Leijonhufvud supplied a much needed boost to morale.

To my parents, who supported me during my work on my PhD, and to my typists, Pam Tupe and Robyn Wieland, who struggled through the drafts, I also extend my thanks.

Financial support through the Baillieu Research Scholarship during my studies is gratefully acknowledged.

I am grateful for permission to quote from Donald E. Moggridge (ed.), *The Collected Writings of John Maynard Keynes*, and thank the Royal Economic Society and Macmillan (London and Basingstoke).

For permission to quote from Axel Leijonhufvud, *On Keynesian Economics and the Economics of Keynes; a study in monetary theory* and *Information and Coordination; essays in macroeconomic theory*, I thank Oxford University Press, New York.

Professor Leijonhufvud kindly supplied me with some of his lesser-known writings and gave permission to quote his unpublished UCLA discussion paper, 'The varieties of price theory...'.

Part one

Chapter one

Introduction

The inherited literature

Over the decades since the publication of Keynes's *The General Theory of Employment Interest and Money*[1] there has emerged a 'Keynesian' macroeconomic model which has become deeply entrenched in the textbook literature and loyally upheld by a substantial group of academic economists. Although differences of emphasis and detail exist amongst the adherents of the orthodox position, there remains a broad consensus that their formalized model is a useful, albeit highly simplified, representation of Keynes's basic position.

These established views, however, have been subjected to increasing scrutiny and criticism during the 1960s and 1970s.[2] Academic interest in this area has continued into the 1980s without any apparent sign of abatement. Dissent has not merely focused upon matters pertaining to the recognition of Keynes's rightful status in the history of economic thought. It is not solely concerned with setting the record straight as to whether Keynes or somebody else should be credited with the discovery of particular theoretical concepts and be recognized as the first advocate of counter-cyclical fiscal policy. On the contrary, strident controversy surrounds the very theoretical foundations of *The General Theory* itself. The purpose of the rebellion against the orthodox position is to demonstrate that a true understanding of Keynes's perception of the forces governing aggregate behaviour cannot be properly assimilated into the conventional model.

Objections have been raised against the orthodox view which held that Keynes had not really developed a revolutionary general theory as he himself had believed. The standard approach was to argue that Keynes's insights could be incorporated with established classical theory to form the neoclassical synthesis, thereby converting his theory into a special case characterized by rigid money wages and absolute liquidity preference.[3] Discussion within the majority school proceeded to centre around whether the liquidity trap was empirically significant or whether such a narrow and artificial concept deserved to be regarded as a critical assumption required to explain persistent unemployment. Many of the dominant school have come to accept the theoretical proposition that balanced deflation will raise the real value of money balances beyond the amount which would plausibly be hoarded in speculative reserves. On this ground they believed that price flexibility would result in increased expenditure sufficient to restore full employment. They conceded, however, that in practice one ought not to rely on this means of generating the required level of real demand. This remorseless logic has led many to believe that only the assumption of wage rigidity, based on Keynes's alleged reliance on money illusion, should sensibly be regarded as being essential to his doctrine of persistent unemployment. But classical economists had already argued that trade union monopolies caused unemployment through their excessive wage demands and refusal to accept cuts in money wages. The inescapable conclusion was that Keynes had added virtually nothing to established theory.[4] Even the so-called 'new Keynesians' uphold the long-term tendency for full employment to be attained but modify what they see as Keynes's approach based on rigid money wages by making them merely sticky.

This chain of reasoning implies that much of *The General Theory* is superfluous and that, although his works contained rich insight, Keynes was not a rigorous theoretician, but rather 'a great man dabbling in economics'.[5] The quest for rigour really began after Keynes.

Johnson accused Keynes of dilating

> rather pretentiously.... And above all there is the pervading influence of Keynes the born propagandist, with his instinct for dramatizing his ideas...fortified as polemicists often are by a certain obtuseness in understanding the arguments of his adversaries.[6]

Obviously such attitudes give rise to considerable latitude in the interpretation of Keynes's writings. As Leijonhufvud points out:

> If Keynes does not fit, so much the worse for him – the [standard] model represents what Keynes actually meant or really intended and, consequently, what he should have said.... The impression of Keynes that one gains from such comments is that of a Delphic oracle, half hidden in billowing fumes, mouthing earth-shattering profundities whilst in a senseless trance – an oracle revered for his powers, to be sure, but not worthy of the same respect as that accorded the High Priests whose function it is to interpret the revelations.[7]

The academic economist has recently been exposed to a plethora of rival models intended to convey the substance of Keynesian macrotheory.[8] The adherents of particular approaches seem to have great difficulty in convincing others both of the internal consistency of their own models and of the legitimacy in attributing such models to Keynes himself. Examples are abundant. Don Patinkin is troubled by David Roberts' approach regarding the synthesis of the concepts of aggregate supply and aggregate demand.[9] Sidney Weintraub is similarly concerned about how these concepts are to be properly presented. He argues that some modern attempts to develop an alternative diagrammatic representation, which explains the breakdown of nominal income into its price and quantity components, are seriously misleading.[10] Kregel[11] is hostile to Shackle's preference for an analysis proceeding in terms of *ex ante* and *ex post* phraseology. Neither is Kregel impressed by the accounts given by Clower, Grossman, Phelps and Arrow who treat Keynes's economics as an analysis of disequilibrium behaviour. He suggests that Keynes adopted an equilibrium approach and that Keynes had three models between which he slipped backward and forward.

Not only is there disagreement about the exact specification of the model truly reflecting Keynes's intentions. Models are being suggested which are of vastly different character and which use fundamentally different analytical techniques. Theoreticians now must reflect upon the worth of fix-price systems, which involve the non-Walrasian feature of quantity adjustments, as a means of representing Keynes's views. There is also a newcomer, catastrophe theory, which is a controversial form of analysis occasionally adopted to cast light upon features of disequilibrium behaviour.[12]

There are now many models currently being employed apart from the usual IS-LM and 45° constructions, but disputes are not simply confined to the problem of formalizing the problem of unemployment. There appear to be substantive differences between the various alternatives. Coddington has identified three broad categories within which the major styles of analysis can be subsumed.[13]

First, there is the 'fundamentalist' view that Keynes's recognition of uncertainty about the future implies that economies are inherently unstable and that aggregate behaviour is unpredictable. Formalized model building and econometric studies are seen by extreme fundamentalists as largely a waste of time. There is also 'hydraulic' Keynesianism, which flourished in the 1940s and 1950s, and became the textbook orthodoxy. Adherents of this school have faith in the study of national accounting aggregates which can be manipulated, and, it is hoped, fine-tuned, by government policy. The third approach, which has gained in popularity due to the efforts of Clower and Leijonhufvud, is that of 'reconstituted reductionism' in which the process of disequilibrium is considered from the viewpoint of the individual transactor so that rigour in the analysis can be achieved. This resort to methodological individualism is designed to ensure that processes, which are argued to occur at the aggregate level, in fact are logically possible outcomes of individual actions and choices.[14]

To commence with the hydraulic approach, Leijonhufvud argues that standard 'Keynesian' models misinterpret Keynes and he considers that neither the diagrammatic *IS-LM* approach nor the static, mathematical, simultaneous-equation method grasp the essence of Keynes's revolutionary contribution. This at least is one area where the fundamentalists and reductionists agree. They have a common enemy. The initial misunderstanding of Keynes has resulted in the later factional differences which merely centred around the slopes of the *IS* and *LM* curves. Because Keynes was thought simply to have revised classical economics by making restrictive assumptions about certain interest elasticities which he supposedly thought were more realistic, the main value of his writings was believed to be in their practical relevance in justifying fiscal policy. Policy makers could hardly rely on the Pigou effect automatically to restore full employment in the long run, and discussion concerned the form which intervention should take.

Nowadays, a 'Keynesian' is anyone who believes that there is any useful scope for demand management regardless of whether monetary or fiscal policy is the chosen instrument. Debate now centres on devising theories to explain real-world pricing behaviour and devising feedback rules likely to improve macroeconomic performance.

One purpose of this work is to examine the arguments made by Leijonhufvud and the fundamentalists that the orthodox school at its birth misunderstood Keynes's theoretical position. Responses to internal and external pressures were shaped by what was regarded, most likely erroneously, as central to Keynes's system. First-generation Keynesians had mistakenly attributed an unqualified support for fiscal policy to him. Attempts to rationalize the need for fiscal policy pointed attention to irrelevant issues. Leijonhufvud maintains that the majority school were in error to describe *The General Theory* as an entirely clean break from the *Treatise*.[15] He prefers to read the former in the light of the latter and suggests that a continuity of thought exists between the two. Only then can theoretical innovations of *The General Theory* be identified and Keynes's change of stance in relation to policy be understood. Fundamentalists, by contrast, maintain that Keynes advocated profound social and institutional reforms. Bastard Keynesianism is criticized by fundamentalist post Keynesians for fostering the cult of fine-tuning and for overlooking, if not positively suppressing, Keynes's true message.

In order to assess the contribution of Keynes's interpreters we shall be required to follow in their footsteps. If exegetical legend has formed a smokescreen around 'what Keynes really said' then it will be necessary to examine the relevant texts and make up our own minds.

This is no mean task for *The General Theory* is considered by some to be poorly written. Furthermore, Keynes does not tell us unambiguously what he himself considers to be the relationship between *The General Theory* and the *Treatise*. He writes: 'The relation between this book and my *Treatise on Money*...is probably clearer to myself than it will be to others; and what in my own mind is a natural evolution in a line of thought...may sometimes strike the reader as a confusing change of view.'[16]

Another problem which makes any interpretation of Keynes somewhat hazardous is the necessity to interpret *silence*. *The General Theory* focuses on the determination of employment in a simplified financial environment. Was this because he considered monetary matters of less importance than before or was it that he had already written his *Treatise* and was therefore content to abbreviate his discussion of the monetary and financial sector so that he could concentrate on the determination of employment where his contribution was the more original and provocative?[17] *The General Theory* provides no explicit answer and we are left to ponder the meaning of Keynes's change of emphasis.

Although it may be difficult to determine what Keynes really said, sometimes it will prove easier to show that some popular interpretations are what Keynes never said. Apart from these instances where Keynes explicitly contradicts his interpreters, the argument might sometimes depend on 'many small indications, not lending themselves to quotation, by which one writer can feel whether another writer has at the back of his head the same root ideas or different ones'.[18] Consequently there will sometimes be a speculative tenor to the subsequent exposition. To be able to deal with delicate problems of textual exegesis in such a fashion requires considerable reliance upon the readers' willingness to attempt to divest themselves of preconceptions about the fundamental character of Keynes's analysis. This asks a great deal especially because the tincture of personal predilections might be detected in the position to be taken by the writer himself.

The question naturally arises as to whether such an exercise in comparing Keynes with his interpreters merely provides entertainment to a handful of academics who happen to be interested in the history of economic thought. It is argued that this is not so. On the surface it would seem that the recent flurry of activity in reinterpreting Keynes is simply to set the historical record straight. In fact, the contributors are often using Keynes's words to express their own views. How else can the passion and the persistence of the debate be explained? There is much to be said for Patinkin's view that nowadays we ought to be able to speak for ourselves and not fanatically seek support from the ancient and holy text.[19] But, on the other hand, if one believes that we can still learn something useful from *The General Theory*, then surely we are entitled to re-examine it.

Sufficient time has also passed for a substantial literature on interpreting the interpreters to have accumulated and for further confusion and misunderstandings to have become entrenched. It would be impossible to refer to all the literature which has emerged on the subject of stating in detail what Keynes said and whether his arguments were sound. So many permutations of viewpoint abound that it would add needless complexity to keep track scrupulously of which authority said exactly what. Too many decades have passed for it to be possible to disentangle the imbroglio of what Keynes said, what interpreters think Keynes said, whether the classicists said what Keynes thought they said, whether the classicists had already said what Keynes said and whether what Keynes said was valid. To compound the confusion, misunderstandings about the meaning of the terminology used by the protagonists have been rife. (One need only refer to the infamous savings equals investment debate for ample evidence of this.)

In view of such considerations, the goal here is not to build a comprehensive and precisely specified model which is true to the letter (or spirit) of *The General Theory*. Little attention will be paid to certain isolated issues, which are thought by some to be of great importance, such as whether employment should be measured in wage units, whether the capital stock can be measured at all or whether Keynes had, or ought to have had, a more diverse menu of financial assets in his theory of liquidity preference. There are many issues like these which are able to inflame the ardour of some economists. The concern here is of a more pristine variety. An attempt will be made to explain, at the logical and intuitive level, the nature and causes of involuntary unemployment. In the process, what are regarded as rival perspectives on Keynes can be reconciled. This is a worthwhile project in view of the increasing popularity of recently formulated search and rational expectations models in which the idea of involuntary unemployment, as Keynes understood it, is denied and with it the desirability of some forms of macroeconomic intervention.[20]

This is therefore to some degree both a 'Reconsideration of *The General Theory*', to employ the sub-title of Victoria Chick's recent book, as well as a sort of 'Guide to Keynes's Interpreters'.[21]

This work attempts to tread a path through a confusing array of alternative means by which Keynes's insights have been, with varying degrees of success, conveyed. A primary intention of this work is to argue within a history-of-thought framework, though it is hoped there is something of interest in it both for the theoretician[22] and the methodologist.

Why historians of thought disagree: psychological and methodological factors

A few words need to be said on the methodological aspect. It is commonplace now to describe revolutionary developments in science in Kuhnian terms, but in the context of the history of economic thought it seems at times as though theology rather than science is involved. Paradigms have inspirers, and, in crises, it is natural to return to the founding father to see if our problems arise not because his insight was essentially mistaken and now outmoded but rather because we failed to grasp the fundamentals from the very outset. We do not readily surrender that to which we once adhered. Instead, we re-examine the very foundations in the hope that formal adjustments and shifts in emphasis and degree can save the system. As in theology and political philosophy, economics is a discipline in which self-doubt causes many to look backwards. The physical sciences do not seem to respond to crises in that way, and whether this is due to the subject of enquiry or the temperaments of the enquirers is a difficult question.

The development of Keynesian economics has an (alarming?) affinity to the history of Christian theology. The dominant Catholic view reigned until some of the excesses of the creed and its ceremonies became too much for many to endure. The spirit of the Reformation, however, was short lived. New dogma and new heresies emerged. Fact and fiction once more became entangled. In a more modern era, some post Keynesians (without the hyphen!)[23] appear to loathe the post-Keynesians in much the same way as Protestants once saw Catholicism as an abomination. Fundamentalism aptly describes the disposition of some post Keynesians (Shackle being a notable exception). Just as Christians, prior to the ecumenical movement, were divided among themselves (evidently feeling that to distort the true teachings was a more insidious crime than to reject them openly or ignore them entirely), so too are the professed followers of Keynes in dispute with each other. Cynics have suggested that Christians have moved together not because past sins are now forgiven, but simply because they need each other to resist forces liable to promote their extinction. Yet, despite the emergence of new classical economics, many Keynesians seem intent on continuing to denigrate others. One hopes that the flippancy of the analogy does not detract from the substantive point being made.

Evidence exists which suggests that any *rapprochement* is unlikely to occur over the short period. Indeed, polarization could be emerging in so far as post Keynesians and their neo-Ricardian collaborators seem to be distancing themselves from the new Keynesian and new classical debate. The disequilibrium theoreticians such as Clower, Leijonhufvud and Patinkin no longer inspire new developments and they seem to occupy the eroding middle ground.[24]

It is surprisingly pertinent to pursue the theological analogy by briefly considering difficulties that have confronted scholars in biblical interpretation, especially in their attempts to reconcile the letter and spirit of the New and Old Testaments. Leijonhufvud is prepared to see greater consistency and continuity between *The General Theory* and the *Treatise* than, say, Patinkin. It is also worth remarking that it was the priests who invented the art of exegesis.

What saves the history of economic thought from being 'confused controversy...better left to theology'[25] is that science cannot be practised without an underlying vision which enables data to be interpreted and organized. Visions themselves require elucidation, and some would say rational justification as well. Logical consistency and a degree of intuitive plausibility would be desirable qualities, although success need not require either or both. Cynics have indeed considered Keynes's very obscurity to have aided the spreading of his teachings, but this work is written in the naïve hope that rival visions can be understood and sensibly evaluated.

It is important to note that the methodological approach taken in this work lies between two extremes. At one end stands Leijonhufvud who is prepared to use a vision to impose ordering principles upon Keynes's writings. His concern was one of rational reconstruction. The opposing approach is typified by Patinkin who examines the literal text of Keynes with painstaking care and who is unwilling to make intuitive leaps to fill in any gaps. While Leijonhufvud can be accused of reading things into Keynes, Patinkin can sometimes seem unduly pedantic. Patinkin requires the clearest of evidence before attributing to Keynes any particular view.

Leijonhufvud was acutely aware of how his interpretation was exactly that, an inevitably subjective perspective on Keynes.[26] His primary goal was to show that textbook Keynesians had made serious mistakes. The secondary goal was to put forward a coherent, positive alternative which deserved preference. Many reviewers fail to recognize this. Leijonhufvud puts the argument that his interpretation is to be considered as a superior, but not absolutely true, alternative:

> *The General Theory*...will not lend itself to a tightly formalized interpretation – any fully consistent axiomatic 'model' of the theory of that work is bound to leave something out or bring something in that was not there.[27]

It is curious that so many interpretations of Keynes have appeared. The evidence is, after all, fixed in black and white. Usually when economists disagree, one explanation is that the object under study varies as time passes. Historians of thought need to find a different excuse.

The virulence of disputes is also a prominent feature. Frequently, the issue seems trivial and important only to the participants and their egos. Views of rivals are often dismissed summarily on the basis of one or two snippets of supposedly conclusive evidence of patent error. One is often left with the feeling that passages are quoted but that the accompanying commentary cannot logically be derived from the evidence supplied. Sometimes a passage cited strikes the reader as contradicting the position the author is striving to make.

Furthermore, why do demonstrably false views (for example, concerning Keynes) persist for generations in a supposedly free society? Historians of thought are virtually united in attributing to Keynes that chapters 2 and 19 indicate that *The General Theory* does not have rigid wages as a special, and highly limiting, assumption. Apparently, systematic errors do persist contrary to new classical teaching. Perhaps, however, acting on a 'true' view of Keynes confers no profits.

If such doubts are ever raised, the most usual answer is that historians of thought face the same problem that scientists do when confronted with data to weigh and interpret. Prior theoretical judgements influence the perception of the evidence. Paradigms are incommensurable and members of rival schools cannot communicate effectively. Kuhnian arguments are sometimes made which emphasize problems of Gestalt switches. There is, however, frequently a noticeable asymmetry. Our school has no difficulty understanding your school, but your school remains locked in its paradigm, which explains why you fail to agree with us. A kind of subjectivism results, even though other members of any one school or community can provide interpersonal, quasi-objective confirmations of their colleague's work.

It is possible that such sophisticated explanations of scientific disagreement represent an over-reaction to the earlier, more commonsense, view which was simply that human failings, such as pride, obstinacy, lack of clarity and ordinary misunderstandings, play an important role. Debates in the 1930s between Keynes and his critics have already been seen in this way only one side blames Robertson, Hawtrey, Ohlin and others while others point to Keynes's confusion and frequent shifting of ground.[28] Modern debates about Keynes's essential message can, it is argued, also be seen in this light. In particular, the fundamentalist and reductionist renditions of Keynes have far more in common with each other than is generally appreciated.

The human factor is suggested as an important, though incomplete, explanation of disagreements among interpreters of Keynes. Not only perfectly understandable personal failings are relied on. Bounded rationality plays some part too. No reader is able to absorb nuance fully or to appreciate that a certain passage was written with another, possibly yet to be drafted, in mind. While comprehension cannot be perfect, it is also true that authors are themselves rarely entirely exact and consistent. Indeed, language can be elastic, poetic and persuasive rather than a reliable and unambiguous means by which precise concepts are accurately conveyed. Authors themselves, and Keynes is a good example, are often content to present a satisfactory account of their views rather than an ideal one. Readers can therefore be left with a feeling that they agree up to a point but to precisely what point eludes formal and scholastic expression.

While it is possible in principle that disagreements can be lessened if reasonable discourse is employed, even Keynes simply got fed up with Hawtrey and Robertson.[29] The great believer in the value of persuasion and the notion of degrees of rational belief by which final judgements can be suspended to allow the evidence to continue to be accumulated and weighed grew impatient with those who seemed to quibble over matters of terminology and dynamic detail.

Once schools form, authors cite each other and identify themselves with the group. The foundations are not questioned. Appeals to authority and to conventional judgements replace independent investigation. Unfortunately, those who lay the foundations are themselves those the most likely to be hot-blooded and partisan. It is left for those who follow years later to search for syntheses. Only when passions have cooled, confusions are identified and texts disinterestedly dissected does the prospect of reconciliation seriously arise. Later generations have the advantage of being able to read early in their education the accumulated literature within a relatively brief space of time. The ability to compare and contrast the well-developed positions of the rival schools is presented to the second generation but denied to the first.

When the logical structures of the rival models are worked out, differences in details of dynamic adjustment can more readily be distinguished from genuine differences in paradigms.

A complex of urges moves a thinker exploring a new paradigm. Discovery implies that something once cherished is cast aside, and conservatism counsels caution. Inherited wisdom provides evolutionary continuity. It is easier to explore within sight of the reassuringly familiar. To probe, test and question is restless and individualistic.[30] Urges to create, conserve and reconcile co-exist uneasily. While initial discoveries surprise and excite, a yearning for order and coherence can follow.

Creation implies an extension or transformation of vision. Rivals are deemed to have been left behind clutching to the wreckage of the old. But for those without the exhilaration of fresh discovery to drive them, change is unsettling and painful. In economics, where victories are seldom decisively won, the urge to find a workable synthesis, therefore, ultimately finds expression. A successful synthesis channels the disparate motivations constructively in the sense that most people are kept busy and happy. Incommen- surable paradigms, on the other hand, prevent communication and foster frustration.

There is a sense in which intellectual thought, and science specifically, evolves in a Darwinistic manner. What survives is not necessarily an intrinsically higher form but is simply the fittest for the environment prevailing. While co-operation has known survival value, during the emergence and growth of a new branch of thought the very forces behind its impetus encourage an intense and single-minded narrowness of those at the frontier.

It seems that both individual and group psychology play some role in explaining the creation and propagation of schools of thought.

Too readily, however, are paradigms deemed to be incommensurable. The urge to form clubs to carve out a research programme is strong. Intellectual sect appeal sways many. Yet rival interpreters of Keynes share a common culture. It is not as though spacemen are trying to communicate with primitive tribesmen. Logic therefore can be used to pare away the superficial differences and to locate which disagreements can be traced to the structure of the chains of logic and which to the texture of the paradigms themselves.

There is a mischievous propensity, however, not to take rivals seriously.[31] What they say they cannot mean. Arguments, though heavily qualified, are reduced to their essence in the helpful explanations supplied by the other side. The practice is widespread. For example, new classical economics is portrayed in new Keynesian textbooks[32] as implying the policy ineffectiveness postulate, which in turn requires a rather preposterous assumption of perfect price flexibility. Prices are imperfectly flexible in reality, therefore scope for stabilization policy remains. Overlooked are the denials by new classicists that this is a worthwhile counter-argument. Barro accepts that prices are not all determined on auction markets and that long-term contracts are prevalent, but simply responds, 'So what?' Even though it is possible to increase aggregate demand after agents have locked themselves into price agreements, it is not clear that the increase in output is desirable from a welfare point of view. Agents are being forced to vectors they did not expect to be pushed towards.[33] The policy ineffectiveness postulate was simply a rhetorical device intended to put the ball into the Keynesian court. Under very simple assumptions (price flexibility and rational expectations), demand management was difficult to justify. Keynesians were forced to search for some justification, and the question is whether they have succeeded yet.[34]

If the new classical–new Keynesian debate is really about the justification for feedback policy-rules, then the debate is being side-tracked and a misleading synthesis is being formed. New Keynesians seem to view the debate in terms similar to that resolved temporarily under the standard textbook synthesis. The old Keynesians believed that prices are rigid. Classicists believe they are highly flexible. Reasonable people are being urged to take the middle (i.e. new Keynesian) ground and recognize significant short-run inflexibility and correspondingly accept some role for stabilization policy.[35]

Other examples are easy to find.

During the 1970s Friedman and his critics appeared to be at cross-purposes concerning whether their differences could be expressed in terms of the neoclassical synthesis. The notion that monetarists believed in a vertical *LM* curve seemed the obvious means to formalize Friedman's critique. This occurred despite Friedman's protests.[36]

The reconciliation of rival bodies of thought on meaningful terms is therefore no simple task.

Even if it is accepted that exegesis can be more objective than it has been, a normative issue arises. The practice of historians of thought must depend on the purpose of the mode of enquiry.

Three particular exegetical styles can be identified, the *rhetorical*, the *heuristic* and the *archaeological*. The categories are not mutually exclusive and no ranking in terms of intrinsic merit is offered.

The *rhetorical* technique is not advocated merely to justify selective quotation simply to confuse or silence an opponent. The term is used in a higher sense in the style of Donald McCloskey.[37] It refers to the effort to strike responsive chords in others with whom you engage in discourse. In practice, authors strive to persuade, sermonize, convert, inspire and legitimize. Arguments are in favour of a particular theoretical system and not, at least directly, in support of policies that reflect value judgements.

There is a real risk of one-sided and rather subjective advocacy. The honest hope is that out of exuberant competition progress in some sense occurs. Many doubt, however, that two barristers acting as adversaries promote just outcomes, even if liberty and freedom of expression are thereby protected. Sophistry is rhetoric's degenerative form, and it is rather common in doctrinal analyses of Keynes. The aim becomes to knock down your opponent, and little care is taken to strike fair blows.

Real discourse, however, is two-way. Parties are then good-naturedly prepared to accept reasonable counter-arguments. The Socratic dialectic is perhaps its highest form, unless your view of Plato – and this appears to be McCloskey's view – is that he endeavours ultimately to claim authority to legislate on the basis of certain philosophical knowledge which supposedly emerges. A genuine spirit of conciliation requires an acceptance that propositions of interest can usually only be justified in terms of a degree of rational belief.

Sheila Dow[38] argues that schools compete with each other to gain converts by persuasion. No school is correct because all are equally constrained by their own visions. Despite the relativistic undercurrent, at least some fruitful communication and cross-fertilization is possible in Dow's system. Appreciation of the methodological foundations of your own and your rivals' positions is claimed to aid the process.[39] Arjo Klamer also seems to champion a methodological technique which exalts persuasiveness.[40]

But to sway an audience they need to understand you, and communication can be impeded by formal style. The cultivated and the literary are doubtless considered to be devoid of rigour by the modernist and the technocrat. Differences in style can sometimes reflect differences in substance. The subject matter of enquiry cannot always be precisely defined and analysed. Fuzzy language can be chosen deliberately. Its poetic and impressionistic quality can be deemed a virtue. If this is recognized, some of the barriers to mutual understanding can be removed.[41] Even so, effective communication is very much a trial-and-error process. Keynes, for example, could not know in advance what others would regard as too obvious for words and what would require the most patient and carefully framed analysis. After years of debate with critics such as Robertson, Hawtrey and Hayek, one feels that Keynes became ever less patient. Effective dialogue is rarely sustained.

Keynes's antagonism towards excessive mathematical formalization is well known.[42] His comments gain in weight when we realize that Keynes, for his time, was a mathematical economist of some ability. Early in his career, he was the author of the formidable *A Treatise on Probability*, a work which combined the literary and mathematical styles. Later, although he continued to use algebra to supplement the text,[43] he emphasized that the manipulation of equations can never convey the subtle complexity of economic interactions. Furthermore, algebra in particular is not only tedious but can also obscure one's meaning. He wrote to Hugh Townshend after the publication of *The General Theory*:

> When I come to revise the book properly, I am not at all sure that the right solution may not lie in leaving out all this sort of stuff altogether, since I am extremely doubtful whether it adds anything at all which is significant to the argument as a whole.[44]

Keynes himself was more interested in conveying his basic ideas than in building an overall model with painstaking precision.[45]

It is, I think, of the essential nature of economic exposition that it gives, not a complete statement, which, even if it were possible, would be prolix and complicated to the point of obscurity but a sample statement, so to speak, out of all the things which could be said, intended to suggest to the reader the whole bundle of associated ideas, so that, if he catches the bundle, he will not in the least be confused or impeded by the technical incompleteness of the mere words which the author has written down, taken by themselves.

The *heuristic* approach, by contrast, views the inherited literature as a quarry to be mined. Branches of thought can be abruptly cut short by the sudden emergence of new research programmes and a change in the nature of problems relevant to society at the time. Circumstances can change so that old ideas become fashionable again, and old books can profitably be re-read with new spectacles. As Leijonhufvud notes, to search for illumination necessarily brings in some subjectivity. To identify significant features of one body of thought to contrast them with those of another often involves judgements about the appropriateness and likely fruitfulness of any rational reconstruction. Critics would point to the relativism which such an approach appears to invite. They can complain that interpretations of Keynes seem to be justified merely by pointing to the needs of the age. For example, the profession at large, concerned increasingly with providing greater rigour and generality to macroeconomic analysis by looking for its microfoundations, had become uncomfortable in the 1960s about simple and highly aggregated renditions of Keynes based on the *IS-LM* framework. To search for passages in Keynes indicating insight about processes at the atomistic level was then a useful thing to do. For a follower of the heuristic approach, to focus on an author's stated 'central message' is not necessarily the best procedure, especially if the purpose of the examination is to reveal the not-so-obvious elements hasty readers have hitherto overlooked. Searching for an illuminating and characteristic cluster of themes is a sensible alternative. The reader's role can be active, and, in extreme cases, the author need not know best.[46]

The third approach is the *archaeological*. It strives to be as objective as possible and has the strongest empiricist and positivist connotations. The aim is to 'let the texts speak' so that the 'central message' can be discerned. The 'noise–signal' distinction reflects a kind of sophisticated falsificationism. Although the search for conflicting textual evidence can unearth it, the anomalous passages can be put aside if the great weight of evidence still favours the hypothesis. Patinkin can reasonably be assigned to this branch. Whether what the texts say depends on the reader's ears is, of course, a difficulty in employing this approach in practice. What is 'central' to one interpreter is often peripheral to another, and whether a particular passage really does say, or signify, what one interpreter maintains can still be a matter of contention. The exegetical style is sometimes labelled 'Talmudic', with a discernibly pejorative connotation.

Patinkin's concern, in part, is to rescue Keynes from his interpreters and those who seek to use Keynes's writings to bolster arguments of their own.[47] Non-archeological approaches sometimes utilize a technique which can be termed 'sophisticated verificationism'. Only passages reflecting Keynes's true intentions can be regarded as corroborative evidence. (All swans are white. This swan is black. Therefore, this is not really a swan.) Adherence to the text certainly promotes discipline and reduces the temptation to indulge in writing fiction.

Vision and the process of interpretation

In the previous section, emphasis was placed on such dynamically shifting factors as moods, personality conflicts, loyalty and matters of taste and purpose. Separate consideration can be given to the individual's act of interpretation which is of a rather less unstable nature.

Evidence is examined on the basis of a relatively fixed internal frame of reference; that is, a Gestalt, vision or set of beliefs about how the world works. Perceptions about how societies function form part of an individual's vision. So do higher philosophical beliefs.

Some controversies in economics involve differences which might, in principle, be settled by the appeal to empirical evidence. Not all controversies are like this. Those involving fundamental differences of vision seem impossible to resolve. Any evidence offered by one side simply does not convince the other; they interpret the evidence in a manner which conforms to their own preconceptions of how a system functions. There still exist apparently irreconcilable beliefs regarding whether observed unemployment can be interpreted as being 'natural' or induced by a deficiency of aggregate demand. We are also no closer to attaining professional consensus regarding the direction of causality between changes in the quantity of money and changes in nominal income – Paul Davidson and Milton Friedman will never agree on exactly what the evidence indicates.

Unfortunately, exactly the same problem exists for interpreting Keynes's own writings. Some think that one chapter is *the* chapter and that others do not matter so much. It is hoped that the interpretation given here does not give undue influence to any portion of Keynes's writings to the exclusion of others.[48]

Ideally, one would interpret Keynes best by studying his entire works as a mutually consistent whole, including those in areas outside economics. If we could grasp how Keynes saw the world generally, we could perhaps better comprehend his economic writings. Many others have realized that Keynes's liberal philosophy is closely related to his views about economics.[49] Such an investigation would not be possible within the terms of reference of this work, but one observation can be made which shows that the view of Keynes's economics offered here is consistent with his general philosophy.

Keynes was an extraordinary blend of conservative and radical. His view was that wise management would remove the worst ill-effects of a system of unregulated capitalism, yet he was never clearly sympathetic to fine-tuning.[50] His contemptuous views on contemporary Marxism are well known and yet he remained friendly to the radical views of the Bloomsbury group. Is this really so paradoxical?[51] Research might reveal that Keynes was conservative enough to see merit in stabilizing conventions of all kinds, political as well as economic; conventions of justice and fair play which constrain the conduct of individuals and nations in order to comply with the standards accepted by all English gentlemen. On the other hand, he rejected the stern Edwardian conventions about sound finance and the virtue of abstinence from consumption which are mirrored by those which seek to impose limits upon personal behaviour under the guise of the improvement of morality. Absurd conventions must go, yet Keynes accepted that the rational rules of conduct set by the wise were superior to the maxim of the absolute freedom of the many. Intervention is needed in the sphere of politics as well, but none of the kind which is harsh and authoritarian.

His liberalism is perhaps that of Aristotle rather than Mill.[52] Furthermore, it may be that a study of his seemingly unrelated views on the nature of probability and the use of Benthamite, utilitarian calculus could well dovetail to form a coherent picture of Keynes's overall vision in which man is not an isolated, calculating individual but a social creature inclined to reasonable behaviour. This line of argument is speculative but seems worthy of further examination. Such a complicated vision could profitably be compared with that of the adherents of the Chicago school whose open acceptance of radical individualism and the rational, atomistic, economic man, unmistakably pervades their writings on economics and the nature of freedom. The clarity of their exposition of their views has meant that the profession has easily recognized it.

Unfortunately, many accuse the Chicagoans of twisting economics to conform with their normative predilections. The implication is that their economic analysis is thereby discredited. Perhaps the accusers should look at themselves. Those whose social vision is that the world is too complicated for simple 'as if' laws to succeed in serving the common good often believe that complicated forms of regulation are necessary. The more optimistic of them believe in fine-tuning, their faith in fiscalism perhaps being reflected in their faith in all kinds of government regulation and social welfare programmes. These people are 'liberals' in the American sense of the word. Their politics and economics are just as intimately connected as the Chicagoans'. In every case, however, it is not necessarily the case that politics and value judgements have influenced economics but rather that the anterior social vision has governed both.

Writing anything about what Keynes said inevitably involves some risk once the influence of divergent visions of society is recognized. Keynes had grand ideas, ones which provoked the hostile response of many, but an enthusiastic response from others. It is inherently controversial because he sought to attack the classical vision of an economy, a vision which has connections to an all-embracing view of how a society functions. Perhaps this is why we often find that questions of what Keynes said and whether he was right are debated with such vigour even today.

The area of research is an active one again, but there are basic methodological questions which are not discussed. Is it proper to argue from the top down; that is, to ascertain the philosophical position of an author in order to systematically formulate the structure, texture and purpose of the economics? Or is it better to work from the bottom up by examining the economics in terms of its internal logic and grafting onto it only the minimum philosophical accompaniment?[53] Furthermore, if a bundle of ideas about epistemology, values, social goals, and economic and political forces are correlated, is it necessarily the case that any one element causes the other? Or is there some common cause, such as a unifying philosophical principle? Alternatively, an urge to see reality consistently in a particular way can be the thread connecting the parts. A pessimist can see disorder in philosophy, the universe and in mankind, while an optimist is inclined to find order and harmony in all things.

Controversy stemming from differences in vision is unlikely to be resolved but, if logic and vision can clearly be separated, the smaller questions about details of adjustment can perhaps be resolved. The process by which perturbations send pulses through a system are in principle capable of identification. Simple sequence models can be built to show how a disturbance in one market spills over into the next. The dynamic loanable funds–liquidity preference debate is an example of a controversy mainly about logic. However, these issues have become entangled with those concerning vision. The nature of the destination is the real quarrel. Does the interest rate ultimately depend on thrift and productivity or on bootstraps speculation?

While Frank Hahn is justified in striving to reduce as much as possible to the level of logic, others see competition and pluralism as creative forces which promote breadth as well as rigour.[54] A possible rejoinder to Hahn is that vision statements and judgements about the appropriateness of particular models to particular circumstances are not amenable to logical and mathematical dissection. Similarly, one cannot prove that any one interpretation of Keynes is the best.

Fundamentalism and reductionism: similarities and differences

When comparing fundamentalism and Keynesian reductionism, it is unclear whether the two views are best seen as complements or substitutes. There is a natural tendency for writers to disagree with each other to promote product differentiation.

One reductionist, Leijonhufvud, is happy to accept the fundamentalist message about the instability of investment. It constitutes the primary shock which sets off the multiplier repercussions. Shackle[55] wrote a respectful, but lukewarm, review of Leijonhufvud's book, though Leijonhufvud has subsequently spoken to Shackle to acknowledge the extent of agreement which exists between them.[56] The amplification of the initial shock due to objective liquidity constraints is distinct from the subjective loss of confidence behind what triggered the decline in income in the first place. Leijonhufvud now claims that full-employment, Walrasian optimum is not something he necessarily believes to exist, but is merely an idealized benchmark against which reality, and alternative theoretical models to explain it, can be compared.[57]

In simple terms, both factions agree that the problem is not, as the orthodox view held, that there was a spanner in the works in the form of rigid prices. The problem of macroeconomic disturbances ultimately lies in the fact that agents do not have full information upon which to decide correctly what to do.

Reductionists tend to stress their own innovations. In disequilibrium, false information frustrates processes that allow agents to grope towards the Walrasian optimum, a benchmark and a special type of full-employment outcome in which all markets, present and future, clear. Fundamentalists, in effect, respond that agents are groping in a darkened room for the black cat that is not there. The Walrasian optimum vector does not even exist. Fundamentalists stress the lack of confidence of investors and bears rather than the lack of money in the hands of the unemployed. The two ideas, however, hardly seem mutually exclusive, especially if uncertainty initially triggers the decline in income and the subsequent liquidity constraints. While there is some difference of emphasis, this does not mean that this is a symptom of some underlying incompatibility.

Fundamentalism is more concerned with pointing to those expectations which are autonomous. The instability of behavioural functions is thought to follow from an emphasis on speculation. Money is seen to be important as a store of wealth.

Reductionism gives greater scope to objective factors to which expectations adapt. Lower sales generate the belief over time in the need to reduce output and to reduce inventory accumulation. Eventually, dismal outcomes adversely influence the MEI curve. Money is a fickle messenger. Information is withheld whenever it is not spent.

To some extent, fundamentalism can be seen, in a manner similar to how Coddington[58] viewed Keynesian reductionism, as a means to define the domain over which the hydraulic approach can sensibly apply. Many markets are governed by conventional rules of conduct which, upon examination, have little firm and objective foundation. Wise policy-makers would therefore avoid experimental and unsettling policies. Stabilizing and benign conventions need to be nurtured. If behavioural relationships are sufficiently stable, demand management has some scope.

Nevertheless, fundamentalism has its critics. Some maintain that its focus is too narrow and that its adherents are too set in their beliefs. While Shackle's prose is lucid and evocative, his insights do not carry economics forward very far. The message is often construed as a negative one. 'Don't believe in orthodox Keynesian fine-tuning.' 'Disasters can occur at any moment.' A simple, if perhaps only partial, reply to the critics is that policy-makers humbly need to face the fact that they cannot control the economy. Their scientific pretensions need to be recognized as too ambitious. Goals must be lowered and economics be seen as an art rather than an exact science.[59]

Similarly, Leijonhufvud argues that the limited circumstances under which Keynes advocated fiscal policy need to be identified. If bear speculation makes monetary policy impracticable, and if there is a serious departure from full employment, fiscal stimulus is warranted. To take an analogy, suppose that you prick your little finger. Clearly, the body's restorative mechanisms can normally cope with this disturbance without the need for surgery. Contrast the case of a gunshot wound. A naïve classicist, who argues that no man could ever design, understand and therefore improve upon the performance of a system as miraculous and complex as the human body, would be a positive menace to have as your doctor. Even rudimentary first-aid is better than doing nothing.

The respective parties have enough in common to make rational debate possible. Both visions of Keynes emerged in the 1960s and 1970s and were responses to a common problem, the feeling that traditional Keynesian macroeconomics had perceivably been unable to supply intellectually satisfying insights into events of the 1960s and into the deeper nature of the monetarist controversy.

There would be little point reconciling vastly disparate paradigms. This can be achieved, somewhat trivially, by assigning each to its legitimate domain. For example, if classical theory arose to analyse the engine of growth, whereas marginalism was directed towards the allocative question in a relatively quiescent environment, there is little scope for dialogue.[60]

In a sense there is nothing really new about pointing to similarities between reductionism and fundamentalist versions of post Keynesianism. Two sources[61] juxtapose the two when portraying schools of thought on a spectrum. What is novel is to argue how close the two are and that a worthwhile synthesis seems viable.

A notable feature of the diagram shown in Figure 1 concerns the positioning of the Austrians next to the fundamentalists, but the Austrians are prepared in some ways to adopt, as did the young Hayek, a Walrasian spirit which emphasizes tendencies towards co-ordination and the restorative properties of market systems.

The Austrians begin to close the loop. They emphasize creative disorder. Entrepreneurship and individual action are described by the Austrians as progressive. There is a sense of ascent, a climbing towards some goal even if it (the Walrasian vector) is never reached. The process is the important and interesting thing rather than some hypothesized destination where the market opportunities have come to be exploited.

Similarities between the Austrian and the fundamentalist approaches[62] must raise questions about the validity of the latter as a rendition of Keynes.

Two points can be made here. First, it is only selected aspects of the Austrian vision upon which the fundamentalists have drawn. Surely, you can agree with some of the things your rivals believe in without conceding your entire cause. Second, fundamentalists take a more pessimistic view than do the Austrians. In a sense, the darker side of the Austrian vision is stressed by the fundamentalist Keynesians. Austrians recognize Knightian (or unquantifiable) uncertainty and see in it the justification for the existence of the entrepreneur, a heroic figure central to the progress of Western civilization. On the other hand, fundamentalists worry about the potential for instability should entrepreneurs lose their faith in the future. They point to the potential fragility of the system while the Austrians point to its progressive vigour.

Fundamentalist post Keynesians have a number of concerns about elements of Leijonhufvud's interpretation. A reconciliation requires that these concerns are dealt with. Some involve simple misunderstandings while others raise more difficult problems.

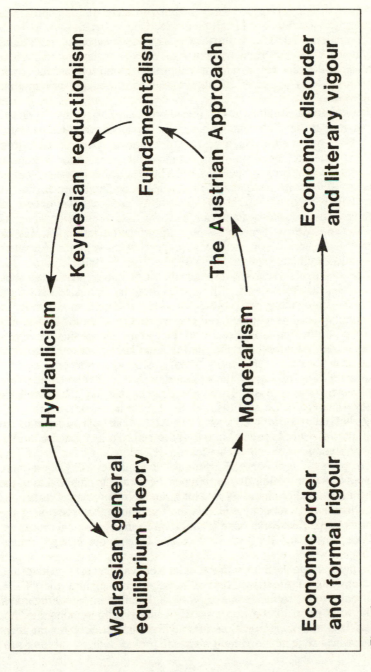

Figure 1

Three steps are required for a meaningful reconciliation. First, the parties need to understand each other. Second, important parts of each interpretation need to be established as exegetically accurate renditions of Keynes. Third, the respective positions must be logically compatible, because, if they are not, Keynes has contradicted himself and the 'true' interpretation is a matter of choice and assertion and not mutual compromise.

Leijonhufvud certainly has an image problem. Suspicions are raised by his very use of Walrasian language. Leijonhufvud (and Clower) are seen by some as fighting a rearguard action to prop up an ailing Walrasian research programme by, paradoxically, expanding its domain to cover disequilibrium phenomena.[63] There is a feeling that genuine monetary theory in a sequential production economy set in historical time and bathed in Knightian uncertainty cannot be couched in Walrasian, or even atomistic, terms.[64]

The very use of the expression, 'co-ordination failure' seems to connote that there is some classical process which is being prevented from succeeding to operate by virtue of some 'imperfection'. An account of Keynes as a disequilibrium theorist seems to presuppose that one accepts the Walrasian equilibrium vector as the state towards which the system ultimately converges. As with the neoclassical synthesis Leijonhufvud claims to attack, full employment is generated in the long run. A co-ordination failure seems to refer to the supply side being too disorganized, the problem being that false relative prices emerge as a result of imperfect search activity. If only agents were not confused and were all willing to supply the appropriate level of output, then full employment would result. This sounds rather like Say's Law and an analysis merely of voluntary unemployment. Furthermore, Leijonhufvud's corridor concept reserves for classical economics at least partial validity even in the short run. To a fundamentalist, Leijonhufvud is just another classical apologist.

To make things worse, Leijonhufvud approves of Robertson's critique of Keynes's liquidity preference theory and is prepared to see a role for thrift and productivity in a long-run theory of interest rates.

Leijonhufvud's reputation has also suffered through the company his theories keep. His works have been allied to the theoretical works of Patinkin and to the fix-price, or non-Walrasian, general equilibrium theorists.

To group Leijonhufvud with Patinkin, who was the first to pursue the implications of viewing Keynes as a disequilibrium theorist,[65] contributes to the former's image problem. Patinkin is widely regarded as the high priest of the neoclassical synthesis who demonstrated to Hicks that the incorporation of real balance effects meant that Keynesians had to abandon their claims to provide a theory of long-run unemployment equilibrium. There are, however, obvious differences between Leijonhufvud and Patinkin. Leijonhufvud looks more to the mechanics of money-using systems. He is sceptical about the theoretical significance of real balance effects considering that they drive money wages further away from their 'correct', sustainable long-run values. He gives greater emphasis to intertemporal considerations including interest rates and the speculative demand for money.[66] Patinkin also favours the old Hansen–Klein formulation of *The General Theory* on account of its emphasis on effective demand and the process of income equilibration.[67]

Distrust of Leijonhufvud perhaps also stems from the more obvious drawbacks of a branch of theory which has explicitly claimed him as a forbear. The fix-price approach is of such uncertain theoretical soundness that Barro felt obliged to abandon the project he commenced with Grossman. There is some irony here because the fix-price approach is precisely what the crudest version of hydraulicism embodied, and this is the very target of Leijonhufvud's critique of textbook orthodoxy and its 'spanner-in-the-works' view of Keynes.

Overall, the list of objections initially appears impressive. Of the complaints listed, however, some can be readily dismissed because they involve either uncharitable or simply erroneous readings of Leijonhufvud. The major finding, so far as views on behaviour in the short run are concerned, is that there are no significant differences between Leijonhufvud and his post Keynesian critics. Matters concerning the long run, over which there has been rather less debate, are not so easily settled. Portions of Leijonhufvud's (and the fundamentalist post Keynesians') discussions are unsatisfactory, but can be repaired without creating serious internal inconsistencies. Nevertheless, passages in Leijonhufvud indicate that he is not prepared to press his preference for long-run elements of classical thought to extremes. Furthermore, the more nihilistic claims of the fundamentalists can be challenged as intrinsically dubious and exegetically inaccurate.[68] Even Shackle and Davidson themselves moderate their attacks on rationality by speaking of reasonable behaviour rather than urging us to accept irrationality. Wild instability is often no more than a potentiality. Such attitudes enhance the prospects of reconciliation.

But, if anything, fundamentalists have become more hostile to Leijonhufvud and Clower as the years have passed. Finding fault with them has become popular sport lately.[69]

Dow and Earl[70] are ambivalent about how Clower and Leijonhufvud should be regarded by the fundamentalists.

Clower and Leijonhufvud's many writings have influenced the arguments in this book considerably yet their tendencies to use

Walrasian modes of analysis in formal arguments rather imply that they cannot rest easily in the Post Keynesian camp alongside the purists, even though their emphasis on coordination problems and the failings of the IS-LM approach to macroeconomic theory also prevents them from full membership of the neoclassical Keynesian group. There is a world of difference between the neoclassical Keynesian 'quantity-constrained' and so-called 'disequilibrium' approaches to macroeconomics associated with Barro and Grossman...or Malinvaud..., and the earlier work of Clower and Leijonhufvud from which the new approaches have clearly descended. Perhaps Clower and Leijonhufvud occupy a no-man's-land between neoclassical and Post Keynesians with attempts to force them into either camp doomed always to failure, yet never completely fruitless since they help illuminate the nature of the differences between the two groups.

It is easy to sympathize with this view. Nevertheless, the evidence marshalled by Dow and Earl to support the existence of grounds to separate the reductionists from the fundamentalists is rather unconvincing. They state that their work

> was partly inspired by Leijonhufvud's work on Keynes. But only partly. Leijonhufvud has performed a great service in showing how economists have often read Keynes' work in a very blinkered manner but we view *his* interpretation of Keynes with rather mixed feelings. His Walrasian blinkers have caused him to evolve a view of unemployment disequilibria and the multiplier which leaves out much that we see as important in Keynes' theory.[71]

Two specific defects are supplied:

> For Leijonhufvud, the spread of chaos has nothing to do with the instability of underlying behaviour functions in the face of falsified expectations and changes in the state of 'the news'; it has everything to do with inelastic expectations causing inertia in price adjustments.... Although he treats behaviour functions as stable, Leijonhufvud seems haunted by the spectre of an utterly explosive multiplier rather than the system eventually settling down either in a full-employment state or in the liquidity trap. If behaviour functions are stable one would have expected either of these outcomes to be the end result if no prices turn out ultimately to be rigid rather than merely sticky. Which outcome actually arose would depend on the power of real balance effects. Yet he continually writes as though the only thing which stops a worker's loss of earnings from causing an *equal* loss of expenditure, and hence an infinite multiplier contraction, is the possibility that the

worker may be able to borrow or use up liquid reserves. In all of his descriptions of the multiplier he fails to mention that a worker who loses her income would otherwise probably have saved part of it. An ability and willingness to spend from liquid reserves *does* act as a buffer when an effective demand failure occurs, but in the *General Theory* it is a fractional marginal propensity to consume which acts as the main brake on the multiplier.[72]

Both allegations are questionable. The latter, in particular, is probably just wrong.

First, the initial shock to which the system fails perfectly and instantaneously to respond in the absence of the Walrasian auctioneer specifically relates in Leijonhufvud to the instability of the investment function. It is true, however, that, apart from the initial shock, the underlying functions then remain stable while the short-run equilibrium is being reached. But Keynes in chapter 18 of *The General Theory* made the same *ceteris paribus* assumptions. In this respect, Leijonhufvud's attempt to portray Keynes's basic model can reasonably be criticized for its focus on a model which is too basic. Recall, however, that the standard hydraulic model embodies the same assumptions, yet the multiplier does still operate. In Leijonhufvud, enough chaos can be spread by false signals being sent without the need to superimpose, in a fundamentalist style, the effects of induced shifts in behavioural functions.

The second objection of Dow and Earl is simply extraordinary. They supply no direct textual evidence whatever to support the statement that Leijonhufvud's model incorporates an explosive multiplier.[73] Leijonhufvud never speaks of an equilibrium income of zero. He does indeed argue that the presence of buffers (stocks of wealth) sufficiently large to create a corridor around full employment cause the multiplier to be somewhat muffled. Behaviour outside the corridor involves the deviation-amplifying multiplier being sufficiently strong to overcome the buffers. The multiplier would operate at full strength if financial buffers are entirely non-existent (and Leijonhufvud considers that Keynes implicitly dealt with only this special case). The unimpeded multiplier is not infinite. It is equal to the expressions derived in elementary Keynesian texts. There is no reason to attribute to him any other view.

Dow and Earl overlook two relevant pieces of evidence. First, Leijonhufvud clearly accepts that the hydraulic account of the multiplier, in which leakages govern its size, is correct although the micro-foundations are not supplied in orthodox textbooks.

Although in the comparative statics of the New Economics the income-constrained process survives only in the form of the multiplier, that 'inexhaustibly versatile mechanical toy' is surely a major factor in the continued influence of this *otherwise emasculated* version of Keynes' theory.[74]

Secondly, Leijonhufvud clearly considers that stable equilibria involving positive output levels do emerge.[75]

Leijonhufvud is entitled to expect that his readers are charitable enough to assume that he understands the basic principles of first-year economics. Evidently, he was prepared to assume that his readers understood these things too. Why do Dow and Earl construe the absence of a clear statement of the obvious as evidence of confusion and fundamental error?[76]

Dow and Earl are not being singled out. It almost seems to be the general rule of inter-school dialogue that opportunities for misunderstanding seldom remain unexploited. Examples, alas, abound.

The role of uncertainty and the significance of conventions

Keynes's attack on classical economics has been recognized to have objective and subjective aspects. The former, where the hydraulic approach has its legitimate domain, concerns the mechanical operation of the multiplier and the endogenous means by which income reaches an equilibrium. The latter concerns the role played by expectations and by psychological factors. Dispute over which of the two is the more crucial departure has been intense.

To some extent, Keynes did remain influenced by his classical upbringing. Keynes was clearly prepared to make certain classical assumptions about the labour and goods markets.[77] A discussion of whether he did this (1) so that he could adopt as many classical assumptions as possible and therefore more convincingly refute their arguments, (2) because he believed those assumptions to be true, (3) because he was confused or (4) because his line of thought had not become sufficiently developed to 'escape from habitual modes of thought' is not the concern of this work. Joan Robinson[78] has speculated along these lines, but the position taken in this work is that Keynes, for whatever reason, accepted much of the classical wisdom and that his targets for attack were carefully selected.

As indicated above, Keynes's assault can be regarded as two-pronged. First, there is the objective aspect, rightly stressed by Leijonhufvud, that, in the absence of the auctioneer, the optimal vector of relative prices is not likely to be generated (even if it exists) through the decisions of isolated transactors. Second, decision-making is not governed by the principles of actuarial calculus that are generally recognized by classical economists. Fundamentalists have centred their interpretation around this axis. Uncertainty, particularly in relation to decisions to invest, means that other factors require analysis for aggregate behaviour to be understood. In particular, the role of psychological forces should not be overlooked. Keynes stresses

> the three fundamental psychological factors, namely the psychological propensity to consume, the psychological attitude to liquidity and the psychological expectation of future yield from capital-assets.[79]

It must be admitted that the classicists have recognized 'waves of optimism and pessimism' arguments as explanations of the trade cycle.[80] Keynes was clearly aware of such theories, although he was evidently not greatly impressed by them. He considered such oversimplified accounts to be 'somewhat mythical'.[81]

What Keynes did, however, was to realize that such psychological factors not only might influence the motion of the system but also govern how the economy can gravitate to a particular position involving a persistent state of involuntary unemployment. These factors are of pivotal importance in explaining why a system can remain in a sub-optimal state of rest sometimes for a period of considerable duration. Indeed, Keynes probably accepted, contrary (it appears) to Leijonhufvud, that a long-run involuntary unemployment equilibrium was a theoretical possibility. In this respect, the hydraulicists would have a point (provided that the fundamentalist argument about the inconsistency of the concepts of equilibrium and uncertainty are neutralized).

To understand how psychology can govern aggregate behaviour, it is necessary to recognize that one of Keynes's most important innovations lay in the realization of the significance of conventions that arise when transactors, confronted by an uncertain environment, are psychologically disposed to act in a manner in which they study and imitate the actions of others. There need not be any collusion or any form of anti-competitive behaviour. Free individuals spontaneously enter into these informal relationships with each other. The existence of conventions in *The General Theory* is plainest in his treatment of the labour, equities and bond markets.[82] Keynes is most explicit in his famous 1937 *QJE* article so stressed by Shackle.

> Knowing that our own individual judgment is worthless, we endeavour to fall back on the judgment of the rest of the world, which is perhaps better informed. That is, we endeavour to conform with the behaviour of the majority or the average. The psychology of a society of individuals each of whom is endeavouring to copy the others leads to what we may strictly term a *conventional* judgment.[83]

The importance of conventions is that they can promote stability and, if they are breached by a disequilibrating shock of sufficient magnitude, then the initial deviation from full employment can be amplified considerably. For example, if the share market were to collapse during a sudden downturn because the panic-stricken public abruptly lost faith in the values conventionally given to their shares,[84] then investment will be depressed and employment will decline still further. This disturbance is in addition to the multiplier effects caused by the initial shock. So long as the share market remains placid, aggregate demand will remain higher than it would otherwise have been.

Although conventions can promote stability, it is possible, indeed, probable, that inflexibilities can result which will prevent price adjustments from being made even in markets capable in principle of virtually instantaneous changes. For example, Keynes stresses that the interest rate is set by convention rather than by the classical forces of thrift and productivity.[85] This implies that the interest rate will be sticky and an initial decline in the marginal efficiency of investment (MEI) schedule will fail to be neutralized by its immediate reduction.

Conventions, then, can explain why a system can depart from an initial position of full employment.

Furthermore, conventions can also explain how it is possible for a system to settle at some point far removed from full employment. For example, despite the existence of involuntary unemployment, a convention between labourers, which, as we shall subsequently see, can be rationalized in microeconomic terms, can permanently prevent the money wage falling below some lower limit. Consequently, complete equilibrium at less than full employment will be possible because the price level becomes anchored. This means that Leijonhufvud's argument that money wages are, on account of job search, simply too slow to fall during the disequilibrium phase of the downturn can be questioned. It also means that the theoretical possibility of the restoration of full employment by sundry real balance effects can be swept aside.

We shall see in Part four that different conventions arise in different markets, have different properties and have different roles to play. The picture is one of greater complexity than that painted by either Leijonhufvud or the hydraulic Keynesians. A system's mode of adjustment depends on the durability of critical conventions and on the manner in which disruptions in one market can spread to others. For example, a crisis in the share market might spread to the bond market because the demand for precautionary balances might rise. This will generate pressures which will raise interest rates and exacerbate the problem of the deficiency of planned investment. Markets are not insulated from each other. Changes in tastes which appear in one market can be accompanied by sympathetic responses in others. Advanced models ought to incorporate such features as these.

Most textbooks have focused on the simplest model contained in *The General Theory* where the demand for money, the MEI curve and the propensity to consume are given as independent variables. The forces which lie behind the positions of these curves have not received as much attention. The writings of Shackle and Davidson have not influenced textbook writers. Instead, the standard approach has been to take these curves as given and to assume a rigid money wage. The static short-run equilibrium position can thus be determined. Comparative-static experiments can then be made, given the curves as independent data. This procedure has caused the dynamics of the process of adjustment to be suppressed. Leijonhufvud has gone some way towards stirring interest in this relatively neglected area and he has done much to delve into the intuitive and microeconomic foundations of the independent variables so that a better understanding of the implicit dynamics can be achieved. This is a proper approach since, as Keynes notes, those variables are 'capable of being subjected to further analysis, and are not, so to speak, our ultimate atomic independent elements'.[86]

However, even Leijonhufvud has presented a rather simplified view of things, although, to be fair, his primary task was simply to find whether the textbook-Keynesian story captured the feeling and recognized the major themes of Keynes's writings. He never sought to identify the more sophisticated theoretical structures, his interest being in the basic model. He has inserted a probe into *The General Theory* and the sampled cross-section revealed to him a series of ideas that were both so mutually self-supporting and so intellectually elegant that he felt that he had struck the core of what Keynes was driving at. The enquiry into the nature and importance of conventions to be undertaken here is an attempt to drill one layer deeper and it enables an examination of the interdependencies both between individual transactors and between markets. The story can then be seen to be considerably more complicated than is often appreciated. The position where an economy can settle is not simple to specify or predict.

We can now see why Keynes was more concerned with the system's trend and with the process of convergence to it than with the cyclical deviations from full employment, the latter attracting the attention of classical theorists.[87]

Conventions can cast light on the properties of a suboptimal equilibrium state, the existence of which is itself of theoretical interest. These are the sorts of quotations from Keynes which catch the eye and which form the axis around which the interpretation here will gravitate.

> [I]t is an outstanding characteristic of the economic system in which we live that, whilst it is subject to severe fluctuations in respect of output and employment, it is not violently unstable. Indeed it seems capable of remaining in a chronic condition of subnormal activity for a considerable period without any marked tendency either towards recovery or complete collapse.[88]

> [One of] the outstanding features of our actual experience...[is] that we oscillate, avoiding the gravest extremes of fluctuations in employment and in prices in both directions, round an intermediate position appreciably below full employment.[89]

It is conceded that conventions are not part of Keynes's formal model. They do, however, stand in the background and influence the nature of the environment within which individuals must function. Their stability stands behind crucial functional relationships. It is the existence of the conventions that lie behind the propensity to consume, the willingness to invest, the desire to hold money and the behaviour of the money wage which together can explain stability in a system that is patently far removed from a position of Walrasian full employment.

If the incorporation of uncertainty is an important aspect of Keynes's departure from classical economics, then it is necessary to pursue the manner in which the fundamentalist and reductionist approaches take account of uncertainty. It is argued that a reconciliation is possible if each camp shifts ground slightly.

In order to render the two approaches commensurable, more is required than simply to identify passages where some misinterpretation has occurred. It is not here the case simply that poor communication has prevented both sides appreciating that their positions are in fact extremely close. A new theme must be introduced into each as logical extensions of their respective theoretical structures. In order to bridge the remaining gap, the introduction of the notion of a 'conventional equilibrium' is suggested.

The hope is that it can give fundamentalism more backbone. To posit tendencies towards locally stable outcomes gives scope to the potential for orderly behaviour and thereby would reduce what some see as an excessively pessimistic emphasis on volatility. Stable conventions reduce the likelihood of unsettling surprise. Conventions can supply fences, albeit rickety ones which can collapse under pressure, within which activity is perceived to be safe. Price changes can be confined to a range, and bullish and bearish sentiments can normally be contained within. Conventional behaviour does not imply complete conformity or unanimously held beliefs or expectations.

Fundamentalists already recognize that behaviour can be 'sensible' and based on a judicious acceptance of conventional norms.[90] In addition, tendencies exist already within the reductionist programme to adopt the middle ground. Hahn's concept of a conjectural equilibrium is a kindred one. Indeed, some of the examples chosen by Hahn can be regarded as conventions and possibly even as verging on the customary, the latter arising from sociological forces.[91] The evocative illustration of the persistence over the centuries of human sacrifices to placate the gods clearly indicates that Hahn's vision is not narrowly economic. Nevertheless, Hahn's primary point is that the conjectural equilibria which interest him are those which result in price stability in the face of perceived unemployment. If agents believe that they face inelastic demand curves below the current price, a stable price–quantity vector can result.[92]

Under a conventional equilibrium change is sometimes scarcely even contemplated by agents. Furthermore, conventional behaviour suggests a process of convergence where agents look at what others are doing. The more who congregate in a vicinity, the more who join them. People enter crowded restaurants and are often too shy or suspicious to enter an empty one. Once inside they do not all sit at the same table or order the same meals. Within orderly constraints, diversity is possible. Indeed, the menu can offer exotic dishes and diners can try what they have never tasted before (quite possibly though after glancing at other tables to see what others have ordered and whether they seem to be enjoying their meals).

As Coddington observed:

> Reductionist choice theory *as it has been developed* does not shed any light on decisions involving such immediate and strong interdependence as this.[93]

Nevertheless, there is no reason why this could not be done. Certainly, at the literary and intuitive level, conventions can be incorporated into an essentially atomistic framework. It is likely to be true, however, that interdependencies work against mathematical tractability.[94] As with Leijonhufvud, prose can persuade and tempt, but the mainstream economist insists on a model. Without one, the impact is softened.

For reductionist thinking, the infusion of conventional equilibria would quell complaints based on the supposed defect of seeing Keynes's contribution in terms of disequilibrium. Suppose that the maximum sustainable level of output is regarded as the relevant Walrasian benchmark. In so far as a conventional equilibrium is associated with a non-Walrasian vector, the divergence can be regarded as reflecting disequilibrium in the non-market-clearing sense even though the system is, until exogenously disturbed, in a state of rest. Furthermore, conventional behaviour arises naturally under conditions of Knightian uncertainty. Central elements of fundamentalist thinking can then be absorbed into the reductionist programme.

Conventional behaviour lies between what may be regarded as two extremes, the fully rational and the fully irrational. Full information enables optimizing behaviour. Blind adherence to custom denies it. The former connotes agility and flexibility, the latter mindless inertia. Neither party would really wish to be seen as adopting a stance at either extreme. There is an opportunity for reconciliation.

Indeed, there is no reason why an analysis incorporating the notion of conventions should be at all inconsistent with any of the three broad approaches to interpreting Keynes, including the hydraulic. On the contrary, the recognition of conventions could promote greater unity by transforming these apparent rivals into complementary approaches. To do this it is necessary, however, to moderate the zeal of the fundamentalists whose almost nihilistic outlook involves the rejection of all models which seem either deterministic or are tainted with notions implying the stability of macroeconomic activity.

At the same time the pervasive character of uncertainty which they stress needs due recognition. A compromise between the fundamentalist and those of more orthodox persuasion could be reached if conventions are not seen as always being frail and liable to sudden collapse. There can then be equilibrium in a system composed of individuals facing uncertainty. We need not reject the reductionist perspective *per se* on the grounds either that it supposedly requires that each transactor makes choices subject to well-defined constraints or that it conceals the forces which animate the system during the process of change. It is possible that an understanding of conventions can allow a reductionist model to be built which explains the ultimate position of equilibrium and yet incorporates the wildly unstable processes in the transitional phase.[95]

Furthermore, the dynamics themselves may be capable of more rigorous analysis. If different markets are governed by conventions of different character and durability, we can argue that a system can be stable in the face of relatively small shocks, but can career away into situations of severe unemployment or inflation (or both) if the initial shock is beyond some critical threshold level.

Behaviour of this kind is analogous to Leijonhufvud's idea that, if a shock is small enough to be able to be neutralized by self-correcting market forces, full employment will be preserved; whereas, if a shock is too great, the deviation-amplifying multiplier will overwhelm the benign forces of equilibrating price adjustments. Leijonhufvud refers to a 'corridor' outside of which the system cannot move without being subjected to forces which exacerbate the initial disequilibrating perturbation.[96] Leijonhufvud does not, however, attribute the notion of the corridor to Keynes.[97]

34

One can conclude, therefore, that some scope exists for integrating reductionist and fundamentalist ideas.

Notes

1 J.M. Keynes, *The General Theory of Employment Interest and Money*, London, Macmillan, 1936 (hereafter referred to as *The General Theory*).

2 For example, Robert W. Clower, 'The Keynesian revolution: a theoretical appraisal' and 'A reconsideration of the microfoundations of monetary theory', both in R. Clower (ed.), *Monetary Theory*, Harmondsworth, Penguin, 1969; Axel Leijonhufvud, *On Keynesian Economics and the Economics of Keynes: a study in monetary theory*, New York, Oxford University Press, 1968; Hyman P. Minsky, *John Maynard Keynes*, New York, Columbia University Press, 1967; G.L.S. Shackle, *Keynesian Kaleidics*, Edinburgh, Edinburgh University Press, 1974; A.G. Hines, *On the Reappraisal of Keynesian Economics*, London, Martin Robertson, 1971; Paul Davidson, *Money and the Real World*, London, Macmillan, 1978, 2nd edn.

Later assessments of the writings of Keynes and the Keynesians have been aided by the publication of *The Collected Writings of John Maynard Keynes*, edited by Donald Moggridge, London, Macmillan, 1971, the volumes of which will be identified, for example, as follows: *Collected Writings*, vol. xiv. Leijonhufvud's book is referred to as *On Keynesian Economics*.

3 Franco Modigliani, 'Liquidity preference and the theory of interest and money', *Econometrica*, vol. 12, January 1944, pp. 45–88.

4 Axel Leijonhufvud, 'Keynes and the classics: two lectures on Keynes' contribution to economic theory', London, Institute of Economic Affairs, 1969, Occasional Paper 30, pp. 13–17.

5 Leijonhufvud, *On Keynesian Economics*, p. 17.

6 Harry G. Johnson, 'The general theory after twenty-five years', *American Economic Review*, vol. 51, May 1961, pp. 1–17, at p. 2.

7 Leijonhufvud, *On Keynesian Economics*, p. 35.

8 For samples of modern developments in macrotheory see Robert J. Barro and Herschel I. Grossman, *Money, Employment and Inflation*, Cambridge, NY, Cambridge University Press, 1976; Edmund S. Phelps, *Microeconomic Foundations of Employment and Inflation Theory*, New York, W.W. Norton, 1970; Geoffrey C. Harcourt (ed.), *The Microeconomic Foundations of Macroeconomics*, Boulder, Colorado, Westview Press, 1977; E. Malinvaud, *The Theory of Unemployment Reconsidered*, Oxford, Basil Blackwell, 1977; Michio Morishima, *The Economic Theory of Modern Society*, Cambridge, Cambridge University Press, 1976; E. Roy Weintraub, *Microfoundations: the compatibility of microeconomics and macroeconomics*, Cambridge, Cambridge University Press, 1979.

9 See David L. Roberts, 'Patinkin, Keynes and aggregate supply and demand analysis'; Don Patinkin, 'Keynes' aggregate supply function: a

plea for common sense', in *History of Political Economy*, vol. 10, no. 4, 1978, pp. 549–76 and 577–96 respectively.

10 S. Weintraub, 'Comment on aggregate demand and price level diagrammatics', *Journal of Post Keynesian Economics*, vol. 3, no. 1, Fall 1980, pp. 79–87, especially pp. 83–4.

11 J.A. Kregel, 'Economic methodology in the face of uncertainty: the modelling methods of Keynes and the post-Keynesians', *Economic Journal*, vol. 86, June 1976, pp. 209–25.

12 For the use of catastrophe theory specifically to elucidate Keynes's macrodynamics see Laurence Harris, 'Catastrophe theory, utility theory and animal spirit expectations', *Australian Economic Papers*, vol. 19, December 1979, pp. 268–82, especially pp. 278 *et seq.*; Hal R. Varian, 'Catastrophe theory and the business cycle', *Economic Inquiry*, vol. 17, 1979, pp. 14–28, especially p. 21.

13 Alan Coddington, 'Keynesian economics: the search for first principles', *Journal of Economic Literature*, vol. xiv, no. 4, pp. 1258–73.

14 Leijonhufvud is taken as the principal representative of the reductionist camp. Clower's views are not examined in as much detail, and there are three reasons for this. First, Clower simply does not engage in lengthy exegesis. Second, there are indications of differences between the two upon which it would be a digression to expound. Clower, for example, is not particularly concerned about inter-temporal co-ordination failures. Apparently, he views his examination of false trading as representing the more general and illuminating case. His interest in the missing microfoundations of Keynes has tended to focus on behaviour in thin markets. ('New directions for Keynesian economics', Universita Degli Studi di Siena, Quaderni Dell'istituto di Economia, no. 63, 1987.) Clower's own arguments have not yet attracted the same critical attention as Leijonhufvud's. Third, Clower's views deserve more intensive scrutiny than is feasible here. One certainly cannot say that what applies to Clower automatically applies to Leijonhufvud despite their close collaboration.

15 J.M. Keynes, *A Treatise on Money*, London, Macmillan, 1930, 2 vols, which is reprinted with different pagination in *Collected Writings*, vols v and vi.

16 Keynes, *The General Theory*, p. vi.

17 Leijonhufvud, *On Keynesian Economics*, p. 26.

18 Keynes, *Collected Writings*, vol. v, p. 177, n. 3.

19 Don Patinkin, *Anticipations of the General Theory?*, Oxford, Basil Blackwell, 1982, p. 158.

20 The development of models which rationalize policies of non-intervention has been noted by Frank Hahn who expresses concern that these models 'cure' involuntary unemployment by virtually assuming it away. See 'Monetarism and economic theory' and 'Unemployment from a theoretical viewpoint', in *Economica*, vol. 47, February 1980, pp. 1–17 and August 1980, pp. 285–98. A similar view is held by James Tobin. See 'How dead is Keynes?', *Economic Inquiry*,

vol. 15, October 1977, pp. 459–68, esp. 463–4. Furthermore, the extent to which the rational expectations hypothesis (REH) applies to reality has also been questioned. See, for example, Robert J. Gordon, 'Recent developments in the theory of inflation and unemployment', *Journal of Monetary Economics*, vol. 2, 1976, pp. 185–219, esp. pp. 201–2, and George A. Akerlof, 'The case against conservative macroeconomics: an inaugural lecture', *Economica*, vol. 46, August 1979, pp. 219–37. Lawrence Klein, *The Economics of Supply and Demand*, Oxford, Basil Blackwell, 1983, ch. 6, expresses concern over how younger economists have too eagerly embraced the REH as both a theoretical tool and as a guide for policy-making. Indeed, a measure of the extent to which the economics of Keynes is seen as increasingly irrelevant is supplied by Daniel K. Benjamin and Levis A. Kochin, 'Searching for an explanation of unemployment in interwar Britain', *Journal of Political Economy*, vol. 87, no. 3, June 1979, pp. 441–78. This is an empirically based paper without the REH being relied upon, but it has assisted in creating an intellectual environment far more hostile to Keynes.

21 These remarks are prompted by Robert Solow's review of Victoria Chick's *Macroeconomics after Keynes: a reconsideration of the General Theory*, Deddington, Oxford, Philip Allan, 1983, in the *Journal of Political Economy*, vol. 92, no. 4, August 1984, pp. 784–7.

22 John Fender, *Understanding Keynes: an analysis of 'The General Theory'*, Brighton, Wheatsheaf Books, 1981, pp. 2–4, expresses similar hopes.

23 See Paul Davidson and Sidney Weintraub, 'Jacob and Paul Samuelson, post-Keynesian', *Journal of Post Keynesian Economics*, vol. 3, no. 4, Summer 1981, pp. 602–3. Throughout this work, I likewise use 'post Keynesian' to refer to those such as Shackle and Davidson, who strive to extract Keynes's essential insights, whereas the 'post-Keynesians' are those who have built upon the hydraulic, or bastardized, rendition of Keynes.

24 See Katherine W. McCain, 'Longitudinal author cocitation mapping: the changing structure of macroeconomics', *Journal of the American Society for Information Science*, January 1984, pp. 351–9. I am grateful to Professor Don Lamberton for this reference.

25 Keynes, *Collected Writings*, vol. xiv, p. 226. He was referring to the lengthy exegesis surrounding the interest-rate controversy.

26 Leijonhufvud, *On Keynesian Economics*, pp. 387–9.

27 Axel Leijonhufvud, 'Schools, "revolutions", and research programmes in economic theory', in *Information and Coordination: essays in macroeconomic theory*, New York, Oxford University Press, 1981, pp. 291–345, at p. 317, n. 40.

28 Compare Gordon A. Fletcher, *The Keynesian Revolution and its Critics: issues of theory and policy for the monetary production economy*, New York, St Martin's Press, 1987 and John R. Presley, *Robertsonian Economics: an examination of the works of Sir D.H. Robertson on industrial fluctuation*, London, Macmillan, 1979.

29 *Collected Writings*, vol. xiv, pp. 23–8; xiii, p. 520.

30 For a grumpy critique of newfangled falsificationism, which treats knowledge as temporary and disposable, see D.C. Stove, 'Karl Popper and the jazz age', *Encounter*, vol. 65, June 1985, pp. 65–74. Running parallel to counter-intuitive attacks on Newtonian physics was jazz, which likewise scorned discipline, predictability and order. Keynes's notion of open-ended, indeterminate uncertainty also fits the feel of the jazz age. Perhaps Hayek and Schumpeter can be added to the band.

31 Recent history confirms this assertion. Robert E. Lucas Jr has objected to modern caricatures of new classical arguments. See 'Tobin and monetarism: a review article', *Journal of Economic Literature*, vol. xix, June 1981, pp. 558–67. Incidentally, the often-told joke about the professor, his student and the money on the sidewalk must irritate new classicists, not simply because it is rhetoric but for the reason that it indicates the teller has missed the point. Money is, of course, found on sidewalks, but not systematically. The professor is entitled to deny that he can find money costlessly and predictably.

32 For example, Robert E. Hall and John B. Taylor, *Macro-economics: theory, performance, and policy*, New York, W.W. Norton and Company, 1988, 2nd edn.

33 Robert J. Barro, 'Discussion', *American Economic Review, Papers and Proceedings*, vol. 74, May 1984, pp. 416–17.

34 Robert Lucas, 'Tobin and monetarism: a review article', pp. 564–5.

35 Robert Gordon, 'Output fluctuations and gradual price adjustment', *Journal of Economic Literature*, vol. xix, no. 2, June 1981, pp. 493–530. The urge to synthesize finds form in suggestions to stabilize neither P (Barro's suggestion) nor Y (the old Keynesian approach) but PY instead, a proposal which seemingly strives to embrace the insights and motives of each camp.

36 Milton Friedman, 'Comments on the critics', *Journal of Political Economy*, vol. 80, no. 5, September–October 1972, pp. 906–50, at p. 913.

37 Donald N. McCloskey, 'The rhetoric of economics', *Journal of Economic Literature*, vol. xxi, no. 2, June 1983, pp. 481–517.

38 Sheila Dow, *Macroeconomic Thought: a methodological approach*, Oxford, Basil Blackwell, 1985, pp. 244–5.

39 Vision and methodology are linked. Friedman's view of the world is that it is essentially simple and predictable. Instrumentalism, therefore, is a natural methodological choice. The belief that appreciation of methodological issues will somehow have a considerable effect on resolving differences about economic theory is held by Tony Lawson, 'Realism and instrumentalism in the development of econometrics', *Oxford Economic Papers*, vol. 41, no. 1, January 1989, pp. 236–58.

40 Arjo Klamer, *The New Classical Macroeconomics: conversations with the new classical economists and their opponents*, Brighton, Wheatsheaf Books, 1984.

41 For observations on the connection between poetry and science, see Jacob Bronowski, *The Identity of Man*, Harmondsworth, Penguin, 1965, esp. pp. 62–3. See also Arjo Klamer, op. cit., p. 50 concerning Lucas on

Keynes's style: Henry Y. Wan Jr, *Economic Growth*, Harcourt Brace Jovanovich, New York, 1971, p. 12 concerning Harrod; G.L.S. Shackle, 'A student's pilgrimage', *Banca Nazionale del Lavoro Quarterly Review*, no. 145, June 1983, pp. 107–16, at p. 116.

42 Keynes, *The General Theory*, pp. 297–8.

43 See Don Patinkin, *Keynes' Monetary Thought: A Study in its Development*, Durham, North Carolina, Duke University Press, 1976, p. 22.

44 Keynes, *Collected Writings*, vol. xxix, p. 246.

45 Keynes, *Collected Writings* vol. xiii, p. 470. See also Lawrence E. Fouraker, 'The Cambridge didactic style', *Journal of Political Economy*, vol. 66, no. 1, February 1958, pp. 65–73, esp. 65–7; Michael G. Phelps, 'Laments, ancient and modern: Keynes on mathematical and econometric methodology', *Journal of Post Keynesian Economics*, vol. 2, no. 4, Summer 1980, pp. 482–93; Joseph Schumpeter, 'Keynes, the economist', in Seymour E. Harris (ed.), *The New Economics: Keynes' influence on theory and public policy*, London, Dennis Dobson, 1948, pp. 73–101, at pp. 74–5; Keynes, *Collected Writings*, vol. xxix, pp. 35–8, 150–1, 246.

46 Axel Leijonhufvud, 'Schools, "revolutions", and research programmes', in *Information and Coordination*, pp. 291–345, at p. 314, n. 33. Furthermore, scholars have found value in Karl Marx's early writings even though the author did not want them published. See Dirk J. Struik (ed.), *Economic and Philosophic Manuscripts of 1844*, New York, International Publishers, 1964, p. 49.

47 See Alan Coddington, *Keynesian Economics: the search for first principles*, London, George Allen and Unwin, 1983, p. 113, n. 1, where Patinkin seems to be driving at what amounts to the distinction between a fundamentalist interest in extracting the essential insight from a text and a dry, academic, and archaeological one. In response to Patinkin though, there is nothing unusual, surely, in describing as a 'fundamentalist' someone who reads texts somewhat selectively as this is exactly what Christian and Islamic fundamentalists are widely claimed to do. The real distinction is between reasonable and unreasonable selectivity.

48 Allan H. Meltzer deserves praise, even if it has not proved to be beyond criticism, for his well-balanced account of the features of Keynes's model, which draws from many portions of *The General Theory* interpreted conscientiously and literally. See Alan H. Meltzer, 'Keynes's *General Theory*: a different perspective', *Journal of Economic Literature*, vol. 19, March 1981, pp. 34–64.

49 See Roy F. Harrod, *The Life of John Maynard Keynes*, London, Macmillan, 1951. See Samuelson in Seymour E. Harris (ed.), *The New Economics*, pp. 15–52; Minsky, *John Maynard Keynes*, chapter 8; Dudley Dillard, *The Economics of John Maynard Keynes: the theory of a monetary economy*, London, Crosley Lockwood, 1948, ch. 12; Donald E. Moggridge, *John Maynard Keynes*, Harmondsworth, Penguin, 1976, ch. 1; Donald E. Moggridge (ed.), *Keynes: Aspects of the Man and His Work: the first Keynes seminar held at the University of Kent at*

Canterbury, 1972, London, Macmillan, 1974; Derek Crabtree and A.P. Thirlwall, *Keynes and the Bloomsbury Group: the fourth Keynes seminar held at the University of Kent at Canterbury, 1978*; Robert Skidelsky (ed.), *The End of the Keynesian Era: essays on the disintegration of Keynesian political economy*, London, Macmillan, 1977. Compare the caustic tone of Elizabeth S. and Harry G. Johnson, *The Shadow of Keynes: understanding Keynes, Cambridge and Keynesian Economics*, Oxford, Basil Blackwell, 1978, pp. 14–15. For a recent contribution, see Robert Skidelsky, 'Keynes's political legacy', in Omar F. Hamouda and John N. Smithin, *Keynes and Public Policy After Fifty Years Volume 1: Economics and Policy*, New York, New York University Press, 1988, pp. 3–28.

50 J. Ronnie Davis, *The New Economics and the Old Economics*, Ames, Iowa, Iowa State University Press, 1971, pp. 144–5, shows Keynes's reluctance to accept compensatory public finance in the early 1930s. See also Meltzer, op. cit., p. 42 and Keynes, *Collected Writings*, vol. xxvii, pp. 319–20, 326.

51 See Derek Crabtree in Crabtree and Thirlwall, *Keynes and the Bloomsbury Group*, p. 16 for an example of Keynes's seemingly contradictory stance. See also Quentin Bell, ibid., pp. 78–9 and Hutchison at p. 98.

52 Athol Fitzgibbons, *Keynes's Vision: a new political economy*, Oxford, Oxford University Press, 1988, traces things back to Plato instead.

53 Skidelsky and Fitzgibbons appear to favour the former with Fitzgibbons reconstructing Keynes from the very top, the level of epistemology. Skidelsky begins with Keynes's attitudes to personal and political life.

54 Sheila Dow springs to mind.

55 G.L.S. Shackle, 'Keynes and today's establishment in economic theory: a view', *Journal of Economic Literature*, vol. 11, no. 2, June 1973, pp. 516–19.

56 Leijonhufvud did not say much about Knightian uncertainty in his book. (See, e.g. *On Keynesian Economics*, pp. 374–5.) His explanation (disclosed in conversation in April 1987) is that he felt that Shackle had already said as much as required and that he chose to give greater emphasis to the formal underpinnings of Keynes's attack on Say's Law than the fundamentalists had.

57 Leijonhufvud, *Information and Coordination*, ch. 7.

58 Alan Coddington, *Keynesian Economics*, p. 112.

59 See also Peter E. Earl and Neil M. Kay, 'How economists can accept Shackle's critique of economic doctrines without arguing themselves out of their jobs', *Journal of Economic Studies*, vol. 12, no. 1/2, 1985, pp. 34–48.

60 Compare A. K. Dasgupta, *Epochs of Economic Theory*, Basil Blackwell, 1985.

61 Paul Davidson, *International Money and the Real World*, London, Macmillan, 1982, p. 2; Sheila C. Dow and Peter E. Earl, *Money Matters: a Keynesian approach to monetary economics*, Oxford, Martin Robertson, 1982, pp. 167–70.

62 This judgement is corroborated by S. C. Littlechild, 'Comment: radical subjectivism or radical subversion?', in Mario J. Rizzo (ed.), *Time, Uncertainty, and Disequilibrium: exploration of Austrian themes*, Lexington, Mass., Lexington Books, 1979, pp. 32–49, at p. 38, where it is argued that Shackle and the Austrians share radical subjectivism but that the former's view is more radical so far as potentialities are created rather than discovered. For something to be discovered it must be part of the givens in a world which, in principle, can be fully specified. Nevertheless, I note that the creative acts of one can be regarded as exogenous discoverable data by others.

63 Paul Davidson, *International Money and the Real World*, p. 72; Anna M. Carabelli, *On Keynes's Method*, Macmillan, London, 1988, p. 2.

64 Paul Davidson, 'Reviving Keynes's revolution', *Journal of Post Keynesian Economics*, vol. vi, no. 4, Summer 1984, pp. 561–75, reduces Keynes's revolution to the rejection of three neoclassical axioms (of gross substitutability, of reals and of ergodicity).

65 Don Patinkin, *Money Interest and Prices: an integration of monetary and value theory*, New York, Harper and Row, 1st edn, 1956, ch. 13.

66 Leijonhufvud, *Information and Coordination*, pp. 164–5, n. 48, p. 182, n. 85.

67 Don Patinkin, *Anticipations of the General Theory? And other essays on Keynes*, Oxford, Basil Blackwell, 1982, p. 84, n. 8.

68 To some extent, Coddington's efforts in *Keynesian Economics*, ch. 4, are to be taken further here.

69 Paul Davidson, *International Money and the Real World*, pp. 67–73; Christopher Torr, *Equilibrium, Expectations and Information: a study of the General Theory and modern classical economics*, Cambridge, Polity Press, 1988, pp. 78–84; Warren Young, *Interpreting Mr Keynes: the IS-LM enigma*, Cambridge, Polity Press, 1987, ch. 5. 2.

70 Dow and Earl, *Money Matters*, pp. 167–71. I doubt that, despite the stated eclecticism and discernible inclination towards a 'Babylonian' style, either author would strongly object to being assigned to the fundamentalist camp for the present purposes.

71 Dow and Earl, *Money Matters*, p. 181.

72 ibid., pp. 181–2.

73 Another (internal) defect in their argument is that the liquidity trap *does* involve a rigid price, the interest rate. Furthermore, the price level can fall freely even if quantities are in an unemployment equilibrium. Leijonhufvud's views on the role of real balance effects cannot, however, be pursued here.

74 Leijonhufvud, *On Keynesian Economics*, p. 59 (emphasis added).

75 ibid., pp. 86–9.

76 A conversation with Leijonhufvud (Perugia, April 1987) confirms that he accepts that the marginal propensity to save plays the role usually assigned to it. He was surprised to learn that his writings had been interpreted in any other way.

77 Keynes, *The General Theory*, pp. 5, 378–9. See also pp. v–vi, 146.

78 Joan Robinson, 'What has become of the Keynesian revolution?', in Milo Keynes (ed.), *Essays on John Maynard Keynes*, Cambridge, Cambridge University Press, 1975, pp. 123–31, at pp. 124–5; and 'The theory of money and the analysis of output', *Review of Economic Studies*, vol. 1, no. 1, October 1933, pp. 22–6, at pp. 24–5.

79 Keynes, *The General Theory*, pp. 246–7.

80 See, for example, W. Stanley Jevons, *Political Economy*, London, Macmillan, 1913.

81 Keynes, *Collected Writings*, vol. xiii, p. 89. See also *The General Theory*, ch. 22 where such forces are seen as a partial explanation of cyclical behaviour. Keynes sees such factors as working in conjunction with several others.

82 Note that the bond market and the share market will not be subsumed in this work under the one heading as does Leijonhufvud (but see *On Keynesian Economics*, p. 136, n. 9). The reason for keeping these markets distinct is that the MEI curve is not always fixed in the short run in Keynes's model (cf. ibid., p. 42). To anticipate findings in later chapters, this is because of fairly *elastic* price expectations prevailing in the commodities sectors. The bond market, on the other hand, is usually governed by inelastic price expectations as Leijonhufvud maintains.

83 Keynes, *Collected Writings*, vol. xiv, p. 114, emphasis in the original.

84 For the idea that conventions apply in the valuation of shares see Keynes, *The General Theory*, p. 152.

85 ibid., pp. 203–4, 325. The rate of interest 'is a highly conventional ...phenomenon', p. 203.

86 ibid., p. 247.

87 Sir John Hicks, 'Mr Keynes' theory of employment', *Economic Journal*, vol. 46, June 1936, pp. 238–53, at p. 239, but compare Hicks's 'Recollections and documents', *Economica*, vol. 40, February 1973, pp. 2–11, at p. 7, n. 1.

88 Keynes, *The General Theory*, p. 249.

89 ibid., p. 254. Not everyone accepts that such an intermediate position is a centre of gravity towards which the system converges. For example, see Athanasios Asimakopulos, *Investment, Employment and Income Distribution*, Cambridge, Polity Press, 1988, pp. 138–9. He regards such paragraphs as being simply descriptive. However, if speculators prevent interest rates from falling sufficiently to ensure full employment, average performance will surely systematically lie below full employment.

90 Paul Davidson, 'Rational expectations: a fallacious foundation for studying crucial decision-making processes', *Journal of Post Keynesian Economics*, vol. v, no. 2, Winter 1982–3, pp. 182–98; Tony Lawson, 'Uncertainty and economic analysis', *Economic Journal*, vol. 95, December 1985, pp. 907–27.

91 Herbert A. Simon writes that conventional behaviour lies at 'the farthest remove from neoclassical economics' and discussions of it 'do not rest at all on rationality assumptions'. He appears to have in mind customs rather than endogenously determined conventions which emerge from

the acts of rational, but uncertain, individuals. See his entry, 'Behavioural economics', in John Eatwell, Murray Milgate and Peter Newman (eds), *The New Palgrave: a dictionary of economics*, London, Macmillan, 1987, in 4 vols, vol. 1, pp. 221–5, at p. 222.

92 Frank Hahn, 'Exercises in conjectural equilibria', *Scandinavian Journal of Economics*, vol. 79, 1977, no. 2, pp. 210–26.

93 Coddington, *Keynesian Economics*, p. 96, emphasis added.

94 Dow and Earl, *Money Matters*, p. 178. Even if 'causing horrendous mathematical complications', I note that theoretical physics, for example, has not proved sterile on account of it.

95 This view conflicts with Coddington, 'Keynesian Economics...', pp. 1260–70, who sees Keynes's retention of the notion of equilibrium as a classical ball and chain which impeded his 'long struggle of escape' from 'habitual modes of thought and expression' (*The General Theory*, p. viii). W. Robert Brazelton, in 'A survey of some textbook misinterpretations of Keynes', *Journal of Post Keynesian Economics*, vol. 3, no. 2, Winter 1980–81, pp. 256–70, at p. 264, alludes to Coddington's argument without clearly agreeing or disagreeing.

96 It can be argued that a kind of corridor surrounds any conventional equilibrium regardless of whether it coincides with full employment.

97 Leijonhufvud, 'Effective demand failures', in *Information and Coordination*, p. 112, n. 16.

Part two

Chapter two

Leijonhufvud on unemployment and effective demand

Leijonhufvud's interpretation: a preliminary overview

In his book *On Keynesian Economics and the Economics of Keynes*, Leijonhufvud's aim is to distil the essence of Keynes's vision of how a modern capitalist system behaves. This vision is contrasted with that of the post-war 'New Economics' which claimed Keynes as its progenitor.[1]

Leijonhufvud argues that the orthodox majority school has failed to comprehend the true nature of Keynes's revolution. This has led to the revisionism which has resulted in Keynes's contribution being considered to be merely a special case of the neoclassical synthesis where the IS and LM curves are of peculiar elasticity.

He draws a distinction as suggested by the title of his book, between the writings of the 'Keynesians' – scholars who profess to follow Keynes – and those of Keynes himself. What is the Keynesian economics that is claimed to be in fundamental error?

> Keynesian economics...is far from being a homogeneous doctrine. The common denominator, which lends some justification to the identification of a majority school, is the class of models generally used. These short-run, simultaneous equation models have their prototype in the famous, early 'Keynes and the Classics' paper by Hicks. The basic analytical framework, which these models have in common, one finds conventionally summarized in most textbooks in the familiar Hicks–Hansen IS-LM apparatus. This framework will hereafter be (not altogether adequately) referred to as 'the Income–Expenditure model'.[2]

Harry Johnson has commented:

> [The Keynesians] are to be identified with an American-led group of economists oriented towards mathematical and econometric model-building.... To put the point in terms of personalities: both Milton Friedman...and Joan Robinson...can with a clear

conscience commend Leijonhufvud's book to their students; Paul Samuelson, leader of the American Keynesian tradition, will find it embarrassing to do so.[3]

Leijonhufvud is no less blunt:

> Almost the entire corpus of fiscal policy theory identified with the 'New Economics' has been a post Keynes development. One does not find Lerner's 'Functional Finance' concept explicitly elaborated in the *General Theory*. The concept of the 'deflationary (or inflationary) gap' and the associated array of algebraic exercises on the income-expenditure model, such as the balanced budget multiplier theorems, belong to a later period.[4]

Although it might not be easy to name many figures who confidently upheld all these articles of faith, Leijonhufvud, as recently as 1978, commented that he could not recall being criticized for attacking a non-existent school of Keynesian straw-men.[5]

According to Leijonhufvud, these conventional schematic representations are inadequate means to explain the process by which the system moves from one level of income to another. Econometric models merely measure quantitative differences between initial and final equilibrium states. Neither does the mechanical manipulation of *IS* and *LM* curves highlight the dynamic process of transition. Leijonhufvud notes

> that comparative static experiments with the standard simultaneous equation model cannot yield any statements relating to the process connecting the initial and terminal 'equilibria'. The seeming precision of the algebraic manipulation disguises the fact that 'equation-skipping' sketches of intervening events are altogether impressionistic.[6]

An appropriate model would focus upon the factors which govern individual choice. Aggregate models abstract from the conditions facing individual transactors thereby concealing the changes in relative prices and budget constraints which are at the heart of the very process under study. To obtain 'an empathic grasp of Keynes' vision'[7] it is necessary to discover the implicit microeconomic analysis which explains how a system can, in the aggregate, both move to and remain in, a state of substantial unemployment.

What follows is a highly simplified account of what appear to be the more salient features of Leijonhufvud's 1968 version of the essentials of Keynes's macrodynamics. (Modifications made since the publication of his book will be discussed subsequently when his arguments are critically examined.) Certainly this is not a thorough compendium of his book because the predominant concern is in interpreting Keynes and not in discussing capital theory, the pure theory of the Keynes and the windfall effects, or the other subsidiary issues into which Leijonhufvud delves deeply. Why Leijonhufvud saw it to be necessary to discuss such matters and the conclusions he reached will, however, be given attention. Furthermore, as this work will be hard pressed even to deal fully with all the arguments pertaining directly to Keynes, certainly this section will not attempt to amount to more than a fairly comprehensive summary of his position. Leijonhufvud's contribution is both broad and deep. The arguments stream through the text and cascade into the footnotes below. Any interpretation of his book therefore (and indeed, of *The General Theory* as well) must be somewhat selective, and the reader inevitably chooses as important those topics which made the greatest impression on him or her. Subjective judgements creep in from the outset. Consequently, what is here dismissed as peripheral, some may hold to be central. This cannot be helped. One can only hope that the reader will be swayed on the balance of probability. A proof beyond reasonable doubt is impossible.

The summary to be given below will tend to focus on chapters II and V of his book. These form the two central pillars which support his account of the meaning and significance of the dynamics implicit in Keynes's comparative-statics analysis. Details of other aspects of his position will receive individual attention during the topic-by-topic treatment that is adopted subsequently.

Leijonhufvud rejects the Keynesian interpretation which reduces Keynes's arguments to merely a 'special case' of the neoclassical synthesis where either money wages are fixed, the liquidity trap prevails or investment expenditure is interest inelastic. An interpretation of Keynes on these lines allows the possibility of some sort of equilibrium at less than full employment but gives fiscal policy too much emphasis. Leijonhufvud argues that an examination of *The General Theory*, when read in conjunction with his *Treatise*, enables us to reject that Keynes upheld any of the three conditions upon which the special case depends.

Neither did Keynes, contrary to Keynesian teaching, hold that an unemployment equilibrium could exist in which no automatic forces could plausibly restore full employment in the long run.[8] Keynes's theoretical contribution lay first in discovering how a system could be in disequilibrium in the short run,[9] and second in elaborating upon the mechanisms which could restore full employment in the long run. In this section, the former will be considered and the latter will be dealt with in the next.

Keynes, in Leijonhufvud's view, did not completely overthrow classical economics and he did not adopt the radical Keynesian arguments that either certain prices (primarily money wages and the interest rate) are rigid or transactors do not respond to price incentives. The latter occurs when animal spirits so dominate the investment decision that interest rates play no significant part. Instead, Keynes's objection to classical theory was considerably more subtle. His only modification of the classical model was to remove the assumption that economies operated as if there existed a Walrasian auctioneer who set optimum prices so that exogenous shocks would be immediately neutralized without causing unemployment.

Few would deny that it is absurd to suggest that the real-world economy acts as if there exists the mythical Walrasian auctioneer who instantly and costlessly informs all agents of the equilibrium prices that will clear all markets.[10] In reality, transactors must search for the most favourable terms of purchase and sale, and, being ignorant of the new price vector required to maintain full employment after a disequilibrating shock, their reservation prices might be too slow to adjust to the changed circumstances. It then becomes possible that transactors can trade at 'false' or disequilibrium prices resulting in the undesired accumulation of unsold stocks at the end of the market day. Prices need not be rigid for this to occur. Anything less than instantaneous adjustment suffices.

Leijonhufvud suggests that the main reason why prices are not quick enough to adjust is that transactors are imperfectly informed about the true state of the demand for whatever it is that they supply. Buyers and sellers do not communicate except through price offers and their rejection or acceptance. Price signals can be misinterpreted and expectations can exist which in fact are mistaken. Sellers might erroneously believe that today's reduction in demand is only temporary. They might believe that business will soon return to normal. It follows that they will be reluctant to contract for the sale of their product at a lower price than before. They will prefer to speculate that tomorrow they will be able to sell their stocks at nearly the old price. This seems preferable to selling everything today at whatever price they can get. In other words, price expectations are inelastic with the result that quantities sold will adjust more rapidly than prices.

To be more specific, suppose that a downward shift in the MEI schedule disrupts an initial state of full employment. Also suppose that investment is responsive to changes in the interest rate. Now, if the interest rate were to fall by a sufficient amount (remaining positive in the process), then entrepreneurial pessimism could be offset and investment would not fall. (Ignored is the fact that lower interest rates might affect consumption and therefore the amount of investment required to preserve full employment.) An initial excess of planned saving over planned investment would cause bond prices to rise and interest rates to fall unless bears hoard money and do not lend it to investors. But because bears possess inelastic price expectations, they are reluctant to pay higher security prices fearing an imminent capital loss. Consequently savings are withheld from investors. (Output and income have yet to fall so aggregate saving can be regarded as given.) Leijonhufvud suggests that the effect of bear speculation is to interfere with communications between savers and investors. The true perception of the economic environment conveyed by savers to investors through price signals (that is, through changes in the interest rate) does not arise as automatically as the classicists assumed. They had maintained that lower interest rates would occur and that this would induce the same behaviour of investors as would have taken place if they had been in direct, verbal (or perhaps even telepathic) communication with savers. It would be as if they had been told the following: 'I am prepared to save now so that you can use the resources I release to make capital goods and thereby satisfy my future consumption desires.' Instead bears, in effect, transmit another message: 'I want more money *per se*. I neither wish to consume nor invest.' Decisions are made, therefore, by individual investors in the light of false perceptions of savings and future consumption plans.[11]

The nexus between saving and investment is made even less reliable by the fact that savers do not inform sellers of precisely what items they wish to consume at some specified time in the future. Investors simply have to form their own estimates about the pattern and composition of future consumption.[12] There is, to repeat, no direct communication between savers and investors.

Consequently, investment may not rise to offset lower consumption and aggregate employment can therefore fall, but the story does not stop here. Producers of investment goods might attempt to persuade their employees to accept, say, a 5 per cent wage-cut in order to reduce their money costs and thereby counteract the recent decline in sales revenue and profits. However, workers may be ignorant of the fact that aggregate demand has fallen and that jobs at their initial wage cannot be obtained elsewhere. Because consumers and investors as a whole do not directly communicate with these workers, the latter might erroneously believe that other employers can still afford to pay them their original wage or close to it. These workers would rather quit and engage in job search because they possess inelastic expectations regarding their money wage. While searching for jobs, the ex-workers curtail their consumption because they are no longer earning income and have little accumulated savings.[13] This causes the shock to the investment-goods industry to become amplified so that spillover effects are felt by the consumption sector. Employers in the consumption sector now insist that their employees accept a wage-cut to keep their jobs.[14] These workers likewise refuse the lower offer and search for alternative employment, and the process of falling aggregate demand continues with a multiplying effect.

It is the multiplier that is the outstanding innovation of *The General Theory*. It exposes the major weakness of the classical model, the absence of a valid theory of short-run dynamic adjustment. In the classical scheme the greater the divergence of current false prices and the equilibrium prices, the greater the incentive for parties to profit (or minimize losses) by exchange and thereby to return to full employment. Any disequilibrium at the end of the market day would be temporary and Walrasian equilibrium would be restored within the short run. If transactors happen to hold inelastic price expectations, then any stocks that they choose not to sell on the market day in the hope of attaining a higher price tomorrow reflect voluntary unemployment because transactors have simply priced themselves out of the market.

Keynes attacked this kind of reasoning which does not recognize that a deviation from an initial state of full employment might become cumulative and generate more and more involuntary unemployment. If worker A becomes unemployed then those who previously made the goods once consumed by A will also become unemployed and, once this multiplier process is initiated, restoration of full employment becomes problematic within the short run. When workers eventually realize that lower wages must be accepted to regain their old jobs, employers are no longer willing to hire them at that wage. Employers are now confronted with additional multiplier-induced reductions in demand. They will be willing to hire workers and pay them in cash only if they expect to gain the marginal revenue in cash needed to cover the marginal cost. No single producer can pay his newly employed worker in kind or rely on him spending his entire wage on the items he produces. No single employer can expect to be able to sell additional output and cover his costs. Only if all employers agreed as a group to hire all the unemployed simultaneously, would it be possible for the additional output made by one firm to be bought out of the wages paid by other employers to their newly employed workers.[15] Acts of production and exchange which would occur at full employment do not occur now for the simple reason that the money required by a worker to effect these transactions is not possessed by him on account of his own current unemployment. In a barter economy, however, no such problem could arise because workers could be paid in kind the marginal physical product of the last worker engaged. The employer need not fear being unable to cover his additional production costs through additional sales. This can be contrasted to a monetary economy in which workers can produce output for which there is no buyer. The budget lines of the unemployed workers shift inwards after they are dismissed or they quit. This reduction in their expenditure reduces the income earned by the employers. If commodity prices are sticky, unsold stocks increase and employers suffer further disruptions of their cash flows.

In a money-using system one needs money to communicate a desire to exchange, and in disequilibrium the wrong signals are sent.[16] Transactors face a prolonged decline in demand which they interpret as meaning, 'People don't want my product as much as before.' In fact, the unemployed are prepared to work and to consume, but employers are not informed of the workers' 'notional' demand. They only know of the state of 'effective' demand which involves the desire to exchange backed up with the means of payment required to effect the purchase. Two parties may be prevented from trading because the medium of exchange might not be possessed by the potential purchaser until he is able to sell his goods to a third party.

Reasoning of this kind is alien to the short-run dynamics of the classical school which had largely concerned itself with analysing the causes both of the trade cycle and of temporary financial crises. Attention was not paid to the study of effective demand which could expose the workings of the multiplier and explain the persistence of a state of demand-deficient unemployment. This is because the classicists had relied upon the cardinal tenet that any excess supply in one market must be offset by an excess demand elsewhere so that there would be strong pressures to cause equilibrating adjustments of relative prices. For example, in order to eliminate an excess supply of labour and a corresponding excess demand for goods, competitive pressure will cause wages to fall relative to the prices of commodities.

Clower has objected that only notional demands need necessarily offset excess supplies. No effective excess demand for goods corresponding to the excess supply of labour exists which will drive production to full-employment levels. It is only if you are already at full employment that notional and effective demands are equal because only then are all transactors able to acquire the money needed to effect their mutually consistent desires for trade.[17]

Leijonhufvud agrees with Clower that unemployment stems from a lack of purchasing power in the hands of the unemployed. To repeat, Leijonhufvud's position is that Keynes's short-run dynamics depends upon the realization that communication failures can occur which in turn can cause an initial shock to be amplified by multiplier effects. Not only are savers and investors unable to co-ordinate their activities to ensure full employment, but also consumers and producers. The classical assumption of the possession of full information by all transactors is merely a special case of Keynes's general theory.[18] It is the lack of perfect (and the presence of misleading) information upon which to base one's decision which is at the heart of the dislocations suffered by monetary economies.

Furthermore, because conventional models cannot analyse the flow of information from its source to its destination where it must be interpreted and responded to, a new 'cybernetic' approach is needed.[19] In this way the stages of a dynamic process can be meaningfully and consistently linked. Leijonhufvud complains:

> The Walrasian model is admirably suited to the study of the incentive function of prices, the performance of which is a necessary but not sufficient condition for the coordination of a decentralized system. But from the standpoint of dynamic theory, it remains what cyberneticians term a Clockwork model – a strictly deterministic, Newtonian mechanism in which prices perform the function of levers and pulleys.... Yet might it not be the time to consider whether the direction in which the Newtonian conception leads us is really the most fruitful for 'purely' theoretical inquiry to pursue?[20]

Although things become progressively worse in the short run by virtue of the multiplier, full employment could still be restored in the long run. This aspect is discussed at length in Part three of this work.

As money wages fall, workers gradually become prepared to accept lower wages after a fruitless search for jobs paying their old wage. As a consequence, various real balance effects will be generated. In particular, deflation will increase the real value of idle balances and will cause, in the absence of the liquidity trap (which, according to Leijonhufvud, Keynes explicitly repudiated[21]), a decline in the interest rate. It should be remembered that the interest rate being 'wrong' was the cause of all the trouble in the first place.[22]

The decline in the MEI curve which disrupted the investment sector was on account of bear speculation not offset by an immediate reduction in the rate of interest sufficient to preserve full employment. In the long run, however, the forces of thrift and productivity would ultimately prevail over speculation.[23] Interest rates would fall and, because investment is, contrary to the Keynesians, interest elastic,[24] aggregate demand would grow. Furthermore, Keynes realized that lower interest rates would affect consumption by increasing the value of the stock of wealth and thereby generating a 'windfall effect'. Leijonhufvud therefore defends Keynes from the neoclassicists who disparage him for having overlooked how deflation could restore full employment.[25]

Full employment could be restored by belated wage reductions, but the road would be very bumpy and the burden of adjustment would be thrown on to the money wage which would fluctuate violently during the transitional period. If workers had accepted a wage cut initially, a small one would have sufficed, but, once the multiplier effect has caused income to decline sharply, much greater reductions are required subsequently to trigger the various real balance effects. The dislocative effects of the deflation required to eventually restore full employment are severe.[26] Things get much worse before they can possibly get better if the system is allowed to flounder without fiscal intervention.

It is in this light that we should interpret Keynes's policy recommendations. At the theoretical level there is little to divide Keynes from the classicists regarding long-run considerations. Only the dynamics of short-run disequilibrium were radically different. The Keynesians failed to realize that Keynes's apparent advocacy of fiscal policy simply stemmed from the recognition of the short-run potency of the multiplier effect. It was not that there was a 'clean break' from his faith, expressed in the *Treatise*, in the power of monetary policy. Keynes never ceased to believe in the long-run importance of low long-term interest rates.[27] *The General Theory* simply argued that bear speculation made it impossible for interest rates to adjust quickly enough and by a large enough amount to overcome large changes in income induced by the multiplier.

The response to Leijonhufvud's challenge

One might have expected that Leijonhufvud's extensive criticism of the orthodox school would have provoked immediate and impassioned denunciations. This did not occur. His work appears to have been favourably received by the profession as a whole and his interpretation has been acknowledged and discussed in the textbooks.[28] Friedman has described Leijonhufvud's book as 'brilliant' and 'penetrating'.[29] Johnson found it to be 'monumentally scholarly' and 'enjoyably readable'.[30] Even Joan Robinson gave a friendly review.[31] But as time has gone by discontentment has grown. According to Blaug:

> ...Leijonhufvud's book was well received. Indeed, it was too well received: it was swallowed whole, despite the fact that its central message is uncertain, its style of exposition subtle to the point of being obscure and its target more or less the whole of received macroeconomics.[32]

Unfortunately, these assertions were not substantiated, and I am not aware of Blaug ever elaborating at length upon the particular issues where he believes Leijonhufvud is mistaken. Other writers, however, have made more formal attempts to assess Leijonhufvud's interpretation.[33] These contributions tend to reflect a growing opinion that, however valuable Leijonhufvud's analysis may be on its own terms, it is too speculative and cannot be fairly attributed to Keynes himself. Alan Coddington remarks that it 'can be read into the *General Theory* only with what seems to me to be a great deal of ingenuity and determination'.[34] Richard Jackman's critique is more vigorous in that he claims that 'Leijonhufvud's interpretation...is unfaithful to Keynes' writings and...misrepresents Keynes on a number of major issues'.[35]

Interest in his interpretation has waned. As James Trevithick[36] notes:

> Leijonhufvud's book was greeted with a considerable critical acclaim but I think it is fair to say that, partly because of the manner in which it was written, it has not had very much impact on the way in which macroeconomics is taught, even at a graduate level.

Leijonhufvud's book, being largely one of doctrinal history, did not capture the attention of textbook writers in the sense that a model could be drawn directly from its pages and presented in simple diagrams capable of being grasped by undergraduates. There are no diagrams which convey simply Leijonhufvud's theoretical discoveries either. It was left to the French school, who, among others, built fix-price and general equilibrium models, to attempt, with only partial success, to represent Leijonhufvud's views on Keynes.

On the whole, however, we can say that Leijonhufvud's book was considerably better received than was *The General Theory* itself. A cynic would suggest that this must mean that Leijonhufvud's thesis is easily incorporated into established doctrine and remains essentially neoclassical despite the many well-aimed jibes directed against orthodox teachings.[37] An alternative view, however, is that Leijonhufvud does not engage in the sweeping polemical attacks which have alienated some modern thinkers from *The General Theory*. We shall find that each possibility can be fairly argued as being part of the explanation.

It may prove helpful, even at this early stage, to provide the reader with an indication of the position to be taken in this work. On some specific issues I shall argue that Leijonhufvud's interpretation is open to criticism. However, this assessment will probably be friendlier than some of those previously cited because it is maintained that many of the foundations of his position are quite secure. In particular, (a) the recognition of the role of money in generating multiplier effects, (b) the emphasis given to information flows in explaining co-ordination failures, (c) the pivotal importance of interest rates and (d) the existence of real balance effects in Keynes's writings constitute the major areas of agreement. Several disagreements with Leijonhufvud appear with regard to what might be thought of as relatively trifling and pedantic points. However, it is submitted that there is enough of a pattern to these objections to show that the view of Keynes that one gets through Leijonhufvud's spectacles is significantly different.[38] Nevertheless, the differences are not fundamental.

First, it is argued that Leijonhufvud tends to present somewhat artificial arguments in his efforts to portray the transactors in Keynes's model as typically possessing inelastic price expectations. It is doubtful, contrary to Leijonhufvud, that Keynes held this adage to be generally true: 'Things are seldom as good or bad as they are first reported.'[39] Price expectations may be elastic or inelastic depending on the particular circumstances of the moment. Economic agents do, it is agreed, need to form expectations in the absence of costless and complete information, but whether these price expectations need to be universally inelastic is another question.[40] Instability and falling income can also be consistent with price expectations being greater than unity. For example, if a sudden fall in share prices bursts a speculative bubble, panic sales in anticipation of further falls are perfectly possible. It can be argued that Leijonhufvud's view that expectations are generally inelastic is really only a special case of Keynes's more general theory of individual behaviour when decisions need to be made in an environment of uncertainty, confusion and disarray. To allow more scope for discoordinated behaviour allows fundamental insights to be absorbed.

Secondly, there are crucial steps in the argument (for example, in relation to the properties of the MEI and liquidity preference schedules) where the *Treatise* has been cited, despite the existence in *The General Theory* of evidence seeming to indicate a contrary view. This is symptomatic of Leijonhufvud's faith in the strongly complementary character of these two works. In disposing of the Keynesian notion that *The General Theory* is a 'clean break' from his earlier writings, Leijonhufvud seems to have gone to the opposite extreme and to have exaggerated their similarities.

It cannot be denied that there are similarities between these works however. Indeed, a case can be made that some of the revolutionary concepts of *The General Theory* can be found in the *Treatise*.[41] Leijonhufvud's position though is quite different. His view is that the later book should be interpreted in the light of the less radical and extreme discussions of the earlier.

The third general objection is that Leijonhufvud's interpretation as a whole is rather too friendly to classical economics. Keynes's more radical statements against the classical school sometimes are not treated as centrepieces but as mere qualifications, provocative overstatements or fundamental mistakes. For example, despite Keynes's denunciation of the classical theory of the determination of the interest rate, Leijonhufvud still argues that Keynes should be taken to have recognized the importance of thrift and productivity in the long run. One must admit that the interest rate controversy was (and, indeed, still is) marred by apparently endless dispute, but to brush Keynes aside does conceal that there may be other areas, apart from the theory of short-run, multiplier-induced dynamics, where Keynes and the classicists were in sharp disagreement.

It seems that Leijonhufvud, in a praiseworthy attempt to avoid terminological snarls and polemical distractions, has unduly softened the tone of the controversy between Keynes and the classicists. Certain statements about the stability of the MEI schedule and the absence of the liquidity trap, also indicate a slight but clear leaning towards classical modes of thought.

Leijonhufvud on unemployment

Leijonhufvud relies on Clower's analysis of the microfoundations of Keynes's revolution in monetary theory. Clower argues that the fundamental characteristic of a monetary economy is: *'Money buys goods and goods buy money; but goods do not buy goods.'*[42] Consequently, an individual may have notional demand without having effective demand. The former relates to the desire to acquire goods backed up with the means to barter goods or labour in exchange for it. The latter pertains to the desire to acquire something backed up with the means of payment, that is, money.

In disequilibrium, the problem is that

> we may be caught in the vicious circle where the unemployed cannot make their consumption demand *effective* until they have sold their services for money, and producers with excess capacity cannot bid for labour until they have sold their goods – which the unemployed do not have the cash to purchase, and so on.[43]

It is claimed that such a phenomenon is totally alien to classical short-run dynamics because it involves the denial of a cardinal tenet of classical faith, namely, Walras' Law that any excess supply in one market must be offset by at least one excess demand in other markets. The existence of an excess supply and a matching excess demand causes equilibrating price changes to ensue.[44] For example, in order to eliminate any excess supply of labour and its corresponding excess demand for commodities, competitive pressure will cause wages to fall relative to the price of consumption goods.

Clower's objection is that only notional demands need necessarily offset excess supplies. No effective excess demand need exist to inform producers of the willingness of labour to work in exchange for the money required to purchase commodities. Only at the full employment price vector are notional and effective demands equal,[45] because only then do all transactors possess the liquidity to effect their mutually consistent desires to purchase and to offer their given goods and services in return. Keynes's emphasis on the concept of effective demand and his attack on the classical teaching that supply creates its own demand should be taken at their face value as a denial of Walras' Law.[46]

The classicists, according to Leijonhufvud's view of the state of pre-Keynesian theory, have overlooked that, in the real world without the Walrasian auctioneer, false trades can occur. Even Hicks, who expressly considered the problem, did not believe that false trading would be empirically significant in inducing income effects: 'I think we may reasonably suppose that the transactions which take place at "very false" prices are limited in volume.'[47] Clower comments tartly:

> It is heartening to know that income effects can be ignored if they are sufficiently unimportant to be neglected; but this is hardly a solution to the problem at issue. The essential question is whether the supply-and-demand functions of traditional analysis are in any way relevant to the formation of market prices in situations where disequilibrium transactions *cannot* be ignored.[48]

Under competitive equilibrium conditions, everybody can sell as much of their initial endowment as they desire. Any seller can immediately find a buyer at the prevailing price.[49] Traders are price takers and the demand for their product is perfectly elastic, buyers being aware of the prices that other sellers offer.[50]

Things are very different in competitive disequilibrium. Traders are unaware of the slope or position of the demand curves for their products.[51] Prices are not parameters; sellers need to be price makers. Once the initial equilibrium has been disturbed, transactors are likely to offer to sell at false prices because they simply do not know what the new equilibrium vector is.[52]

Keynes's short-run disequilibrium state can be explained, according to Leijonhufvud, by the inelastic expectations of transactors preventing instantaneous re-equilibrating price adjustments. Agents know that a 'normal' price has been established for their product and will maintain this as a reservation price while they gather more information.[53]

Some workers, being ignorant of the necessity to accept a money (and real) wage cut if equilibrium in a changed environment is to be restored, prefer to forego current earnings to devote their efforts to finding alternative employment. Consumption falls because it is largely dependent on realized income in the absence of a significant stock of past savings.[54] Aggregate demand falls even further as a consequence and employers sack still more workers,[55] especially if they are accumulating unsold stocks and are illiquid.

Market signals then tend to create unemployment instead of alleviating it. As Leijonhufvud explains:

The workers looking for jobs ask for *money*, not commodities. Their notional demand for commodities is *not communicated* to producers; not being able to perceive this potential demand for their products, producers will not be willing to absorb the excess supply of labour at a wage corresponding to the real wage that would 'solve' the Walrasian problem.... The fact that there exists a potential barter bargain of goods for labour services that would be agreeable to producers *as a group* and labour *as a group* is irrelevant to the motion of the system. The individual steel-producer cannot pay the newly hired worker by handing over to him his physical product (nor will the worker try to feed his family on a ton-and-a-half of cold-rolled sheet a week).[56]

Producers and workers alike have idle capacity. The cause is that the wage rate does not immediately fall to its optimal value. Neither money illusion[57] nor wage rigidities caused by trade unions is required to explain the existence of unemployment. Leijonhufvud is justified in commenting:

Is it not rather strange...that a model with wage-rigidity acknowledged to be its main distinguishing feature should become widely accepted as crystallizing the experience of the unprecedented wage-deflation of the Great Depression?[58]

But has Leijonhufvud succeeded in discovering Keynes's implicit rationalization of the existence of involuntary unemployment? Leijonhufvud writes:

Alchian's [search-theory] analysis remains perfectly applicable to the explanation of individual behaviour in a state of 'involuntary' unemployment, and the initial 'inflexibility' of reservation prices that his analysis implies is, indeed, a necessary condition for the emergence of such a state. But it is not sufficient. Keynes's involuntary unemployment is fundamentally a product of the cumulative process which he assumed the initial increase in unemployment would trigger.[59]

Did Keynes rely implicitly on all, or even any, of the analysis presented by Leijonhufvud?

Leijonhufvud's evidence from Keynes

Leijonhufvud finds evidence for the denial of Walras' Law[60] in Keynes's critique of the second classical postulate:[61] 'The utility of the wage when a given volume of labour is employed is equal to the marginal disutility of that amount of employment.'[62] If wages are greater than the marginal disutility involved in the supply of labour, involuntary unemployment exists.

Leijonhufvud stresses that Keynes's definition of voluntary unemployment is very wide. Keynes treated the frictional and structural changes in demand as being subsumed under the heading of voluntary unemployment.[63] The definition also embraces

> the refusal or inability of a unit of labour, as a result of legislation or social practices or of combination for collective bargaining or of slow response to change or of mere human obstinacy, to accept a reward corresponding to the value of the product attributable to its marginal productivity.[64]

Keynes did not, therefore, attribute involuntary unemployment to the willed actions of any group, such as a trade union.

This point is amplified by his definition of involuntary unemployment which makes it clear that both parties are constrained to forego mutually advantageous exchanges.

> Men are involuntarily unemployed if, in the event of a small rise in the price of wage-goods relative to the money-wage, both the aggregate supply of labour willing to work for the current money-wage and the aggregate demand for it at that wage would be greater than the existing volume of employment.[65]

Keynes was concerned with the existence of unemployment despite both the willingness of workers to receive lower real wages and the willingness of employers to pay workers the value of their marginal product. Keynes abstracted from the distortions caused by monopolies.[66] He assumed the existence of free competition.

Keynes's message, however, has been misunderstood because of his juxtaposition of the two concepts that workers are willing to receive lower real wages brought about by inflation but will resist cuts in money wages.[67] Keynes was taken to have assumed money illusion on the part of transactors. Leijonhufvud shows that this interpretation is inadequate. He cites Keynes's statement that consumption expenditure 'is obviously much more a function of (in some sense) *real* income than of money-income'.[68] As Leijonhufvud observes:

> Is it really plausible to interpret him as attributing at the same time 'money illusion' to workers in planning to sell their services and sober 'realism' in planning to spend the proceeds?[69]

How then is Keynes to be interpreted? Leijonhufvud claims:

> In disequilibrium, the system is 'confused' and transactors act on the basis of faulty information. In a sense, then, though hardly a

useful sense, they may be said to act under an 'illusion' of one sort or another. But Keynes had no patience with this semantic point.[70]

He goes on to suggest, however, that the resistance to cuts in money wages can be interpreted in two ways and that Keynes has failed to make it clear which he would stress.[71] First, ill-informed workers with inelastic expectations maintain excessive reservation prices while searching for alternative employment. Second, workers, not being able to achieve a general wage cut, obstinately refuse to accept lower remuneration relative to other workers.[72] Leijonhufvud favours the former because it 'lends a pleasing unity of conception'[73] to Keynes's theory. In either case, wages do not change instantly to their new equilibrium values and quantity adjustments become inevitable. A fundamentalist objection is, however, that the preference for the former is blatantly subjective and that Leijonhufvud elevates what he regards as implicit over what Keynes said explicitly. In so far as Keynes's own explanation relies on the interdependence of utility functions, whereas Leijonhufvud's is more firmly individualist and amenable to a neoclassical analysis, it can be argued that the options reflect different visions.

Keynes did not rely solely on wage inflexibility in his denial of the second classical postulate. Indeed, Keynes considered that 'the actual attitude of workers towards real wages and money-wages respectively...is not theoretically fundamental'.[74] Leijonhufvud overcomes Keynes's apparent depreciation of the importance of the behaviour of workers by noting:

> Actually, while it is not 'fundamental' to Keynes' explanation of why a situation of involuntary unemployment is not quickly remedied by automatic forces, it *is* fundamental to the explanation of how the situation can develop that some lag in price adjustments is present.[75]

Keynes's 'theoretically fundamental' objection was that 'the classical theory assumes that it is always open to labour to reduce its real wage by accepting a cut in its money-wage'.[76] The Keynesians have not fully understood the significance of this objection. They have, correctly, realized that Keynes argued that money-wage cuts lead to a *pari passu* fall in aggregate demand in money terms, leaving real wages unchanged. The implication that Walras' Law was being attacked, however, had not been drawn. Keynes was denying emphatically and repeatedly that effective demand can be increased in a monetary economy despite the existence of opportunities for mutually favourable barters of real physical products.[77] Goods themselves are not the means of payment as Keynes took Mill to have asserted.[78] Keynes is most explicit:

The conviction, which runs, for example, through almost all of Professor Pigou's work, that money makes no difference except frictionally and that the theory of production and employment can be worked out (like Mill's) as being based on 'real' exchanges with money introduced perfunctorily in a later chapter, is the modern version of the classical tradition.[79]

The classicists argue

by false analogy from some kind of non-exchange Robinson Crusoe economy, in which the income which individuals consume or retain...is...the output *in specie*.... But, apart from this, the conclusion that the *costs* of production are always covered in the aggregate by the sale-proceeds resulting from demand, has great plausibility, because it is difficult to distinguish it from another, similar-looking proposition.., that the income derived...has a value exactly equal to the *value* of the output.[80]

Leijonhufvud notes that Keynes highlighted the role played by money in the act of exchange in order to deny Walras' Law. The orthodox interpretation has misrepresented Keynes's position in its attempt to argue that Keynes was really *affirming* Walras' Law.[81] Keynes, in this view, merely denied the alleged classical belief that the money market always clears.[82] In the orthodox view, Keynes had (wrongly) assumed that the classicists held that the sum of notional excess demands in non-money markets is always equal to zero, the excess demand for money being always equal to zero. Keynes realized that an excess demand for money is possible and the essence of his revolution is to attack the invalid dichotomy between the real and monetary sectors. Leijonhufvud validly objects:

This standard interpretation...fails to explain why Keynes should insist that the crucial error of the classical economists lay in their misrepresentation of the nature of the wage bargain and in their conviction 'that the theory of production and employment can be worked out as being based on..."real" exchanges'.[83]

Moreover, Keynes's statement that, 'Nevertheless, [Walras' Law] still underlies the whole classical theory, which would collapse without it'[84] is left unexplained.[85]

Certainly, crucial features of Leijonhufvud's argument sharply distinguish Keynes and the classicists. The reductionist account is novel and differs from the hydraulic one. Fundamentalists can agree with Leijonhufvud, though one aspect, the claim that the inelastic wage expectations of workers is central, is contentious.

Some objections to Leijonhufvud's portrayal of expectations

If prices moved instantly and remained at their re-equilibrating values, quantity adjustments would not occur. Leijonhufvud attributes the absence of the required price adjustments to the inelastic price expectations of transactors.[86] It is doubtful that Keynes explained involuntary unemployment in the same way Leijonhufvud does.

> All that Keynes needed to assert is that the worker who is threatened with a lay-off will not offer to take *any* cut necessary to retain his job. Nor, having been laid off, will he immediately resign himself to shining shoes or selling apples.[87]

Although all that Keynes needed to do was assert this, he did not. Leijonhufvud continues:

> One reason, of course, is that his views of what his services should be worth unavoidably are related to what he was paid only yesterday...[H]is expectations are 'inelastic' in the Hicksian sense and his decision to withhold his services from the market may therefore be described as *speculation* on the future course of (obtainable) wages. This is the way Keynes described the behaviour of producers.[88]

Here is the evidence that Leijonhufvud draws from Keynes:[89]

> For, although output and employment are determined by the producer's short-term expectations and not by past results, *the most recent results* usually play a predominant part in determining what these expectations are.[90]

Two points can be made. To attribute to workers similar behaviour to that of producers begs the question which is whether it is true that all agents possess inelastic price expectations. An alternative approach is to examine each market in isolation. Doing this reveals answers different from Leijonhufvud's. Second, if anything, this passage supports the opposite contention to that made by Leijonhufvud. Expectations are quite elastic when 'the most recent results...play a predominant part', but to the behaviour of producers we devote individual attention in the next section.

Some general remarks, however, can conveniently be made here. According to Leijonhufvud, Keynes collapsed short-term expectations and realized results 'for convenience'.[91] He states: 'Although it would have been cumbersome and tiresome to carry the distinction between expected and realised magnitudes through every passage of the book, it might still have been worthwhile to do so...'[92]

Is it not more reasonable to explain Keynes's position by recognizing his belief that expectations are fairly elastic? Leijonhufvud is, in effect, blaming Keynes for not conforming to Leijonhufvud's interpretation. Perhaps Keynes meant what he said. *Ex ante* values depend on *ex post* values so far as short-term production decisions are concerned. This could be a meaningful part of Keynes's analysis and not merely an expedient simplification.

The interpretation based on elastic expectations is also in accordance with Keynes's views about the multiplier process. Let us take

the extreme case where the expansion of employment in the capital-goods industries is so entirely unforeseen that in the first instance there is no increase whatever in the output of consumption-goods. In this event the efforts of those newly employed in the capital-goods industries to consume a proportion of their increased incomes will raise the prices of consumption-goods until a temporary equilibrium between supply and demand has been brought about....As time goes on..., the consumption-goods industries adjust themselves to the new demand...[T]here is no reason to suppose that more than a *brief interval of time* need elapse before employment in the consumption industries is advancing *pari passu* with employment in the capital-goods industry.[93]

In other words, the producers of consumption goods expect the shift in demand to be maintained and will quickly expand production. They do not require a prolonged period where realized results are in excess of their expectations of sale proceeds before they revise their expectations. If their expectations were inelastic, they would not greatly increase the flow of output because they would fear that the additional demand could disappear. They would be left then with undesired inventories. Output would advance *pari passu* with the capital-goods sector only if the producers of consumption goods expected to be able to sell the additional, and more costly, output at a sustained level of higher prices. Keynes envisaged that transactors would respond quickly to changes in the prices offered for their products. Keynes, therefore, held that elastic expectations were conceivably typical in the short run.[94] One thing that is clear is that Keynes held that, even if price expectations were elastic in the commodity market, multiplier effects would occur. Transactors, believing a slump to be more than transient, can anticipate that if they continue to produce at past levels losses and illiquidity will result. Therefore, they can reduce their output before actually making losses. (One can conjecture that liquidity constraints can relatively effectively apply the brakes to an upswing, whereas it is always possible to spend less money than you currently possess if you anticipate lower demand.)

The elasticity of price expectations merely affects the path by which the system moves towards a new level of income. If the marginal propensity to consume is four-fifths and if the initial shock increases income by $10, then equilibrium income will rise by $50 irrespective of the elasticity of price expectations. Keynes draws attention to the

> confusion between the logical theory of the multiplier, which holds good continuously, without time-lag, at all moments of time, and the consequences of an expansion in the capital-goods industries which take gradual effect, subject to a time-lag and only after an interval.[95]

The more quickly increased demand is anticipated, the quicker is the expansion to a higher income level. If changes were foreseen perfectly, the multiplier could work instantaneously.[96] Because Keynes considered that output would expand quickly, he must have held that current results could influence producers' anticipations strongly.

Leijonhufvud's formula of taking a general equilibrium model, subtracting the auctioneer and adding inelastic price expectations cannot readily be attributed to Keynes. The formation of expectations cannot be reduced to such conceptually simple terms.

The behaviour of producers

This section deals with the issue of the flexibility of the prices of output. Examined are the roles played by inventories. The behaviour of firms over the short, and very short, run are discussed. We can then evaluate Leijonhufvud's arguments that inventories can exacerbate the liquidity problems suffered by firms in a downswing. A related point is also considered: how reasonable is it to attribute to Keynes the inelasticity of price expectations of producers?

It is not clear that Keynes had any simple rule about the price (and quantity) expectations of suppliers in the two commodities markets (consumption and investment goods). Several passages can be cited without a clear pattern emerging, but it is evident that Leijonhufvud oversimplifies by attributing inelastic expectations to all agents.

Consider the following. After complaining of the Austrian practice of taking the ratio of the supply price of new consumer goods and producer goods as measuring the marginal efficiency of capital – a 'drastic simplification' in Keynes's eyes – he writes: 'But when the prices in question are prices prevailing in slump conditions, the simplification of supposing that the entrepreneur will, in forming his expectations, assume these prices to be permanent, is certain to be misleading.'[97]

On one occasion, however, Keynes was happy to consider that an increase in effective demand can be initiated by 'an increase in working capital *in anticipation* of increased consumers' demand'.[98] This accords with his later view[99] where changes in demand that are foreseen can fit comfortably into his model.

Clearly, Keynes's views are complex. An important passage appears in the *Treatise*[100] which confirms the view that current variables unduly influence expected values, but he also indicates that it is not just the level of prices but also the duration (rather than the rate of change) of their increase which matters:

> For, with the existing mentality of entrepreneurs, today's spot price for finished goods, which is certain, has far more influence in determining entrepreneurs' decisions as to the rate of new input into the machine of process than the prospective price at the end of the production time, which is to them quite uncertain; whereas it is wholly the latter price and not at all the former which ought to influence them. The result is that, when spot prices are rising, especially if they have been rising steadily for some six months, the rate of input is unduly accelerated, and if they have been falling it is unduly retarded – with obvious subsequent consequences.

Note that after a time expectations overshoot feasible short-run values. This entire passage suggests that the elasticity of price expectations can at least equal unity.

Keynes, one feels, was deliberately non-committal. The actions of individuals are by no means simple to determine. Perhaps, as Leijonhufvud[101] notes, the approach of G.B. Richardson[102] is liable to be fruitful. One agent cannot be confident about his actions until he knows what the others are doing, but the others are in the same position. That Richardson's approach is relevant is clear from Keynes's remarks in the *Treatise*:

> Moreover, where there are a number of entrepreneurs making independent decisions, which they take pains to conceal from one another, involving an increased rate of input, it is quite impossible for any of them to foresee with accuracy the increased rate of output, and consequently the reaction on prices by the time that one production period has passed by.[103]

Keynes refused to pledge loyalty to any simple rule of adjustment: 'Evidently the possible ramifications and extensions of the foregoing argument are so numerous that one could continue for many more pages amplifying, qualifying and generalising it.'[104]

Perhaps the following is a fair interpretation and summary.

Keynes accepted that producers probably had inelastic expectations in practice, but gave it little theoretical weight considering that, even if they could anticipate future demand correctly, involuntary unemployment could still emerge. For the most part, it was reasonable simply to allow the decisions of producers to respond quickly to changes in demand. It is the state of expectations of the investor, rather than the producer, which is of central importance, as we shall see in subsequent chapters.

While the results of his 1968 book can be obtained if interest rates and money wages are prevented by speculation from instantaneously reaching their Walrasian values, Leijonhufvud chose to incorporate inventory accumulations because this would conform to an interpretation of Keynes founded upon inelastic price expectations.

Leijonhufvud has, however, retreated from the view that Keynes reversed in all markets the adjustment velocities of prices and quantities. Leijonhufvud admits that, in the short run, prices and quantities of commodities move in step. (This reflects Leijonhufvud's increasing tendency to explain Keynes's insights in Marshallian terms.) Paul Davidson[105] asserts that Leijonhufvud has changed his mind in a fundamental way, but Leijonhufvud's retreat was a strategic one and not a rout. His concession is a rather minor one upon investigation. His new position, and one that is difficult for any fundamentalist to condemn, is explained in a little known and unpublished work.[106] It supplements another important paper[107] written at about the same time.

It is curious that Davidson points to Leijonhufvud's change of emphasis merely as evidence of the latter recognizing his mistakes rather than instead praising Leijonhufvud for contributing to the common enterprise.[108] There are two ways to view Leijonhufvud's reformulation. It can be seen as a confession of error, a sign that the paradigm is breaking down, an invitation to attack with greater vigour once weaknesses begin to appear. Alternatively, it can be taken as evidence that the original creed is far more flexible than its critics appreciate. The changes can be taken as a sign of a healthy interest in how real-world markets function, a question which spontaneously appears on the research agenda once the Walrasian auctioneer is discarded.

Leijonhufvud now attributes to Keynes a different view on supply responses by producers. Although it glosses over the various plausible adjustment processes on the market day, Keynes's tacit views can still make perfectly good sense. Leijonhufvud writes: 'We could go half-way. Instead of reversing Marshall's ranking we could consider equalizing price and output adjustment speeds.'[109]

Leijonhufvud now prefers to construe Keynes as follows. Keynes implicitly has output and its prices changing on the same brief timescale ('minutes') whereas money wages change over a longer period ('weeks'). Consequently, within the market day, expected and realized sales become equal and price comes to equal marginal cost.[110] This brutally suppresses the details of adjustment on the market day, during which inventories could well accumulate, but clearly Keynes chose not to proceed in a way which specifically focuses attention on inventories. He complains: 'One will search [Keynes' writings] in vain for a coherent account of firm behavior in the very short run.'[111]

Keynes systematically assumes that, in the short run, flow supplies of commodities clear. Leijonhufvud points out[112] that Keynes casually skips between 'expected price', 'expected sales proceeds' and 'expected sales volume'. This is valid only if *ex post* market clearing is being assumed under conditions where *ex ante* variables have indeed been realized. It is the almost complete overlapping of expected and realized results in the commodity markets which makes sense of it all.[113] Keynes, in effect, held that, minute by minute, expected and realized demands were being brought into equality by adjustments of output, the price being offered at any time, in the absence of any clearly superior alternative, sensibly being equal to the marginal cost.[114]

Leijonhufvud sees Keynes's procedure as a rather shoddy corner-cutting exercise rather than as representing a serious conflict between what Keynes in fact wrote and how Leijonhufvud had construed him in 1968. Keynes's procedure assumes away too much of interest, namely the exact nature of price adjustments during the short period itself. Similarly, as he wrote in a recent paper, his 1968 position suffered also from a different, but somewhat contrived, theory of short-run price dynamics.

To say, as I once did, to my frequent regret, that 'In the Keynesian macrosystem the Marshallian ranking of price – and quantity – adjustment speeds is reversed' is too mechanical to be helpful. It reads an open invitation to fix-price rationing modelling of the sort that pays little attention to the determination of prices.[115]

Leijonhufvud has also had second thoughts about the use of the theory of monopolistic competition as a means to examine conduct under conditions of disequilibrium and to provide a plausible account of Keynes's implicit microtheory.

It was suggested by Arrow[116] that, under disequilibrium conditions, atomistic firms will be obliged to set their own prices and become transitory monopolists until a market price emerged. Leijonhufvud is now suspicious of such suggestions. He casts doubts on attempts

to model the firm as...trying to keep track of the position and elasticity of a negatively-sloped demand-curve for his own output – which lives its shadowy existence only when the industry is out of equilibrium – in order to capture what he can of these most evanescent monopoly profits...[O]ne has to make assumptions about information possessed by the firm that seem most unpalatable, even when dressed up as stochastic expectations.[117]

The objection is a reasonable one. A firm in disequilibrium operating in a world where demand curves are shifting cannot grope for a given curve.[118] The firm is, by contrast, more aware of its own cost conditions which makes marginal-cost pricing a more reasonable strategy. Applying Arrow's theory in conditions of macrodisequilibrium is doubtful. It is not clear that firms are liable to be taking advantage of the ignorance and confusion of their customers. (One notes the recent tendency of new Keynesians to rediscover monopolistic competition to counter new classical assertions that their models are not soundly based on principles of individual optimization. They appear to be talking about short-run equilibrium states rather than adjustment processes though.)

Though Leijonhufvud does not say so, it can be further argued that pure competition can be preserved. If there is a decline in aggregate demand, then there is a decline for the representative, normal good. If a market demand curve shifts on account of a decline in the income of consumers, the perfectly elastic demand curve shifts downwards. If, when short-run equilibrium is generated or when the decline in demand proceeds at a smooth pace, consumers are well aware of the prevailing market price, then demand curves for firms can be perfectly elastic and price can equal marginal revenue and marginal cost. Flow supplies of output clear. This is not inconsistent with Keynes's views.[119] It is possible to have involuntary unemployment in a world of pure competition on the output side. Sellers can be painfully aware that the demand for their product is low and that prices cannot fall any lower given their cost structure and given the money wage.

On the other hand, in so far as inelastic price expectations can lead to the accumulation of stocks with possibility of lower revenues being received to finance subsequent purchases of inputs, the illiquidity of producers could have a significance of its own. Keynes does refer to inventories in *The General Theory* but he does not consider their existence as central to the process of disequilibrium. He considers that, in response to increased fixed investment,

> there is no reason to suppose that more than a brief interval of time need elapse before employment in the consumption industries is advancing *pari passu* with employment in the capital goods industries.[120]

The reason for the rapid adjustment of output in the consumption sector could be that the sellers' expectations adjust rapidly or it could be, as Leijonhufvud would prefer it, 'that wage-goods have a high carrying-cost'[121] which deters holding inventories as buffers.

On the latter point, Keynes is somewhat less than helpful. He refers to 'the carrying-costs of surplus stocks which force their absorption within a certain period, neither very short, nor very long'.[122] This, if anything, also supports Leijonhufvud. Keynes is also prepared to acknowledge the role of inventories in causing merely 'minor oscillations within the main movement of the Trade Cycle'.[123]

Note that Keynes wrote (in 1933):

[I]t is a characteristic of finished goods, which are neither consumed nor used but carried in stock, that they incur substantial carrying charges for storage, risk and deterioration, so that they are yielding a negative return for so long as they are held...If it were not for this consideration, the effective demand at a given moment would be governed by more permanent considerations concerning the direction of popular expenditure averaged over a considerable period of time, and would be less subject to rapid fluctuations such as characterise boom and depression.[124]

This passage by its recognition of inelastic expectations supports Leijonhufvud, despite the denial that in practice stock holdings are likely to be significant. (Note, however, that inventory accumulations could promote stability rather than exacerbate liquidity problems – a point against Leijonhufvud.)

This general outlook seems representative of Keynes's views. He accepts, perhaps partly out of courtesy to Hawtrey, that inventory fluctuations are of some, but not prime, importance.[125] Keynes did concede to Hawtrey:[126] 'I have seen much evidence that the changes in traders' stocks are quite large enough to be an important factor.' In partial support of Leijonhufvud, Keynes in a draft of *The General Theory* does admit that

in my *Treatise on Money* I overestimated, as a result of the insufficient attention given in that book to the distinction between actual and anticipated demand, the importance of transitional changes in the stock of *unfinished* consumption goods.[127]

This deficiency was not made good in the final draft but it does suggest that buffer stocks of one kind are of some significance.[128] Presumably, carrying costs for unfinished goods are, however, relatively low. So far as unfinished goods are concerned, Keynes subsumes them under the heading of investment.[129]

So far as an increase in consumer demand is initially unforeseen, disinvestment in stocks bears the brunt of adjustment and reduces the multiplier unless windfall profits happen to provoke optimism. This suggests that producers' expectations might adjust rapidly or they might not. This view is reinforced by Keynes's letter to Hawtrey where he states, though perhaps exaggerating to jolt Hawtrey into understanding his point, that 'it is not relevant to my immediate purpose for me to superimpose the complication of entrepreneurs' making mistakes...[I]t really makes no difference if their foresight is *momentarily* incorrect.'[130] Keynes is largely indifferent about whether expectations of actual demand are 'arrived at by a careful attempt at elaborate foresight...or merely by revision at short intervals on the basis of trial and error'.[131]

What evidence there is from volume xiii does therefore suggest that Keynes held that for a simple theoretical model, the revision of expectations can be deemed to be quite rapid. Corroboration can be found in volume xiv where disinvesting in stocks is evidenced 'only momentarily'.[132] In 1937, rough lecture notes reveal that the issue of making mistakes in short-period expectations is 'of secondary importance, emphasis on it obscuring the real argument'. The theory of effective demand 'is substantially the same if we assume that short-period expectations are always fulfilled'.[133]

Producers seem rather quick to learn about their environment. In a rather patronizing response to Hawtrey, Keynes wrote (in a manner of interest to an advocate of rational expectations):

> But it really makes no difference if their foresight is momentarily incorrect, unless you are asserting a psychological law, that employers are chronically subject to a particular type of false expectation which leads them...to fail to curtail employment to the proper level and hence habitually to make a loss.[134]

Leijonhufvud is entitled to retort that what *triggers* the motion is the failure of prices to instantaneously adjust and that Keynes should not have swept aside the transitional stages as mere complications. Keynes was not denying the inelasticity of expectations of producers, he simply did not consider that anything would be achieved by making his theory still more complex. This is a reasonable view particularly if Keynes was writing in an effort to convince Hawtrey. By putting aside the Marshallian process of trial and error he could highlight a fundamental point: 'Now Hawtrey, it seems to me, mistakes this higgling process by which the equilibrium position is discovered for the much more fundamental forces which determine what the equilibrium position is.'[135]

Keynes therefore did not see inventories, and the resulting miscalculations (and possible illiquidity) of producers, as particularly important. While Keynes considered differences between *ex antes* and *ex posts* to be of little direct relevance to the fundamental problem, it was only natural for Leijonhufvud, in view of his origins, to have greater sympathy for the approach of the Swedish school. Furthermore, at the time when Leijonhufvud wrote his thesis, search theory was an imagination-capturing development. For Leijonhufvud to have a vision based on Clower, the Swedish school and search theory is hardly surprising, and for that vision to be used to organize and interpret the subject-matter of examination was likewise only to be expected.

It is perhaps a little demanding of Leijonhufvud to have expected Keynes to have given more on the details of market-day dynamics. Keynes's remarks about Hawtrey's undue concern for the process of groping, higgling and bargaining apply equally to Leijonhufvud.

You do not need to have producers constrained by unplanned inventories as Leijonhufvud would prefer. Neither do you even need to emphasize inventory-cycle considerations whereby declines in output can be amplified by the reductions of current inventories to their planned levels as orthodox Keynesians might consider important. Keynes deliberately chose to avoid these complicating factors. Why should Keynes give a reviewer an opportunity to misconstrue him and hold erroneously that transitional problems of matching *ex antes* and *ex posts* were at the heart of the matter?[136] Keynes sought to demonstrate a much stronger proposition than that; namely that an involuntary-unemployment state was a logical possibility even if *ex antes* were realized. The picture is made more complex if inventories emerge which drive the system from the marginal-product-of-labour locus, and, presumably, also make the specification of the aggregate supply curve problematic. The absence of emphasis on inventories in *The General Theory* is explained by Leijonhufvud by arguing that Keynes was more concerned with developing a theory of how to avoid major catastrophes. He was not concerned with relatively 'minor oscillations' in which inventories play a major role.[137] On this point, it is easy enough to agree with Leijonhufvud.

Some conclusions can now be drawn.

The role played by producers is a relatively unimportant one in the sense that they seem to respond fairly quickly to the changes in demand which truly govern the motion of the system. Whether inventories play a major role is not really in dispute. Leijonhufvud concedes that, in Keynes, inventories are not stressed. It is curious that this is one point where Keynesians clearly differ from Keynes and yet Leijonhufvud does not point this out.

It is difficult to explain why inventories play only a relatively small role. Perhaps it is due to their high storage costs or perhaps producers are quick to curtail output by virtue of their having relatively elastic expectations. Both possibilities are plausible and can claim support from Keynes's writings.

Leijonhufvud rightly observes that the details of adjustment are missing in Keynes's analysis. It is not clear, however, that

Leijonhufvud's attempts to fill the gap are entirely appropriate. Certainly, Leijonhufvud's views cannot be dismissed out of hand as some have done. Leijonhufvud is now prepared to examine Keynes's views in a Marshallian style. Doing so does not greatly change his original interpretation which was framed in Walrasian language.

Too much has been made of Leijonhufvud's concessions on the matter of price flexibility in the short run. It remains essential, in Leijonhufvud's scheme, that no auctioneer exists to generate the correct price vector instantaneously. If prices and quantities of output are allowed to move together at equal speed, it is true that he has retreated from his view that the Marshallian ranking has been completely reversed. However, to concede this much does not imply that Leijonhufvud has changed his mind on the essential point that prices have not changed to their new and correct Walrasian values prior to any production decisions being made. Trades are still being made on the basis of false prices. If prices and quantities both fall and flow supplies do clear, the system is still moving away from the Walrasian vector.

Leijonhufvud can jettison the idea that commodity prices are rather sticky without affecting his central argument. The cause of involuntary unemployment can be traced to how money wages cannot be instantaneously cut to offset the failure of interest rates to instantaneously negate a decline in planned investment. The money wage and, in a more fundamental sense, the interest rate, are the true culprits.

All that is lost by granting a considerable degree of flexibility to the prices of commodities is the 'pleasing unity of conception'[138] that Leijonhufvud once perceived in *The General Theory*. Neither does it really matter if some agents have highly elastic expectations. Any confusion and error at all, whether it be an error of optimism or pessimism, can generate false trades. Inelastic price expectations are not a necessary condition for the emergence of false prices.

The real wage and the marginal product of labour

Thanks to the efforts of the fundamentalists, it is nowadays more appreciated among historians of thought that the marginal-product-of-labour curve is not a demand curve for labour in Keynes's chapter two but a locus of market equilibria. The chain of causality is not that high real wages cause unemployment but that both phenomena stem from a common cause, a deficiency of aggregate demand. If one accepts the law of diminishing returns, competitive markets and the clearing of the goods market,[139] the real wage equals the marginal product. This is because lower levels of demand cause employment to fall, which raises the marginal product of labour (assuming, of course, that variable proportions are technically possible[140]), which, in turn, brings about higher real wages. High real wages are not to blame for unemployment. They are merely its symptom.

When discussing non-instantaneous cuts in money wages, Leijonhufvud[141] did not, in 1968, grasp this point. He considered that the real wage would respond to lower levels of money wages. Perhaps this was because he held goods-prices as fairly constant and allowed inventory accumulations, with subsequent growth of illiquidity, to be of importance.[142]

Since the publication of his book, however, Leijonhufvud has had second thoughts[143] and has modified his views in two ways. First, he allows commodity prices to be flexible. Second, he accepts the essence of the argument outlined above about the nature of the causative processes at work. Leijonhufvud's concessions therefore allow a relatively brief account to be given of his position, though a few words are needed on how significant his shift of view has been.

In reply to Grossman's assertions that Keynes accepted the classical demand function,[144] Leijonhufvud writes, with justice:

> Grossman is completely wrong on the pivotal point of his entire argument – which was that 'the *General Theory* repeatedly assumes that firms refer only to the real wage in determining their demand for labor, and Keynes never even suggests the notion of a sales constraint'. (Grossman argues this case without once making reference to either chapter 5 or chapter 20 of the *General Theory*!) Our analysis above also shows, however, that Grossman was right in his criticism of my book on another point: it is *not* correct to attribute to Keynes a general reversal of the Marshallian ranking of relative price and quantity adjustment velocities. In the 'short-est run' for which system behavior can be defined in Keynes' model, output-prices *must* be treated as perfectly flexible. The Marshallian ground rules of his analysis will not accommodate a still shorter Hicksian 'fix-price market day'.[145]

In so far as Grossman was right, we have seen how Leijonhufvud revises his views to accommodate the criticism. Leijonhufvud, however, denounces as invalid Grossman's 'pivotal point'. In so doing he fully accepts an argument made by fundamentalist followers of Keynes such as Davidson, further evidence that Leijonhufvud is closer to Davidson than the latter is prepared to acknowledge.

Leijonhufvud accepts that it makes sense in theory to see the curve of the marginal product of labour as an equilibrium locus. Furthermore, he accepts that Keynes saw it in the same light. It is now known, however, that, if anything, real wages move procyclically, contrary to Keynes's belief. Leijonhufvud sees a natural explanation in the stickiness of prices and the accumulation of inventories in the slump and finds Keynes's reply to the arguments of Tarshis and Dunlop as rather contrived.[146]

Whatever Leijonhufvud considers to be a more useful way to look at reality, and he is perfectly entitled to stress the role of inventories as his personal view on the subject, one must note that motion off the real wage–marginal product locus is difficult to model in a simple fashion. Many schedules are market equilibrium curves. For the MEI schedule to be derived, flow supplies of investment goods are assumed to clear. Likewise, the given consumption function is based on the two assumptions that, at current income levels, effective demands for goods are satisfied and second that prices have settled to equilibrium values. Therefore real consumption at any level of income and employment does not suddenly change with changes in prices and inventory accumulations.

Keynes's simplification can well seem naïve to Leijonhufvud, but the advantages of the procedure are manifest. If the real wage is a passive variable, which cannot be said to *cause* involuntary unemployment, it is convenient to show how a unique real wage for each output level can plausibly emerge. It has taken decades for it to be recognized by even a relatively small group that the real wage is passively determined in the short run. Additional complications would obscure the essential point.[147]

Instantaneous versus sticky wage adjustment

We have seen that Leijonhufvud's initial attempt of 1968 to show that Keynes relied on inelastic expectations in the commodity market is not fully convincing. If Leijonhufvud is mistaken about the nature of the commodity market, the question arises whether he is on firmer ground so far as the labour market is concerned.

From the outset it should be pointed out that Leijonhufvud's views about the labour market have been seen merely as a refinement of the classical position. As Chick observes, 'The only improvement offered by the new over the old classical view is that labour is now merely ignorant, rather than stubborn.'[148] There is in any case nothing explicit in Keynes to support the view that inelastic expectations prevent the wage adjustments that would restore full employment. Keynes did, however, say something about the obstinacy of workers imparting inflexibility to the money wage by their refusal to accept reductions relative to other groups of workers.[149] Leijonhufvud, however, fails to appreciate that, even though Keynes assumed that money wages are not perfectly flexible, the obstinate behaviour of workers neither clearly causes, sustains nor amplifies involuntary unemployment. Leijonhufvud agrees that if money wages were highly flexible (though this, of course, is not the same as being perfectly flexible), unemployment would probably increase.[150] If money wages did instantly adjust to their correct level, agents would have no way of knowing that this new nominal wage rate was indeed 'correct'. However willing the parties are to accept a market-clearing wage, nobody knows what it is because no auctioneer exists both to cry out a vector, and to assure agents that this is indeed the true vector which would avoid false trades.

Keynes and Leijonhufvud differ in their analysis of the effects of falling money wages on the real wage and the level of employment. Leijonhufvud argues as follows:

> As an illustration suppose that, following the initial reduction in aggregate demand, an instantaneous across-the-board wage cut of $X/unit time would have been sufficient to induce employers to maintain full employment through period one. This did not happen; instead, some workers lost their jobs and the income-constrained process came into operation.[151]

It is essential to Leijonhufvud's case that temporary wage inflexibility caused by inelastic expectations prevents an instantaneous reduction in both the money and the real wage. Had money wages fallen, full employment would have been maintained and real wages would have fallen too. If money wages fall and if commodity prices fall *pari passu*, the resulting deflation increases the quantity of real balances and lowers the rate of interest.[152] Employment rises and the real wage falls on account of diminishing returns.

Keynes, however, was adamant that money wage settlements do not cause involuntary unemployment: 'There may exist no expedient by which labour as a whole can reduce its *real* wage to a given figure by making revised *money* bargains with the entrepreneurs.'[153] Leijonhufvud takes this to mean that *once the multiplier has taken hold*,[154] money-wage reductions are of no help, but it is not clear that his view has a clear theoretical foundation, as we shall see shortly.

Keynes stated that

> the Classical Theory has been accustomed to rest the supposedly self-adjusting character of the economic system on an assumed fluidity of money-wages; and, when there is rigidity, to lay on this rigidity the blame of maladjustment.[155]

These passages could mean more than the statement that once involuntary unemployment exists, belated money-wage cuts need not do any good. It could be, however, that Keynes would equally reject the view that 'instantaneous' money-wage cuts would work. Keynes's own words could amount to an attack on Leijonhufvud's analysis of involuntary unemployment. Contrary to classical teaching, an offer of a lower money wage need not result in an increase in the quantity of labour demanded and a decline in the real wage.[156] Keynes denied that a cut in money wages (whether instantaneous or otherwise could well make no difference) would restore full employment.

The first of Keynes's arguments sought to 'rebut the crude conclusion that a reduction in money-wages will increase employment "because it reduces the cost of production"'.[157] Apparently Leijonhufvud is prepared to accept the validity of this objection.[158] The argument was that, although lower money wages enable employers to hire more workers with the same aggregate wage bill as before, any increase in employment need not be permanent. If the marginal propensity to consume is less than unity, the newly employed workers will not consume all of the additional output. To prevent the accumulation of commodity inventories, producers will need to make unanticipated price reductions, thereby incurring losses. These losses will induce the curtailment of the flow of output until the initial level of employment is restored. Lower commodity prices will increase the real wage so that it returns to its former value, the lower real wage brought about by the lower money wage being momentary.[159] Keynes's argument is well known. It has been discussed at length by Tobin[160] and Lerner.[161] Leijonhufvud only mentions it in passing with seeming acceptance.[162]

Keynes's second argument was that lower money wages could only restore full employment by an indirect (and extremely unlikely) favourable effect on the propensity to consume, the marginal efficiency of capital or the rate of interest.[163] It is possible that here Leijonhufvud and Keynes part company. Leijonhufvud seems to argue that Keynes meant that deflation necessarily has the required favourable effects provided that the wage-cut is instantaneous. One can fairly ask why it would matter exactly when the wage-cut would occur. If an instantaneous money-wage cut can offset a decline in the MEI curve or induce a Keynes effect, why can't a belated one? Were there an auctioneer, he could just as easily call out a correct vector later as immediately. Were he absent, then, whether cuts were instantaneous or belated, employers and employees would find it extremely difficult, if not impossible, to acquire information about money wages required to induce exactly the appropriate shifts in the aggregate demand curve. No two agents have any way of knowing the macroeconomic 'externalities' whereby their own actions play a part in governing the price level itself which in turn influences the decisions of other agents. While there may be acute difficulties in deferred wage cuts, in that declining income could well have caused such pessimism that larger money-wage cuts are necessary to induce the required shift in the aggregate demand curve,[164] it is not clear that any substantive differences are involved. Key arguments in his 1968 book do not seem fully thought out.

Leijonhufvud claims that while money-wage inflexibility caused by inelastic price expectations

> is not 'fundamental' to Keynes' explanation of why a situation of involuntary unemployment is not quickly remedied by automatic forces, it *is* fundamental to the explanation of how the situation can develop that some lag in price adjustments is present.[165]

It can be argued, however, that within Leijonhufvud's own paradigm and despite his belief to the contrary, price inflexibilities are required not only to initiate, but also to maintain, a state of involuntary unemployment. If money wages had fallen instantly without being impeded by inelastic expectations, and if *pari passu* reductions in the price of commodities had resulted, then the quantity of real money balances would have increased sufficiently to lower the rate of interest and restore full employment immediately. If, however, inelastic expectations cause the multiplier to amplify the initial shock and if pessimism gradually grows, then a larger fall in the rate of interest, and, consequently, greater deflation is required.[166] This deflation will surely be forthcoming as soon as workers are willing to sell their labour at whatever price is necessary to clear the market through real balance and investment-demand effects. The very fact that sufficient deflation has not eventuated means, within Leijonhufvud's terms of reference, that wages are not adequately flexible during that period.

If Leijonhufvud's argument were followed to its logical conclusion, workers must be held to have only themselves to blame for their unemployment. The upshot is that, because money-wage cuts must restore full employment, Leijonhufvud seems to have no theory of involuntary unemployment! If workers have the power to lower the rate of interest at will, then their failure to do so must be interpreted as an obstinate refusal to work for a lower real wage. How can Leijonhufvud escape from this dilemma?

A resolution of the contradiction is that, for instantaneous adjustments, agents trust the auctioneer whereas, in the real world, where wage cuts are belated, agents only have their own fallible judgements upon which to depend. Only in the Walrasian fantasy world can instantaneous cuts succeed.

Leijonhufvud, however, seems questionably to assert, as earlier indicated, that instantaneous cuts would work in the real world too, but we have seen that agents do not have the information required to settle instantly upon the same vector which the auctioneer would have selected. Furthermore, imagine someone standing in the town square announcing the Walrasian vector. It is not enough for the townsfolk to

79

know the vector. They also must believe that others are prepared to contract on these terms. In the real world, therefore, workers only have a slender, hypothetical chance of alleviating their own unemployment. Therefore, involuntary unemployment occurs in a meaningful sense.

Leijonhufvud's interpretation bears the marks of a classical theory, but we must not be too quick to judge. Instead of blaming unemployment on absolute wage rigidity, he ascribes it to imperfect wage flexibility. This appears to be merely a difference in degree, but involuntary unemployment can sensibly be explained none the less. Despite Leijonhufvud's position being reasonable, however, Keynes did not clearly rely on wage inflexibilities to explain what triggers involuntary unemployment. Keynes's denial of the wage-cut mechanism was without qualification and he did not mention the possibility of an auctioneer, or well-informed agents, being capable in principle of selecting appropriate money wages to prevent a departure from full employment. Perhaps, of course, Keynes was wrong – or simply never directed his mind towards the unrealistic notion of instantaneous adjustments when making his generalizations about the adverse effects stemming from having highly flexible money wages.

To conclude, Leijonhufvud's interpretation largely remains intact despite probing criticisms by fundamentalists and others.

Notes

1 Axel Leijonhufvud, *On Keynesian Economics and the Economics of Keynes: a study in monetary theory*, New York, Oxford University Press, 1968, pp. 6–10.
2 ibid., p. 4.
3 Harry Johnson, 'Keynes and the Keynesians: some intellectual legends', *Encounter*, vol. 34, January 1970, pp. 70–2, at p. 71.
4 Leijonhufvud, *On Keynesian Economics*, p. 403. See also 'Keynes and the effectiveness of monetary policy', *Western Economic Journal*, vol. 6, March 1968, pp. 97–111, at p. 98. In view of David Colander, 'Was Keynes a Keynesian or a Lernerian?', *Journal of Economic Literature*, vol. 22, December 1984, pp. 1572–5, this contention is capable of some debate because Keynes retracted his objections to aspects of Lerner's position.
5 Axel Leijonhufvud, 'The Wicksell connection: variations on a theme', in *Information and Coordination: essays in macroeconomic theory*, New York, Oxford University Press, 1981, p. 177, n. 74.
6 Leijonhufvud, *On Keynesian Economics*, p. 301, n. 27. A second strand (e.g. ibid., pp. 30–1) is that not only is the process unexplained, sometimes the steps are simply logically impossible.
7 ibid., p. 12.
8 ibid., ch. V.
9 ibid., ch. II.

10 ibid., pp. 36–8, 75 *et seq.*, 394.
11 ibid., pp. 280–1. Leijonhufvud in fact did not put the matter as fully or emphatically as it appears here.
12 ibid., pp. 278–9.
13 In so far as buffer savings exist, consumption would not so rigidly depend upon currently realized income. See Leijonhufvud, 'Effective demand failures', in *Information and Coordination*, pp. 103–29, at p. 123. Consumption habits, however, might also be slow to adjust. See Keynes's *A Treatise on Money*, vol. 2, *Collected Writings*, vol. vi, p. 26, and *The General Theory of Employment Interest and Money*, London, Macmillan, 1936, p. 97.
14 Throughout this argument Leijonhufvud eliminates the ambiguity about real and money wages by assuming that commodity prices are held roughly constant so that inventories mount in the face of falling demand. These inventories exacerbate the problem by reducing the aggregate sales revenue out of which employers pay wages in the next period.
15 Whether autonomous planned investment needs to return to its initial level is a matter for later discussion. Christopher Torr, *Equilibrium, Expectations and Information: a study of the General Theory and modern classical economics*, Polity Press, Cambridge, 1988, pp. 10–11, 30–1, 78–84 considers Leijonhufvud's case to be defective in this regard.
16 Axel Leijonhufvud, *Keynes and the Classics*, Institute of Economic Affairs Occasional Paper no. 30, London, 1971, pp. 30, 36.
17 Victoria Chick, 'The nature of the Keynesian revolution: a reassessment', *Australian Economic Papers*, vol. 17, no. 30, June 1978, pp. 1–20, criticized Clower for, among other things, the inadequately rigorous specification of his model. My interest is confined to the elaboration of the gist of Clower's argument and I am not relying upon his mathematical formulation in any way.
18 Leijonhufvud, *On Keynesian Economics*, p. 394.
19 This approach has not (yet) proved popular. See 'Cybernetics and macroeconomics' by James L. Cochrane and John A. Graham, and the comment by Masanao Oaki and Leijonhufvud in *Economic Inquiry*, vol. 14, June 1976, pp. 241–50 and pp. 251–8 respectively.
20 Leijonhufvud, *On Keynesian Economics*, pp. 394–5.
21 ibid., p. 158.
22 ibid., p. 336. See also Leijonhufvud's 'The Wicksell connection' in which his arguments about the pivotal role of the interest rate are expounded.
23 Leijonhufvud, *On Keynesian Economics*, pp. 12, 30.
24 ibid., esp. pp. 163–8.
25 ibid., pp. 325, *et seq.*
26 ibid., p. 353.
27 ibid., pp. 14–15.
28 See, for example, Robert L. Crouch, *Macroeconomics*, New York, Harcourt Brace Jovanovich, 1972; Paul Wonnacott, *Macroeconomics*, Homewood, Ill., Richard D. Irwin, 1978, revised edn; John B. Beare, *Macroeconomics: cycles, growth and policy in a monetary economy*,

New York, Macmillan, 1978; Charles W. Baird, *Elements of Macroeconomics*, New York, West Publishing, 1977, and (with Alexander E. Cassuto) *Macroeconomics: monetary, search, and income theories*, Chicago, Science Research Associates, 1981, 2nd edn.

29 See Robert J. Gordon (ed.), *Milton Friedman's Monetary Framework: a debate with his critics*, Chicago, Chicago University Press, 1974, pp. 16–17, n. 7. A similar view is expressed by James Tobin, 'Inflation and unemployment', *American Economic Review*, vol. 62, no. 1, March 1972, pp. 1–18, at p. 4. See also Sir John Hicks, *The Crisis in Keynesian Economics*, Oxford, Basil Blackwell, 1974, p. 32. Also Robert L. Crouch in his review in *Econometrica*, vol. 39, no. 2, March 1971, pp. 407–8 expresses 'unreserved praise' and says that it is 'the thesis of the decade and the book of 1968'. Shackle's response ('Keynes and today's establishment in economic theory: a view', *Journal of Economic Literature*, vol. 11, June 1973, pp. 516–19) is a peculiar blend of compliments and criticisms. He expresses a deep respect for Leijonhufvud's scholarship and yet there is also a profound disquietude about the substance of the interpretation.

30 Johnson, 'Keynes and the Keynesians', p. 70. Similar comments can be found in 'The Keynesian revolution and the monetarist counter revolution', *American Economic Review*, vol. 61, no. 2, May 1971, pp. 1–14, at pp. 6, 11 and *On Economics and Society*, Chicago, University of Chicago Press, 1975, pp. 97, 104.

31 Joan Robinson, *Economic Journal*, vol. 79, September 1969, pp. 581–3.

32 See 'Discussion' of C.J. Bliss, 'The reappraisal of Keynes' economics: an appraisal', in Michael Parkin and Aveline Nobay (eds), *Current Economic Problems: the proceedings of the Association of University Teachers of Economics, Manchester, 1974*, Cambridge, Cambridge University Press, 1975, p. 213.

33 See John F. Brothwell, 'A simple Keynesian's response to Leijonhufvud', *Bulletin of Economic Research*, vol. 27, 1975, pp. 3–21; Richard T. Froyen, 'The aggregative structure of Keynes's general theory', *Quarterly Journal of Economics*, vol. 90, August 1976, pp. 369–87; Herschel Grossman, 'Was Keynes a "Keynesian"? A review article', *Journal of Economic Literature*, vol. 10, March 1982, pp. 26–30; Richard Jackman, 'Keynes and Leijonhufvud', *Oxford Economic Papers*, vol. 26, no. 2, July 1974, pp. 259–72.

34 Alan Coddington, 'Keynesian economics: a search for first principles', *Journal of Economic Literature*, vol. 14, no. 4, December 1976, pp. 1258–73, at p. 1268. See also Leland B. Yeager, 'The Keynesian diversion', *Western Economic Journal*, vol. 11, 1973, pp. 150–63, at p. 156.

35 Jackman, 'Keynes and Leijonhufvud', p. 259.

36 James Trevithick, 'Recent developments in the theory of employment', *Scottish Journal of Political Economy*, vol. 25, no. 1, February 1978, pp. 107–18, at p. 108.

37 Compare Claes-Henric Siven, 'Book review', *Swedish Journal of Economics*, vol. 72, 1970, pp. 93–6, at p. 96.

38 Keynes, *Collected Writings*, vol. xiii, p. 627, used the same analogy.
39 Leijonhufvud, *On Keynesian Economics*, p. 375. Of course, even if this maxim is not implicit in Keynes, it could still be a valid reflection of the attitudes of real-world transactors, but this is an entirely distinct issue.
40 Jackman, 'Keynes and Leijonhufvud', pp. 265 *et seq.*, objects to attributing inelastic price expectations to all transactors. He prefers to analyse each market separately. Crouch, in his book review in *Econometrica*, op.cit., also rejects the idea of the universality of such expectations. Compare Leijonhufvud, *On Keynesian Economics*, pp. 69–72, 77, 85 for hints of a more general perspective regarding the co-ordination problems confronting atomistic transactors than the one which focuses solely on the existence of inelastic price expectations.
41 See Ghanshyam Mehta, *The Structure of the Keynesian Revolution*, London, Martin Robertson, 1977; B. Littleboy and G. Mehta, 'Patinkin on Keynes' theory of effective demand', *History of Political Economy*, vol. 19, no. 2, 1987, pp. 311–28; Don Patinkin, 'Keynes' theory of effective demand: a reply', *HOPE*, vol. 19, no. 4, 1987, pp. 647–58; Littleboy and Mehta, 'Patinkin on Keynes's theory of effective demand: a rejoinder', *HOPE*, vol. 21, no. 4, pp. 711–21.
42 Robert Clower, 'Foundations of monetary theory', in Clower (ed.), *Monetary Theory: selected readings*, Harmondsworth, Penguin, 1969, pp. 202–11, at pp. 207–8.
43 See Leijonhufvud's 'Effective demand failures', *Swedish Journal of Economics*, vol. 75, 1973, pp. 27–48, at p. 40, reproduced in *Information and Coordination*, pp. 103–29, at p. 119.
44 Clower, 'The Keynesian counter-revolution...', in Clower (ed.), *Monetary Theory*, p. 291.
45 ibid., p. 292.
46 See Clower, 'The Keynesian counter-revolution...', p. 278 and Leijonhufvud, *On Keynesian Economics*, pp. 67, 68 (esp. n. 1). The reader should note that confusing terminological differences exist. Writers have drawn distinctions between Walras' Law, Say's Law, Say's Principle, Say's Identity and so on. What is bothersome is that different writers sometimes give different meanings to the same term. Keynes attacked 'Say's Law' according to Leijonhufvud, but here the term 'Walras' Law' will be used instead. See Leijonhufvud, *On Keynesian Economics*, p. 91.
47 Sir John Hicks, *Value and Capital*, Oxford, Clarendon, 1946, 2nd edn, p. 129. See also Leijonhufvud, *On Keynesian Economics*, pp. 54–5 for an elaboration of Hicks's position.
48 Clower, 'The Keynesian counter-revolution...', p. 281 (emphasis in original). See also Leijonhufvud, *On Keynesian Economics*, p. 55 for an endorsement of Clower's argument.
49 Leijonhufvud, *On Keynesian Economics*, p. 79.
50 ibid., pp. 69, 76, 77.
51 ibid., p. 76.
52 ibid., pp. 69–70.

53 Leijonhufvud relies upon the writings of Alchian. See ibid., pp. 76 *et seq.*

54 This reference to the existence of a buffer stock of savings is Leijonhufvud's modification of Keynes's pure case where consumption is a function of realized income.

55 Leijonhufvud, *On Keynesian Economics*, pp. 57, 84–5.

56 ibid., p. 90 (emphasis in original).

57 ibid., p. 80.

58 ibid., p. 49.

59 ibid., p. 81.

60 See note 46.

61 In this section I am paraphrasing Leijonhufvud and reproducing some of the passages from *The General Theory* which Leijonhufvud cites. The reason is that later I will be interpreting many of the passages cited by Leijonhufvud in a different way.

62 J.M. Keynes, *The General Theory of Employment, Interest and Money*, London, Macmillan, 1936, p. 5 (emphasis in original deleted).

63 ibid., pp. 6, 15. See also Leijonhufvud, *On Keynesian Economics*, p. 92, especially n. 20.

64 Keynes, *The General Theory*, p. 6.

65 ibid., p. 15 (emphasis in original deleted).

66 ibid., pp. 5–6, 11. See Leijonhufvud, *On Keynesian Economics*, pp. 92–4. Note that Keynes retained the first classical postulate. See Keynes, *The General Theory*, p. 17.

67 'Whilst workers will usually resist a reduction of money-wages, it is not their practice to withdraw their labour whenever there is a rise in the price of wage-goods' (Keynes, *The General Theory*, p. 9).

68 ibid., p. 91.

69 Leijonhufvud, *On Keynesian Economics*, p. 95, n. 22. See also Don Patinkin, *Keynes' Monetary Thought: a study of its development*, Durham, North Carolina, Duke University Press, 1976, p. 109.

70 Leijonhufvud, *On Keynesian Economics*, p. 95. Leijonhufvud goes on to cite: 'It is sometimes said that it would be illogical for labour to resist a reduction in money-wages...' (Keynes, *The General Theory*, p. 9).

71 Leijonhufvud, *On Keynesian Economics*, pp. 95–7.

72 Keynes, *The General Theory*, pp. 13–15.

73 Leijonhufvud, *On Keynesian Economics*, p. 96.

74 Keynes, *The General Theory*, p. 8.

75 Leijonhufvud, *On Keynesian Economics*, p. 95, n. 23. Note that voluntary search *initiates* involuntary unemployment which is generated by the multiplier.

76 Keynes, *The General Theory*, p. 11.

77 See ibid., pp. 10–13, Appendix to ch. 19. See also Leijonhufvud, *On Keynesian Economics*, pp. 97–8.

78 See Keynes, *The General Theory*, p. 18. Whether or not Keynes misinterpreted Mill will be discussed later.

79 ibid., pp. 19–20.

80 ibid., p. 20 (emphasis in original). See Leijonhufvud, *On Keynesian Economics*, pp. 98–100.
81 Included 'in Keynes' indictment is the denial of the relevance of Walras' Law...Most later writers...have argued either than this portion of Keynes' indictment is wrong, or that the proposition which Keynes attacks is not in fact the one he thought he was attacking. Most economists have opted for the second explanation...' (Clower, 'The Keynesian counter-revolution...', p. 278).
82 For a discussion of classical monetary economics, see G. Becker and W. Baumol, 'The classical monetary theory: the outcome of the discussion', *Economica*, vol. 19, 1952, pp. 355–76.
83 Leijonhufvud, *On Keynesian Economics*, p. 100.
84 Keynes, *The General Theory*, p. 19.
85 Leijonhufvud, *On Keynesian Economics*, p. 101.
86 Unitary elasticity is a modern 'Keynesian' assumption. See ibid., p. 368.
87 ibid., pp. 95–6.
88 ibid., p. 96.
89 ibid., p. 96, n. 24.
90 Keynes, *The General Theory*, pp. 50–1 (Leijonhufvud's emphasis).
91 Leijonhufvud, 'Effective demand failures', *Information and Coordination*, p. 115, n. 25.
92 Leijonhufvud, *On Keynesian Economics*, p. 74. Leijonhufvud continues (p. 74) to point out that Keynes did not clearly distinguish his process analysis from his description of the final unemployment state. This is not being disputed.
93 Keynes, *The General Theory*, pp. 123–5 (emphasis added).
94 Keynes's point has not received the attention that it deserves, even from otherwise sympathetic interpreters. See Paul Davidson, *Money and the Real World*, London, Macmillan, 1978, 2nd edn, p. 27; David G. Champernowne, 'Expectations and the links between the economic future and the present', in Robert Lekachman (ed.), *Keynes' General Theory: reports of three decades*, New York, St Martin's Press, 1964, pp. 174–202, at p. 181; Albert G. Hart, 'Keynes' analysis of expectations and uncertainty', in Seymour E. Harris (ed.), *The New Economics*, London, Dennis Dobson, 1948, pp. 415–24, at p. 420. Compare Henry Hazlitt, *The Failure of the "New Economics": an analysis of Keynesian fallacies*, London, Van Nostrand, 1959, pp. 141–4.
95 Keynes, *The General Theory*, pp. 122–3.
96 Compare Leijonhufvud, *On Keynesian Economics*, p. 62.
97 Keynes, *The General Theory*, p. 192, n. 2.
98 *The Collected Writings of John Maynard Keynes*, London, Macmillan, 1971, vol. xiii, p. 457 (with added emphasis).
99 Keynes, *The General Theory*, p. 123.
100 Keynes, *Collected Writings*, vol. v, p. 292.
101 Leijonhufvud, *On Keynesian Economics*, pp. 69–70.
102 G.B. Richardson, 'Equilibrium, expectations and information', *Economic Journal*, vol. 69, no. 274, June 1959, pp. 223–37.
103 Keynes, *Collected Writings*, vol. v, p. 292.

104 ibid.
105 Paul Davidson, 'Disequilibrium market adjustment: Marshall revisited', *Economic Inquiry*, vol. 12, no. 2, June 1974, pp. 146–58, at p. 159.
106 Axel Leijonhufvud, 'The varieties of price theory: what microfoundations for macrotheory?', UCLA Discussion Paper, no. 44, January 1974.
107 Axel Leijonhufvud, 'Keynes' employment function (comment)', *History of Political Economy*, vol. 6, 1974, pp. 164–70.
108 See Paul Davidson, 'Why money matters: lessons from a half-century of monetary theory', *Journal of Post Keynesian Economics*, vol. 1, no. 1, Fall 1978, pp. 46–70, at pp. 50, 61–2.
109 Leijonhufvud, 'The varieties of price theory...', p. 39.
110 ibid., pp. 39–41.
111 ibid., p. 39.
112 ibid., p. 43 (citing *The General Theory*, pp. 47, 50–1, 282). Leijonhufvud, however, cannot criticize Keynes too strenuously. As he admits, he does not himself clearly distinguish price and quantity expectations (*On Keynesian Economics*, p. 277, n. 25).
113 In 1968, Leijonhufvud also complained that Keynes could have painted the picture more sharply. In effect, he has chided Keynes for not fitting into the framework which Leijonhufvud felt he ought to have. See *On Keynesian Economics*, pp. 73–4. An alternative view, of course, is that Keynes did not universally uphold quite inelastic price expectations and instead incorporated into his model a very rapid adjustment of expectations by suppliers. While one can disagree with Leijonhufvud, one still has to concede the plausibility of his case however.
114 Leijonhufvud's use of the Hicksian 'minute' is legitimate in substance. Keynes (*The General Theory*, p. 47, n. 1) described as 'daily', 'the shortest interval after which the firm is free to revise its decision as to how much employment to offer'.
115 Axel Leijonhufvud, 'What would Keynes have thought of rational expectations?', in David Worswick and James Trevithick (eds), *Keynes and the Modern World*, Cambridge, Cambridge University Press, 1983, pp. 179–205, at p. 197. Note the hostility to fix-price models, which share with the *IS-LM* approach an oversimplified view of dynamic adjustment. Leijonhufvud cannot be held responsible for the outgrowth of fix-price models which fell prey so easily to the charges of Lucas and the defector, Barro, that such disequilibrium models made little sense and embodied irrational pricing behaviour.
116 Kenneth J. Arrow, 'Toward a theory of price adjustment', M. Abramowitz (ed.), in *The Allocation of Economic Resources: essays in honour of Bernard Francis Haley*, Stanford, Stanford University Press, 1959, pp. 41–51. See Leijonhufvud, *On Keynesian Economics*, pp. 69, n. 3, 76, 79. Nowadays it is realized that, under conditions of persistent imperfect knowledge prices can remain dispersed. For developments in the analysis of the role of imperfect knowledge in the model of monopolistic competition see, for example, S.A. Ozga, 'Imperfect markets through lack of knowledge', *Quarterly Journal of Economics*,

vol. 74, 1960, pp. 29–52; Steve Salop, 'Information and monopolistic competition', and Michael E. Porter, 'Interbrand choice, media mix and market performance', both in *American Economic Review Papers and Proceedings*, vol. 66, no. 2, May 1976, pp. 240–5 and pp. 398–406 respectively. A (not entirely random) sample of the voluminous literature examining the manner in which agents, in the absence of the auctioneer, are allowed to set prices and transmit signals even in atomistic markets is: Franklin M. Fisher, 'Quasi-competitive price adjustment by individual firms: a preliminary paper', *Journal of Economic Theory*, vol. 2, 1970, pp. 195–206. David Laidler, 'Information, money and the macro-economics of inflation', *Swedish Journal of Economics*, vol. 76, 1974, pp. 26–40.

117 Leijonhufvud, 'The varieties of price theory...', p. 42.

118 Arrow (op. cit., pp. 45–6) also notes that the curves can shift but the point is entangled with his observations about their slope.

119 On the issue of price flexibility, Keynes, interestingly in view of Hicks's distinction between the fix- and flex-price sectors, refers to administered prices and to those 'produced in the full blast of competition' (*Collected Writings*, vol. xiii, p. 628). In 'Relative movements of real wages and output', (*Collected Writings*, vol. vii, pp. 394–412, at pp. 410–12), Keynes doubts that imperfect competition is an important factor. See also *The General Theory*, pp. 378–9.

Because Nicholas Kaldor, 'Keynesian economics after fifty years', in David Worswick and James Trevithick (eds), *Keynes and the Modern World*, p. 13, takes a view similar to Arrow (though he seems to have in mind Robinson's version of monopolistic competition), likewise can his views be rejected as being supposedly essential to Keynes's argument.

120 Keynes, *The General Theory*, pp. 124–5.

121 ibid., p. 239.

122 ibid., p. 318.

123 ibid, p. 332. See also p. 317, where Keynes notes that inventory holdings help to explain the periodicity of cycles.

124 Keynes, *Collected Writings*, vol. xxix, pp. 86–7.

125 Keynes, *Collected Writings*, vol. xiii, pp. 131, 147, 582, 628–9.

126 ibid., p. 614.

127 ibid., p. 434 (emphasis added).

128 Contrast ibid., p. 472, where Keynes refers to 'the *gradual* absorption of stocks during a slump' (emphasis added).

129 While Keynes considered it important to treat newly produced and unsold consumption goods (and unfinished goods as well) as 'investment' this perhaps is stressed because of its *logical* importance so that terms can be used with water-tight exactitude and 'income' can be defined. (Keynes's concern with user cost can also be seen in this light.) There is consequently no reason to consider either that inventories play a theoretically important or active role or that they are of great empirical significance. (This issue also crops up when considering 'the' aggregation procedure in part three.)

130 Keynes, *Collected Writings*, vol. xiii, pp. 602–3 (emphasis added).

131 ibid., p. 603.
132 Keynes, *Collected Writings*, vol. xiv, pp. 71–2.
133 See ibid., p. 181 for both passages. The importance of the *ex ante* and *ex post* distinction has been examined by Jan Kregel, 'Economic methodology in the face of uncertainty: the modelling methods of Keynes and the post-Keynesians', *Economic Journal*, vol. 86, June 1976, pp. 209–25. See also Davidson, *Money and the Real World*, pp. 377–8.
134 Keynes, *Collected Writings*, vol. xiii, p. 603. That pessimism can take root quickly is also clear from *Collected Writings*, vol. xiii, p. 383, where a decline in income can trigger a decline in net investment due to decreased investment in working capital. Investment in fixed capital was also seen as depending largely on the *existing* rate of profit (ibid., p. 385). Such statements indicate a fairly high elasticity of expectations, but one which could still be less than unity. Expectations seem to be based on current far more than on past evidence. Indeed, the past is seldom mentioned.
135 Keynes, *Collected Writings*, vol. xiv, p. 182.
136 Another reason, suggested by Paul Davidson ('Disequilibrium market adjustment: Marshall revisited', *Economic Inquiry*, vol. 12, no. 2, June 1974, pp. 146–58), and endorsed by John Brothwell ('Rejoinder', *Bulletin of Economic Research*, vol. 28, 1976, pp. 123–6, at p. 125) is that Keynes's model is forward looking and is largely concerned with the flow supplies of newly produced goods. Spot markets therefore fall into the background and output flows and prices move together without any overall reversal of adjustment velocities of prices and quantities.
137 Leijonhufvud, *On Keynesian Economics*, p. 152, n. 28. Note, however, that inventory cycles are demand-side phenomena induced by sudden revisions of planned inventories. Illiquidity induced by inventory holdings do not play a role.
138 ibid., p. 96. See also pp. 37, 378–9 but compare p. 52 where it is sufficient that 'one or more prices are given', the last, incidentally, having a rather hydraulic ring to it if the short run is in mind.
139 Edmond Malinvaud, *The Theory of Unemployment Reconsidered*, Oxford, Basil Blackwell, 1977, pp. 31–2, n. 26. Compare Patinkin, *Money, Interest and Prices*, ch. 13, pp. 320–2 and his discussion, now superseded, of point K in fig. XIII–1, Paul Davidson, 'A Keynesian view of Patinkin's theory of employment', *Economic Journal*, vol. 77, September 1967, pp. 559–78 and E. Mishan, 'The demand for labor in a classical and Keynesian framework', *Journal of Political Economy*, vol. 72, December 1964, pp. 610–16, were also pioneers.
140 Faith in the law of diminishing returns gave rise to Keynes's chapter 2 definition of involuntary unemployment whereby the fall in the real wage consequent upon a reflationary increase in aggregate demand must not be resisted. In 1933, he considered constant returns to be one of a set of 'fancy cases' (*Collected Writings*, vol. xxix, p. 90, n.). Keynes's views on the inverse relationship between employment and the real wage (where he disagreed with Pigou) persisted. In 1937, he refers to

diminishing returns as 'one of the very few incontrovertible propositions of our miserable subject' (*Collected Writings*, vol. xiv, p. 190).

141 Leijonhufvud, *On Keynesian Economics*, pp. 57–8.

142 Leijonhufvud's views are rather confusing because in ibid., p. 108, he expressly recognizes that money-wage cuts can lead to equiproportional declines in prices, which, of course, would leave the real wage unaffected.

143 Leijonhufvud, 'Keynes' employment function (comment)'.

144 Mark Blaug (*Economic Theory in Retrospect*, London, Cambridge University Press, 1978, 3rd edn, pp. 676, 682) seems to hold views similar to those of Grossman.

145 Leijonhufvud, 'Keynes' employment function (comment)', p. 269, quoting Grossman, 'Was Keynes a Keynesian?', p. 29, n. 13.

146 Leijonhufvud, 'The varieties of price theory...', p. 52, n. 14; and 'Keynes' employment function (comment)', p. 169.

147 Not only do inventories create complications. A change in the composition of output also would affect the real-wage locus. For example, an increase in the investment share would reduce real wages because those in the investment-goods sector consume wage goods but do not produce them. See Keynes, *The General Theory*, p. 7. This point is discussed further when dealing with the aggregation question, i.e. whether the consumption and investment sectors can legitimately be subsumed under one heading, 'commodities'.

148 Victoria Chick, 'The nature of the Keynesian revolution: a reassessment', *Australian Economic Papers*, vol. 17, no. 30, June 1978, pp. 1–20, at p. 2, n. 5.

149 Keynes also hinted that even an all-round proportional money-wage cut would be resisted: 'It is only in a highly authoritarian society, where sudden, substantial, all-round changes could be decreed...' But, on the other hand, 'the contention that...unemployment...is due to a refusal by labour to accept a reduction of money-wages is not clearly supported by the facts'. See *The General Theory*, p. 260 and p. 9 respectively.

150 See ibid., p. 269. See also Jacob Viner, 'Mr Keynes on the causes of unemployment', *Quarterly Journal of Economics*, vol. 51, November 1936, pp. 147–67, at p. 149. On the theoretical point that an increased variance in money wages destabilizes employment, see Peter Howitt, 'Wage flexibility and employment', in Omar F. Hamouda and John N. Smithin (eds), *Keynes and Public Policy After Fifty Years*, vol. II: *Theories and Method*, New York, New York University Press, 1988, pp. 61–9.

151 Leijonhufvud, *On Keynesian Economics*, pp. 57–8.

152 ibid., p. 58, n. 16.

153 Keynes, *The General Theory*, p. 13.

154 Leijonhufvud, *On Keynesian Economics*, p. 95, n. 23.

155 Keynes, *The General Theory*, p. 257.

156 See Jackman, 'Keynes and Leijonhufvud', p. 268.

157 Keynes, *The General Theory*, p. 261.

158 Leijonhufvud, *On Keynesian Economics*, pp. 108–9.

159 Keynes, *The General Theory*, pp. 12, 261.
160 Tobin's position is a little strange. He claims that money illusion is a necessary condition for involuntary unemployment. As we have seen, Keynes did not rely on money illusion, at least not in the sense of involving irrationality. Tobin then accuses Keynes of contradicting himself because, if money illusion prevailed in all markets, lower money wages would increase employment. See James Tobin, 'Money wage rates and employment', in Seymour E. Harris (ed.), *The New Economics*, London, Dennis Dobson, 1948, pp. 580, 586.
161 Abba Lerner, 'The general theory', in Robert Lekachman (ed.), *Keynes' General Theory: reports of three decades*, New York, St Martin's Press, 1964, pp. 203–22, especially pp. 206–10.
162 Leijonhufvud, *On Keynesian Economics*, pp. 87, 98, 108, 317.
163 Keynes, *The General Theory*, pp. 260 *et seq.*
164 Furthermore, the larger the departure from 'correct' nominal price values, the more confused agents become and the greater the problems in achieving a 'correct' vector. Leijonhufvud would agree with this statement which simply says that belated adjustments make groping all the more difficult, but he seems to believe that, for 'instantaneous' wage adjustments, problems of finding the correct vector are readily solvable. 'All that Keynes needed to assert is that the worker who is threatened with a lay-off will not offer to take *any* cut necessary to retain his job' (*On Keynesian Economics*, pp. 95–6). But how is the employer to select an appropriate wage? And what guarantee is there that the aggregate wage bill won't fall thereby effecting a change in the distribution of income with a further effect on the consumption function?
165 Leijonhufvud, *On Keynesian Economics*, p. 95, n. 23. See also p. 81.
166 ibid., p. 58, n. 16.

Chapter three

Involuntary unemployment in the history of economic thought

Fundamentalists and reductionists share scepticism over the hydraulic rendition of Keynes's assault on classical economics. If the American Keynesians indeed portrayed Keynes's attack on the classicists in a manner that was quickly subsumed under the neoclassical synthesis, what is there then in Keynes's theory that is a unique and valid criticism of classical economics?

It is not that investment is unstable and depends on the volatile expectations and stock market speculation. Pigou himself said in his initial review, which was largely of virulent hostility, that

> his description of the precarious character of business forecasts and of the consequences of experts in this matter being chiefly interested in short-run developments (chapter xii), are all admirable.[1]

After quoting Keynes's statement that share purchases should be made indissoluble like marriage, he continues: 'Admirable too is much of his "Notes on the Trade Cycle".'[2]

Keynes himself wrote that 'the fact of fluctuations in the volume of fixed investment and their correlation with the credit cycle has long been familiar'.[3]

Neither is it that mass psychology is important and that there are waves of optimism and pessimism. The potential for instability and herdlike behaviour was recognized by many before Keynes.[4] Some classicists were also fully prepared to accept that agents base their actions on expectations which must be formed in a world of Knightian uncertainty. In such an environment the future is unknowable and the prospects of surprise are great. It is not a world of quantifiable, probabilistic risk. One must admit that modern mathematical accounts tend to reduce all decision-making problems to ones where the probability and the prospective gain can be assigned to each alternative.[5] We should be reluctant, however, to ascribe any deficiencies of modern versions of classical economics to its founders who were prepared to expound their views in a free-ranging literary style. They did not feel obliged to equate worthwhile economic analysis with that which can be expressed in mathematical form. Knightian uncertainty is by its nature difficult (impossible?) to treat in such a fashion. Consequently, since only a portion of any transactor's decision-making can reasonably be analysed using a framework of contingent contracts, our understanding of economic behaviour will remain incomplete if we rely on mathematics. Knight himself considered that the existence of genuine uncertainty was virtually the reason for an entrepreneur's very existence. Yet Knight gave *The General Theory* a rather scathing review (gleefully reproduced by Henry Hazlitt).[6] There must have been something in it that he did not like, and it could not have been the recognition of Knightian uncertainty!

Keynes's opinion of Knight's review is illuminating.

> I read his passionate expiring cries, but, controversial-minded though I am, I could not discover any concrete criticism to reply to. In fact, I really felt that there was nothing at all to be said. Indeed with Professor Knight's two main conclusions, namely, that my book caused him intense irritation, and that he had great difficulty in understanding it, I am in agreement... [T]he truth is, I feel sure, that our minds have not met, and that there is scarcely a single particular in which he has seen what I was driving at.[7]

We should, therefore, reject the view that the novelty of *The General Theory* lies in its stressing the importance of expectations, uncertainty and the like. Indeed, since Keynes's analysis of expectations is not comprehensive and detailed,[8] we could not even say that he systematically formalized what had hitherto been observed by the best classical thinkers. What is regarded as novel herein is how Keynes argues that uncertainty gives rise to conventions which alter the functioning of the macro-system and prevent it attaining full employment. Uncertainty, then, plays a vital and novel role, but indirectly.[9] This is explored in Part four.

There is also the view that the essence of Keynes lies in his recognition of the importance of the financial instability of the capitalist system. Again, the best of classical theory clearly incorporates this, and indeed, the notion has an extremely long history. The idea even crops up in Defoe.[10] A great tradesman or man of commerce is

> like a great tree in a thick wood, if he falls, he is sure to crush a great deal of the underwood which lies within the reach of his boughs and branches. A young tradesman miscarries, and it reaches but a little way; a few creditors are affected, and some hurt is done; but if the overgrown tradesman falls, he shakes the

exchange, as we call it; he pulls down here half a dozen, and there half a score; and they pull down others, and, like rolling ninepins, they tumble down one another.

Mill emphasizes the notion of the financial crisis in response to prior expansionary recklessness by traders.[11] So does Jevons.[12] Consequently, Minsky's arguments that Keynes himself emphasized this cannot be accepted as validly identifying 'the essence of Keynes' (although it must be taken as being consistent with it).[13] There is nothing uniquely Keynesian in stressing financial instability. Vision is not inextricably involved. Classical economists can and have recognized these themes. So have Clower and Leijonhufvud.[14] They are modular pieces of logic which can be slotted into any research programme.

There is a theme common to these explanations of unemployment that are acceptable to the classicists. They involve the acceptance of the idea that there is a *dialectic* at work which causes the system to be subject to cyclical fluctuations. The explanation of the business cycle is as mechanical as the story of how a system spirals in towards full employment if structurally or randomly shocked. There are regular waves of optimism and pessimism in classical stories.[15] For every upswing, the downswing is inevitable and there are *laws* of motion governing aggregate behaviour and steering the economy back to full employment. In Keynes's system, uncertainty, psychology and expectations, which govern investment, are not always bound by laws which give rise to predictable behaviour. Cycle theory was not Keynes's primary concern. Chapter 22 is only one chapter of *The General Theory* and it is not particularly mechanical in terms of how turning points are described. If conventions survive, then so does relative stability. If they do not, fluctuations will be more violent. If more than just the multiplier is involved, it would be helpful to incorporate a theory of the creation, persistence and destruction of conventions. It would then be possible to question the classical tenet that, in the long run, full employment will be restored in the absence both of further exogenous or random shocks and of endogenous, or cyclical disturbances, which everyone agrees might disrupt this tendency. To achieve this, it shall be argued in Part three that Keynes validly denied that the optimal rate of interest will be generated even in the long run.

This work upholds the earlier 'radical' view that

Keynes' main achievement...was to show that there is no automatic self-righting mechanism tending to establish full employment in an unplanned private-enterprise economy.[16]

Involuntary unemployment, it is argued, can exist in the long run, whether money wages are perfectly flexible, absolutely rigid or anything in between. Classicists could not accept this, whereas Keynes could accept portions of their theory of business cycles to supplement his writings on unemployment. In this way we can dismiss the claims that Keynes was not a revolutionary and that he was ignorant of the works of his predecessors. So far as Keynes was concerned, the classicists had little of direct interest to say. (One might concede, however, that Keynes was impolite not to give credit to others for ideas which he borrowed and then transformed.) This sounds both sweeping and dogmatic, but the divergence between Keynes and the classicists must be put starkly and bluntly to avoid the conclusion that the arguments of this work stem merely from exegetical hairsplitting. The conflict between the paradigms is both real and substantial; even in the abstract the market system cannot generate full employment. On the contrary, without conventions to limit certain price variations, the supposedly self-adjusting system will prove to be extremely unstable. Differences of vision separate Keynes from the classicists far more deeply than any differences separate the fundamentalists and reductionists.

To accept these efforts to magnify certain differences between Keynes and the classicists appears to involve struggling against the current of modern academic opinion. Many seem to have been swayed by the efforts of scholars to uncover the elements of Keynes's analysis in earlier writings of the better classical thinkers.[17] These forerunners of Keynes avoided polemics and considered that they were merely extending and qualifying economic theory as it stood at that time.[18]

As we have just seen, one can argue that what many see as innovatory was neither novel nor even essential to Keynes's argument. Furthermore, some of the efforts to identify anticipators of Keynes are considerably more persuasive than others. In the case of Jacob Viner,[19] the very obscurity of some of the suggested precursors that he unearths (such as Hugo Bilgram and an anonymous reviewer of Mill) tends only to indicate how little the respectable members of the profession had questioned whether there were serious problems preventing any powerful tendency for a competitive economy to approach full employment.

More recently, the view is increasingly becoming that Keynes's contribution was more along the lines of being an important reorganizer who tied together the arguments made by many others into a coherent analytical form.[20] Much of his work can indeed be fairly seen in this light, and it is generally accepted this by no means lessens the respect one should extend to Keynes.[21]

Ronnie Davis finds that there was a widespread belief in the United States, prior to 1936, that automatic self-adjustment by money-wage cuts could not be relied upon,[22] that there was a multiplier[23] at work which exacerbated the problem of a deficiency of aggregate demand, and that fiscal policy should be used to combat cyclical fluctuations.

Whether crucial elements of Keynes's system were anticipated by major figures in the United States is discussed by Davis. While he certainly supplies evidence against the myth that Keynes stood alone against the dark forces of classicism and ignorance, a cynic is entitled to speculate that here lies a possible explanation of the predominantly American phenomenon of bastard Keynesianism. What was already congenial to the American mind was embraced.[24] What was not was left out. The mechanical aspects of the multiplier and a preference for counter-cyclical fiscal policy were willingly seen as Keynes's central message because these aspects were the most assimilable.[25]

Herbert Stein even remarked of Keynes that 'it is possible to describe the evolution of fiscal policy in America up to 1940 without reference to him'.[26] Stein also notes that the *theory* which justified such policies in the early 1930s was, however, far from sophisticated. It is not my purpose to examine this literature with a view to assessing the extent to which the Chicago tradition or other major strands of classical thought had embodied the principal features of Keynes's analysis.[27] Neither will the Swedish school be examined. It is conceded that much in Keynes is capable of incorporation into the classical way of thinking, but the analysis framed in terms of conventional behaviour remains an innovation. It is also agreed that Keynes attacked more appropriately only the most extreme versions of orthodox thought, which stemmed largely from Anglo-Saxon and Austrian sources.[28] Keynes was certainly not alone in criticizing those with extreme faith in the restorative powers of the market mechanism, and the earlier Keynesians who painted the picture of Keynes as the lone hero have been soundly rebuked.[29]

George Garvy perhaps expresses what many modern scholars believe:

> One of the most perplexing riddles in the history of social science is how a man of the intellect of Keynes could have laboured for years on what he considered to be a revelation without becoming aware of its multifarious antecedents, and how a large segment of the English-speaking community of economists could have accepted his analysis and policy conclusions as such.[30]

Modern views have indeed changed. That the 'Treasury view' reflected the beliefs of the bulk of informed academics in the early 1930s is now generally denied,[31] although historians might wish to research into the question of whether Keynes led the profession prior to the early 1930s, by which time many had realized the need for public-works programmes. It is also pertinent to note that those in government were not convinced by the best of the available advice, and neither were the financial press. Both of these groups remained rigidly classical, and in its most vulgar form.[32]

It can be argued that, to some extent, this modern view has overshot the mark in its reversal from the earlier belief that Keynes was a revolutionary with a grasp of macroeconomic phenomena far superior to any predecessor. There remains something which those of classical vision did not realize; conventions can cause a long-run equilibrium at less than full employment.

Some might see a conventional equilibrium as being analogous to a conjectural equilibrium,[33] where one's expectations, upon which decisions are made, depend on our beliefs about the actions of others. They might go on to hold, however, that these conventions will disappear in the long run or that conventional beliefs will gradually change until they conform to expectations consistent with Walrasian equilibrium. There is, it might be suggested, an automatic long-run tendency for conventions to become 'optimal'. Although such recognition of conventions would be some concession to Keynes, it would still be fair to characterize such views as non-Keynesian and, in a sense, classical.

One useful dividing line between the best of classical thought and the views of Keynes can be suggested. So long as the parameters of tastes, population, technology and the like remain unchanged, conventions that persist govern the position of equilibrium. Keynes held that it is desirable for one convention in particular, that which operates in the labour market and which imparts inflexibility to the money wage, to persist in the long run, because without it a money using system would be most likely to collapse. Some are prepared to take this step. They include Lerner, Hansen and Davidson.[34] Leijonhufvud is prepared to accept this too. Hydraulicists, fundamentalists and reductionists are united on at least one issue.

There is a difference of vision between those of pragmatic classical persuasion, who agree that money-wage cuts would be a foolish policy to adopt when more reliable monetary or fiscal intervention will achieve the same result more quickly and with much less dislocation, and those who believe that such a policy would be sheer madness and one which will cause us to revert to primitive bartering. Similarly, there is a difference of vision separating those who believe that the convention governing the interest rate will at the most impede adjustment and those who believe that the longer this convention lasts the stronger will be the belief that it will continue.

It is not the case that there is merely a difference in the degree to which the parties uphold the restorative powers of the market system.

Keynes and Mill

Considerable attention has been focused on the question of the extent to which Mill was fairly criticized by Keynes for allegedly denying the critical importance of money and for upholding Say's Law which denies the possibility of prolonged unemployment. There has been speculation about the sense in which Mill was understood, or misunderstood.[35]

Keynes has been accused of tearing a passage of Mill out of context in order to refute a proposition Mill never made.[36] Keynes is believed to have falsely held that Mill failed to recognize the significance of the distinction between the means to purchase and the desire to purchase. Keynes sought to reduce classical economics to the principle that 'supply creates its own demand'. He proceeded to (mis)quote Mill's famous statement in support:

> What constitutes the means of payment for commodities is simply commodities.[37]

Mill, however, went on to say that, if conditions of commercial crisis prevailed, a general glut could exist. Keynes did not mention Mill's later qualifications that a desire to hoard may exist in abnormal times, and that dislocations emerge during periods of financial crisis.

The reason for Keynes's incomplete account has been the subject of conjecture. Professor Mundell has stated, 'Whether this omission was by design or carelessness is not clear.'[38] Davis and Casey have taken a slightly more moderate stance. They write, 'Keynes was merely careless....Keynes was relying on secondary sources which, unknown to him, had taken licence to edit the passage. We conclude that Keynes did not read Mill's chapter at all.'[39]

Not only are these views patronizing and insulting to Keynes, they are also obviously wrong. The classicists held that general gluts can occur, but *only* in times of commercial crisis. Keynes's whole argument is that the level of aggregate demand can cause the system to be at rest *anywhere* between full employment and crisis levels of unemployment. Therefore, Keynes held that a commercial crisis is not a necessary condition for the existence of general gluts. Voluntary panic-induced hoarding of money is not a necessary condition either.

Keynes was well aware of the classical notion that people hoard during crises. Keynes's only error was to attribute the notion to Marshall instead of tracing it back to Mill.

> Mr. J.A. Hobson after quoting...the above passage of Mill points out that Marshall commented as follows... 'But though men have the power to purchase, they may not choose to use it.' 'But', Mr. Hobson continues, 'he fails to grasp the critical importance of this

fact, and appears to *limit its action to periods of "crisis."*' This has remained fair comment, I think, in the light of Marshall's later work.⁴⁰

It is amazing that not only Davis and Casey, but also Pigou, have cited this paragraph and seem to have failed to grasp its literal meaning.⁴¹

Indeed, the relationship between Marshall and Mill also has had a peculiar history. There are differences of opinion as to whether Hobson correctly held that Marshall had extended Mill.⁴² After referring to Mill, Marshall, as indicated above, remarked, 'But though men have the power to purchase they may not choose to use it.' Some suggest that Marshall *qualified* Mill,⁴³ others that he had *summarized* him.⁴⁴ Perhaps we should therefore not be so hard on Keynes. What modern commentators think Keynes and Hobson thought Marshall thought Mill thought are matters which ought not detain us long, although such questions manifestly have their intellectual charm.

Whatever Marshall meant, it remains clear that Keynes oversimplified Mill's position, but it was an easy mistake to make. There are passages which appear to involve a confident acceptance of Say's Law at its most extreme: general gluts are impossible because an act of supply implies an act of demand. Only later is Mill's meaning clearer where he does allow that errors can occur in the selection of the particular kinds of goods one should produce. He also recognizes hoarding as a likely outcome of a commercial crisis. These are, however, the exceptions which serve only to highlight the fundamental belief that there are normally powerful tendencies operating to eliminate maladjustments and to cause full employment in the long run.⁴⁵

Even if we accept that Mill's views were more reasonable than those attributed to him by Keynes, it nevertheless remains true that the classical recognition of unemployment stemming from frictional, speculative or other causes is different to the sort of unemployment envisaged by Keynes. It is one thing to say, as did Mill, that there is a potential desire to exchange as evidenced by the existence of goods supplied, and that this potential to exchange will be realized except in temporary and abnormal circumstances. It is another thing to say that gluts can persist in the long run even if the potential and the desire exist but cannot be fulfilled for the want of effective demand. Even Mill at his best, where nothing is torn from its context, is susceptible to frontal attack. His qualifications do not rescue him.⁴⁶

It is true that in the passage taken from Mill, Keynes stopped short of including Mill's statement:⁴⁷ 'Besides money is a commodity; and if all commodities are supposed to be doubled in quantity, we must suppose money to be doubled too, and then prices would no more fall than values would.' Neither did Keynes refer to Mill's recognition that in times of commercial crisis 'there is really an excess of all commodities above the money demand: in other words, there is an under-supply of money'.[48] Mill cannot be taken to have held that the excess demand for money was identically equal to zero and that money played no essential role in what was virtually a barter economy.[49] This is all conceded. But, in Keynes's defence, his allegation against the classical school can be interpreted as charging that money was to them important and essential to disequilibrium *only under abnormal conditions*. Their analysis proceeded along the lines that it was reasonable to assume that under normal conditions it was 'as if' barter prevailed, money being a mere veil.[50] Mill makes it clear that this is his position. After stating, in a manner reminiscent of chapter xiv of his *Principles*, that there

> can never...be a want of buyers for all commodities; because whoever offers a commodity for sale, desires to obtain a commodity in exchange for it, and is therefore a buyer by the mere fact of his being a seller.

He continues:

> This argument is evidently founded on the supposition of a state of barter... If, however, we suppose that money is used, these propositions cease to be exactly true.[51]

He proceeds to explain that, in a monetary system, exchange takes place in two stages and there may be a delay between the sale of a commodity and the expenditure of the money received on the commodities of others. When there is a 'general disinclination to buy' we have a 'general excess...which is of no uncommon occurrence' but which 'can only be temporary'.[52]

Mill's position in chapter xiv also seems clear: all goods will be sold because the goods produced are the ultimate means of purchase (section 2), provided we assume the 'right' goods are being made (section 3) and that there is no state of commercial crisis (section 4). The interpretation given here to Mill's section 2 is therefore stronger than Patinkin's[53] view that no more is involved that the unobjectionable national accounting identity that national income equals the value of the output. Section 2 ought to be treated as a piece of analysis showing faith in the essential capacity of an economy to avoid problems of a deficiency of aggregate demand and behave as if money was normally a convenient, intermediary device. It is evident that Keynes understood this to be the position of the classicists. Although *The General Theory* itself does not discuss the differences between a barter and a monetary economy in a systematic way, earlier drafts and lectures do attempt to draw the distinction formally and this is pursued in the next section.[54]

The role of money

Keynes contrasted a 'barter', 'co-operative', 'real-wage', 'real-exchange' or 'neutral' economy with an 'entrepreneur' or a 'monetary' one. In the former, the factors of production can share the output (or sales revenue) in agreed amounts and proportions. In particular, the real wage can be negotiated and the equilibrium level of output consistent with that wage can be specified so that 'only miscalculation or stupid obstinacy can stand in the way of production'.[55] Money would be merely of 'transitory convenience'[56] and 'a neutral link between transactions in real things and real assets'.[57] It facilitates trade and does not distort relative prices. In the other type of economy, the one which prevails in the real world, money plays an essential role. 'Money is *par excellence* the means of remuneration in an entrepreneur economy which lends itself to fluctuations in effective demand.'[58] A decline in aggregate money expenditure is possible and its effect will be to reduce employment. This is because production will not be undertaken 'unless the *money* proceeds expected from the sale of the output are at least equal to the *money* costs' that are avoidable.[59]

Keynes plainly held that to proceed along the grounds that money was a veil was inadequate for a general theory:

> The classical theory..., as exemplified in the tradition from Ricardo to Marshall and Professor Pigou, appears to me to presume that the conditions for a Neutral Economy are substantially fulfilled in general; – though it has been a source of great confusion that its assumptions have been *tacit*...[60]

Note that Keynes[61] cites Ricardo (who had been quoted by Hobson and Mummery[62]): 'Productions are always bought by productions or services; money is only the medium by which the exchange is effected.' Clearly, Ricardo (in this passage) does not see money as having any disruptive influence; the idea of money effecting exchanges was clearly seen, but this was deemed to be of little importance.[63]

Further evidence of Keynes's recognition of the importance of money and his belief that the classicists had given it inadequate attention can be found in his later writings also. When writing on post-war reconstruction and employment policies, he specifically drew attention to the popular objection of where the money to finance such grandiose schemes was supposed to come from. So long as the potential to produce was there (that is, the bricks and mortar, the architects, the labourers and their means of subsistence) buildings can be constructed. 'Anything we can actually *do* we can afford.'[64] Keynes complained of the 'very usual confusion between the problem of finance for an individual and the problem for the community as a whole'.[65] At the aggregate level, finance was purely 'a technical problem';[66] everybody realizes that, at the individual level, there are genuine financial constraints.[67] This is plainly a reference to the conservative adherents of 'sound finance'.

Even if we accept that many classicists did at least say something about unemployment and monetary disturbances in the short run, it is still possible to argue that their account was partial and that their faith in the restoration of full employment was unwarranted. Joan Robinson once commented on the manner in which violations of Say's Law were treated:

> Marshall had a foxy way of saving his conscience by mentioning exceptions, but doing so in such a way that his pupils would continue to believe in the rule.[68]

Therefore, the extent to which Keynes was anticipated should not be exaggerated. The classical view was that an economy (if not prone to fits of hoarding) tends to be stable, except so far as entrepreneurial confidence inevitably waxes and wanes and about which little can be done. Hoarding panics are relatively rare. Hutchison observes that Smith describes hoarding as 'crazy' under ordinary, stable conditions.[69] Compare Keynes, who may even have had Smith in mind when writing that, although it was well known that money served as a store of wealth, it would be an 'insane' use to which to put it in a classical world devoid of uncertainty. 'Why should anyone outside a lunatic asylum wish to use money as a store of wealth?'[70] This may be a coincidence, but perhaps Keynes's knowledge of classical thought was more comprehensive than many have suggested.

A classical theory, in Keynes's eyes and probably in truth, held that money was usually neutral except in crises and during transitional stages.[71] A general theory, however, must examine the impact of indirect monetary exchange between remote traders on aggregate behaviour. On this point, Keynes for once agreed with Hayek,[72] though the latter argued that it was largely governmental mismanagement that caused the problem of monetary shocks and that money could and should assume a neutral role. Hayek, therefore, remains in the classical fold in view of his belief that money need not prevent the attainment of full employment if markets were to operate freely.

Having argued that the notion of effective demand was recognized by both the classicists and Keynes, but that Keynes alone argued that any monetary dislocation is not unnatural or temporary, it is now possible to judge their relative levels of sophistication in their incorporation of money.

Certainly, the classicists accepted that an excess demand for money could exist and that there could be excess supplies in other markets as a result. At the existing money wage, commodity price level and interest rate, hoarders could demand more money to hoard than there was in supply. Money would then be drawn out of active circulation. That an excess demand for money was behind the problem of widespread unemployment was so clear to the classicists that they even suggested gold mining, to increase the money supply, as an occupation for the idle.[73] Keynes was fully aware of this view, but reasoned that the supply of money or gold would be too inelastic for any reliance to be reasonably placed on this automatic remedy.[74] Consequently, if Keynes had merely pointed out that hoarding was possible and mining gold impracticable, he would have added little to the existing state of knowledge, except so far as the non-temporary nature of hoarding was concerned. Leijonhufvud does not pause to consider whether to give Keynes credit for this because he sees Keynes's primary assault involving something deeper.[75] Perhaps this is why he does not dwell on whether Keynes treated Mill fairly.[76]

Leijonhufvud argues that Keynes denied the principle that any excess supply had to be matched somewhere by an effective excess demand. According to classical logic, any thrift which caused an excess supply of consumption goods would, in the absence of hoarding, cause an effective excess demand for investment goods as savings would be invested. Alternatively, classicists would reason that the real wage could be adjusted to eliminate an excess supply of labour and that the additional output would be demanded by the newly employed. According to Leijonhufvud, Keynes, in denying that these things would occur in a money using system, instead maintained, in effect, that the only positive demand for money in a short-run equilibrium would be the notional demand of the unemployed workers for the money they would have used to purchase bonds or consumption goods had they been employed.[77] In Keynes's scheme, the money market could rapidly clear (the interest rate having equated the quantities of money effectively demanded and supplied) and yet excess supplies could exist in other markets. The classicists had stressed that the money market need not clear on the grounds of continuing panic-induced hoarding in periods of financial crisis, but this is not a necessary condition for an inadequacy of aggregate demand.

There is some evidence, however, that the classicists would have been prepared to accept money was so important because hoarding it, *even if the money market cleared*, would withdraw money from active circulation and generate unemployment. Pigou is one economist who immediately accepted the multiplier and did not consider it to be a revolutionary insight. Perhaps Pigou is a special case and the relationship of his and Keynes's economics will require separate consideration.[78]

It can be argued that Leijonhufvud gives too little sympathy to the classicists in this respect. After all, the very fact that they acknowledged that hoarding, if it occurred, would be serious, indicates that money can potentially play a part in explaining the cumulative motion of the system away from full employment. It was the hoarding of money that was argued over, not that of peanuts.[79] Money had a special role even to the classicists, but the full significance of that role with regard to the multiplier, bear speculation and the effect of money wage cuts was not generally appreciated. The classical understanding (with the possible exception of Pigou, whom, ironically, Keynes chose to criticize the most vehemently) was relatively rudimentary.

The classicists had seen that an excess demand for money existed, but it is unlikely that they anticipated Keynes in two major respects. First, did they recognize that an excess demand for money can be associated with the *equilibrium* in the securities and commodities markets? Was the additional demand for hoarding forever unsatisfied since interest rates never rose sufficiently? Was their understanding confined to disequilibrium motion whereby cycles were seen as a violent flux where transactors were incessantly striving to sell securities and commodities and to economize on input purchases and consumption expenditure in a frenzied effort to secure cash in hand? In Keynes, a short-run equilibrium was possible, the securities and commodities markets conceivably had no tendency to change (if money wages are assumed constant). There were the idle labourers, with an unsatisfied demand for money (given the relative price vector), who were in excess supply.

Second – and this is the fundamental difference between Keynes and the hypothetical classicist – supposing that a review of classical monetary thought revealed that the securities market cleared and the flow of output was sold so that there was a glut of idle productive machinery and manpower rather than vast inventories of unsold goods, was there the realization that the excess demand for money corresponding to the excess supply of labour was merely notional and that reductions in the money wage would not allow the labour market to clear so that labour is *involuntarily* unemployed? It is one thing to see, as the classicists did, that hoarding is associated with unemployment, but the details of the analysis of the unemployment state differ sharply. If voluntary hoarding is associated with unemployment – a classicist would accept this – this does not imply that a reduction of consumption reflects voluntary decisions by consumers to save more and 'release resources' to investment. Savings propensities and bearishness require separate analysis. The unemployed are not themselves *choosing* not to spend, they need not possess any money to hoard. They are involuntarily unemployed and are *forced* to curtail expenditure. Hoarders have *chosen* to curtail expenditure, but not labourers.

Leijonhufvud's view, therefore, that the multiplier and an analysis of the perverse dynamics of effective demand was original to Keynes, is accepted. Others apparently would share this view for Leijonhufvud has strengthened the position of the Keynesians. Indeed, this could partly explain their failure to criticize him strenuously.[80] He has provided an analytical framework which justifies the attention which the Keynesians have given to the multiplier. He has relieved them of the unnecessarily strong assumption that prices are rigid and has replaced it with the more realistic assumption that equilibrating price adjustments do not occur instantaneously. He rightly praises the Keynesians for preserving the multiplier concept 'in an otherwise emasculated version of Keynes' theory'.[81]

Keynes and Pigou

What follows is an attempt to distance Leijonhufvud and Keynes on the one hand from Pigou (and Haberler) on the other. By doing this, Leijonhufvud's interpretation of Keynes might not seem, as it does to some, to yield too much to the neoclassicals who claim Pigou and Haberler as intellectual forebears. Leijonhufvud's views can be distinguished from those of Pigou. While Leijonhufvud is prepared to argue that in Keynes, and in the real world, restoration of full employment by deflation is merely a logical possibility, Pigou's position seems rather more extreme.[82]

We must respect Hutchison's re-examination of Pigou, which concludes, correctly, that Pigou did not recommend wage cuts. Instead, Pigou plainly supported Keynes, and others, in their advocacy of fiscal policy. Nevertheless, it is possible to sympathize with Keynes's view that often Pigou's 'good common sense ceases to overbear his bad theory'.[83]

Hutchison has challenged those who have criticized Pigou to produce evidence to support Keynes's assertion.[84] While adequately attempting to respond to Hutchison is outside the scope of this work, the issue is important enough to warrant the presentation of some evidence that suggests that Hutchison, in remedying the distortions of Pigou which have come about, has perhaps unduly flattered him.

Certainly Pigou is not guilty of contradicting himself by allowing scope, in a cautious yet optimistic tone,[85] for discretionary fiscal policy in a world where, in fact, money wages are inflexible and where hypothetical automatic processes work too slowly. As a temporary expedient, the government can sensibly enter the market-place and increase the aggregate demand for labour which, by virtue of cyclical fluctuations, especially of investment,[86] has fallen with resulting unemployment. Nevertheless, wage deflation is an alternative which, according to Pigou, *would work* if the more prudent alternative of fiscal policy were not adopted.[87]

It is wiser to hold that Keynes's complaint in the appendix to chapter 19 was that Pigou's *mathematical* model was such that no involuntary unemployment, for which fiscal policy could be a remedy, could ever emerge. Keynes felt that Pigou held that labour was always in a position to govern its real wage and consequently no involuntary unemployment was possible.[88] The contradiction in Pigou was between his formalized model and the accompanying text which purported to explain real-world processes.[89] Consequently, Keynes ought to have made it clear that his objection was not that the classicists entirely overlooked fluctuations in aggregate demand but that they had failed to realize that their analyses violated their anterior assumptions about the functioning of the labour and money markets.

It also should be noted that Pigou believed that real wages moved pro-cyclically.[90] Keynes's first definition of involuntary unemployment, in which real wage cuts were a necessary effect of recovery but were not opposed by workers if achieved by reflation at a constant money wage, therefore would seem rather bizarre to Pigou, and it is difficult to accuse Pigou of overlooking a possibility which he considered contrary to the facts of the world.[91] Therefore, one should not be too willing to accept Keynes's charge of Pigou's naïvely holding that money and real wages were bound simply to each other. Nevertheless there seems some legitimacy to Keynes's complaint that Pigou naïvely has real-wage bargains.[92] Pigou has retorted[93] that he did not ignore the fact the *money* wages are perceived by workers as important, but Pigou simply resorts to money illusion[94] to identify the cause of the undesirable inflexibility.

One cannot pursue here the topic of whether Keynes correctly understood Pigou and whether these alleged contradictions in Pigou indeed exist. Instead, the cleavage between Keynes and Pigou will be revealed by indicating first that Pigou accepted the efficacy of wage deflation and second that Pigou did not perhaps grasp the relationship between money wages, real wages and involuntary unemployment that was emphasized by Keynes. As the latter is discussed later in this chapter, attention here turns to the former.

Many passages, written before and after *The General Theory*, indicate that Pigou regretted that institutional barriers existed which promoted wage inflexibilities and impeded full employment. His grounds were not confined to the view that micro-allocation suffered; rather, aggregate unemployment can be attributed to excessively high wages.[95] Against the well-known passage describing wealth effects induced by changes in the price of assets as 'academic exercises' not likely to be 'posed on the checker board of actual life'[96] which is taken by many as a recognition not merely of the fact that, in the real world, wage reductions are out of the question politically but also is taken as an acceptance that the beneficial effects might be too slow to appear with any strength, can be placed the following passages.

In *Industrial Fluctuations*, Pigou's views appear unmistakable, at least on a casual reading:

> [W]age-rates in modern conditions are held more or less rigidly at conventional levels higher in bad times than is warranted by the conditions of short-period supply.

In 1936 we find:

> With [interest-rate] policies in any degree resembling actual policies, ...cuts in money wage rates *must* lower real wage rates and increase employment.[97]

In *Employment and Equilibrium*[98] he endorses his view in his *The Theory of Unemployment*:

> With perfectly free competition among workpeople and labour perfectly mobile...there will always be at work a strong tendency for wage-rates to be so related to demand that everybody is employed.

Indeed, *The Theory of Unemployment*, part i (chapter x), is devoted to an attempted refutation of the view – later appearing in chapter 2 of *The General Theory* – that general money-wage cuts will merely cause equiproportional deflation leaving the real wage unaffected.[99] See also *Industrial Fluctuations*, chapter xix for the view that money-wage inflexibilities are a real problem. Incidentally, he also notes the possibility of the elasticity of price and wage expectations exceeding unity,[100] a point of interest to tracing the origins of the Pigou effect.

Pigou also writes (after alluding to the likelihood that employers are likely to expect further wage reductions and defer their outlays):

> [W]hen the impulse driving wage-rates down comes from the pressure of unemployment, everyone will know that, once a *sufficient* cut is made, the pressure will cease and, therefore, the downward tendency will stop.[101]

In *Lapses from Full Employment*[102] appears:

> Thus the policy of reducing money wage rates and that of expanding money demand do not stand on exactly the same footing. As we have seen *exceptional* conditions are possible in which reductions in wage rates would not benefit employment at

all; but...a sufficiently low level of money wage rates would ensure full employment once for all without any need for further manipulation.

It would be a misrepresentation of Pigou to highlight only those passages which show confidence in the deflationary path to full employment. Pigou does understand the problem of nominally fixed contractual obligations and the disruptions to organization caused by bankruptcies.[103]

Other differences of viewpoint could also be cited. For example, it is Pigou, and not Keynes, who took the more extreme 'Keynesian' view[104] on the uselessness of monetary policy in deep depression on the grounds that 'when industrialists see no hope anywhere, there may be *no* positive rate of money interest that will avail'.[105]

It is tentatively concluded that the differences over theory and policy between Keynes and Pigou are real and sharp both before and after *The General Theory*. This casts doubts on the popularly held view that Pigou had substantially acknowledged the soundness of Keynes's contributions and had been obliged to retreat in the face of the Keynesian revolution. His book, *Keynes's 'General Theory'* is laced with comments on the invalidity of many of Keynes's arguments and seems to indicate that Pigou was prepared to concede little of substance.[106] Certainly, tracing the evolution of Pigou's thought would be a worthwhile undertaking.[107] Care would certainly need to be taken in order to avoid the error of quoting Keynes's views of Pigou as indeed representing what Pigou was saying.

Money illusion

One peculiar feature of the evolution of our understanding of the essential characteristics of Keynes's revolution has been the rise to ascendancy at one time of the notion of the pivotal importance of money illusion.[108] In its crudest form it refers to how transactors make decisions on the basis of selected nominal prices and do not take account of changes in the general price level. This is the sense in which it is used here. Money illusion in this context is not intended to embrace all possible reasons as to why the labour-supply equation is not homogeneous with respect to (current) money wages and prices. For example, where monetary injections are temporarily misinterpreted as real, agent-specific, relative improvements in the terms of trade, this is *not* money illusion in the primitive sense employed here which relies on 'irrationality'. Illusion once shared, with minimum wage laws and obstinacy of union officials, the role of explaining the rigidity of the money wage in the face of unemployment.

The position of money illusion is less clear nowadays in view of the plethora of rival microfoundations of Keynes's economics, and, in particular, Leijonhufvud's dismissal[109] of it spurred no passionate rebuttals from the old 'Keynesian' school. It appears that no one wishes to defend the doctrine of money illusion since transactors nowadays are acutely aware of the nominal-real distinction. You either have to reject Keynes as being irrelevant or search further in *The General Theory* for other ways to produce an unemployment equilibrium.

That money illusion has held sway both in textbooks and in the writings of some historians of economic thought can hardly be doubted.[110]

Long ago it was held that Keynes's economics was of practical value largely because workers in a depression did indeed fail to appreciate that the prices of wage-goods had fallen by more than the nominal wage and would resist cuts. Similarly, during a boom, workers could be deceived and unemployment levels could be set by the social planners at some politically desirable figure of, say 2 per cent, which could be sustained by government expenditure even if the 'natural' rate of unemployment – in this context, the maximum sustainable in a market system devoid of illusion – was higher. But, when we look at *The General Theory*, what do we find?

Money illusion in Keynes

The most surprising discovery is that money illusion plays no part whatsoever in Keynes's analysis of the labour market. Workers are fully aware of what the real wage is in comparison to their marginal disutility of labour and are not deceived by a decline in real wages during an upswing. Workers

> do not resist reductions of real wages, which are associated with increases in aggregate employment and leave relative money-wages unchanged, *unless the reduction proceeds so far as to threaten a reduction of the real wage below the marginal disutility of the existing volume of employment.*[111]

In other words, workers fully perceive falls in the real wage, or even if it is about to fall, below the marginal disutility of labour. They know what is happening to each. When the real wage falls in the upswing it is with their open-eyed consent, unless it proceeds too far when it is met with open-eyed opposition.[112] Workers are prepared to accept the lower real wage required in the upswing as determined by their lower marginal productivity. Keynes accepted that the real wage was inversely related to the level of activity, because he accepted that the law of diminishing returns would prevail as output grew.[113]

Before attention can be given to the important question of the nature of labour market responses to disequilibrating shocks, some general remarks on adjustment processes are called for.

In a state of confusion and disarray, even if the 'correct' price vector were to emerge miraculously in the absence of an auctioneer, agents simply would not *know* it to be the appropriate vector. An auctioneer performs two tasks. He cries out a vector and he assures agents that this indeed is the mutually consistent and correct one. Leijonhufvud does not suggest, as some have done, that agents in the absence of an auctioneer have in mind a probability distribution and, on average and in the short run, grope successfully. There is no orderly search in his account whereby agents engage in some optimal number of trials to learn of the true state of demand. Such models could be plausible in dealing with small, or microeconomic, shocks, where much of the environment is intelligible, but under more severe forms of dislocation, about which agents know little from past experience, models incorporating risk, as distinct from Knightian uncertainty, could prove misleading. In the face of large shocks, demand curves are shifting. It is not a simple case, as in Arrow, where agents are merely testing the elasticity of their given demand curves. One can, as does Leijonhufvud, abstain from probabilistic versions of search activity based on perceptions of risk and prospective gain without veering to the opposite extreme, as might some fundamentalists, and to deny that a solution exists even in principle. For all intents and purposes, groping in a darkened room for a black cat which is there but uncooperatively elusive would look to the scientific observer much the same as the groping for one which is in truth not even there. One might sensibly prefer the more radical approach which denies the very existence of the Walrasian vector in an uncertain world and yet feel that to frame an assault on Leijonhufvud in those terms is rather too harsh.

In any event, it is not clear that Keynes himself gave any weight to either uncertainty or merely imperfect knowledge in explaining how labour markets can in logic settle into a state of involuntary unemployment and how labour markets do in fact behave. Uncertainty to Keynes was a problem in other markets. Workers are only too well aware of their own unemployment. The labour market has a passive role. It responds to uncertainties which rock other markets.

Nevertheless, attempts have been made to understand Keynes's money-wage dynamics in terms of uncertainty.[114] Darity and Horn[115] make the interesting suggestion that the suppliers of labour are themselves uncertain about the appropriate real wage, but in fact Keynes never says that himself, choosing instead to emphasize the 'fundamental' point that the nexus between money and real wages is nonexistent. He contents himself with a somewhat hydraulic argument that lower wages reduce expenditure in roughly the same proportion. Uncertainty is not pervasive, and besides, workers know the current real wage and are willing to accept *a* lower real wage even if they do not know *the* Walrasian wage. In Keynes, there is a 'neutral' real wage corresponding to full employment, and it takes on a definite value, the marginal product at full employment. Keynes does not emphasize difficulties in perceiving marginal (revenue) products. On the contrary, he is happy to jump from one comparative-static state to another without giving much thought to the problems of 'groping'. In *The General Theory*, the real wage's equality to the marginal product is not difficult to achieve. It occurs automatically in flow supply equilibrium in the goods market.[116] Workers resist money-wage cuts, it is true, but not because they are uncertain merely about how far the reduction needs to be.[117] They resist *any* nominal cuts.

Why then do labourers reject money-wage cuts in a depression even if they are prepared to accept a real-wage cut? Keynes offers two reasons. The first is 'not theoretically fundamental' although it is the one which has attracted more attention, especially in Britain.[118] Keynes[119] suggests that workers guard their positions relative to those of other workers and resist money-wage reductions 'which are seldom or never of an all-round character'. There is no money illusion here, apparently just some sort of jealousy or pride. Perhaps, as suggested by Leijonhufvud,[120] the remuneration of others is being used as an indicator of one's own marginal revenue product, no direct knowledge of it being possessed by any given labourer.[121] The importance Keynes attached to his alternative objection to classical thought, which does not depend on money illusion either, remains largely unappreciated. There is 'the other, more fundamental, objection':

> There may exist no expedient by which labour as a whole can reduce its *real* wage to a given figure by making revised *money* bargains with the entrepreneurs.[122]

Leijonhufvud rightly elevates this quotation to a position of importance yet appears to grasp only part of its significance to the microfoundations of macroeconomics. Leijonhufvud[123] rightly emphasizes that the dynamics of a monetary system cannot be assumed analogous to one of barter.

> The workers looking for jobs ask for *money*, not commodities.... The fact that there exists a potential barter bargain of goods for labour services that would be mutually agreeable to producers *as a group* and labour *as a group* is irrelevant to the motion of the system.

Leijonhufvud,[124] however, sees no further microeconomic ideas behind what Keynes wrote and argues that the representative worker is engaged in job search and this imparts inflexibility to the money wage in view of inelastic price expectations. He does not consider that the workers themselves might rationally *choose* not to attempt to counter involuntary unemployment 'through a *futile* competition for employment between the unemployed labourers'.[125] If a worker realizes that others will simply retaliate, then the incentive to undercut others largely disappears and the opportunity for a collective truce, policed by the unions, exists. It cannot be said, however, that Keynes clearly had this in mind.

What Keynes felt to be the microfoundations of resistance to cuts in money wages is uncertain.[126]

One can look at changes in the real wage, *assuming that money wages are not falling*, so that the relationship between the real wage and the marginal disutility of labour – the subject of the second classical postulate which Keynes sought to attack – can be studied in isolation.

If the inability of workers to reduce their real wage even if money wages were flexible downwards, is the 'fundamental' issue, then the difficulties which exist in exactly specifying Keynes's supply-of-labour function can be dispensed with.[127] If workers resisted money-wage cuts it was not because they confused nominals and reals, but it was for a completely different reason. For a discussion of involuntary unemployment, it is the non-resistance to real-wage cuts *per se* which is of direct concern. Money-wage behaviour in the real world is a different issue.

If money illusion is rejected as an essential property of transactor behaviour in the labour market, did Keynes assign any role to it in his analysis of other markets?

If we examine Keynes's views on consumption expenditure we find that habits may, among other things, impart some degree of stickiness[128] but as Leijonhufvud once again rightly points out,[129] workers are free of money illusion. Also suggestive of denying any more than the passing relevance of money illusion is a passage from a draft of *The General Theory*:

> An increment of 'voluntary' saving...is only to be welcomed... when employment is supra-optimal and earners are finding themselves tricked by the industrial machine into exerting themselves on a scale, the marginal disutility of which is not adequately rewarded by their marginal product – a state of affairs which actually in the modern world is very infrequent.[130]

Keynes's views are illuminated by his treatment of illusion so far as it applies in the industrial sector.

For a time at least, rising prices may *delude* entrepreneurs into increasing employment beyond the level which maximises their individual profits measured in terms of the product. For they are so accustomed to regard rising sale-proceeds in terms of money as a signal for expanding production, that they may continue to do so when this policy has in fact ceased to be to their best advantage; i.e. they may underestimate their marginal user cost in the new price environment.[131]

Keynes is clearly aware of what money illusion is, and expressly gives it a minor and peripheral role in explaining temporary deviations which constitute 'certain practical qualifications'[132] of his basic model.

Further evidence of the unimportance of money illusion can be obtained from his discussion of the determination of interest rates and his dispute with Irving Fisher about whether inflationary expectations could cause nominal interest rates to rise to preserve a real return for wealth holders. Whether Keynes or Fisher was correct is not the issue here. What matters is that Keynes could easily have chosen to resort to the argument that savers were overcome by money illusion and for that reason nominal interest rates would not rise. Keynes[133] did not, even though he was fully aware of Pigou's argument that borrowers and lenders might at different rates appreciate the fact that the price level was changing.

A conclusion which now clearly emerges is that, while Keynes knew what money illusion was, at no stage did he rely on it in his attack on orthodox thought.

Money illusion in classical economics

Attention is now turned to a remarkable aspect of the controversy between Keynes and the classicists. Examining writings prior to *The General Theory* indicates that it was the *classical* economics where money illusion had a significant role to play. Note that Keynes, rightly or wrongly, considered Pigou and Mill to be major representatives of the classical school, and money illusion appears in the works of both.

The notion makes an appearance as early as Mill when he sought to identify the limited circumstances in which a general glut of commodities could occur. If all classes of producers are endeavouring to expand operations beyond the level which can profitably be sold,

it is a certain proof that some general delusion is afloat. The commonest cause of such delusion is some general, or very extensive, rise of prices (whether caused by speculation or by the currency) which persuades all dealers that they are growing rich. And hence, an increase of production really takes place during the process of depreciation, as long as the existence of the depreciation is not suspected.... But when the delusion vanishes and the truth is disclosed,...they will be likely to repent at leisure.[134]

Pigou certainly incorporated money illusion into his analysis. It played an important role, along with the immobility of labour, in explaining why fluctuations in employment can become pronounced.[135]

When prices rise, business men become more prosperous.... Furthermore, besides the real change in their fortunes there is also an element of imagined change. For when people have more or less money than usual, even though prices have changed in precise correspondence, the natural tendency to 'think in gold' is apt to make them imagine themselves really richer or really poorer.

Pigou also specifically refers to money illusion in the labour market. He states:

that the tendency of workpeople to 'think in gold' leads them to resist reductions in money wages when prices are falling and to acquiesce in refusals to raise money wages when prices are rising, thus in effect demanding an increase in the rate of real wages in times of depression and assenting to a decrease in times of prosperity.[136]

Pigou repeats that appropriate adjustments to real wages are thwarted by 'factors of inertia...which...in a money economy tend to keep money wages stable. To a great extent people – employers and employed alike – think in money.'[137]

In his review of *The General Theory*,[138] Pigou objects to Keynes's accusations that the classicists had overlooked how changes in the price level, at a given money wages, alters the real supply schedule of labour. His point was that money illusion matters and he later repeats the claim.[139]

It is also clear that Keynes knew that money illusion was important to Pigou, and he even criticized Pigou for depending on such a limited assumption to justify the fiscal intervention which Pigou had advocated with Keynes ten years earlier.

I was already arguing at that time that the good effect of an expansionist investment policy on employment, the fact of which no one denied, was due to the stimulant which it gave to effective demand. Professor Pigou, on the other hand, and many other economists explained the observed result by the reduction in real wages *covertly* effected by the rise in prices which ensued on the increase in effective demand. It was held that public investment policies (and also an improvement in the trade balance through tariffs) produced their effect by *deceiving*, so to speak, the working classes into accepting a lower real wage, effecting by this means the same favourable influence on employment which, according to these economists, would have resulted from a more direct attack on real wages (e.g. by reducing money wages whilst enforcing a credit policy calculated to leave prices unchanged).[140]

Consequently, even though Pigou did recommend fiscal policy along with Keynes, his theoretical justification could have differed markedly.

It can be concluded that money illusion sometimes was relied upon by some classical writers to explain why prices need not adjust to maintain equilibrium at full employment. Keynes plainly knew what money illusion was. He fully realized that it played a significant role in the writings of others, but that it did not in his own.

Money illusion and the post-Keynesians

What is strange is that theoreticians and historians of economic thought have not viewed the debate between Keynes and the classicists in this light. Instead of an interpretation of Keynes based on money illusion being spurned at its birth, it has been clasped warmly against the bosom.

James Tobin[141] provides an interesting example. In order to protect Keynes's outcome of involuntary unemployment in the face of falling money wages, Tobin reasons that money illusion could be extended to all markets. It should be noted, however, that Tobin, in a manner resembling that of his 1972 Presidential Address, treats 'money illusion' in a broader fashion to include such things, other than naïve deception, as inelastic price expectations, ignorance of prevailing states of demand and administrative lags in contractual renegotiations, all of which impede price flexibility.

More striking, however, is Patinkin's[142] extension of money illusion into Keynes's theory of the speculative demand for money.[143] His argument is an involved one, the full details of which cannot be discussed here. Put crudely, Patinkin maintains that Keynes's failure to clearly and validly distinguish between real and money balances indicates that Keynes felt that money-holders do not draw that distinction either and were therefore afflicted with money illusion. Perhaps Keynes's blurring of the two – accepting that Patinkin's textual evidence does indicate this – suggests mere obscurity and looseness, and one ought not to maintain that a tacit assumption of illusion in some sense is the explanation. It might be that in some passages Keynes was

tacitly assuming constant money wages while in others, where the effects of wage deflation were under direct examination, he did not.[144]
One passage is sufficient to illustrate.[145]

Unless we measure liquidity-preference in terms of wage units rather than of money (which is convenient in some contexts), similar results follow if the increased employment ensuing on a fall in the rate of interest leads to *an increase of wages, i.e. to an increase in the money value of the wage unit.*

Keynes clearly indicates that to measure liquidity preference in terms of wage units 'is convenient in some contexts'.

Plainly Keynes's model usually has constant money wages and only in 'some contexts' (such as examining the effects of money wage cuts on the MEI schedule and the interest rate) does Keynes consider there to be a need to differentiate real and nominal balances.

Patinkin[146] wonders why Keynes did not recognize that greater real balances can increasingly satisfy the speculative demand for money if that too were measured in real terms. Whether Keynes made a mistake or not in overlooking this – assuming that he did indeed fail to consider the issue – it is not clear that this lapse should be construed as meaning that money illusion in Patinkin's broad sense (let alone in the narrow and primitive sense used here) can be attributed by Keynes to the speculators. It is too strong a conclusion to draw from circumstantial evidence.[147] Keynes's whole theory of liquidity preference bore the marks of being in only semi-finished form, and whether or not he could or would have specified the demand for real balances while preserving the (long-run) non-neutrality of money one cannot say, of course.

Whether or not agreement with either Tobin or Patinkin is ultimately arrived at, it certainly emerges that money illusion is often relied upon to give some insight into aspects of Keynes's arguments found difficult to understand clearly at the literal level. The profession has often and willingly adopted it, yet it is argued that, in its simplest form, Keynes plainly rejected it. It appears that the once official version of the history of economic thought is completely at variance with the facts. The 'problem' with Keynes's allegedly naïve theory of expectations based on money illusion in the labour market never existed.

In conclusion, Leijonhufvud is certainly correct to reject money illusion, but an alternative account of money-wage inflexibilities can be offered which has considerably more exegetical support than Leijonhufvud's speculative suggestion about inelastic wage expectations. Not only is money illusion rejected in the labour market. It is rejected as a characteristic of any market. Ironically, it was Pigou who saw it as important, not Keynes.

One final comment needs to be made. To anticipate possible misunderstandings, it is not intended that, by denying illusion and by considering real variables important Keynes is being taken to trivialize actions that use money. Money matters even if agents think in real terms. Labour can *think* in reals without being able to *act* in reals. The non-neutrality of money is not being denied.[148] Neither does this stance necessarily prevent the incorporation of the additional problems agents could have in judging appropriate wage offers, in real terms, under conditions of uncertainty. The argument also is fully consistent with the view that agents in money-using systems are unable reliably to effect desired real exchanges even if all parties were aware of the possibility of mutually beneficial real trades.

Some modern views on involuntary unemployment

All Keynesian factions agree that a lack of effective demand explains a state of involuntary unemployment. Hydraulicists portray the phenomenon in mechanical terms, fundamentalists (such as Davidson) in institutional terms such as the financial and credit structure, and the reductionists point to the role of money as a means to express demand. The subjectivism prevalent in so much of fundamentalist literature is evident so far as a mere lack of volition explains involuntary unemployment. The urge to spend and the willingness to extend credit are central themes. In Leijonhufvud there are constraints beyond the psychological. Ironically, the restoration of confidence, as in classical cycle theory, restores full employment in fundamentalist accounts. It is not clear, therefore, that fundamentalists can legitimately lay claim to identifying the essence of things.

One new classicist, Barro, is unconvinced by the efforts of reductionists to connect involuntary unemployment, the consumption function, the multiplier and liquidity constraints.

> We mentioned before that liquidity constraints, where some people cannot borrow readily at the going interest rate, could be a basis for the Keynesian consumption function. But if such constraints were important, we would expect recessions to exhibit major shortfalls in consumer expenditures on non-durables and services. In fact, the data show relatively little fluctuation in these categories of spending. The components that do decline substantially during recessions are – aside from business investment – the purchases of consumer durables, including residential housing, automobiles, and appliances. These goods are relatively easy to buy on credit because durables serve as good

collateral for loans. Therefore, the data suggest that liquidity constraints do not play a major role in U.S. business fluctuations.[149]

The argument would amaze most Keynesians. The unemployed do not buy houses or cars even if the asset is partial collateral because the liquidity-constrained are unable to meet the interest payments or convince the lender that they would be able to. The income-inelastic necessities make the first claim to household disposable income, and outlays on durables are therefore deferred or cancelled. The data have a natural, commonsense explanation, but the obvious seems to have become invisible to Barro who appears constrained by his new classical vision.[150]

If Barro's argument can be put aside, then two distinct issues arise. What is the nature of the constraints, preferences and opportunity sets which explain involuntary unemployment? Why are attempts not made to regain employment by accepting lower money wages? The second question is of little practical relevance if no reliable mechanism exists by which money-wage cuts can indeed restore full employment. Nevertheless, it is of intellectual interest to discover possible reasons why it is rational not to even attempt to relieve involuntary unemployment by money-wage cuts. This is a separate issue from that which simply describes how labour markets in fact behave because many aspects of actual behaviour can reasonably be grouped under the heading of the 'voluntary' effects, in some sense, of consciously made decisions.

Much attention has been devoted to the issue of explaining price inflexibilities in general and wage inflexibilities in particular. The underlying rationale is that, in the absence of such impediments, full employment would emerge – assuming that a vector of prices exist and that adjustment processes are stable.

Many attempts have been made to isolate properties of the labour market which give rise to behaviour which is in some sense 'involuntary'. Sometimes suggestions are offered as interpretations of Keynes and sometimes as positive contributions in their own right, perhaps to supply what is felt to be the missing link in Keynes, a coherent theory of money-wage and real-wage determination.

One strand of thought sees the resistance to money-wage cuts as being rational even in the face of unemployment on the simple ground that there is a real subsistence floor.[151] This possibility would be of no help if real wages moved countercyclically.

Other explanations look to the role of unions[152] and how the preferences of individual rank and file workers are not reflected in the conduct of the leadership. Furthermore, a recent contribution suggests that the firm's unionized and employed labourers cannot be replaced by the *currently* unskilled 'outsiders'. There are costs of hiring and firing which are barriers to entry which the 'insiders' happily exploit.[153]

Some emphasize Keynes's argument[154] about relativities and the interdependence of utility functions. Surprisingly, Davidson and Smolensky[155] adopt the 'bastard Keynesian' view that involuntary unemployment (as distinct from real-world, money-wage inflexibility) is *caused* by unionization and minimum-wage legislation. It is for this reason that workers are left powerless to reduce their real wage and must await an increase in aggregate demand.

Albert Rees[156] referred long ago to a few possibilities to explain the absence of pressure from employers to drive down the money wage including fear of public disapproval, loss of reputation and inability in future to recruit higher-quality labour, unionization and – an unexplored possibility, it seems – the fear that management has that the stockholders or directors would insist on a similar cut in managerial salaries. Managers do not want to rock the boat.

Other attempts to explain why price inflexibilities are rational under conditions of unemployment include Takashi Negishi's[157] attempt to use oligopoly theory in circumstances where the agents perceive (or conjecture) that price cuts will not work because of high search costs. Cuts in prices will cause total revenue to drop because so few new sales are attracted, yet a price increase has the same effect because it prods an existing customer to search for a lower price elsewhere.

By contrast to Negishi's approach this work takes a slightly different tack. Instead of agents being unable to communicate lower money prices to prospective purchasers, they perceive that the effort would be futile because, just as in an oligopolistic model, the other workers will retaliate to preserve their position of employment. Unions evolve to prevent such leapfrogging wage cuts.

Search theory was popular for a time and, so far as Leijonhufvud relied on inelastic price expectations as a trigger mechanism for the multiplier, he could be considered an adherent of that approach. Critics have considered such theories as unable to deal satisfactorily with layoffs, as distinct from quits, a common complaint being that search unemployment is entirely 'voluntary'.[158] Alchian[159] was prepared to speculate, like Leijonhufvud, that Keynes had some kind of search-theory notion in mind and that workers cannot distinguish specific and aggregate declines in the demand for labour. Donald F. Gordon and Allan Hynes[160] were among the first to explain involuntary unemployment (and overemployment) as due to unpredictable macroeconomic shocks that 'temporarily fool the economy' into departing from the long-run, vertical Phillips curve.

Another important and well-developed strand of the literature[161] considers the role of implicit contracts whereby workers and firms agree to an inflexible wage rather than settle on an arrangement whereby labour is bought on a spot basis. Firms relieve workers of the risks of wage flexibility. Also there exists the 'invisible handshake' strand of implicit contract theory of Arthur Okun.[162]

Leijonhufvud has responded to those strands of argument. To him, *the* issue is the non-instantaneous adjustment of money wages. He has no particular regard for any theory which attributes involuntary unemployment to belated money-wage cuts, because he believes that, once the income-constrained process is under way, such cuts would not deal with the problem in any significant way. 'Keynesians' (including Okun, Gordon and others), Leijonhufvud complains:

> who should have no particular use for the assumption [of short-term wage rigidity have]...eventually made it the touchstone of Keynesian doctrine.[163]

What new Keynesian and new classical economists share is the belief that, but for impediments to the absolutely free play of market forces, employment would be higher. New classicists[164] can argue that seeming inflexibilities are better seen as a manifestation of market choices. Maximum short-period employment is not a good indicator of welfare and there is no valid scope for governments to make this a target of social policy.

If Leijonhufvud is right to hold that there is no theoretical need for impediments to wage flexibility after an initial stickiness, there is a practical need to explain contemporary, labour-market behaviour in plausible terms. When Leijonhufvud responded to the discussion of his paper,[165] he is reported to have stated that

> Many Keynesians hold on to some nominal wage rigidity, whether from implicit contract theory or elsewhere, because they think it is what makes them characteristically Keynesians. Professor Leijonhufvud thinks that the move over to this mish-mash and away from Keynes's intertemporal [dis-?]equilibrium story makes Keynesian economics easy prey to monetarism.

This seems fair comment.

Robert E. Lucas, evaluating attempts to explain Keynes by resorting to implicit contracts, rejects the view that the voluntary-involuntary distinction even makes much sense or is of much value to an empirical economist.[166] You cannot look into people's heads to determine their subjective states of mind towards their unemployment. Furthermore, if they choose to operate under institutions which involve inflexibilities in the setting of the nominal wage, this is their free choice.[167]

Leijonhufvud rejects the view that a Keynes–Wicksell type of intertemporal co-ordination failure can be rejected on purely methodological grounds as Lucas suggests:

He [Lucas] may be right that we have no operational way to distinguish voluntary from involuntary unemployment or to measure excess demands and supplies. But whether we have a good analytical and empirical handle on it or not, the coordination problem is a real one.[168]

Leijonhufvud is prepared to consider that Keynes's insights are of greatest value 'outside the corridor' where the system is afflicted by large, unforeseen and ill-understood shocks. In contrast to Lucas:

If the lesson is that we have no reliable way of using past data to predict quantitatively how the economy will react to unprecedented change, we would still like to understand qualitatively how the system reacts to unforeseen and ill-understood developments, such as the Great Depression. Such explanation will have to make use of the concepts of excess demand and supply that have no place in Lucas' approach. One hesitates to suggest it but the despised notion of economic policy as an 'art' (rather than a quantitative science) might even have a place in such circumstances.

He draws a medical analogy to show the sorts of questions with which the NCE approach cannot successfully cope. He seeks to deal with

problems of reduced immunological capacity or infections either of a 'massive' nature or by novel strains of bacteria.

By contrast, Lucas would see this 'pursuit...as productive of nothing but quackery in medical practice'.[169]

Lucas once wrote:

Thus there is an involuntary element in *all* unemployment, in the sense that noone chooses bad luck over good; there is also a voluntary element in all unemployment, in the sense that however miserable one's current options, one can always choose to accept them.[170]

Ten years earlier, Leijonhufvud, in a somewhat different context, had supplied a counter-argument:

The man who lost his job yesterday may be 'willingly' unemployed in the sense that the option of shining shoes or selling apples is open to him today. But he is certainly 'unwillingly' unemployed in that were he offered the option of changing places with one of his fellows who remains employed...he would take it.[171]

Leijonhufvud here puts his finger on the point: can even a 'voluntary' dismissal be reversed if one changes one's mind?

The very issue is addressed by Martin Neil Baily[172] who makes a stimulating comment in favour of the relevance of implicit contract theory to a modern attempt to rationalize involuntary unemployment.

> Workers *are* assumed to be aware that their employment situation is risky and that workers in unstable industries...receive higher hourly wage rates...than workers in stable industries.... But an enlisted man in the army who gets his head blown off would hardly be described as dying voluntarily, just because he knew ahead of time that army life was dangerous. Many people have reacted negatively to contract theory because they think that a model of efficient layoffs means unemployment is voluntary.... When people react efficiently to adverse circumstances, it does not mean they like their situations.

The issue here boils down to one of taking a chance and losing, rather like Lucas's remark that 'noone chooses bad luck over good'.[173]

Baily's analogy is somewhat misleading. The real issue is whether, during the *next* negotiations the unfortunate error of the past can be remedied. Decapitated soldiers are in no position to try an alternative tactic next time around.

Some new classicists would appear confident that a renegotiation of wages in the light of improved information about the state of the world in general, and the rate of inflation in particular, would allow employment to increase towards the natural rate. Leijonhufvud contests this considering that perverse multiplier effects can dominate and that the fundamental problem, being the 'wrong' interest rate in Keynes–Wicksell stories, is not reliably dealt with by money-wage adjustments.

The question arises as to how much the various attempts to explain 'involuntary unemployment' use the term in a sense similar to that of Keynes. Has Leijonhufvud done a better or worse job than others in trying to find a reasonable explanation of such a state?

The answer to that question is yes, if you consider irreversibility to be an essential ingredient to involuntary unemployment. Having lost your job, it is too late to change your mind. Once you miss the boat (or are pushed overboard), you are left stranded. It bears repeating that, in Leijonhufvud, *voluntary* search causes non-instantaneous money-wage cuts, but thereafter, once the multiplier has taken hold, unemployment can no longer be attributed entirely to search. Once the deviation is amplified restoration of full employment, in the short run at least, is problematic.

This point does not seem well appreciated. Consider C.J. Bliss who makes a criticism of Tobin, which equally is one of Leijonhufvud:

> Tobin is simply incorrect to support Keynes in saying that workers have no effective way to signal to employers their willingness to work for a lower real wage. A cut in the money wage demanded is such a signal.... It is true that large changes in money wages may be required to bring about small changes in real wage rates. But in this case large changes in money wages are not disruptive, at least not of the labour market. It is usually thought to be a good feature of a control that it has low leverage on the magnitude to be controlled. This facilitates fine-tuning and avoids serious overshooting.[174]

The whole of Tobin's argument is that to signal one's preparedness to work at a lower real wage is not the way to actually achieve the targeted real wage. Employers are not made aware of the notional demands for goods which would become effective if those workers were employed (and if aggregate investment, the culprit, were to return to a full-employment level). Furthermore, after the real balance effect, the nominal wage has become vastly distant from the Walrasian value consistent with full employment. This exacerbates the problem because at a later date the money wage must move back. Groping for the right nominal values becomes very much more difficult under the regime postulated by Bliss.

Once the system has departed from full employment, the choice of prices to set becomes ever more difficult and false trades are liable to persist. If perfect information had been available to all agents at the outset, no amplification of the initial shock would have occurred. Now, even if, despite the confusion and disarray of the new and deflationary environments, agents were somehow to learn of the possibility of mutually beneficial trades at particular relative prices, these positions need not be attainable in a system sucked dry of liquidity by bears and by the constriction of credit pipelines. On top of this, in practice, entrepreneurial pessimism is likely to have grown and an even larger profit share is needed to entice businesses to invest.

The reversal of erroneous decisions cannot simply be assumed possible, as it appears to be in some new classical stories. This branch of thinking is impatient with disequilibrium processes. Nothing, it is argued, can be clearly observed and, even if they could, rational agents would simply learn to anticipate the process and jump immediately to the final outcome. To put a Leijonhufvudian counter-argument, if the system does experience a deficiency of aggregate demand, however, an injection of spending is a necessary condition for recovery. One cannot spend anticipated, but not yet realized, income if one is an ordinary worker without access to credit. The restoration of a cash flow is a necessary condition for an upturn.

Information about potentially beneficial trades is of no use if no effective means exist to achieve those exchanges. That Leijonhufvud believes this, however, is not generally known. For example, Boris Pesek,[175] an early reviewer of Leijonhufvud's book, wrote:

Imperfect information may be responsible for a given outcome only if it were true that perfect information would change this outcome. But...even if perfectly informed consumers realized that common good and prosperity lies in consuming more (and hiring more), could and would each individual act accordingly?

Pesek seems to think that there must be something more fundamental than imperfect information at the heart of an unemployment state and he is right, but Leijonhufvud looks at mistakes made on the supply side only in order to explain the trigger-mechanism which sets forth the multiplier. Thereafter, the absence of purchasing power, which persists even after agents realize that they have made mistakes (if they ever do), is the source of the persistent unemployment. Pesek's logic is dubious. Would he argue as follows: smoking does not cause lung cancer because when the victims give up smoking they still need not recover? (The logic makes more sense, however, if we consider a smoker's cough instead.)

The system, once it departs significantly from full employment, is transformed. This is what Leijonhufvud tried to make clearer in his 'Effective demand failures',[176] although the ideas were already in chapter vi: 1 of his 1968 book. Leijonhufvud quotes Trygve Haavelmo:[177]

There is no reason why the *form* of a realistic model (the form of its equations) should be the same under all values of its variables. We must face the fact that the form of the model may have to be regarded as a function of the values of the variables involved. This will usually be the case if the values of some of the variables affect the basic conditions of choice under which the behaviour equations in the model are derived.

In the face of large disturbances, adjustments could occur along unfamiliar chains of trade. New sequences need to be tested if the regular clientele cannot send effective signals. Under such circumstances, Knightian uncertainty is liable to arise. Income constraints can propel the system into the unknown. Fundamentalist and reductionist insights can be wedded.

Involuntary unemployment that emerges and persists is rational from the viewpoint of each agent maximizing perceivable and attainable gains. Timidity in the financial and investment sectors generates objective spending constraints elsewhere. Price conventions, however, can remain undisturbed. Because learning occurs only on the basis of the signals generated by the system, agents can only come to understand and adjust to their current predicament. Knowledge of some superior and attainable state need not emerge endogenously. Even if it did, unless the hoarders (or the suppliers of trade and bank credit) and investors knew somehow that the others knew of and were inclined to act upon that belief, nothing would change. Only they have the power to change the plight of the economy because workers and producers of consumption goods have no effective power to produce and sell more without the earlier co-operation of the hoarders and investors. Those affected by the multiplier are unemployed on account of the actions of third parties and cannot directly improve their positions if starved of liquidity.

Having stressed that irreversibility is essential to the involuntary unemployment of labour, a further point requires attention. Up to now the argument has been framed in terms of how employment has fallen and the real wage has risen and how the return to the initial point requires reflation and not money-wage cuts. (Fundamentalists and reductionists can agree on this.) Part of the story has been that the labour market does not clear and that the real wage is higher than at its full employment figure. This accords with Keynes's famous definition of involuntary unemployment in chapter 2. Yet in 1939, and occasionally in *The General Theory*[178] itself, Keynes flirted with an alternative which, while stressing how powerless is labour to redress the situation, does relax the condition that real wages are too high. If real wages fall far enough, it is possible that workers will not attempt to gain employment by reducing the money wage. No real balance effects would arise. If involuntary unemployment is what a lasting increase in aggregate demand would diminish, then it exists whenever the aggregate supply curve is not perfectly inelastic. The recent consensus is that no particular significance attaches to the real wage. A few remarks can be made on such points but a recent paper[179] renders unnecessary a lengthy textual examination of Keynes's evolving views.

In his 'Relative movements of real wages and output',[180] he suggests why, as Dunlop and Tarshis had shown, a procyclical relationship exists. Most of his suggestions seem relevant to short-term factors applicable to a closed economy. He refers to house rents, but these cannot be held to be sticky in nominal terms in the long run. Furthermore, he mentions that changes in the terms of trade can cause the price of imported wage goods to rise thus driving the real wage down, but this cannot apply at the purely theoretical level to the world at large.[181] Of the reasons

Keynes gives,[182] only one seems capable of persisting in the long run and therefore able to cause any revision of the notion of the long-run state of involuntary unemployment. Keynes suggests that imperfect competition could emerge in slumps and thus, if demand remains low, concentration remains high and wages low.

Keynes considers that the finding of procyclical behaviour does not weaken his case:

[I]t would be possible to simplify considerably the more complicated version of my fundamental explanation which I have expounded in my 'General Theory'. [Footnote: Particularly in chapter 2, which is the portion of my book which most needs to be revised.] My practical conclusions would have, in that case, a fortiori force.[183]

Richard Kahn's[184] views are thus, to a degree, validated. He felt that 'Keynes made unnecessarily heavy weather' of the concept. Curiously, Kahn feels that Pigou's (and Robertson's) occasional use of the term 'involuntary unemployment' of itself indicates substantial agreement with Keynes. Pigou (as cited by Kahn) held that employment was involuntary if the worker could not gain employment except under 'conditions less favourable than those which he habitually maintained'.[185] It is far from clear that Pigou would have agreed with Keynes's 1936 definition which deals with the possibility that the real wage was too high but could not fall. Pigou had his own model, his own views about the forces governing the real wage and his own reason for favouring fiscal policy. One cannot say, therefore, that Keynes's subsequent simplification represents any significant retreat or an acknowledgement of the superiority, on this point, of the views of other Cambridge economists.

Suppose that we follow Keynes and accept that his 1936 definition was unduly restrictive. Following the definition of 1939 and accepting the empirical findings that real wages move procyclically has an interesting implication. If the real-wage locus is upward sloping, it could cut the supply-of-labour curve at more than one point. Indeed, it is possible that the two curves are coincident giving an infinite number of points where the real wage equals the marginal disutility of labour. At such points the labour market would clear in some sense, as could all other markets. There would be no pressure at all for the money wage to fall and the system would remain in a state of long-run equilibrium given the real wage.

Of still greater theoretical interest is that, because no excess supplies appear in any market, the sum of effective and notional excess demands is zero. Full employment, the Pareto optimal point, would not be the only place where the sum of notional excess demands was zero. Clower and Leijonhufvud do not consider this possibility, but in view of Keynes's modifications of 1939, Walras' Law needs further qualification.[186]

In suboptimal equilibrium states, all parties would be better off were demand to grow but no one has any incentive to strive to reduce their relative price. Were the unemployed to awaken one morning with pockets full of money, additional consumption-spending would drive employment, the real wage and real profits upwards. It remains true that the role of money is central.[187]

The 1939 account also captures the spirit of the prisoner's dilemma.[188] There is no hope for the participants to move the system towards full employment. Even the slender hope offered by money-wage cuts has no appeal if a decline in money wages immediately reduces the real wage below a value corresponding to the real marginal disutility of labour. No individual worker can assume that others will follow suit so that recovery, and with it higher real wages sufficient to compensate for the temporary cut of wages below the marginal disutility of labour, will emerge.

Peculiar possibilities emerge from the viewpoint of policy-making. If the real-wage locus is upward sloping and cuts the labour-supply curve more than once, workers could resist an expansion of aggregate demand and reflation. Perhaps indirect tax cuts would be the best option. These problems can, however, be put aside if the real-wage locus is not mapped during the system's process of adjustment upwards. Government policy could drive the system towards full employment without treading into areas below the supply curve. Equilibrium loci cannot be used naïvely. In the analysis of disequilibrium processes, there is no need for movement to be along such curves.

Whatever is assumed about the behaviour of the real wage and about why money wages are sticky downwards, there remains the question of the role played by money in any modern analysis of a state of involuntary unemployment. Should the distinction between a money-using system and a barter system be regarded as essential nowadays?

If the only problem were a substantial decline in investment, then the process would reverse if, by chance, confidence returned. Investors would then borrow from the banks (or from the bears) at a mutually acceptable interest rate. Those employed in the investment sector purchase consumption goods and liquidity constraints relax in sequence. In a real-world economy, bankruptcies and the dislocation of supply resulting in the loss of customer goodwill impede symmetrical reversal. While barter economies can simply revert to full employment if prices are flexible enough to converge to the Walrasian vector, reversibility is a genuine problem when the financial structure of a monetary economy has been fractured. Reflation need not restore what deflation destroyed. Money is of crucial, independent importance. If it were not, why do the collapse of credit pyramids and the offsetting presence of buffer holdings of money influence the quantity outcomes associated with any given price vector? The absence of a universally trusted and credible auctioneer, the illiquidity of endowments and outputs, and the dependence of the system on money together create the conditions under which involuntary unemployment can exist. Mistakes made in a barter world are reversible and unemployment is voluntary in a significant sense. Dudley Dillard observes that in classical and neoclassical economics 'money occupies virtually no place...[M]oney is there but it doesn't do anything'. It is as if barter prevailed. Dillard condemns 'barter illusion'.[189]

In a barter world relative prices are crucial, but things can be different in a money-using system according to a reductionist outlook. In the wake of any demand disturbance – and a decline in aggregate investment can be regarded both as a sectoral and a structural perturbation – suppose that involuntary unemployment emerges. While worsening prospects in one part of an economy can be consistent with the *relative* desirability of being elsewhere, it is doubtful that relative price signals can be deemed to encourage appropriate resource flows. Only effective excess demands in one sector attract resources to it. If, however, prospects across the board are poor and merely less unattractive in some sectors, then the choice is not between the poor and the very poor. A third possibility is to opt out and remain liquid. There is no reason why adverse, effective, structural shocks in one sector (say, a decline in export commodity prices) need be offset by effective signals in other markets, especially if the initial shock is large enough to generate multiplier effects sufficient to drown out effective excess demands (if any) being received elsewhere. Being pushed out of an industry by ruinous losses is not symmetrical with, or analytically equivalent to, being enticed elsewhere by effective excess profits. (In an international context, the J curve may need to dip even lower to overcome the effects of the multiplier and thereby to spur excess demand sufficient to encourage the restructuring of the export sector.) Reductionist and fundamentalist insights woven together here are not solely of interest to historians of thought.

Some[190] question the practical and operational relevance of the notion of involuntary unemployment because it is difficult to demonstrate empirically whether it is prevalent in any particular case. But why should doubt preclude governmental action? Day-to-day decisions are made with degrees of rational belief and no one insists on infallibility. If the self-confident, clinical and technocratic attitude to fine-tuning is disappearing, the new agnosticism is finding expression in

127

such proposals as stabilizing nominal income. If some of the unemployment is involuntary, such a rule is liable to mop up at least some of it. If policy-makers are uncertain, it seems reasonable for them to behave as others do in such circumstances, to follow sensible rules of thumb. Fundamentalists need not be nihilists, and reductionists lay no claims to be able to fine-tune. The approaches are compatible, intellectually defensible and are consistent with modern policy proposals.

Notes

1 Arthur C. Pigou, 'Mr J.M. Keynes' general theory of employment, interest and money', *Economica*, vol. 3, February 1936, pp. 115–32, at pp. 131–2. Alvin Hansen has also stressed that investment behaviour was of importance in pre-Keynesian theories of business fluctuations. See his *Monetary Theory and Fiscal Policy*, New York, McGraw-Hill, 1949, pp. 145, 149 and *Business Cycles and National Income*, London, Allen and Unwin, 1964, expanded edn, ch. 16.

2 Pigou, 'Mr J.M. Keynes' general theory...',p. 132.

3 J.M. Keynes, *A Treatise on Money*, London, Macmillan, 1930, vol. 2 (*The Collected Writings of John Maynard Keynes*, London, Macmillan, 1971, vol. vi, p. 89).

4 See Hansen, *Business Cycles and National Income*, ch. 15 and p. 303.

5 See Jacques H. Drèze (ed.), *Allocation Under Uncertainty: equilibrium and optimality*, London, Macmillan, 1974. Compare John D. Hey, *Uncertainty in Microeconomics*, Oxford, Martin Robertson, 1979, who suggests an alternative line of enquiry worthy of pursuit (esp. pp. 41, 233–4).

6 Henry Hazlitt (ed.), *The Critics of Keynesian Economics*, New York, Arlington House, 1977, pp. 67–95.

7 Keynes, *Collected Writings*, vol. xxix, pp. 217–18.

8 See Samuelson's well-known view in Seymour E. Harris (ed.), *The New Economics: Keynes' influence on theory and public policy*, London, Dennis Dobson, 1948, at p. 150 and Albert Hart's comments at pp. 419–22. Compare Hicks's opinion in his review that 'the use of the method of expectations is perhaps the most revolutionary thing about this book'. See 'Mr Keynes' theory of employment', *Economic Journal*, vol. 46, June 1936, pp. 238–53, at p. 240. Arthur W. Marget's account of the existence of expectations in orthodox analyses is convincing. See *The Theory of Prices: an examination of the central problems of monetary theory*, New York, Prentice-Hall, 1942, vol. 2, pp. 177 *et seq.*, especially pp. 179–80, n. 72.

9 This view differs slightly from that of Terence W. Hutchison, *On Revolutions and Progress in Economic Knowledge*, Cambridge, Cambridge University Press, 1978, ch. 7.

10 James Sutherland, *Defoe*, London, Methuen, 1950, 2nd edn, p. 33.

11 John Stuart Mill, *Principles of Political Economy: with their applications to social philosophy*, edited by Sir William Askley (1909), Fairfield, New Jersey, Augustus M. Kelley, 1976, pp. 641, 644, 651 *et seq.*, 709, 734. See Hansen, *Business Cycles*, pp. 213 *et seq.*

12 Mill, *Principles*, pp. 116, *et seq.* See also Gottfried Haberler, *Prosperity and Depression: a theoretical analysis of cyclical movements*, London, Allen and Unwin, 1964, 5th edn, pp. 60–1.

13 One must partly agree with Patinkin, 'Keynes' aggregate supply function: a plea for common sense', *History of Political Economy*, vol. 10, no. 4, Winter 1978, pp. 577–96, at p. 582, fn. 12. I do not wish to be taken, however, as equating classical economics with bad economics because much in Minsky is, of course, good economics. Neither am I denying that Keynes's approval of the *IS-LM* construction makes it impossible for Keynes, unlike the American Keynesians, to have held financial instability to be of considerable importance. I differ from the fundamentalist, Minsky, in that the classicists did have good theories of regular oscillations, but not of why the trend was persistently below full employment.

14 'The coordination of economic activities: a Keynesian perspective', *American Economic Review*, vol. 65, no. 2, May 1975, pp. 182–8.

15 Compare Shackle's approach which is to avoid deterministic accounts of the formation of expectations.

16 Joan Robinson, *Collected Economic Papers*, vol. 1, Oxford, Basil Blackwell, 1951, p. 134. Samuelson, in *The New Economics*, p. 151, adopts the same stance. Contrast Axel Leijonhufvud in *On Keynesian Economics and the Economics of Keynes: a study in monetary theory*, New York, Oxford University Press, 1968, p. 53, n. 6.

17 Curiously, Marget's work of impressive scholarship has attracted little attention. Perhaps the reason is that most economists believe that no idea is ever completely new – Marget even cites Aristotle. Consequently, to hold that Keynes had been anticipated by many others in their isolated *obiter dicta* or in fragments of qualifying arguments, in no way lessens the accolade Keynes deserves.

18 For example, Hansen refers to J.M. Clark's doubts about the real-world effectiveness of the price mechanism in A.H. Hansen, *A Guide to Keynes*, New York, McGraw-Hill, 1953, pp. 7–11.

19 Jacob Viner, 'Comment on my 1936 review of Keynes' *General Theory*', in Robert Lekachman (ed.), *Keynes' General Theory: reports of three decades*, New York, St Martin's Press, 1964, pp. 253–66, at p. 257.

20 This view is not entirely new. Note Haberler's agreement in 'Sixteen years later', in Lekachman (ed.), *Keynes' General Theory*, esp. 290–1. Similar views are expressed in his 'The general theory after ten years' in the preceding chapter of Lekachman.

21 Axel Leijonhufvud, *Keynes and the Classics: two lectures on Keynes' contribution to economic theory*, Institute of Economic Affairs, Occasional Paper, 30, 1969, pp. 9–10. A similar view is expressed by J. Ronnie Davis, *The New Economics and the Old Economists*, Ames,

Iowa State University Press, 1971, pp. 7, 83–4. Leijonhufvud, however, disagrees with aspects of Davis' case. See Leijonhufvud, 'Schools, "revolutions"...', in *Information and Coordination: essays in macroeconomic theory*, New York, Oxford University Press, 1981, p. 314, n. 33. Part of his complaint, no doubt, would be that Keynes was not anticipated so far as the communication-failure angle was concerned, especially with regard to the stickiness of interest rates.

22 Davis, *The New Economics*, pp. 94–9, 115.

23 ibid., pp. 21, 54, 81.

24 This perhaps explains what some would regard as an impertinent observation by Paul Wonnacott, *Macroeconomics*, Homewood, Ill. Richard D. Irwin, 1978, rev. edn, p. 288, fn. 13, that the 'British head start with the Depression may partially explain why the *General Theory* was written by an Englishman'.

25 To interpret an author in the light of how you are currently pondering the same questions seems to be ordinary human nature. Criticisms of Hicks's *IS-LM* framework stem in part from how he imposed his own simultaneous-equation technique on *The General Theory* in order to formalize aspects of it. Cf. Warren Young, *Interpreting Mr Keynes: the IS-LM enigma*, Cambridge, Polity Press, 1987.

26 Herbert Stein, *The Fiscal Revolution in America*, Chicago, University of Chicago Press, 1969, p. 163 and p. 9.

27 The interested reader could consult Don Patinkin, 'The Chicago tradition, the quantity theory and Friedman', *Journal of Money, Credit and Banking*, vol. 1, no. 1, February 1969, pp. 46–70; Elizabeth S. Johnson and Harry G. Johnson, *The Shadow of Keynes*, Oxford, Basil Blackwell, 1978, p. 198.

28 See Friedman, in Robert J. Gordon (ed.), *Milton Friedman's Monetary Framework: a debate with his critics*, Chicago, Chicago University Press, 1974, pp. 164–5. One has in mind Robbins and Hayek. It is curious that Austrians can simultaneously stress uncertainty and yet have faith in the long-run powers of thrift and productivity.

29 Hutchison's arguments are particularly forceful. See Terence Wilmot Hutchison, *On Revolutions and Progress in Economic Knowledge*, Cambridge, Cambridge University Press, 1978, ch. 6.

30 George Garvy, 'Keynes and the economic activists of the pre-Hitler Germany', *Journal of Political Economy*, vol. 83, no. 2, April 1975, pp. 391–405 at p. 391.

31 Interestingly, Colin Clark recalls a conversation with Hawtrey that he was on leave when the notorious Treasury paper was written. He disassociated himself from it with disdain and he was irritated by the lack of recognition of his theory of the importance of short-term interest rates. Hawtrey is often (mistakenly, it appears) blamed for being the mastermind behind the Treasury view.

32 This assessment of the level of sophistication of economic analysis prevailing at that time in less academic circles stems from conversations with Colin Clark. See also Keynes himself, *Collected Writings*, vol. xxix, p. 68.

33 The works of Hahn and Negishi will be discussed in the final section on involuntary unemployment. Murray Milgate pejoratively labels conjectural models as 'imperfectionist' believing that they rely on 'frictions' which inhibit a tendency to full employment and 'merely' render very slow the self-correcting forces in an economy which ultimately eliminate disequilibrium. Whatever Hahn's intention may be, the view offered here is that conventional equilibria can, in logic at least, persist even in the long run. See Frank Hahn, 'John Maynard Keynes: a Centenary estimate', *The History of Economic Thought Society of Australia Newsletter*, no. 5, Autumn 1985, pp. 1–18, at p. 11. Hahn's position is perhaps closer to that of Leijonhufvud than to that taken in this thesis. A conjectural equilibrium is sometimes seen by Hahn as a short-run phenomenon. See Frank Hahn, 'Wages and employment', *Oxford Economic Papers*, vol. 36 (n.s.), supp., November 1984, pp. 47–58, at p. 54.

34 That stable money wages gives money a relatively stable real purchasing power, and makes it useful as a medium of exchange, is stressed in Paul Davidson's *Money and the Real World*, London, Macmillan, 1978, 2nd edn, pp. 237–8. Curiously, Leijonhufvud (*On Keynesian Economics*, p. 108, n. 9) fails to recognize that this is one aspect of the infamous chapter 17 which Hansen described as 'highly significant' and 'obviously something which deserves serious consideration' (Hansen, *A Guide to Keynes*, p. 164). It would be possible to argue that Hansen became a Keynesian only when he realized this. He had always accepted the importance of investment in cyclical fluctuations and was sympathetic to the substance of the notion presented in the *Treatise* that the relationship between savings and investment was crucial (A. H. Hansen, Francis M. Boddy and John K. Langum, 'Recent trends in business cycle literature', *Review of Economic Statistics*, vol. 18, no. 2, May 1936, pp. 53–61; A.H. Hansen and Herbert Tout, 'Annual survey of business cycle theory: investment and saving in business-cycle literature', *Econometrica*, vol. 1, 1933, pp. 119–47. Absent from Hansen's 'Mr Keynes on underemployment equilibrium', *Journal of Political Economy*, vol. 44, October 1936, pp. 667–86 at pp. 677–8 was his recognition of the importance of wage inflexibility for a money-using system.

35 Leijonhufvud, *On Keynesian Economics*, p. 101, esp. n. 29.

36 See John Stuart Mill, *Principles of Political Economy: with their applications to social philosophy*, edited by Sir William Askley, Fairfield, New Jersey, Augustus M. Kelley, 1976; Don Patinkin, *Money, Interest, and Prices: an integration of monetary and value theory*, New York, Harper and Row, 1965, 2nd edn, pp. 646–7; and 'Keynes' misquotation of Mill: comment', *Economic Journal*, vol. 88, June 1978, pp. 341–2. Compare Henry Hazlitt, *The Failure of the New Economics*, Princeton, Van Nostrand, 1959, pp. 34–5.

37 Keynes, *The General Theory*, p. 18. A simple explanation of Keynes's misquoting Mill might be that, because he was in a hurry, he copied the passage from Hobson's book which was nearer at hand.

38 Robert A. Mundell, *Man and Economics*, New York, McGraw-Hill, 1968, p. 110.
39 J. Ronnie Davis and Francis J. Casey Jr., 'Keynes' misquotation of Mill', *Economic Journal*, vol. 87, June 1977, pp. 329–30, at p. 329. Patinkin, 'Keynes' misquotation of Mill: comment', criticizes Davis and Casey, but his observations do not attack the orthodox view that Keynes misread Mill. Keynes, incidentally, owned two copies of *Principles*. See Pascal Bridel, 'On Keynes' quotations from Mill: a note', *Economic Journal*, vol. 89, September 1979, pp. 660–2.
40 Keynes, *The General Theory*, p. 19, n. 2 (italics added).
41 Davis and Casey, 'Keynes's misquotation of Mill', p. 300; Arthur C. Pigou, 'Mr J.M. Keynes' general theory of employment, interest and money', *Economica*, vol. 3, May 1936, pp. 115–32, at pp. 116–17.
42 J.A. Hobson and A.F. Mummery, *The Physiology of Industry: being an exposure of certain fallacies in existing theories of economics*, New York, Kelley and Millman, 1956, p. 102, n. 1.
43 Patinkin, 'Keynes's misquotation of Mill: comment'; Hansen, *A Guide to Keynes*, New York, McGraw-Hill, 1953, p. 13.
44 J. Ronnie Davis, 'Keynes's misquotation of Mill: further comment', *Economic Journal*, vol. 89, September 1979, pp. 658–9.
45 Consequently, Patinkin, *Money, Interest, and Prices*, p. 648, is not entirely convincing. Mill (and Ricardo) must have had faith in Say's Law in the long-run sense – in the ordinary macroeconomic sense as distinct from the secular-historical sense – because their short-run analysis of unemployment involved the explanations of the exceptions to the general rule of full employment.
46 Consequently, Benjamin M. Anderson's objection in Henry Hazlitt, *The Critics of Keynesian Economics*, New Rochelle, NY, Arlington House, 1977, p. 188 can be rejected.
47 Mill, *Principles*, p. 558.
48 ibid., p. 561.
49 Barbara S. Henneberry and James G. Witte, 'The unemployment–inflation dilemma in macroeconomics: some contradictory aspects of contemporary theory and policy', *Scottish Journal of Political Economy*, vol. 23, no. 1, February 1976, pp. 17–25, at p. 26, n. 9.
50 Compare A.H. Hansen, 'Keynes on economic policy', in Seymour E. Harris (ed.), *The New Economics*, London, Dennis Dobson, 1948, pp. 197–207, at p. 202.
51 Mill, *Essays on Some Unsettled Questions of Political Economy*, cited by Hazlitt, *The Critics of Keynesian Economics*, p. 41.
52 ibid., p. 42.
53 Patinkin, *Money, Interest and Prices*, p. 647.
54 A lengthy treatment here of the materials found in Keynes, *Collected Writings*, vol. xxix has been rendered unnecessary by Roy J. Rotheim's 'Keynes' monetary theory of value (1933)', *Journal of Post Keynesian Economics*, vol. 3, no. 4, Summer 1981, pp. 568–85.
55 Keynes, *Collected Writings*, vol. xiii, p. 408.

56 Keynes, *Collected Writings*, vol. xxix, p. 67. See also p. 97 and vol. xiii, pp. 353, 408–12.

57 Keynes, *Collected Writings*, vol. xxix, p. 67.

58 ibid., p. 86.

59 ibid., p. 78 (emphasis added).

60 ibid., p. 79 (Keynes's emphasis).

61 Keynes, *The General Theory*, p. 369.

62 One hopes that the passage was accurately quoted by Hobson and Mummery. Otherwise, there might emerge a debate as to whether Keynes had ever read Ricardo.

63 Although he saw that money merely served that role, this does not necessarily render his theory as objectionable as those of his followers in the Ricardian tradition, since Ricardo's main concern was with the long-run proportions of output rather than short-run absolutes. See *The General Theory*, pp. 4, n. 1; 5, n. 1; 339–40, for some kinder words about Ricardo.

64 Keynes, *Collected Writings*, vol. xxvii, p. 270.

65 ibid., p. 266.

66 ibid.

67 See I.F. Pearce, 'The pathology of Keynes' general theory', (unpublished), Seventh Conference of Economists, Sydney, Macquarie University, 1978, Appendix B for a remarkable misreading of Keynes on the question of whether both money and material inputs would be required.

68 Joan Robinson, 'What has become of the Keynesian revolution?', in Milo Keynes (ed.), *Essays on John Maynard Keynes*, Cambridge, Cambridge University Press, 1975, p. 124.
   Similar views are shared by Eprime Eshag, who acknowledges his indebtedness to Robinson in his *From Marshall to Keynes: an essay on the monetary theory of the Cambridge school*, Oxford, Basil Blackwell, 1963, pp. xiv, 59, 87, 108.

69 Hutchison, *On Revolutions and Progress in Economic Knowledge*, p. 144. J.A. Kregel, 'Effective demand: origins and development of the notion', in J.A. Kregel (ed.), *Distribution, Effective Demand and International Economic Relations*, New York, St Martin's Press, 1983, pp. 50–68, at p. 53, identifies the passage from Smith as being from *The Wealth of Nations*, New York, Modern Library, 1776, E. Cannan (ed.), p. 268.

70 J.M. Keynes, 'The general theory of employment', in Robert W. Clower (ed.), *Monetary Theory: selected readings*, Harmondsworth, Penguin, 1969, p. 218.

71 Keynes, *The General Theory*, p. 343, n. 3.

72 Keynes, *Collected Writings*, vol. xiii, p. 254.

73 See W. Stanley Jevons, *Political Economy (Science Primer)*, London, Macmillan, 1898, p. 22; Jacques Rueff, 'The fallacies of Lord Keynes' general theory', *Quarterly Journal of Economics*, vol. 61, May 1947, pp. 343–67, at pp. 348–9. Tobin notes the existence of what he calls 'Rueff's law' that the 'demand for money creates its own supply'. See

Tobin, 'The fallacies of Lord Keynes' general theory: comment', *Quarterly Journal of Economics*, vol. 62, November 1948, pp. 763–70, at p. 765.

74 Keynes, *The General Theory*, pp. 130, 230; and *Collected Writings*, vol. xxix, pp. 85–6. That the elasticity of supply for money is virtually zero has been stressed in modern times by Paul Davidson.

75 Leijonhufvud, *On Keynesian Economics*, pp. 100–1.

76 Curiously, Davis and Casey ('Keynes's misquotation of Mill', p. 329) suggest that Leijonhufvud shows that Keynes did not bother to read Mill, but compare Leijonhufvud, *On Keynesian Economics*, p. 101, n. 29.

77 Leijonhufvud, *On Keynesian Economics*, pp. 87–9, 280.

78 Arthur C. Pigou, *Industrial Fluctuations*, London, Macmillan, 1927, pp. 114–15, but compare pp. 57–9. See also Pigou's review in *Economica* ('Mr J.M. Keynes' general theory...', p. 123) where the logic of the multiplier, with some qualifications, is accepted, at least so far as the upward motion to full employment after a fiscal injection is concerned. Whether he also saw the multiplier as a cumulative, deviation-amplifying mechanism is not clear. A section of this chapter is devoted to the differences between Pigou and Keynes.

79 Compare Leijonhufvud, *On Keynesian Economics*, p. 100.

80 Jacob Cohen has observed, 'What is surprising is how closely the "real" Keynes resembles the Keynes of the "exegetical" literature – despite the author's attempts to show otherwise.' 'Book reviews', *Journal of Economic Literature*, vol. 7, no. 3, September 1969, pp. 841–3, at p. 841.

81 Leijonhufvud, *On Keynesian Economics*, p. 59.

82 Pigou ('Mr J.M. Keynes' general theory...', p. 128) even attributed his more extreme view to Keynes: '[Keynes] allows that in the long period, if money wages are permitted to move freely, the various elements in the economic system tend so to adjust themselves that full employment...is maintained.'

83 Keynes, *The General Theory*, p. 277 – taken only slightly out of context. Keynes chose as his target Pigou's *The Theory of Unemployment*, London, Frank Cass, 1933.

84 Hutchison, *On Revolutions and Progress in Economic Knowledge*, pp. 187–90.

85 Arthur C. Pigou, *Lapses from Full Employment*, London, Macmillan, 1945, pp. 67–73. See also *Industrial Fluctuations*, London, Macmillan, 1927, pp. 110, 291, 303, 309–11 for a similar stance. Compare *The Theory of Unemployment*, pp. 248–51 for the view that fiscal policy can only be relied upon as a temporary measure while increases in wage rates are lagged behind the increase in demand. Although Keynes examines Pigou's *Theory of Unemployment*, he apparently did not heed Robertson's advice (*Collected Writings*, vol. xiii, p. 524) to consult Pigou's *Industrial Fluctuations*. Consider the 'astonishing quotation' from Pigou's *Theory of Unemployment*, pp. 170–4, cited by Kahn, *The Making of Keynes' General Theory*, Cambridge, Cambridge University Press, 1983, p. 19. Also note Pigou's defence of the policy-activist,

Mosley, in Kahn (ibid., p. 89). Contrast Kahn (ibid., pp. 96–7) where he tacitly disputes Hutchison's defence of Pigou but without offering evidence to make clear the sense in which Pigou sometimes opposed public works. Neither does Kahn (p. 126) substantiate the claim that Pigou supported money-wage cuts. Unfortunately, Kahn does not refer to Hutchison's arguments directly.

86 Keynes was clearly wrong to have alleged that Pigou overlooked investment and employment fluctuations on account of Pigou's faith in the rapid adjustment of interest rates that is supposedly integral to the loanable funds theory (Keynes, *The General Theory*, pp. 274–5). It is not surprising that Pigou was flabbergasted by Keynes's charge ('Mr J.M. Keynes' general theory...', pp. 117–18).

87 See also Haberler, *Prosperity and Depression*, Appendix, pp. 486–7, for a view that lower money wages are likely to increase the MEI, and that this is a feasible policy option. Compare Pigou, *The Theory of Unemployment*, p. 73.

88 Keynes, *The General Theory*, p. 274. Compare Pigou, 'Mr J.M. Keynes' general theory...', pp. 118–19; and *The Theory of Unemployment*, pp. 28, 33. That Keynes, and others, had difficulty identifying Pigou's supply-of-labour function is clear from *Collected Writings*, vol. xiv, pp. 35–59.

89 For senses in which Keynes saw classical theory as logically inconsistent see *Collected Writings*, vol. xiv, pp. 56–8, 79–80, 105–8 and vol. xiii, pp. 312, 316. Pigou is alleged to have had particular difficulties in grasping the nature of the multiplier despite his advocacy of fiscal policy (*The General Theory*, p. 277). Compare Pigou, *The Theory of Unemployment*, p. 75.

90 Pigou, *Industrial Fluctuations*, p. 217.

91 Of Pigou's understanding of involuntary unemployment, *Industrial Fluctuations*, p. 332 gives us an inkling. See also Kahn, *The Making of Keynes' General Theory*, Cambridge, Cambridge University Press, 1983, pp. 191–4.

92 Pigou, *The Theory of Unemployment*, pp. 28, 33.

93 Pigou, 'Mr J.M. Keynes' general theory...', p. 119.

94 Pigou, *The Theory of Unemployment*, pp. 294–5; and *Employment and Equilibrium*, London, Macmillan, 1949, pp. 92–3.

95 Pigou did not seem to realize that, in terms of Keynes's theory, union pressures which had raised real wages only did so by reducing employment. *Money*-wage reductions need not increase employment, and therefore reduce real wages, to their initial, full-employment values.

96 Cited by Boris Pesek and Thomas Saving, *Money, Wealth and Economic Theory*, New York, Macmillan, 1967, pp. 15, 28.

97 Pigou, 'Mr J.M. Keynes' general theory...', p. 129 (Pigou's emphasis). Pigou's reasoning is far from clear. He elaborated subsequently and, for Keynes's evaluation of it – 'the most frightful rubbish' – see *Collected Writings*, vol. xiv, pp. 234–62, esp. pp. 238, 250. Note that Robertson (ibid., p. 252) claims that Keynes did not grasp Pigou. So did Pigou (ibid., pp. 256–7). Nevertheless, Pigou's views are unclear. Why did he

argue that, *ceteris paribus*, lower money wages would be associated with higher employment if the connection was not intended as causal? Keynes's astonishment with Pigou's reasoning seems thoroughly justifiable. Pigou's reasoning, by the way, resembles that of Martin Weitzman, and A.P. Thirlwall's defence of Weitzman from Davidson's attacks is open to question, 'Reviews', *Economic Journal*, vol. 98, December 1988, pp. 1256–8, at p. 1258.

98 Pigou, *Employment and Equilibrium*, p. 87.

99 Keynes, as early as 1933, saw the need for Pigou to assume that money-wage cuts reduce interest rates. This is another area where Keynes thought that Pigou did not understand the logic of his own position. See *Collected Writings*, vol. xiii, p. 317; vol. xiv, pp. 266–7.

100 ibid., pp. 122, 145–6, 169–70.

101 ibid., p. 94. The passage reads as though it were a statement of his beliefs about real-world events rather than a mere statement of logical existence of a vector consistent with full employment.

102 Pigou, *Lapses from Full Employment*, p. 39 (emphasis added).

103 Pigou, *The Theory of Unemployment*, pp. 234–5.

104 Lawrence Klein, *The Keynesian Revolution*, New York, Macmillan, 1947, p. 85.

105 Pigou, *The Theory of Unemployment*, p. 213.

106 This is a personal view of Pigou's *Keynes's 'General Theory': a retrospective view*, London, Macmillan, 1950. Naturally opinions will differ about the tone and balance of the book as a whole. Not everyone will be left with the impression that Pigou praised in Keynes only what was already in, or could be grafted onto, Pigou's own works. In view of Pigou's 'concessions' about money illusion and the possible need for negative interest rates – principal 'Keynesian' tenets – it is not surprising that Keynesians see Pigou as one who took a decade to see the light. To put the point on its head, perhaps 'Keynesians' are really followers of Pigou.

107 Witness a recent revival of interest in Pigou in David A. Collard, 'Pigou on expectations and the cycle', *Economic Journal*, vol. 93, June 1983, pp. 411–14.

108 Edward Shapiro, *Macroeconomic Analysis*, New York, Harcourt Brace and World, 1966, p. 220, n. 7, attributes the term to Irving Fisher.

109 Leijonhufvud, *On Keynesian Economics*, pp. 94–5.

110 Useful references include Gloria Shatto, 'Was Keynes a "Keynesian"?', *Journal of Economics and Business*, vol. 27, no. 1, Fall 1974, pp. 86–8; John T. Addison and John Burton, 'Keynes's analysis of wages and unemployment revisited', *Manchester School of Economic and Social Studies*, vol. 50, March 1982, pp. 1–23. The former examines textbook interpretations and the latter the role of Leontief in propagating the money-illusion interpretation. See also Mark Blaug, *Economic Theory in Retrospect*, Cambridge, Cambridge University Press, 3rd edn, 1978, pp. 675, 686; Mark Casson, *Unemployment: a disequilibrium approach*, Oxford, Martin Robertson, 1981, p. 12; William H. Hutt, *The Keynesian*

Episode: a reassessment, Indianapolis, Liberty Press, 1979, p. 267; Milton Friedman in Robert J. Gordon (ed.), *Milton Friedman's Monetary Framework: a debate with his critics*, Chicago, University of Chicago Press, 1974, p. 18; Brian J. Loasby, *Choice, Complexity and Ignorance: an enquiry into economic theory and the practice of decision-making*, Cambridge, Cambridge University Press, 1976, p. 14 and Norman P. Barry, *Hayek's Social and Economic Philosophy*, London, Macmillan, 1979, p. 171. Even G.L.S. Shackle, *Keynesian Kaleidics*, Edinburgh, Edinburgh University Press, 1974, pp. 11, 13 considers it a part of chapter 2 of *The General Theory*.

111 Keynes, *The General Theory*, pp. 14–15 (emphasis added).

112 Compare James A. Trevithick, 'Keynes, inflation and money illusion', *Economic Journal*, vol. 85, March 1975, pp. 101–13, who refers to Keynes's view that retaliatory increases in money wages under inflationary conditions were unlikely at least if the commodity price-level rose by only 5 or 10 per cent. Unfortunately Trevithick fails to cite Keynes. Furthermore, must the cause be money illusion? Possibly the costs of strike action in those days was too high relative to the prospective gain. James Tobin, 'Money wage rates and employment', in Seymour E. Harris (ed.), *The New Economics: Keynes' influence on theory and public policy*, London, Dennis Dobson, 1948, p. 3, agrees that workers act 'with eyes open', but he gives no quotations from Keynes to substantiate that view.

113 For example, see Paul Wells, 'Modigliani on flexible wages and prices', *Journal of Post Keynesian Economics*, vol. 2, no. 1, Fall 1979, pp. 82–93, at pp. 85–6.

114 Note that Ingrid Rima, 'Whatever happened to the concept of involuntary unemployment?', *International Journal of Social Economics*, vol. ii, no. 3/4, 1984, pp. 62–71, at p. 66, suggests that Knightian uncertainty would be regarded by Keynes as an adequate reason to question probabilistic versions of job search that occur in logical time.

115 William A. Darity Jr and Bobbie L. Horn, 'Involuntary unemployment reconsidered', *Southern Economic Journal*, vol. 49, no. 3, January 1983, pp. 717–33, at p. 722.

116 The equality of the money wage and the marginal revenue product under conditions of flow supply equilibrium in the goods sector implies a real wage paid by all employers equal to the marginal product of workers in the wage-goods sector. Compare Paul Davidson, 'A Keynesian view of Patinkin's theory of employment', *Economic Journal*, vol. 77, September 1967, pp. 559–78, at p. 567, n. 1.

117 Allan H. Meltzer, 'Keynes's *General Theory*: a different perspective?', *Journal of Economic Literature*, vol. 19, March 1981, pp. 34–64, at p. 50, validly cites *The General Theory*, pp. 266–7, which indicate that workers are unable to select money wages likely to trigger the Keynes effect on interest rates, but Keynes never said anything about whether workers are themselves uncertain about the 'correct' money wage. It is the policy-maker who does not know of the reliability of money-wage cuts to simulate easy monetary policy. Compare *The General Theory*,

p. 265, where employers are indeed uncertain about the *future path* of money wages and, as a consequence, no clear effect on the MEI schedule results.

118 For example, James A. Trevithick, 'Money wage inflexibility and the Keynesian labour supply function', *Economic Journal*, vol. 86, June 1976, pp. 327–32.

119 Keynes, *The General Theory*, p. 14.

120 Leijonhufvud, *On Keynesian Economics*, p. 96.

121 Don Patinkin (*Anticipations of the General Theory? And other essays on Keynes*, Oxford, Basil Blackwell, 1982, pp. 137–8) agrees.

122 Keynes, *The General Theory*, p. 13. Keynes (ibid., pp. 8, 10, 13) uses similar words repeatedly. Victoria Chick, *Macroeconomics after Keynes: a reconsideration of the General Theory*, Deddington, Oxford, Philip Allan, 1983, ch. 7 and John Fender, *Understanding Keynes: an analysis of 'The General Theory'*, Brighton, Wheatsheaf Books, 1981, pp. 10–11, consider that Keynes's fundamental objection deserves greater attention.

123 Leijonhufvud, *On Keynesian Economics*, p. 90.

124 ibid., p. 95, n. 23.

125 Keynes, *The General Theory*, p. 196 (emphasis added).

126 See *The General Theory*, p. 9 where Keynes admits that the actions of workers in resisting money-wage cuts more vehemently than inflation-induced decreases in the real wage is somewhat illogical. Compare Armen A. Alchian's view of how Keynes's definition of involuntary unemployment need not rely on money illusion. If wages were cut everywhere else, and *if* employees knew it, they would not choose unemployment – but they would if they believed wages were cut just in their current job.

Reuven Brenner also finds it hard to understand how money illusion was essential to any of Keynes's arguments. See 'Unemployment, justice, and Keynes's "General Theory"', *Journal of Political Economy*, vol. 87, no. 4, August 1979, pp. 837–50, at p. 839, n. 5.

127 See Thomas Tuschscherer, 'Meltzer on Keynes's labor market theory: a review of the *General Theory*'s second chapter'; Allan H. Meltzer, 'Keynes's labour market: a reply'; and Ingrid H. Rima, 'Involuntary unemployment and the respecified labour supply curve'; all in *Journal of Post Keynesian Economics*, vol. 6, no. 4, Summer 1984, pp. 523–31, 532–9 and 540–50 respectively.

Rima considers that Keynes (*The General Theory*, pp. 8–9) is 'remarkably luminous' (Rima, op. cit., p. 542) but it is far from clear (to me) whether Keynes was saying what he himself thought or what he believed a consistent classicist, confronted with the *fact* that workers do not always withdraw their labour when inflation reduces their real wage, *ought* to have said. That Keynes always fully understood Pigou also ought not to be assumed. Did Keynes really mean that *he* believed that the supply curve (as a function of real wages) would *shift* or just that the quantity supplied would increase? Perhaps Rima is ingeniously rationalizing Keynes's slip of the pen (assuming that she has construed the passage from Keynes correctly). Given a money wage, Rima seems to argue in favour of a supply curve which, when plotted against real wages, is backward bending – a curious outcome indeed.

128 Keynes, *The General Theory*, p. 97.
129 Leijonhufvud (*On Keynesian Economics*, p. 95, n. 22), cites *The General Theory*, pp. 91–2.
130 Keynes, *Collected Writings*, vol. xxix, p. 111. This could be taken as arguing that workers are seldom tricked or, alternatively, that supra-optimal states themselves are very infrequent. The context suggests the former.
131 Keynes, *The General Theory*, p. 290 (emphasis added). Note the distinct shift in view by contrast to *Collected Writings*, vol. xxix, p. 82.
132 Keynes, *The General Theory*, pp. 289–90.
133 ibid., pp. 141–2.
134 John Stuart Mill, 'On the influence of consumption on production', in Henry Hazlitt (ed.), *The Critics of Keynesian Economics*, New York, Arlington House, 1977, pp. 24–45, at p. 40. One cannot say that illusion played any important role in Mill on the basis of one quotation, of course. Neither can it be assumed that Keynes was aware of this passage.
135 Pigou, *Industrial Fluctuations*, p. 165. David Collard, 'Pigou on expectations and the cycle', *Economic Journal*, vol. 93, June 1983, pp. 411–14, has argued that in Pigou there are key elements of the rational expectations hypothesis, but, surely, in analysing the real world Pigou gave greater emphasis to money illusion – and one doubts that Collard would deny that.
136 Pigou, *Industrial Fluctuations*, p. 283.
137 Arthur C. Pigou, *The Theory of Unemployment*, London, Frank Cass, 1933, p. 294.
138 Pigou, 'Mr J.M. Keynes' general theory...' pp. 118–19.
139 Pigou, *Employment and Equilibrium*, pp. 92–3.
140 Keynes, 'Relative movements of real wages and output', *Economic Journal*, vol. 49, March 1939, pp. 34–51, at p. 40 (emphasis is added).
141 James Tobin, 'Money wage rates and employment', in Seymour E. Harris (ed.), *The New Economics: Keynes' influence on theory and public policy*, London, Dennis Dobson, 1948, pp. 579–85.
142 Patinkin, *Money, Interest and Prices*, pp. 637–42.
143 Blaug (*Economic Theory in Retrospect*, pp. 168, 675) seems to agree, but Patinkin (*Keynes' Monetary Thought*, p. 119) later writes that money illusion was Keynes's 'implicit (and I would conjecture, unintentional) assumption'. See also Harry G. Johnson, 'The general theory after twenty-five years', *American Economic Review*, vol. 51, May 1961, pp. 1–17, at p. 9 for Keynes's 'heinous crime'.
144 Furthermore, Leijonhufvud's (*On Keynesian Economics*, pp. 325–9) sharp attack on Patinkin's failure to see wealth effects in Keynes. Reductions of the money wage increase *real* balances. This lowers interest rates and increases asset prices. Consumption therefore rises. This issue is taken up in Chapter 8.

145 Patinkin, *Money, Interest and Prices*, p. 639, citing *The General Theory*, pp. 171–2 (with Patinkin's emphasis). Neither is Leijonhufvud convinced by Patinkin, but he does not elaborate. See *On Keynesian Economics*, pp. 384–5.

146 Patinkin, *Money, Interest and Prices*, pp. 640–4 (esp. n. 22).

147 Fender, *Understanding Keynes*, p. 129 seems to agree and does not consider Keynes's oversight to be of significance.

148 These remarks are a response to a comment of an anonymous reader. Compare Hyman P. Minsky, 'Frank Hahn's *Money and Inflation*: a review article', *Journal of Post Keynesian Economics*, vol. 6, no. 3, Spring 1984, pp. 449–57, at p. 454, where Minsky expresses his hostility to Hahn's book and his treatment of illusion and neutrality.

149 Robert J. Barro, *Macroeconomics*, New York, John Wiley and Sons, 2nd edn., 1984, p. 512.

150 In so far as 'cash-in-advance' models have been put forward by new classicists, hostile judgements could well prove premature. Furthermore, monetarist models exist which rely on buffer stocks of money being important factors in dynamic adjustment. See David Laidler, 'The "buffer stock" notion in monetary economics', *Economic Journal*, 1984, supplement, pp. 17–34.

151 Nicholas Kaldor, 'What is wrong with economic theory', *Quarterly Journal of Economics*, vol. 89, no. 3, August 1975, pp. 347–57, at pp. 351–2; John Blatt, 'Classical economics of involuntary unemployment', *Journal of Post Keynesian Economics*, vol. 3, no. 4, Summer 1981, pp. 552–9.

152 W.M. Corden, 'Keynes and the others: wage and price rigidities in macro-economic models', *Oxford Economic Papers*, vol. 30, no. 2, July 1978, pp. 159–80, at pp. 172–3. Thorvaldur Gylfason and Assar Lindbeck, 'Union rivalry and wages: an oligopolistic approach', *Economica*, vol. 51, no. 202, May 1984, pp. 129–39.

153 Assar Lindbeck and Dennis Snower, 'Involuntary unemployment as an insider–outsider dilemma', Institute for International Economic Studies, Stockholm, seminar paper no. 282, July 1984.

154 Keynes, *The General Theory*, p. 14. See Hines, 'The "micro-economic foundations of employment and inflation theory": bad old wine in elegant new bottles', in G.D.N. Worswick (ed.), *The Concept and Measurement of Involuntary Unemployment*, London, Allen and Unwin, 1976, p. 79, n. 23. The relativities issue has a long history. See Matthew 20:1–16. See also Reuven Brenner, 'Unemployment, justice and Keynes's "general theory"', *Journal of Political Economy*, vol. 87, no. 4, August 1979, pp. 837–50, where Keynes's own theory of 'involuntary unemployment' is said (p. 838) to depend on a non-utilitarian theory of justice. Sir John Hicks can also be aligned with this group, see his *Value and Capital: an inquiry into some fundamental principles of economic theory*, Clarendon, Oxford University Press, 1946, 2nd edn, pp. 270–1; 'What is wrong with monetarism', *Lloyds Bank Review*, no. 118, October 1975, pp. 1–13, at pp. 2–5. Pigou, as Solow has pointed out, also considered that wage-determination theory

would require the incorporation of fairness. See Robert M. Solow, 'On theories of unemployment', *American Economic Review*, vol. 70, no. 1, March 1980, pp. 1–11, at p. 8. For a recent discussion of wage norms and the status value attaching to wages, see Serge-Christophe Kolm, 'Unemployment resulting from preferences on wages or prices', in Omar F. Hamouda and John N. Smithin (eds), *Keynes and Public Policy After Fifty Years*, vol. II: *Theory and Method*, New York, New York University Press, 1988, pp. 102–18.

155 Paul Davidson and Eugene Smolensky, *Aggregate Supply and Demand Analysis*, New York, Harper and Row, 1964, p. 172. To be fair they later relax this argument (pp. 174–5), but it is not clear why they mentioned it in the first place.

156 Albert Rees, 'Wage determination and involuntary unemployment', *Journal of Political Economy*, vol. 59, no. 2, April 1951, pp. 143–53, at pp. 149–50.

157 Takashi Negishi, 'Involuntary unemployment and market imperfection', *Economic Studies Quarterly*, vol. 25, no. 1, April 1974, pp. 32–41; *Microeconomic Foundations of Keynesian Macroeconomics*, Amsterdam, North-Holland, 1979.

158 See Hines's disappointment with search-theory accounts in David Worswick (ed.), *The Concept and Measurement of Involuntary Unemployment*, ch. 3, 'The "micro-economic foundations of employment and inflation theory"...'

Similarly Richard Jackman, 'Keynes and Leijonhufvud', *Oxford Economic Papers*, vol. 26, 1974, pp. 259–72, at p. 267, considers that search unemployment is voluntary. He overlooks that Leijonhufvud's trigger-device is 'voluntary' but that the multiplier, so far as Leijonhufvud's intentions were concerned, was meant to be an involuntary process whereby agents were powerlessly swept along (*On Keynesian Economics*, p. 95, n. 23).

Robert J. Gordon also labels search theory as 'voluntary', at least so far as they relate to quit decisions by workers and not to firing and layoff activities by firms. See 'Recent developments in the theory of inflation and unemployment', *Journal of Monetary Economics*, vol. 2, 1976, pp. 185–219, at pp. 205–7.

159 Edmund Phelps (ed.), *Microeconomic Foundations of Employment and Inflation Theory*, New York, W.W. Norton, 1970, p. 39, n. 21; p. 44.

160 ibid., p. 386.

161 A handy review of relatively recent developments, though not one which looks either at the voluntary-involuntary distinction or the views of Keynes himself, is Herschel I. Grossman, 'Why does aggregate employment fluctuate?' *American Economic Review*, vol. 69, no. 2, May 1979, pp. 64–9.

162 Inspired by Okun are Tibor Scitovsky, 'The demand-side economics of inflation', in David Worswick and James Trevithick (eds), *Keynes and the Modern World*, Cambridge, Cambridge University Press, 1983, pp. 236–7, where he argues that productivity and morale depend on how well workers are paid (but, curiously, not so much on how stable

are their jobs); George Akerlof, 'The case against conservative macroeconomics: an inaugural lecture', *Economica*, vol. 46, August 1979, pp. 219–37, where fairness and customary behaviour are stressed.

163 Axel Leijonhufvud, 'What would Keynes have thought of rational expectations?', in Worswick and Trevithick (eds), *Keynes and the Modern World*, p. 188.

164 Robert J. Barro, 'Discussion', *American Economic Review, Papers and Proceedings*, vol. 74, no. 2, May 1984, pp. 416–17, at p. 417.

165 Leijonhufvud, 'What would Keynes have thought of rational expectations?', p. 221.

166 See Robert E. Lucas's well-known 'Unemployment policy', *American Economic Review*, vol. 68, no. 2, May 1978, pp. 353–7. Michael Parkin, *Modern Macroeconomics*, Scarborough, Ontario, Prentice Hall Canada, 1982, p. 77, takes a similar view. The notion quite quickly percolated down into an intermediate textbook.

167 Solow, 'On theories of unemployment', p. 8, n. 5, also labels both implicit contract and the social-customs theories as 'in a sense, voluntary'. He continues, 'One can ask [as did Lucas] why workers cling to such costly conventions. It is the job of sociology to answer that question.' Lucas would not accept that, of course. For him, wage-setting institutions are themselves endogenous products of the exercise of free choice. Not everyone would agree with Lucas's view on how people don't have institutions imposed on them. I pursue Lucas's line of argument. The Nazis came to power in Germany because of the actions of individuals operating in an institutional environment which they either shaped or approved of tacitly by their inaction. Obviously, individual stormtroopers bashed individual Jews, and the principle of methodological individualism applies. Given their preferences and the absence of any effective legal constraints, the Nazis were advantageously placed. The Jews later freely chose to clamber onto the trains and jog into the showers. This was optimal behaviour in view of the presence of armed guards and no alternative appearing more attractive given the information then available. Illuminating? Not really.

168 Book Review, *Studies in Business-Cycle Theory*, by Robert E. Lucas in *Journal of Economic Literature*, vol. xxi, March 1983, pp. 107–10, at p. 110. Perhaps his 'the coordination problem is a *real* one' is an intended pun. New classicists give great emphasis to market co-ordination which deals efficiently with *nominal* shocks as though *the* co-ordination problem merely was to bring nominal values, which represent temporarily misperceived real values into line with correct real remuneration. The grave difficulties involved when searching for a moving target, the 'correct' vector changing once the multiplier has taken hold, appear outside the immediate scope of such analysis. Neither does work by new classicists on the real business cycle emphasize how the multiplier frustrates co-ordination.

169 See Lucas's Book Review, *Studies in Business-Cycle Theory*, p. 109 for the last three passages. In contrast to Leijonhufvud, it can be suggested

that Keynes tended to treat the system as normally being susceptible to any passing virus and in need of continual nursing care.

170 Lucas, 'Unemployment Policy', p. 354.

171 Leijonhufvud, 'Comment: is there a meaningful trade-off between inflation and unemployment?', *Journal of Political Economy*, vol. 76, no. 4, July–August 1968, pp. 738–43, at p. 742. Leijonhufvud does not mention whether a slightly lower real wage would be acceptable to the now displaced worker.

172 'Comments by Martin Neil Baily', *Brookings Papers on Economic Activity*, 1980, no. 1, pp. 125–32, at p. 128.

173 Extending the Azariadis–Baily approach is Charles R. Bean, 'Optimal wage bargains', *Economica*, vol. 51, 1984, pp. 141–9, where 'apparently involuntary' (p. 148) unemployment is seen as the side-effect of an implicit contract and where those laid off would have been prepared *ex post* to accept a wage cut to remain with a firm to which their skills were specific.

174 C.J. Bliss, 'Two views of macroeconomics', *Oxford Economic Papers* vol. 35, no. 1, March 1983, pp. 1–12, at p. 8. Compare *On Keynesian Economics*, pp. 336, 408. Whether or not a regime of flexible wages would affect the volatility of employment is a separate question. See Peter Howitt, 'Wage flexibility and employment', in Omar F. Hamouda and John N. Smithin (eds) *Keynes and Public Policy After Fifty Years*, vol. II: *Theories and Method*, pp. 61–9.

175 Boris Pesek, 'Book Review', *Journal of Political Economy*, vol. 77 (1969), no. 4, part i, pp. 559–61, at p. 559.

176 Leijonhufvud, *Information and Coordination*, ch. 6.

177 ibid., p. 103.

178 Keynes, *The General Theory*, e.g. p. 26. In 1936, Keynes considered (p. 15) that the two definitions amounted to the same thing, but that was because he simply assumed that real wages moved countercyclically.

179 Darity and Horn, 'Involuntary unemployment reconsidered', pp. 717–33.

180 Keynes, *Collected Writings*, vol. vii, pp. 394–412. Martin L. Weitzman, 'Increasing returns and the foundations of unemployment theory', *Economic Journal*, vol. 92, December 1982, pp. 787–804, was evidently inspired by Keynes's article.

181 Keynes, *Collected Writings*, vol. vii, p. 404.

182 A list appears ibid., p. 411.

183 ibid., p. 401. See also Darity and Horn, 'Involuntary unemployment reconsidered', p. 723, n. 12.

184 See 'Unemployment as seen by the Keynesians', in Worswick (ed.), *The Concept and Measurement of Involuntary Unemployment*, ch. 1.

185 ibid., pp. 19–20 (with comma deleted). Pigou appeared to include under 'conditions' the nature of the work and its location as well as the rate of pay.

186 Compare Darity and Horn, 'Involuntary unemployment reconsidered', pp. 726–7.

187 Weitzman ('Increasing returns...', p. 792) disagrees. Weitzman has a difficulty. He suggests that increasing returns prevent the unemployed

setting up their own enterprises to escape unemployment, but if there were scope for such expansion why don't existing firms exploit it? The answer is that they are constrained by the lack of demand. Barriers to entry seem of little relevance. Tobin rightly comments, in Worswick and Trevithick (eds), *Keynes and the Modern World*, p. 31, that by focusing on real or supply phenomena, the monetary and intertemporal aspects are missed. No doubt Leijonhufvud would endorse Tobin's remark. Hahn (in ibid., pp. 74–5) and Kaldor (in ibid., pp. 12–15) are, however, friendly to Weitzman. Paul Davidson, 'Liquidity and not increasing returns is the ultimate source of unemployment equilibrium', *Journal of Post Keynesian Economics*, vol. 7, no. 3, Spring 1985, pp. 373–84, condemns Weitzman, but he argues in places in a manner similar to his purported refutation of Clower and Leijonhufvud discussed later.

188 Weitzman ('Increasing returns...', p. 788). He also refers (p. 803) to hysteresis whereby, once the cause of a change is removed, the system need not return to its original position. For example, a slump can persist even when its initial cause has disappeared once expectations of sluggish activity become ingrained.

189 'Effective demand and the monetary theory of employment', in Alain Barrére (ed.), *The Foundations of Keynesian Analysis: proceedings held at a conference held at the University of Paris I-Panthéon-Sorbonne*, London, Macmillan, 1988, pp. 49–64, at p. 49.

190 For example, Alan Coddington, *Keynesian Economics: the search for first principles*, London, Allen and Unwin, 1983, pp. 35–41.

Chapter four

Effective demand: a theoretical and historical perspective

Leijonhufvud provides persuasive evidence that Keynes stressed the vital role played by money in the act of exchange. He concludes

> that Keynes' theory, although obscurely expressed and doubtlessly not all that clear even in his own mind, was still in substance that to which Clower has...given a precise statement.[1]

Such a conclusion is rather tentative and mild, perhaps unduly so. It will be argued here that the idea that transactors require enough purchasing power in the form of cash to attain full employment is almost indisputably present in Keynes. We do not need to infer its existence or read between the lines. Neither do we need to suggest dramatically that either the notion is there or we must reject *The General Theory* as 'theoretical nonsense'.[2] On the contrary, even the classicists recognized the concept of effective demand. The defect in their theory was the unduly optimistic belief that there would be powerful forces at work to ensure that purchasing power would be sufficient to restore full employment in the face of any deflationary shock.[3] Effective demand is not of itself a revolutionary discovery. Rather the forces which *govern* it are the source of dispute.

This is probably a surprising view because there are economists who doubt that Keynes had any sound microfoundation for his multiplier. The main proponent of this view which is so hostile to Leijonhufvud's position is Herschel Grossman.

Grossman's critique

Grossman claims, having in mind Keynes's rationalization of the propensity to consume being in terms of 'fundamental psychological laws' and habits, that 'Keynes had nothing like Clower's conception in mind and...Keynes' own formulation of the consumption function was simply *ad hoc*'.[4]

Grossman has argued that Keynes had no idea of a dual decision hypothesis in mind when he wrote about the consumption function because Keynes did not reject key elements of classical thinking in his accounts of the demand for labour and commodities. Unlike Clower and Patinkin, who deserve the credit for the analysis of behaviour off the notional demand curve, Keynes held that the real wage equalled the marginal product and that the flow supplies of commodities cleared.[5] Entrepreneurs were not involuntarily constrained by illiquidity so why attribute Clower's insights to Keynes so far as the consumption function was concerned?

There is something to Grossman's point. Keynes referred to the fundamental psychological 'rule' and the 'law' as well as to the preservation of habitual norms which cause the consumption function to be rather flat and the multiplier to be rather lower, at least initially.[6] Behaviour is examined by emphasizing tastes rather than purchasing-power constraints. There is no close nexus between income and consumption; Keynes is happy to argue that a stable equilibrium requires that the marginal propensity to consume is less than unity and embraces whatever is convenient to achieve that result.[7]

To meet Grossman's argument, this chapter emphasizes that in other respects Keynes certainly should be taken to have grasped the notion of liquidity constraints and the importance of money to effect expenditures. If Keynes is not explicit when dealing with the consumption function, we can, nevertheless, judge in favour of Leijonhufvud. Keynes saw the possibility that 'a decline in income...may even cause consumption to exceed income'[8] if financial accumulations are run down to cushion the effects of a large decline in income; that is, money holdings matter. That Keynes was aware of the complex relationship between savings and the hoarding of speculative balances suggests his corresponding recognition of consumption being effected through having currency held and earmarked for transaction purposes. Keynes's argument that rising income causes transactions demands to grow and thereby drives up interest rates shows how money is needed to effect expenditure. It is scarce and its price must rise.[9]

In direct answer to Grossman, Keynes's emphasis on psychological forces should not be interpreted as a tacit denial of the role of money as a constraint. As with any demand curve in microeconomics, its position is governed by money (or real) income and subjective tastes and motivation. Examining the latter does not blind us to the importance of the former. Furthermore, although the exact size of the marginal propensity to consume depends on subjective considerations, the fact that it is less than one indicates the fundamental idea that income is not entirely spent on goods and that money can leak from active circulation. The size of the multiplier depends upon the tastes and goals of the consumer (the dynamic multiplier also depending upon the subjective anticipations of entrepreneurs about changes in demand), but whether and how these beliefs and desires are manifested can still depend on objective spending constraints. Indeed the point can be made more sharply. Why does 'psychology' preclude 'rationality' in decision-making in which a budget constraint partially explains a consumer's selection? Is Grossman arguing that the reduction in consumption spending is a mere knee-jerk reaction? Cannot it be said that if a labourer becomes unemployed he is forced to curtail consumption by an objective constraint, and yet the magnitude of that decline in spending depends on a subjective disposition regarding how much of that income would have been spent and how much saved?

However, Grossman could reasonably retort that, since effective demand relates to expected sales proceeds, Keynes cannot be taken to have emphasized that realized income governs subsequent behaviour.[10] Keynes certainly gives the entrepreneur the choice of what to produce. If higher demand is anticipated, entrepreneurs are capable of expanding, and it is not clear how the purchase of additional inputs is to be effected. This is a fair objection, but in so far as the finance is attained through borrowing, interest rates rise on account of the higher transactions demand for money. Keynes clearly saw that.[11] An increase in activity is easily effected by borrowing if need be. The entrepreneur is able to borrow; Keynes never says that workers can borrow, however. The workers are helpless; realized incomes constrain them. Entrepreneurs have buffers of wealth and access to credit which workers do not enjoy.

Monetary versus barter economies

To be sure, it is not clear at times whether Keynes emphasized flows of money, changes of which can induce losses, in order to show that entrepreneurs received *signals* to reduce output or whether they were *constrained* to so do. Keynes's emphasis on expectations of sales to a degree indicates that sellers choose to contract supply. It is not having illiquid inventories which force them to. However, as Brothwell[12] points out, it is only in a monetary economy that the issue of whether savings are invested becomes relevant. In a barter world, the accumulation of goods unconsumed is able to be directly devoted to investment by a Robinson Crusoe or by someone who accumulates wage-goods to feed workers who are to be engaged to build a piece of capital. This would suggest that Keynes saw the essential role of money.

Nevertheless, the idea of savings flows not being offset by an equal investment flow does not of itself convey the idea that falling income is based on constraint rather than voluntary hoarding, so Grossman's stance remains arguable though, on closer examination, it is probably unsound.

It is argued here that Keynes's theory of aggregate demand clearly stresses the essential role of money as a means of payment. It is tempting to say that his very use of the words 'effective demand' indicates this. Why qualify 'demand' with 'effective' if not to distinguish it from 'ineffective demand'; and what sort of demand could be 'ineffective' if it is not a desire without the money to back it?[13] Some possibilities spring to mind but they can be summarily rejected. One option is that someone desires a good but is unwilling to offer anything the seller wants in return. This cannot be taken as an explanation of ineffective demand because it would be a mere unfulfilled dream, an avaricious flight of fancy irrelevant to economic analysis. Besides, mere desires have no reason to fall as effective demand rises; they would never be satisfied anyway for one party gives nothing in return. Another alternative is that demand remains ineffective because willing and able traders do not meet being ignorant of each other's existence. This is plausible. However, if this were the problem, why would governments be able to cure it by burying in mineshafts bottles filled with banknotes?[14] Why would government *expenditure* on objects, whether socially useful or wasteful also be a solution? In so far as it is financed by bond sales, money is being redistributed from those who are not spending to those who are willing to spend so that its velocity increases. It should also be noted that money-wage cuts were rejected as a solution by Keynes, the reason being that money demand, and therefore prices, would fall in roughly the same proportion. In other words, less cash in the hands of the workers leads to less nominal consumption expenditure. Evidently, therefore, the source of the problem *must* be a want of purchasing power in the form of cash, if the injection of cash into the expenditure stream is what cures it.[15] Can this really be interpreted as illegitimately reading something into Keynes? Can it not be argued that ordinary English conveys exactly what Keynes meant even though he chose not to spell it out formally?

There are, however, many other reasons for accepting that Keynes understood the microfoundations of his revolution. A review of classical views on the role of money and Keynes's objections should make this clear. We shall find that even the classicists realized that sufficient effective demand was required for full employment to be generated. This is why they devoted so much effort to show that the hoarding of money was indeed a problem, but only a temporary one. Keynes, however, saw the propensity to hoard as a serious matter. Classical economists also readily seized upon the notion of the real balance, or Pigou, effect whereby consumption expenditure is both desired and *possible* once deflation causes sufficient real balances to exist in the hands of those who had been hoarders.

The role of hoarding in pre-Keynesian thought, especially in connection with Say's Law, can be examined to show that the recognition
of the importance of effective demand was commonplace. One did not
have to be a radical to refer to it, although Hobson, for example did. He
observed that

> a mere desire for 'utilities' and commodities containing them has
> no effect. In order that a desire may be 'effective' it must express
> itself through purchasing power.[16]

What needs to be stressed is that any classical economist would agree;
it is the first thing anyone learns about the microeconomic theory of
demand. It was the *behaviour* of effective demand that caused the
controversy; the cause of a deficiency of demand and whether it would
automatically be corrected were the sources of disagreement.[17] The
notion of effective demand itself was certainly not considered novel by
Hawtrey or Robertson, who saw the concept of Smith, Mill, Pigou and
Marshall.[18] Indeed it seems rather trite to say that if you are unemployed,
you have no money and cannot buy anything. Nevertheless, the writings
of some of the classicists and Keynes's understanding of them will be
examined.

Some theoretical developments

We must take care not to overreact and attribute all unemployment to the
multiplier and liquidity constraints. There has been a recent backlash
against what some see as an undue emphasis on money. The argument
is now made that it is a sufficient but not necessary condition for
breakdown that money fails in its primary function. Even a complex,
non-monetary system (such as one based on computer mediation) is
susceptible to dislocation. Adverse expectations, obstinacy, speculation
and ignorance can thwart trade in any system, monetary or not.[19] There
is also the argument that the existence of any non-reproducible asset, not
necessarily money, can give rise to unemployment.

The substance of the latter argument is that demand can be
channelled into areas which cannot induce employment, the supply of
such things as land or old paintings being fixed.[20] This reasoning,
however, is doubtful since an excess demand for such an asset will
simply increase its nominal price (if it is free to adjust) until the excess
demand is eliminated.[21] (This assumes that there is not speculation that
any increase in the price of the asset is unlikely to last, whereupon the
logic of the liquidity trap will prevail and money will be hoarded.) The
yield on the asset will fall and the cash will return to active circulation
within the short run. Merely assuming the fixed supply of some asset,
such as consols, does not of itself imply the possibility of

unemployment. The problem has already been solved within the short run. The issue of the non-reproducible asset other than money is probably a red herring, despite the view of such authorities as Hahn.[22]

Mention, however, must be made of Davidson's spirited advocacy of the Hahn position.[23] He rejects 'the axiom of gross substitution' and with it the idea that the price of non-reproducibles will ever rise high enough to become close substitutes for reproducibles with which they fundamentally and intrinsically differ. The argument is an extreme one.[24]

A softer option, and one perhaps more in tune with Davidson's (and perhaps Hahn's) true intentions, is to say that even if extremely high nominal (and relative) prices of non-reproducibles did emerge, then the corresponding deflation in the reproducible sector would conceivably be so severe that the money-using system would disintegrate thereby making recovery impossible in any significant sense. Other means exist to explain involuntary unemployment without the need to deny completely that two sets of goods can ever be substitutes no matter how vast the price differential becomes. *Within a relevant range*, the demand for non-reproducibles is a bottomless well. By moderating fundamentalist claims, the claim that Keynesian and Walrasian insights are incommensurable would be weakened.

Why should Clower and Leijonhufvud abandon atomistic analysis? If it is accepted that an inherited stock of dollar denominated debts can prevent full employment emerging through wage and price-level adjustments, certainly this calls into question standard general equilibrium models in which cash flow and bankruptcy do not figure. Keynesian reductionism, however, does not champion the axiom of gross substitution as a reliable dynamic precept. It is simply a device by which the Walrasian vector can be specified under certain hypothetical conditions. There is little reason to believe that Clower or Leijonhufvud would disagree with the scepticism of Arrow and Hahn (endorsed by Davidson) concerning the real-world applicability of standard general equilibrium analyses concerning either the existence or the stability of the Walrasian vector.[25]

Liquidity constraints: Clower and Leijonhufvud versus Davidson *et al.*

It causes some discomfort to be forced into a position of having to reconcile the views given earlier which give strong support to Leijonhufvud with the view of Davidson (and others) that the money supply is endogenous. In Davidson's scheme, *credit extended to effect contracts for goods creates money and money in hand is not needed to buy goods*. How can this objection be met: if there is, in Leijonhufvud, a causal connection flowing from money to goods is this not a version of monetarism?[26]

A simple answer is this: if you are currently unemployed and have neither cash nor access to credit, it is no use entering into a contract to purchase goods. Leijonhufvud's entire argument hinges on the unemployed being constrained. This is behind the demand multiplier. Labour is illiquid and cannot be used as security for a loan or the extension of credit. Firms can obtain credit and the speculators have wealth to draw upon, not the ordinary worker.

Failure to see this simple point seems to be behind Davidson's extraordinary assault on the Clower–Leijonhufvud approach. His argument is that Leijonhufvud unwittingly has embraced Say's Law.[27] One would guess that such a claim would leave Leijonhufvud flabbergasted, and, curiously, the truth is that there is little which separates Leijonhufvud and Davidson on a number of key issues.

Davidson reasons as follows:

> If...Say's Law prevails, then the economy is in neutral equilibrium where actual demand is *constrained* only by actual income (supply). In other words, Say's Law requires that aggregate demand is a *constrained demand function* (in the terminology of Clower...). In the Clower–Leijonhufvud neoclassical synthesis version of the Keynesian system...purchasing decisions are always equal to, and constrained by, *actual* income.... Unemployment is solely due to a 'coordination failure' of the market system to signal entrepreneurs that if they would only hire the full employment level of workers, ...all markets would clear.[28]

He then points out that it is Reaganomics to suggest that unemployment would be ended simply by asking each firm in the nation to hire one more worker.[29]

Davidson's arguments stem, in part, from what simply is a logical error in that he uses the notion of a 'constraint' in two quite different senses. If, under Say's Law, the aggregate supply and demand curves are entirely coincident, then any point can be an equilibrium, but surely there are no 'constraints' in any meaningful sense because there is no obstacle to a movement to full employment. The *choice* to produce and offer more and to take advantage of mutually beneficial trades is not impeded or 'constrained' in any reasonable sense. To say that in a neutral equilibrium 'actual demand is *constrained* by actual income (supply)' involves a peculiar use of words. '*Equal to*' is more appropriate than '*constrained*'.

Contrary to Davidson's unsubstantiated assertion, there exist no passages in either Clower or Leijonhufvud which say that purchasing decisions are always equal to and constrained by income. If this were true, once income began to fall, it would fall without limit and the multiplier would be infinite. The whole of Leijonhufvud's book is, after all, intended to explain Keynes's attack on Say's Law. The point Leijonhufvud tried to make was that actual income imposes an *upper, or effective, limit* on spending (in the absence of buffer savings and personal loans by banks, of course). In Leijonhufvud, savings flows exist and need not be invested which is the same as denying that the average propensity to spend is unity, the foundation of Say's Law.

Davidson's error, however, is not entirely his own fault. Leijonhufvud does give the impression that if workers and producers could meet and decide upon an agreeable real wage, then the multiplier-induced declines in income could, in theory, be negated by a co-ordinated expansion of production. Perhaps Davidson had in mind passages such as this:

> Thus, to repeat, the fact that there exists a potential barter bargain of goods for labor services that would be mutually agreeable to producers as a group and labor as a group is irrelevant to the motion of the system. In economies relying on a means of payment, the excess demand for wage goods corresponding to an excess supply of labor is but 'notional' – it is not communicated to employers as effective demand for output. The resulting miseries are 'involuntary' all around.[30]

This passage seems to suggest that if workers and employers met around a table *and could agree on Walrasian real remuneration*,[31] full employment would be restored. The mere hiring of the unemployed is no sufficient condition for recovery and Davidson cannot fairly attribute that view to Leijonhufvud. If aggregate demand is less than aggregate supply at full employment by virtue of an initial decline in investment then, given the consumption function,[32] an implicit precondition for recovery is an expansion of orders for investment goods. This in turn requires that investors be present at the roundtable conference, and, in an outside-money world,[33] the bears would need to be present too to give their approval.

If there is no credit available to investors, then, in this particular transactions structure, the return of bear hoards to active circulation is essential. Money can then flow in sequence from the investor, to the investment-good producer, to his employees, to the consumption-good producer and then to his employees. Leijonhufvud makes perfect sense on his own terms, but he could have made his point more clearly.

The peculiarity of Davidson's critique of Leijonhufvud has another twist. Davidson emphatically states that the demand for goods produced by labor need never be constrained by income; spending is constrained only by liquidity and/or timidity considerations.[34]

Putting aside the eccentric use of the term 'constrained' to describe a free choice not to spend by virtue of timidity, would Leijonhufvud disagree with this? The answer is no.

> In the analysis of [short-run disequilibrium] processes, money – and 'liquidity' generally – is of particular interest.... Hence our emphasis on aggregate demand *in money terms*.[35]

Furthermore, in Leijonhufvud, the initiating shock is a decline in the confidence of investors (or undue timidity, if you prefer).[36]

Finally, it is noted that Davidson is right to say that demand is governed ultimately by the

> *monetary*, and not the real, expected return on liquid assets. The rate of interest, which is strictly a monetary phenomenon rules the roost.[37]

Unfortunately for Davidson, Leijonhufvud stresses the pivotal importance paid by the expectations of bears in affecting the interest rate. Davidson seems closer to Keynes only in so far as Davidson believes in the *long-run* non-neutrality of money and in the long-run persistence of speculation. By comparison, Leijonhufvud defends the symbolic importance of the long-run validity of the thrift and productivity theory. A viable synthesis could well emerge: if bearishness persists in the financial sector, so do constraints in the real sector.

In short, Davidson's criticisms of Leijonhufvud's explanation of short-run multiplier effects can, for the most part, be dismissed.[38]

Running parallel to his critique of Leijonhufvud is Davidson's assault on Clower. Davidson criticizes Clower for accepting 'Say's Principle' that those who plan to buy something must also plan to sell something first in a money-using system. Davidson[39] notes that this is no fundamental maxim because governments can flout it by printing money without needing to contemplate selling goods and services in return. One doubts, however, that Clower meant anything more controversial than to say that households cannot expect to get something for nothing in their dealings with each other. Davidson's criticism seems somewhat captious because Clower's intention was to build a humble prototypic model to illuminate the means-of-payment function of money.

Similarly, Davidson[40] points to the importance of credit where out-lays occur prior to the receipt of income and therefore cannot be regarded as being 'induced' by them. An expectation of income can 'induce' current outlays which are financed by credit.[41] Surely this is an extension of Clower rather than a refutation. The exact sequence of events and the extent of complexity and interdependence are clarified by incorporating a financial sector, but the essence of Say's Principle still applies. Banks do not plan to extend credit unless they plan on being repaid. Similarly, honest investors contemplating autonomous outlays plan to be able to repay those from whom they borrow, even if they cannot be sure they will be able to.[42]

Davidson considers that credit and finance must be given meaningful roles in any useful model, but Clower's primary purpose was to point to the difference between notional and effective demand, not to supply a complete monetary theory. If Clower focuses too much on induced expenditure and employs a simple sequence by which only cash in hand finances purchases, the analysis would be improved by the extension of the model. But to concede this implies that Clower's and Davidson's approaches are ultimately commensurable in at least some respects. Surely, the mechanics of a monetary system are matters of logic. The transactions structure and sequencing can be formally portrayed and can be assimilated by anyone. The addition of a pervasive financial sector which in principle can break down under sufficient stress, can exacerbate the initial shock and effectively increase the multiplier. Minsky's theories of financial instability can be grafted on. Indeed Clower and Leijonhufvud would be friendly towards this.[43] The dispute is really over logic rather than vision.

Davidson and others have pointed to deficiencies, obscurities and over-simplifications but seem completely unwilling to believe that the defects can be repaired within a reductionist framework.

Consider how shocking Clower and Leijonhufvud must seem to fundamentalist post Keynesians. Equilibrium income is autonomous expenditure times the multiplier, but the emphasis of the reductionists is on induced expenditure and the equilibrating role of saving is scarcely mentioned.[44] If the preceding arguments have merit, such criticisms of the reductionists have little force on close examination.

Some of the dispute can be explained by recognizing that the reductionists have narrow goals. Leijonhufvud was more concerned with pointing to the defects in the *IS-LM* renditions and supplying some of the missing microfoundations. Davidson's aims are more sweeping and he strives to define what Keynes really said and to render it applicable to contemporary problems.

If Leijonhufvud stresses induced expenditure, his purpose was to explain the *change* in income and the foundations of the multiplier. It was not to completely define Keynes's theory of effective demand. The hydraulicists had already specified the short-run equilibrium level of income. If consideration of the financing of autonomous expenditure is not adequately dealt with by Clower, for example, why say that Clower is wrong rather than say that his account is incomplete?

Davidson tries to argue that Clower–Leijonhufvud are as different from Keynes as Euclidean and non-Euclidean geometry are from each other. If the rival approaches are to be instead regarded as complementary, Davidson's statements must attract rebuttal on the grounds that he reads too much into what are really superficial differences.

It is noteworthy, however, that Davidson does not stand alone in viewing Leijonhufvud's discussion as seriously defective.

Christopher Torr has recently claimed that Leijonhufvud's analysis dwells in the realm of the co-operative, or quasi-barter, economy.[45] This is a surprising charge in view of Leijonhufvud's emphasis that Keynes's revolution was based on the recognition of fundamental differences between money-using and barter economies. Torr considers that Leijonhufvud explains neither the foundations of Keynes's theory of effective demand nor the notion of involuntary unemployment.

In a manner similar to Davidson, Torr points to Leijonhufvud's failure to place autonomous expenditure at the centre of a theory of effective demand. The focus on induced expenditure takes attention away from the need for investment to rise to a level sufficient to offset full employment savings flows.

Torr points out that even if workers (as distinct from the community as a whole[46]) had a marginal propensity to consume of unity, or if they were prepared to be paid in kind to guarantee a market for their production, aggregate demand would remain deficient because profits fail to rise.[47] Higher profits result only from the restoration of investment.[48] All factors of production need to supply full-employment output, and the community as a whole would need to demand the output for sufficient profits to be earned. Leijonhufvud, by contrast, seems to think that the mere willingness to supply (instead of search for better prospects) would restore full employment.

By contrast to Davidson, Torr's criticisms are clear and non-polemical. One imagines, however, that Leijonhufvud would willingly reframe his argument to avoid giving post Keynesian fundamentalists the wrong impression.

Two comments are called for.

First, if we take the special case where *all* agents are paid in kind, the production of extra bags of wheat would, under conditions of diminishing returns, reduce the real wage and increase producer surplus, the latter itself being in the form of wheat. The rentier or capitalist can regard the wheat as available for direct consumption, as constituting planned investment (in the wages fund sense) or as something to barter for luxury goods. In a simple barter world, where payment in kind is viable, Say's Law does operate. Leijonhufvud's point should have been regarded as innocuous rather than blasphemous.

Second, it can hardly be too charitable to attribute to Leijonhufvud the insight that recovery requires the restoration of autonomous expenditure. Abstracting from the Pigou effect, the solution to the inter-temporal allocation problem is a prerequisite for a return to full employment in spot markets for labour and consumption goods. Achieving the latter is 'predicated on the prior occurrence of the first'.[49] This in turn requires an appropriate reduction in the interest rate or an increase in the marginal efficiency of investment.

Torr also considers that Leijonhufvud must somehow be bringing Keynes into the tradition of the co-operative economy in which activity is governed as if barter prevailed and only an unwillingness to supply can explain unemployment.[50] Torr finds confirming evidence by pointing to Leijonhufvud's reliance on search theory to explain Walrasian disequilibrium.

There are several problems with Torr's argument. When Leijonhufvud examines *voluntary* unemployment, he points out that Keynes included 'unemployment due to...slow response to change'.[51] For Torr to be right, Leijonhufvud would have to be extremely dim to fail to notice that search behaviour would be included in Keynes's definition of 'voluntary'.

Torr is not right to argue that Leijonhufvud's model is only about voluntary, search unemployment. Leijonhufvud clearly stated:

> Alchian's [search-theory] analysis remains perfectly applicable to the explanation of individual behaviour in a state of 'involuntary' unemployment, and the initial 'inflexibility' of reservation prices that his analysis implies is, indeed, a necessary condition for the emergence of such a state. But it is not sufficient. Keynes' involuntary unemployment is fundamentally a product of the cumulative process which he assumed the initial increase in unemployment would trigger...

> Actually, while it [the search behaviour of workers] is not 'fundamental' to Keynes' explanation of why a situation of involuntary unemployment is not quickly remedied by automatic forces, it *is* fundamental to the explanation of how the situation can develop that some lag in price adjustments is present.[52]

Can Torr's allegation that Leijonhufvud's interpretation cannot deal with the distinction between the co-operative and the entrepreneur economy – where the employer determines the hiring, not the workers – be sustained?

If Leijonhufvud were to have equated involuntary and search unemployment, only then would there be some legitimacy in regarding him as a supporter of the co-operative economy who believed that transient imperfections explain disequilibrium. Yet Leijonhufvud cannot be said to be a supporter even of the long-run applicability of Say's Law.

> Individuals interact on the basis of incomplete information. The consequence is a price vector reflecting the incompleteness of information and a pattern of realized transactions which leaves some agents disappointed. Will this set in motion a learning process that leads to a coordinated solution? If price-adjustments were governed by notional excess demands, then neo-Walrasian stability theorems will tell us under which conditions the answer is 'Yes'. Effective demand theory argues, I think persuasively, that there is no reason to suppose that, whatever the trial-and-error process that capitalist economies rely on, the successive trials will in fact be governed by these notional errors. Consequently *tatonnement* stability theorems are suspect.[53]

The most direct piece of evidence against Torr is this:

> Some time ago, Mr C.W.S. Torr brought to my attention that the 'Tilton laundry hamper' had contained the answer. Much of Vol. XXIX is devoted to some discarded introductions to the *General Theory* in which 'the contract between a Co-operative and an Entrepreneur Economy' is treated as fundamental.
> Keynes' 'Co-operative Economy', as it turned out, was one in which labor is bartered for goods, so that the supply of labor is always an effective demand for goods. In his 'Entrepreneur Economy' the Clowerian rule applies: labor buys money and money buys goods but labor does not buy goods. In the entrepreneur economy, therefore, effective demand failures are possible and so, consequently, is 'involuntary unemployment'.
> That, I think, should settle the matter.[54]

Some regret that the distinction between the co-operative and the entrepreneurial economy was not made in *The General Theory* itself. There are, however, good grounds for Keynes taking the approach he did. It is conceivable that he realized that, at one level, the distinction in those terms was simply misleading and irrelevant. Clearly, even a socialist economy organized on a 'co-operative' basis, is liable to suffer a lack of effective demand if it is a genuine money-using system. If the workers produce 10 cars and outlay $10,000 then, for output to be sustained, $10,000 needs to be received in revenue. Even if profits need not be earned, if sales receipts are only $9,000, current output is not sustainable. Subsidies, a form of fiscal policy in effect, would be needed to bolster demand exogenously. The appropriate distinction is between money-using economies where non-expenditure is a possibility and economies in which sufficient demand is guaranteed, as, for example, when prices adjust so smoothly that expenditure is never deficient and barter models can apply. As praising a co-operative economy would only align him to some distasteful Marxist faction, the deletion of the distinctions would have been seen by Keynes as doubly desirable.

The temptation to make dramatic statements about Keynes's fundamentally new vision about every aspect of economics afflicts many historians of thought. If what matters about the difference between money and barter economies instead can readily be captured by logic, then the urge to draw deep distinctions which separate the wise and true from the shallow and ignorant can be exposed as portentous rhetoric causing unnecessary friction. Too much energy is spent looking for something to criticize if vision so dominates logic that the other side *must* be seriously mistaken.

The representation of Clower and Leijonhufvud by some fundamentalists supplies an interesting example of how schools shape the thoughts of their members. Despite the flashing of the warning lights, the logic is pursued relentlessly. Although Torr realizes that his interpretation makes nonsense out of Leijonhufvud's express claims to explain involuntary unemployment, renders Leijonhufvud a member of the spanner-in-the-works school he claims to attack and flies in the face of a direct statement of support for the distinction in volume xxix between the co-operative and the monetary economy (with unambiguous support for the latter), the outcome is that one deficient section of Leijonhufvud's work is deemed to overturn the rest. Corroboration of one's views is perceived to exist when, to an outsider, there is none. Pre-existing visions are verified rather than falsified. Defects inevitable in anyone's works suffer the glare of the spotlight if they are made by perceived rivals.

But Torr and Davidson cannot fairly be singled out. Their writings support, and find support from, those of others. Individuals must build on the work of others. How else can progress be made? Members also gain confidence from the tacit encouragement of their colleagues. Even able and honest intellects, however, can be captured by a school. Tensions and ambiguities in the evidence are resolved in a way which, at the time, seems to be the least disquieting. To protect what is currently regarded as the central core of the research programme and to resist the absorption of the tenets of other approaches, the immunizing stratagems become ever more contrived. Ironically, the most supple contortionists are said to have the best posture.

Elite circulation plays little role across the schools. Change normally comes from below rather from across. A newcomer's eclecticism, alas, is no badge of merit.

Concluding remarks

The precise role of money in explaining economic fluctuations is still a matter attracting academic attention. Not only is the issue confused from the point of view of the student of the history of economic thought. Theoreticians are still grappling with the problem of macroeconomic disequilibria and its causes. The dynamics of adjustment suggested by the multiplier represent an advance in our understanding, but whether money is necessarily involved, whether price inflexibilities are required to trigger it and whether Keynes's view is properly represented by Leijonhufvud remain questions requiring consideration.

The tone of this chapter is that it is almost self-evident that effective demand, as distinct from notional demand, is central to Keynes's position. Criticisms by some post Keynesians of Clower's and Leijonhufvud's formulations are generally unsatisfactory.

Notes

1 Axel Leijonhufvud, *On Keynesian Economics and the Economics of Keynes: a study in monetary theory*, New York, Oxford University Press, 1968, p. 102.
2 Robert W. Clower, 'The Keynesian counter-revolution', in Clower (ed.), *Monetary Theory: selected readings*, Harmondsworth, Penguin, 1969, p. 290.
3 Consider Marshall. Recovery occurs because, when confidence is restored, 'credit would give increased *means of purchase*, and thus prices would recover'. Alfred Marshall, *The Economics of Industry*, London, Macmillan, 1885, 3rd edn, p. 155 (emphasis added).
4 Herschel Grossman, 'Was Keynes a "Keynesian"? A review article', *Journal of Economic Literature*, vol. 10, no. 1, March 1972, pp.26–30, at p. 27. Grossman is not alone in this view. See Helmut Schuster, 'Keynes' disequilibrium analysis', *Kyklos*, vol. 26, 1973, no. 3, pp. 512–44, at p. 524. Even in *On Keynesian Economics*, p. 187, Leijonhufvud concedes that Keynes did not deduce the consumption-income relation from choice-theoretical foundations.
5 The issue of the equality of the wage and marginal product is dealt with in the chapter dealing with the commodities markets where Keynes's reasons for these seemingly classical ideas are examined. An answer to Grossman is that Keynes was concerned with the final short-run equilibrium state and not with the detailed dynamics. With an instantaneous multiplier it is only the involuntary unemployment of labour that required attention. In his simple comparative-statics model,

the effects of temporary excess flow-supplies of commodities was abstracted from.

6 J.M. Keynes, *The General Theory of Employment Interest and Money*, London, Macmillan, 1936, pp. 97–8.

7 Indeed his treatment of consumption is similar in some respects to that of the *Treatise*.

8 Keynes, *The General Theory*, p. 98.

9 This point is discussed in detail in chapter 5 dealing with *IS-LM* where the importance of liquidity and Keynes's emphasis on the means of financing investment expenditure is considered. It is the crudity of the classical account of how money flows from current savings to investment to which Keynes objected. Money could be diverted into speculative hoards, and bank financing needed separate examination.

10 Keynes, *The General Theory*, pp. 23–5.

11 'In order that producers may be able, as well as willing, to produce at a higher cost of production...they must be able to get command of an appropriate quantity of money...; and in order that they may be willing, as well as able to do this, the rate of interest...must not be so high as to deter them.' *The Collective Writings of John Maynard Keynes*, London, Macmillan, 1971–, vol. v, p. 163.

12 John Brothwell, 'A simple Keynesian's response to Leijonhufvud', *Bulletin of Economic Research*, vol. 27, May 1975, pp. 3–21, at p. 8.

13 It can even be argued that 'effective demand' as used by Keynes is a more sophisticated concept than this. Since his definition involves *expected* receipts, *anticipated* liquidity is what governs the level of output chosen by entrepreneurs during any production period. Furthermore, the instantaneous multiplier is framed in terms of anticipated expenditure. See Keynes, *The General Theory*, pp. 55, 122–4.

14 Keynes, *The General Theory*, p. 129.

15 The question arises whether money is of crucial importance in explaining non-Walrasian outcomes. Money, so far as its involvement in the means-of-payment process is concerned, does not necessarily explain the possibility of reaching a non-Walrasian quantity vector. The maldistribution of money stems from false trading, which in turn can be traced to the primary cause, false prices. Trading at false prices results in non-Walrasian quantities even in a barter world. Money flows in a sense therefore seem epiphenomenal to some and capable of being left out of a model defining comparative-static outcomes. If the false price vector, initial endowments and trading procedures (i.e. shopping, queuing and rationing rules) are specified and fixed it would appear that the quantity vector is determined.

I disagree with this logic. Money matters. For example, the existence of buffer stocks of money can prevent bankruptcies which otherwise would have arisen in the face of interruptions to cash-flow sequences. Forestalling bankruptcies surely would mitigate the effects of a contractionary disturbance and influence the precise quantity vector associated, *ceteris paribus*, with any particular false price vector.

Money, therefore, need not be regarded as 'neutral' even so far as its means-of-payment function is concerned. In the text, an exogenous increase in the money supply (giving cash to the unemployed) could increase aggregate employment and welfare even if the interest rate and other prices were held constant. If prices remained constant on Marshallian grounds, because supply happens to be perfectly elastic (due to, say, constant returns), then one can confidently predict that changes in the money supply would spur recovery. This particular result depends on the absence of a strict regime of output rationing, i.e. a particular form of trading procedure is being tacitly assumed. If the shops selling wage-goods were empty and the shopkeepers were already standing in queues to procure stocks, then receiving more cash would do the workers no good because there would be nothing to buy. In so far as prices could be held constant, on the grounds of any arbitrary, 'spanner-in-the-works', fix-price, 'off-the-supply-curve' assumption, then rationing could still exist and an increase in the money supply could prove ineffective.

Naturally, it is possible to argue, as do Leijonhufvud and Davidson, that the false price vector contains a false rate of interest which itself depends on money's role as a store of value. Money also would matter then. Cf. Paul Davidson, *International Money and the Real World*, London, Macmillan, 1982, pp. 68, 72, concerning the sense in which Clower dismisses the role of money. While Clower only stresses the means-of- payment function, Leijonhufvud cannot be accused of this.

16 J.A. Hobson, *The Science of Wealth*, London, Williams and Norgate, 1911?, p. 185.

17 Consequently those who hold that Keynes, unlike the classicists, perceived that money was the source of effective demand seem to draw too sharp a distinction. See, for example, Pietro Carlo Padoan, 'Interpretations of Keynes, monetary economy and price theories', *Rivista di Politica Economica: Selected Papers*, vol. 69, December 1979, pp. 73–118.

18 Keynes, *Collected Writings*, vol. xiii, pp. 505, 596–7. Curiously, Keynes did not respond to Robertson on this point (ibid., p. 519), and his reply to Hawtrey (ibid., p. 602) is brief and obscure.

19 See Stephen Hall, 'The cause of non-Walrasian equilibria', Imperial College of Science and Technology, University of London, no. 80/2, Discussion Paper in Economics, pp. 10–22. Some valid observations are made by Allan Drazen, 'Recent developments in macroeconomic disequilibrium theory', *Econometrica*, vol. 48, no. 2, March 1980, pp. 283–306, at pp. 299–301.

20 Drazen, op. cit., argues in this way. So does Frank Hahn, 'Keynesian economics and general equilibrium theory: reflections on some current debates', in G. Harcourt (ed.), *The Microeconomic Foundations of Macroeconomics*, Boulder, Colorado, Westview Press, 1977, ch. 1, p. 39.

21 This paragraph draws on L.B. Yeager in Robert W. Clower (ed.), *Monetary Theory: selected readings*, ch. 3, 'The medium of exchange',

pp. 37–60, at pp. 52–3. Of course, things are different if you assume that the price of the non-monetary asset is sticky. See David Currie, 'Effective demand failures: a further comment', *Scandinavian Journal of Economics*, vol. 79, 1977, pp. 350–3. For Keynes's obscure reply to the argument in the text, also made by Reddaway in 1936, see *Collected Writings*, vol. xiii, pp. 68–70.

22 Compare Sheila C. Dow and Peter E. Earl, *Money Matters: a Keynesian approach to monetary economics*, Oxford, Martin Robertson, 1982, pp. 106–7.

23 Paul Davidson, 'The marginal product curve is not the demand curve for labor and Lucas's labor supply function is not the supply curve for labor in the real world', *Journal of Post Keynesian Economics*, vol. 6, no. 1, Fall 1983, pp. 105–17, at p. 115; 'Reviving Keynes's revolution', *Journal of Post Keynesian Economics*, vol. 6, no. 4, Summer 1984, pp. 561–75, at pp. 567–8; 'Liquidity and not increasing returns is the ultimate source of unemployment equilibrium', *Journal of Post Keynesian Economics*, vol. 7, no. 3, Spring 1985, pp. 373–84, at pp. 380, n. 4, 381–3. Edward J. Nell, 'Keynes after Sraffa: the essential properties of Keynes's theory of interest and money: comment on Kregel', in Jan A. Kregel (ed.), *Distribution, Effective Demand and International Economic Relations*, New York, St Martin's Press, 1983, pp. 85–103, at p. 92, in effect agrees with Davidson.

24 Christopher Bliss, 'Two views of macroeconomics', *Oxford Economic Papers*, vol. 35, no. 1, March 1983, pp. 1–12, at p. 4, in a slightly different context, observes that substitution effects will be overcome by income effects. Agents will simply run out of money with which to purchase paintings if prices are forced to rise to extreme values. This, of course, assumes that the supply of bank credit is not perfectly elastic, whereas Davidson is an advocate of the endogeneity of the money supply.

25 Compare Davidson, *International Money and the Real World*, pp. 4, 8–9, 69, 273–4, n. 12.

26 Will E. Mason, 'Some negative thoughts on Friedman's positive economics', *Journal of Post Keynesian Economics*, vol. 3, no. 2, Winter 1980–81, pp. 235–55, at p. 240. Colin Clark also put this objection to me. Such conjecture (that Leijonhufvud is a crypto-monetarist) is not entirely unreasonable. Certainly, however, Leijonhufvud does object to the 'random walk monetary standard' prevalent in reality and, as a policy matter, is friendly to some form of monetary targeting. He also rejects wage-push theories of inflation, but does accept arguments supporting the partial endogeneity of the money supply. See Axel Leijonhufvud, 'Rational expectations and monetary institutions', Working Paper, no. 302, UCLA, Department of Economics, September 1983 (unpublished), and 'Constitutional constraints on the monetary powers of government', *Economia delle Scelte Pubbliche*, vol. 2, 1983, pp. 87–100.

27 This is an amazing charge ('Reviving Keynes's revolution', pp. 561–5), and it was also made belatedly by Joan Robinson. See Richard Kahn,

The Making of Keynes' General Theory, Cambridge, Cambridge University Press, 1983, p. 203.

28 Davidson, 'Reviving Keynes's revolution', p. 564 (emphasis in original).

29 ibid., p. 565.

30 Leijonhufvud, *On Keynesian Economics*, p. 98. Leijonhufvud's use of the term 'involuntary' in describing the generally experienced miseries was somewhat unfortunate. Plausibly, only labour is off its supply curve and trapped where the real wage exceeds the marginal disutility of labour. It is possible that other markets clear and that, (e.g.) given the state of demand, profits are being maximized (MR = MC).

31 Davidson fails to mention that this alone would distinguish Leijonhufvud's views from the Reagan proposal.

32 In other words, Pigou and windfall effects are abstracted from.

33 Remember that Leijonhufvud was writing about a hypothetical barter world when considering the possibility of a centralized solution.

34 Davidson, 'Reviving Keynes's revolution', pp. 566–7.

35 Leijonhufvud, *On Keynesian Economics*, p. 80 (emphasis in original).

36 ibid., p. 86.

37 Davidson, 'Reviving Keynes's revolution', p. 569.

38 Fundamentalists, of course, have other quarrels with Leijonhufvud. They object to his attempts to explain irreversible, sequential and monetary events (whether in the short or long run) in Walrasian terms. Whether Walrasian language can validly be used to discuss such matters, and whether Leijonhufvud gives adequate attention to fundamentalist themes revolving around uncertainty, is discussed later at some length. Davidson does not completely reject Leijonhufvud. Evidently, Davidson approves of the drift by Leijonhufvud towards the Marshallian way of doing microeconomics. See Geoffrey C. Harcourt (ed.), *The Microeconomic Foundations of Macroeconomics*, pp. 316–17.

39 Davidson, *International Money and the Real World*, p. 70.

40 ibid., p. 71.

41 Induced expenditure usually refers to expenditure which is a function of income. It does not necessarily mean that the prior receipt of income 'causes' it because higher anticipated income can be associated with expenditure today and the latter can still be regarded as 'induced'. When investment is described as induced there is no implication that higher sales receipts have directly financed the next period's outlay.

42 There is the question whether the irrationality behind the animal spirits said to govern autonomous investment can override the rationality implied by Say's Principle. In the absence of accumulated hoards, investors need to sell something (securities) to effect their plans, whether they were calculated or spontaneous, otherwise they would remain irrelevant fantasies. Reason wins by brute force, but there is a sense in which lenders can share the same bullish sentiments, supply funds or credit, and give the fantasy an objective existence.

43 Robert Clower and Axel Leijonhufvud, 'The coordination of economic activities: a Keynesian perspective', *American Economic Review*, vol. 65, no. 2, May 1975, pp. 182–8.

44 Objections raised by Dow and Earl concerning the multiplier have been discussed in Chapter 1.

45 Christopher Torr, *Equilibrium, Expectations and Information: a study of the General Theory and modern classical economics*, Cambridge, Polity Press, 1988, pp. 30–1, 78–84. See also John F. Brothwell, 'The *General Theory* after fifty years: Why are we not all Keynesians now?', *Journal of Post Keynesian Economics*, Summer 1986, vol. 8, no. 4, pp. 531–47, at pp. 539–41.

46 Compare Keynes, *The General Theory*, p. 261.

47 Torr, *Equilibrium, Expectations and Information*, p. 30.

48 Increased autonomous consumption of capitalists, rentiers or workers (if they have wealth to draw upon) is another possibility. The average propensity to spend is what is crucial if the community's marginal propensity to spend is less than unity.

49 Axel Leijonhufvud, 'What would Keynes have thought of rational expectations?', in David Worswick and James Trevithick (eds), *Keynes and the Modern World*, Cambridge, Cambridge University Press, 1983, p. 196. Note that *On Keynesian Economics*, part V, examines how autonomous expenditure needs to be raised by the Keynes or Pigou effects for recovery to occur. Leijonhufvud hardly overlooked the point.

50 Torr, *Equilibrium, Expectations and Information*, p. 6.

51 Leijonhufvud, 'What would Keynes have thought of rational expectations?', p. 196, n. 25, citing Keynes, *The General Theory*, p. 6.

52 Leijonhufvud, *On Keynesian Economics*, pp. 81; 95, n. 23 respectively (emphasis in original).

53 Leijonhufvud, 'What would Keynes have thought of rational expectations?', p. 198.

54 ibid., p. 198, n. 31.

Part three

Chapter five

IS-LM and the interest-rate dynamics

Introduction[1]

The longstanding loanable funds-liquidity preference debate remains unresolved. Textbook Keynesians, Leijonhufvud and the fundamentalists have made their quite distinct contributions.

The textbook version of how interest rates (r) vary with changes in income (Y) stems from Hansen. Saving flows affect r only *indirectly* by first reducing nominal income and thereby the transactions demand for money. Leijonhufvud[2] has criticized Hansen's analysis on the grounds that dynamic liquidity preference theory makes little sense. Leijonhufvud supports the loanable funds theory because it allows for the possibility that increased thrift *directly* affects r by increasing the flow of saving relative to the flow of investment. If r immediately fell to clear the initial excess supply of loanable funds, full employment would be preserved. The bears, however, are identified by Leijonhufvud as the agents who syphon the increased savings into speculative hoards and thereby prevent r adjusting fully. The multiplier then causes income to fall. Hansen and Leijonhufvud differ over the sequence of events. In Hansen, r can fall after Y falls because of an excess supply of money spilling over into the financial sector. In Leijonhufvud, Y falls because the prior decline in r was insufficiently large. Because the securities market is the quickest to adjust, r falls only once, and there are no subsequent indirect effects to counteract the downturn.

One writer with fundamentalist leanings, John Brothwell,[3] has pointed to what he regards as defects in Leijonhufvud's critique of Hansen. Brothwell defends Hansen, but only after modifying the textbook account by incorporating Keynes's somewhat neglected 'finance motive' for demanding money. Any reconciliation of the reductionist and fundamentalist perspectives, therefore, requires the resolution of these disagreements.

One finding is that Leijonhufvud's account is consistent with the finance-motive effect. This is because dynamic loanable funds theory can be formulated to encompass it. Second, Leijonhufvud is correct to criticize Hansen's approach, but only on account of its inaccurate expression. A more precisely framed description of the process of contraction reveals that r and Y do fall together through time and that the decline in r would cushion the downturn.

Leijonhufvud's argument can be summarized briefly.[4] In the face of a deflationary disturbance from full employment, the response of a simple, money-using system can be shown in Table 1. The banking system is assumed away and saving is either in the form of money hoards or securities. If the saving flow exceeds investment, then, initially, there is an excess demand for securities. If bears prevent r falling sufficiently, then in the next period, output is curtailed. Output falls until the flow of hoarding is zero.

Table 1 Effective excess demands

Initial	Labour	Commodities	Securities	Money	Sum
Initial	0	0	0	0	0
Stage 1	0	ES	ED	0	0
Stage 2	0	ES	0	ED	0
New	ES	0	0	0	< 0

Leijonhufvud's argument is extraordinary because, while denouncing Hansen repeatedly, he provides no sufficiently detailed alternative. He simply skips the interesting stages between stage two and the new short-run equilibrium and asserts that there are no indirect, or feedback, effects of r on Y.[5]

Brothwell argues that the incorporation of the finance motive preserves Hansen's basic result in that r and Y move together. If investors need to borrow money by selling securities in order to finance subsequent purchases of investment goods, then the demand for money changes prior to the actual transaction. Therefore, contrary to Hansen, r rises prior to the increase in income to which the new investment will later correspond. Conversely, prior to any observed decline in investment, r would fall because funds which are no longer required for investment in the next period are used instead to purchase securities. This implies that in disequilibrium, when saving and investment flows are unequal, r will be changing.

There is nothing to prevent Leijonhufvud from accepting this argument. Indeed, he tacitly relies on it in his stage one. It is couched in terms of the interest rate being determined by effective excess demands for securities. If Leijonhufvud did not make the same case himself, one reason could be that he simply never directed his attention to a full analysis of the adjustment process. Furthermore, Leijonhufvud apparently does not recognize that the finance motive is now used by the fundamentalists to displace the Cambridge argument that mere flows of saving and investment can have *no* direct effect on *r* because *r* is governed by stocks of money and securities.

Incorporating the finance motive allows an increase in investment to raise *r* by initially increasing the flow-supply of securities, and, in so far as greater thriftiness is reflected by an increase in the flow-demand for securities, one supposes that post Keynesians would accept that thrift can have a direct effect too. Indeed Brothwell[6] endorses the argument that a proper stock-flow model must allow for direct effects and that a properly told *IS-LM* story can capture this.[7]

Leijonhufvud apparently has not grasped the significance of the finance motive and how its advocates have used it.[8] He states:

> As far as I can understand, it only introduces a lag in the adjustments of output and loanable funds flows without otherwise affecting the sequence discussed.[9]

To illustrate the sequence of events, a very simple numerical example, which traces money as it circulates, is considered. Thus, it is comparable to the step-by-step approach of Dennis Robertson,[10] and complements Victoria Chick.[11] How much of the story Keynes, at various stages of his faltering ascent, would agree with is not the concern.[12]

Some examples

Take a two-sector system with an initial short-run equilibrium of $100 (*C* = $80, *I* = $20), the multiplier being 5. Money wages are constant although there is unemployment. In the output sector the short-run supply curve is horizontal in the relevant range although prices are assumed flexible to clear all supplied on any market day. The total money stock is $110 and the daily velocity of active balances is constant at 1. The velocity of hoards (idle money) is zero. With income at $100, $100 are active and $10 are idle in bear hoards. Precautionary and speculative demand schedules are held constant as tastes of hoarders are assumed unchanging. Savings out of a given income are not influenced by changes in interest rates. Initially, a permanent, rather than once-off, shift in the MEI schedule is examined.

I shall examine the argument on Leijonhufvud's terms so far as he uses the textbook, 'Keynesian' story attributed, fairly or not, to Hansen and Keynes. This is not a sophisticated account of interest rate dynamics by any means.

As the argument is easier to grasp in the reflationary rather than the deflationary case, we shall suppose that investors become more optimistic. In the absence of credit, the finance required to effect the additional expenditure must be borrowed from the hoarders. This is consistent with Keynes's 'finance motive' for demanding money, which is elevated to importance, with justification, by the fundamentalists, Davidson and Brothwell.

There is an increase in *r* to clear the additional flow supply of securities because, to obtain funds from the hoarders, who are assumed not to share the bullish sentiments of investors, they must be induced to become less liquid. As *r* rises, some envisaged investment projects will be cancelled to an extent depending on their interest elasticity, but this is assumed away for simplicity. Suppose that $21 of investment goods are ordered and produced, the additional $1 being borrowed from the hoarders. With a Robertson lag, consumption spending is unaltered. Day 1 concludes with idle balances of $9.

On day two, the newly engaged factors of production lend an additional 20¢, their increased savings out of yesterday's increased income, to investors.[13] Investors still wish to borrow $1 to sustain investment at $21. They therefore must borrow a further 80¢ from the hoarders and *r* will increase again despite the additional supply of savings (20¢), to induce hoarders to become increasingly illiquid.[14] Note that the consumers have earmarked 80¢ for consumption and it is not available for lending.[15]

We find that spending on day two is $21 + $80.80¢ and, incidentally, if consumption output is assumed lagged, then 'forced saving' – or 'automatic stinting' as Robertson[16] would say – is 80¢ so that the *ex post* *S* and *I* identity is thus explained. Idle balances are $8.20¢.

Table 2

$		Day 0	Day 1	Day 2	Day 3	Day 4	Day n
	C	80	80	80.80	81.44	81.95	84
	I	20	21	21.00	21.00	21.00	21
	V = A	100	101	101.80	102.44	102.95	105
	H	10	9	8.20	7.56	7.05	5
(Units)	*O*	100	101	101	–	–	105

If investment remains at $21 despite ever rising interest rates, then the new equilibrium is with an income of $105 (*C* = $84, *I* = $21), idle money being $5, and planned savings and investment flows being equal at $21. At the start of each day money needed to be borrowed by investors from hoarders and r rose.

For a summary of the process, refer to Table 2 where O is some sort of physical measure of output, V is the value of aggregate sales proceeds (which equals A, the quantity of money in active circulation) and H is the money in hoards. Average daily velocity is A divided by 110. Observe that an exact O figure would depend on how firms estimate daily demand given their uncertainty in disequilibrium.

Note the direction of causality. Hansen's conclusion is correct: income and r rise together. Nevertheless, as more cash is earmarked for consumption, it is repeated investment in excess of savings which, strictly speaking, causes r to rise. Consumers do not bid up interest rates as they already have the money to effect their spending. They have already earned it and do not put pressure on the securities market to satisfy their transactions demand. Those who are employed have plenty of money. Similarly, because consumption-good producers already have the proceeds of yesterday's sales and are enjoying profits, there is no necessary reason for them to borrow to finance the next day's output.[17] There is a subsequent deviation-counteracting factor which asserts itself daily (although the rise in r is cushioned by the daily increase in the flow of savings). Investment on day n will lie between $20 and $21, if the initial assumption of zero interest elasticity is relaxed.

In the converse deflationary case where the MEI schedule falls, every period in which investment remains at a figure lower than its original value will involve declining income and increasing hoards until equilibrium is reached. As more and more money flows into the securities market every day, r will fall to make it sufficiently attractive for bears to hoard. Depending on the interest elasticity of investment, the power of the multiplier is reduced and the decline in income is cushioned.[18]

To examine the effect of changes in r on the multiplier, consider the reflationary case. Had the final investment figure been less than $21 on account of some degree of interest elasticity, in this model the multiplier would still be at least one. A higher r early on day one emerged prior to the investment expenditure so a potentially higher deviation was reduced. Subsequent increases in r exist only if income rises beyond $101, that is, only if idle balances fall below $9. Investment cannot fall so that the new equilibrium is less than $101 simply because, if income fell to that point, r would fall to equal the value required to stimulate $21 of investment which was observed on day one: a *reductio ad absurdum*. Leijonhufvud[19] therefore need not have worried that induced variations in r would completely offset the initial shock, especially if the *LM* curve is fairly elastic so that the new equilibrium r will not have fallen much anyway.

For completeness, the case involving a once-off increase in I is represented in Table 3.

Table 3

$		Day 0	Day 1	Day 2	Day 3	Day 4	Day n
	C	80	80	80.80	80.64	80.51	80
	I	20	21	20.00	20.00	20.00	20
	$A = V$	100	101	100.80	100.64	100.51	100
	H	10	9	9.20	9.36	9.49	10
(Units)	O	100	101	100	–	–	100

The logic is not significantly affected. Falling daily income (which equals expenditure, A and V) is associated with progressive daily declines in r. On day 1, r rises (directly). On day n, initial hoards, r and Y have been restored.

Requiring brief attention is another criticism made by Leijonhufvud of Hansen's account. In the style of Horwich,[20] Leijonhufvud complains:

> Agents discover that they have 'too much cash' only *after* income has fallen; it is not the case, here, that requirements for transactions balances are scaled down already when spending-intentions (by entrepreneurs) are cut back. When people decrease their rate of spending of money on goods – so says the LP theory – the resulting increase in the ratio of their cash balances to their income is unintended and unanticipated.[21]

In other words, Hansen has suppressed an assumption that transactors are taken by surprise and cannot anticipate the decline in income and the reduction in required factor payments (Keynes's business motive). The criticism is a legitimate one as far as it goes, but it affects only the detail of the dynamic process and not the outcome itself because, as we have already seen, interest rates fall as income falls.

Leijonhufvud's objection makes sense if either (a) that day's needs are foreseen and that early in the day only the required balances are held and the rest is passed to the bears – but r and Y fall through time nevertheless, or (b) the new short-run equilibrium is perfectly foreseen and all the required portfolio decisions are effected in stage one so that we find ourselves in the realm of the instantaneous multiplier.

Post Keynesians in the Davidson camp might dismiss all this as nit-picking, and with some justification. They might re-express their portrayal of an upswing as follows. A multiplier-induced increase in household income causes an increase in profit when it is spent, which causes an increase in expected sales by firms in the consumption sector, which causes an increase in planned output, which causes investors again to borrow more from hoarders, and this causes r to rise. Thus, by a chain of logic, a rise in income 'causes' a rise in r! Textbook Keynesians merely have not specified who bids up r and who has 'too little' cash. They have spoken, erroneously, as though agents in general have found themselves with too little cash. Differences between Leijonhufvud and the fundamentalists would then vanish.

To monitor hoarding is neither essentially classical nor Keynesian. To the classicists (such as J.S. Mill), hoarding was considered an exceptional panic-induced increase in liquidity preference (which assumably would raise r). Keynes, I suggest, resisted using the word 'hoarding' because it suggested (to him) that people were merely temporarily *choosing* not to purchase investment and consumption goods. Keynes rightly felt that unemployment in the consumption sector definitely could not be interpreted merely as the necessary effect of voluntary thriftiness which was 'releasing resources for the higher stages of production'. An initiating shock might well be a voluntary decision not to invest, but, in the resulting short-run equilibrium, labour can be trapped in involuntary unemployment.

Nothing in this argument should be taken to suggest that, although the flow of savings influences *movements* in r, the *level* of r depends on thrift and productivity. It might depend even in the long run on self-fulfilling bear speculation as Keynes held (though Leijonhufvud doubts this). Furthermore, the possibility is not denied that changes in the propensity to hoard, which affect the desire to hold old stocks of bonds could outweigh the effect on r of the sales of new securities to investors. Differences of vision really separate Keynes and the classicists, not the logic of the minute details of dynamic adjustment.

The 'finance-your-losses' approach

This section deals with Keynes's views on interest rates and how an idea, pushed aside by Leijonhufvud (and most others), attracted much of Keynes's attention. If Keynes considered a multitude of ways by which to attack received loanable funds doctrine, then this could be seen to cast doubt on Leijonhufvud's view that the idea of inelastic price expectations is central to Keynes's thinking. Leijonhufvud can then be argued to be imposing an organizing vision which makes Keynes's thinking far more simple and readily coherent than it really was. Nevertheless, at the end of this discussion, we must accept that Leijonhufvud's case for inelastic price expectations is at its strongest so far as the bonds and money markets are concerned.

One of Keynes's arguments, which has been rather neglected, is his view that increased thriftiness would induce losses in the consumption sector of equal value and necessitate the borrowing of firms to cover those losses. The increased savings would never reach investors.

A peculiarity of Keynes's argument does not seem to have been stressed. The 'finance-losses' reasoning is very powerful if valid. Increased thrift is always deflationary. Additional saving never leads to investment and all the other arguments about bear speculation and the large stock of securities dominating the flow variables would be rendered superfluous.

Doubts about Keynes's reasoning were first raised by Hayek[22] in his comments on the *Treatise*. If money is borrowed, exactly what is it used to finance? In so far as losers in the consumption sector borrow, they preserve employment in the consumption sector and maintain the status quo. He reasons that Keynes assumes that, despite their losses, investment in the consumption goods sector is (misguidedly) being maintained instead of resources freely flowing to the higher stages of production. On this particular issue, Hayek's intuition is probably sound (if we assume that increased thrift will extend into the future).

Shackle[23] supported Hayek's attack on this point so it is surprising that Harrod[24] alludes to Keynes's arguments in such a favourable manner so many years later and without giving weight to the fact that the innovation gained, at best, lukewarm support when first propounded.

Even Joan Robinson accepted that Keynes's argument required elucidation and was not prepared to let it carry the full burden of preventing adjustments of the interest rate. Indeed in the process of explaining Keynes's *Treatise* she subtly nudges the finance-losses argument into the wings.[25] The finance-losses argument lingered in Keynes's mind and Hawtrey felt moved to raise objections to its re-emergence.[26]

Probably the most precise criticism of the doctrine stemmed from Robertson,[27] but, in the midst of the complexities, Keynes slipped free.[28] During the debate Robertson felt Keynes's case centred upon a 'hitch-up' in the flow of savings to investors. Robertson meant that bears intervened and siphoned off the funds, but Keynes invented a completely different objection and then attacked that instead. The substance of Robertson's objection, *according to Keynes*, was that the loss-makers in the consumption sector would have to telephone their bankers before the workers' savings could be lent to investors at lower interest rates.[29] It is difficult to see how Keynes could have possibly considered such a line of reasoning even implicit in Robertson's counter-argument.

Keynes, we can conclude, did consider that the finance-losses argument played some part in an assault on Say's Law which implied that all savings were invested to assure full employment. Inelastic price expectations play no necessary part in the attack.

To find out who is right a simple model can be built so that we can see the exact sequence of events. Let us consider a very simple economy, in which there are neither precautionary nor speculative demands for money, so that we can examine the 'finance-losses' argument in isolation. Although contrived, the following story illuminates the basic issues.

Suppose the daily income of a fully-employed economy is $100. One hundred workers, the entire labour force, are employed at a wage of 90¢ to make 100 units of output priced at $1. The consumption sector produces 90 units and employs 90 labourers, and investment accounts for 10 units and 10 labourers. The marginal product curves for each sector are the same and, for simplicity, are flat in the relevant range. No banks exist and securities are competitively sold by entrepreneurs if retained earnings are insufficient to effect expenditures.

At full employment, the wage bill (Q) is $90 (100 x 90¢) and the workers initially have an average propensity to consume of unity. Profits and investment equal $10 and employers spend nothing on consumption goods. In equilibrium, $C = 9 + {}^9\!/_{10}\, Q$. To continue in a Cambridge style, to suppress as many complications as possible, assume that, in response to a decline in demand for goods sold at a constant 'cost-plus' price, output is curtailed to that of the previous day's sales. The price of unsold goods does not fall within the market day to clear excess stocks. Inventories accumulate without storage costs, and output decisions are not influenced by the absolute size of unsold stocks.

To trace the circulation of money we assume that there is no bank money and that the quantity of outside money is $100, its maximum income velocity within any day being one. Workers keep their money income overnight and today's income is spent tomorrow morning. Stores selling consumption goods close at noon and today's output is bought with yesterday's income. Securities are sold in the afternoon until 4 p.m. and, as there are no motives to hoard money, borrowings are spent the next day. Workers in both sectors are paid for that day's output at 5 p.m. after the securities market has closed. If an entrepreneur borrows money to purchase investment goods in the afternoon, he places an order with the investment sector which produces and delivers it the next morning. Investors hold borrowings and retained profits overnight to spend the next morning.

On Monday morning workers spend $90, their entire earnings of the previous day, on consumption. The investment sector produces the goods ordered yesterday afternoon and sells them for $10, the level of yesterday's profits. By noon, the consumption employers have $90 in cash and the investment employers have $10. The profits earned by the former are $9 and the latter's is $1. In the afternoon employers pay their workers $90, the consumption sector paying $81 and the investment sector $9. That afternoon $10 of the investment goods are ordered with profits being earmarked for purchasing the goods tomorrow or they are lent to other entrepreneurs who so earmark them.

Suppose on Tuesday morning that workers decide without warning to save $10, reducing consumption to $80. The new comparative-static, consumption function is (if the negative intercept can be forgiven) $C = -1 + \frac{9}{10} Q$. Will this $10 find its way into investment to raise it to $20 and preserve full employment? As yet the investment sector is entirely unaffected by this shock, but consumption producers have produced 90 and only sold 80 units. They have lost $10 because they expected $9 of profit and, having only received $80 in revenue, cannot even afford to pay their workers the $81 wage bill. Certainly they will need to borrow at least $1 to meet their contractual obligation, and, if we assume for the moment that they will also wish to borrow $9 to maintain their autonomous investment at $9, in total they will borrow $10. Suppose that this sum is borrowed from the workers. The unspent $10 in the workers' pockets is handed to the entrepreneurs in return for securities. Because the increased demand for securities was matched by an equal increase in supply, interest rates do not change.[30]

On Wednesday, consumption producers curtail output to 80 and employ only 80 men, but investment spending remains at $10. Suppose workers continue to save $10. It seems that Keynes was right. Both sectors' flow supplies clear. Expenditure is $90 which, by noon, is in the hands of employers. The remaining $10 is held by the thrifty workers.

The consumption sector has received $80, but needs only $72 (90¢ x 80) to pay to workers thereby leaving them with $8 as retained profit which is earmarked for investment too after, perhaps, being lent to other entrepreneurs that afternoon. The investment sector has $10 and has earmarked $1 for investment, putting aside the remaining $9 to pay to its employees at the end of the day. On Wednesday afternoon the $10 held by workers as the unspent portion of Tuesday's income is borrowed but interest rates fall given the demand curve for investment. This $10 is earmarked for investment. Workers finally receive $81 as income. The other $19 are held by the employers.

On Thursday morning, $19 of investment goods are produced. The consumption sector continues to produce 80. We are almost at the result desired by the classicists, despite the detour pointed out by Keynes.

Here we cut off the story abruptly. Having introduced peculiar assumptions and lags we find that a cycle is generated and this obscures the essential point. If the cycle is dampened, the system converges to the classical outcome but we are not concerned – and neither were the discussants of fifty years ago – with the dynamic details. The purpose is simply to cast some light on the intuition involved. The complexities by virtue of the multiplier are not incorporated either.

Table 4

		N	C + I	W	F	L	B
Monday	9 am	–	–	90	10	–	–
	Noon	100	90 + 10	0	100	0	0
	4 pm	–	–	0	100	–	0
	5 pm	–	–	81 + 9	9 + 1	–	–
Tuesday	9 am	–	–	90	10	–	–
	Noon	100	80 + 10	10	90	10	–
	4 pm	–	–	0	100	–	10
	5 pm	–	–	81 + 9	10	–	–
Wednesday	9 am	–	–	90	10	–	–
	Noon	80 + 10	80 + 10	10	90	0	–
	4 pm	–	–	0	100	–	10
	5 pm	–	–	72 + 9	19	–	–
Thursday	9 am	–	–	81	19	–	–
	Noon	80 + 19	71 + 19	10	90	9	–
	4 pm	–	–	0	100	–	10
	5 pm	–	–	89.1	10.9	–	–

Note: *N*: employment (=output); *W*: cash holdings of workers; *F*: cash holdings of firms; *L*: losses (or the expected less the realized surplus for all firms); *B*: bond sales to workers.

The full dynamics depend on the lag structure and the specification of the consumption function. Also relevant was the assumption governing output in the investment sector. Had it been equal to yesterday's sales instead of being pre-ordered, then workers' savings would have been borrowed and spent thereby driving prices up unexpectedly and creating profits in the investment sector. Those profits would have been invested rather than repaid in part to workers and then in part spent on consumption.

Putting such matters aside, it remains puzzling as to exactly what it was that Keynes felt needed financing. In the story just told, only a shortfall of revenue in relation to pre-contracted costs to third parties (such as wages to employees) actually needed financing. The principle had to be stretched[31] to account for the need to finance hitherto internally financed investment. Keynes himself flirted with yet another idea, the need to finance inventory holdings.[32]

One small point requires attention. There is the case where money balances are eroded by entrepreneurs meeting losses from presumably pre-existing emergency funds. If borrowings replenish those dishoardings – and there is no certainty that these funds will be borrowed unless precautionary demands for cash have grown, since the whole point of such funds is that they would fluctuate, smoothing out the effect of erratic sales – money is not lost from circulation. Hitherto inactive funds held by entrepreneurs have been injected and hitherto active funds now hoarded by savers have been withdrawn. The injection of funds from prior hoardings will ultimately find their way to active expenditure unless for some cogent reason some recipient decides to hoard them. There is the case where borrowings are made to replenish funds used by entrepreneurs to engage factors of production. If borrowings are actively used to preserve the initial level of consumption output, it is clear that aggregate output will *grow* since the entrepreneurial dishoardings used previously to pay the factors of production will make their way into active circulation and the average velocity of circulation will rise. Consumption production will be the same in the next period but the re-expenditure of those dishoardings will stimulate the consumption and investment sector beyond their initial levels.

The preceding story has been rather turbid. Can anything of real value be extracted from it or is it just another look at a dead issue in the history of economic thought?

The general style of reasoning adopted here might have wider application to problems which occur when a transactor is constrained and, to effect purchases hitherto financed by past earnings, sells bonds. Furthermore, those who consider that the dynamic loanable funds and liquidity preference theories give different results when the commodity market fails to clear might consider the advantages of building a simple model so that each step and every transaction is made clear so that the pressures causing interest rates to change can be identified. In the story outlined above, the failure of the commodities market to clear was at the heart of the trouble, and the behaviour of the interest rate depended on assumptions made about whether there would be a pressing need to borrow money. Had the initial investment been financed by overdraft and if profits were not the source of investment funds, then the workers' idle savings could only, given an unchanged propensity to hoard, be disposed of at a lower interest rate.

It is not clear that the 'finance-losses' theme in its various forms involves a recognition of the essential nature of a monetary system in which disappointed sales expectations are reflected in a deficiency of purchasing power to effect subsequent transactions. One is tempted to say that Leijonhufvud could have drawn upon the theme as further evidence that, in Keynes's mind, the disruption of cash flows had those consequences. Unfortunately, we must keep a niggling doubt, as a kind of hangover from the *Treatise* with its widow's cruse, jar of Danaid and peculiarly defined terms of the fundamental equations, that 'losses' arise by definition in response to a decline in spending at an initial level of output. Because 'losses' carries with it an idea gained when the word is used in its conventional sense, Keynes perhaps felt that they must simply be covered, or 'financed', somehow.

It was Robertson who sought to go behind such catch-phrases to examine in (tedious) detail exactly where the money stock, which had leaked out of active circulation, had gone. Keynes, however, was hostile even to the notion that his views could be expressed in terms of a declining velocity of circulation or an increase in hoards. At times, Keynes seemed to think that to allow any direct effect of savings on interest rates and investment would restore the form of loanable funds doctrine that was based on Say's Law. Because Keynes's views on details were forever shifting, it is unwise to place too great a weight on any one strand of reasoning by which he sought to break the reliable nexus between saving and investment. Keynes's argument seemed to be that if savings grew as the initial response to an increase in the propensity to save, then income subsequently falls whether the savers hoard or whether they buy old securities.

Robertson's point was that even if savers buy an old security, rather than a new one from an intending investor, the recipient of the money either spends it or hoards it. If a bear hoards it, then it is that decision that causes income to fall. Had a bear not chosen to hoard, the money would have returned to the expenditure stream and income at the end of a relevantly defined period (that is, of sufficient duration to allow cash to flow in a full cycle) would not have fallen. If, to take another possibility, the seller of the bond had been required to 'finance his losses' and meet precontracted obligations, we have seen that unless the recipient firm or household hoards, the money will, after a lag, re-enter active circulation to maintain the initial level of income. What Robertson did not, however, appear to appreciate is that lags here can be of great importance, for example, in generating cycles or in giving rise to hiccoughs in aggregate activity.

The finding that Robertson and Keynes can be ultimately reconciled at a formal level by examining changes in hoards is not entirely trivial because it is by following cash through the system that we see that Keynes's 'finance-losses' argument is valid, but only during the transitional phase. A substantive issue is involved, not just a terminological one. It might even be that such transitional phases are of empirical importance and can, like bear speculation, prevent an instantaneous adjustment of the interest rate. Keynes's disagreement about the initial effects of increased thrift reflects his general attitude that it is naïve to rely on interest-rate adjustments even within a loanable funds context.

Leijonhufvud gives the impression that Keynes's basic contribution to the theory of interest rates was to attack classical theories of interest-rate movements which had overlooked the importance of bear speculation in the short run. If, however, an argument can be made that Keynes had various arguments – some sound, some not – used as devices to overthrow received doctrine in both its long-run and short-run manifestations, then Leijonhufvud can be said to have found a grand design in Keynes which is not really there.

Both the reductionists and the fundamentalists are confident in attributing to Keynes particular views about what governs the level and movements of the interest rate. Robertson's step-by-step method is illuminating because the issue of short-term movement is one of logic. Keynes clearly felt that issues of dynamics were part of his assault on classical theory. By contrast, controversy about the long-run determination of interest rates involves questions of vision. Preferences about future consumption and perceptions of future productivity, so far as they can be expressed in a determinate form which approximates objective reality, govern interest rates in classical models. Speculation based on expectations divorced from objective truth is the rival fundamentalist vision. If perceptions are deemed to be based entirely on imagination, then the conflict is irreconcilable from a fundamentalist point of view. If, however, some objective factors can vaguely be discerned and reasonable estimates of future consumption patterns can be made, then a classical perspective casts some light and a synthesis can be formed. These matters are explored in Chapter 6.

The role of *IS-LM*

Leijonhufvud is one of many economists with doubts about *IS-LM* as a means of capturing the essence of Keynes's insights. His chief claim to fame lies in how he has argued that, in many respects, the once orthodox interpretation of Keynes, which hinged on the peculiar elasticities of the *IS* and *LM* functions, could derive little support from Keynes's writings. He still considers[33] that *IS-LM* has caused us to look for the answers to the wrong questions. He maintains, for example, that the debate around whether the Pigou effect solves the riddle of a long-run equilibrium only indicates how little of Keynes's contribution was grasped. His position is now, and probably always has been, that *IS-LM* can be used but only with the greatest caution. This is because of difficulties in devising coherent dynamic stories to accompany explanations of how an essentially comparative-static model can be used in a disequilibrium context. We have seen how rival dynamic theories of interest-rate adjustment cannot readily be evaluated by employing the model. Similarly, the multiplier process cannot be explained in its dynamic detail. Leijonhufvud's initial complaint[34] was over the 'mechanical manipulation' of the *IS-LM* system rather than over its validity *per se*.[35] When used in the classroom, implicit assumptions about the information possessed by agents in disequilibrium are rarely made clear.[36] Controversy over the process of interest-rate adjustments raises broader questions about the value of using the *IS-LM* model. Reductionists regard it as a generally inadequate means to portray events in money-using systems.

It is not widely recognized that the substance of Leijonhufvud's approach is Marshallian rather than Walrasian. This statement would surprise many fundamentalists in view of how much of Leijonhufvud's 1968 book is devoted to arguments framed in terms of the Walrasian auctioneer and optimal Walrasian vectors. General equilibrium theory is relevant to Leijonhufvud simply because it enables the specification of static equilibria against which the outcome of any alternative system can be compared. He does not believe that general equilibrium theory so much explains reality. His argument is framed in Walrasian terms so that his criticism of it can be understood by the bulk of the profession who, especially in the United States, are themselves Walrasians.

In a little known source, Leijonhufvud contrasts the styles of Walrasian and Marshallian methods, and his point is made with flair:

> Marshallian plots are strong on action and have actors with robust motives of the sort that pre-Freudian authors would naturally capitalize: 'Precaution, Foresight, Calculation, Improvement, Independence, Enterprise, Pride and Avarice...(or) Enjoyment, Short-sightedness, Generosity, Mis-calculation, Ostentation, and Extravagance.' Steadfast shopkeepers compete in the market on center stage, enjoy profits and suffer losses, surrounded by stolid householders out for the thick gravy of Cardinal Utility.... Neo-Walrasian plots have as much action as an existentialist play and characters sicklied over with the pale cast of ordinal utility. With whatever patience can be mustered, one watches individuals, spooked by non-convexities and prone to nightmares over discontinuities, torture themselves with Hamiltonians and such to draw up plans for every conceivable contingency from here to eternity – and never act to either lose or gain.[37]

The *IS-LM* approach does not spell out how liquidity-constrained processes envisaged by Keynes differed in kind from those of quasi-barter models.

The Marshallian approach has features that make it attractive to the macrotheorist. It deals, in principle, with observables. It promises escape from deterministic and teleological riddles. The *ex post*, historical cast of the process analysis, together with the property that each good exchanges directly for money only, makes it the natural tool for the analysis of 'effective demand' problems.[38]

It is tempting to argue that Keynes did not emphasize a dual-decision hypothesis because he was brought up in a Marshallian tradition in which firms used money revenues to meet money costs. To Marshallians, pondering over the behaviour of effective demand is second nature. The importance of money is a shattering discovery only to those who have been educated to disparage Marshall's *ceteris paribus*, partial equilibrium approach in favour of Walrasian microtheory.[39] Indeed, this is exactly what Joan Robinson long ago noted.[40]

Leijonhufvud writes in fundamentalist vein that 'Neo-Walrasian closed system models have so far been inadequate – or, at best, grotesquely cumbersome – vehicles for representing the role of ignorance and the passage of time in human affairs.'[41]

Leijonhufvud's mentor, Clower, is as emphatic as any fundamentalist. He sees neo-Walrasian models whether emanating from Arrow and Debreu or from Modigliani and Patinkin as totally irrelevant to dealing with short-run processes. The transactions structure by which parties effect their exchanges is not specified. To rely on an auctioneer is to tell a 'fairy-tale' and indulge in 'science fiction'.[42] It took decades for the fundamental inadequacy of general equilibrium theory and its more aggregated kinsman, *IS-LM*, to be recognized. As the mathematical structure of the two branches were essentially the same, Clower's assault on the former by implication condemned the latter.[43]

The profession, however, seems reluctant to put *IS-LM* aside. The feeling seems to be that the explanation and description of processes relevant to a money-using system can still be expressed in an *IS-LM* framework, which, while silent on the subject of dynamics, is a handy way of representing some comparative-statics exercises. Similarly, the well-known strength and weakness of *IS-LM* is that it is indifferent to the competing dynamic theories of interest-rate adjustment. You can draw arrows onto your diagram according to whichever theory you embrace. Leijonhufvud himself is only prepared to use *IS-LM* if the assumptions about the transactions structure and information flows upon which postulated motion is said to depend are themselves justified.[44]

Suggested earlier in this chapter is a relatively reliable means to identify impacts of changes in effective demand. Follow money through complete circuits until they become self-replicating. Money flows are empirical whereas to explain processes purely intuitively, whether by relying on logical or mathematical definitions or on utterances by Keynes, is just metaphysics. Simple arithmetic can reveal specific mechanisms, and it is desirable to begin with outside-money models before attempting to incorporate finance and credit. Striving to capture complex processes with prose is difficult. The temptation is to rely on intuitive leaps and employ concepts (such as planned saving and revolving flows of credit) which are difficult to pin down to observable acts of expenditure in specific markets at particular times. For finance to be incorporated, the transactions and credit structures need precise specification and numerical examples are good means to ensure that all effects of a disturbance are followed through so that all parties can see what is happening. The loanable funds-liquidity preference debate would probably then proceed more rapidly.[45]

Notes

1 I gratefully acknowledge the comments of two referees for *The Bulletin of Economic Research*.

2 Axel Leijonhufvud, *On Keynesian Economics and the Economics of Keynes*, New York, Oxford University Press, 1968, pp. 29–30, 86–7, 182–3.

3 John Brothwell, 'A simple Keynesian's response to Leijonhufvud', *Bulletin of Economic Research*, vol. 27, May 1975, pp. 3–21, at pp. 15–21; 'Rejoinder', *Bulletin of Economic Research*, vol. 28, November 1976, pp. 123–6.

4 Leijonhufvud, *On Keynesian Economics*, pp. 86–9. A full discussion of Leijonhufvud's views, his understanding (or otherwise) of George Horwich (*Money, Capital, and Prices*, Homewood. Ill., Richard D. Irwin, 1964), the criticism of Leijonhufvud by Brothwell and by Brian Redhead ('On Keynesian economics and the economics of Keynes: a suggested interpretation', *Bulletin of Economic Research*, vol. 33, no. 1, May 1981, pp. 48–55) and Michael G. Phelp's attempted defence ('A simple Keynesian's response to Leijonhufvud: a comment', *Bulletin of Economic Research*, vol. 28, November 1976, pp. 117–20) cannot be attempted here.

5 Leijonhufvud even claims ('What was the matter with IS-LM?', in Jean-Paul Fitoussi (ed.), *Modern Macroeconomic Theory*, Oxford, Basil Blackwell, 1983, pp. 64–90, at p. 89, n. 26) that Keynesians who believe in dynamic liquidity preference should believe that *r rises* because an excess *demand* for money exists in the third row.

6 Brothwell, 'A simple Keynesian's response to Leijonhufvud', p. 17.

7 Problems persist however. Now that liquidity preference and loanable funds theories come to much (exactly?) the same thing once the finance motive is incorporated – see, for example, A.G. Hines (*On the*

Reappraisal of Keynesian Economics, London, Martin Robertson, 1971, ch. IV) – what has happened to now a seemingly forgotten strand of the debate, viz., whether *r* would move towards the *LM* cure or the curve tracing bond market equilibria? See Harry Johnson, *Macroeconomics and Monetary Theory*, London, Gray-Mills, 1971, pp. 13–14, for a 'bonds-funds relation' which passes through the intersection of the *IS* and *LM* curves. When the *IS* and *LM* curves shift, does the *BF* curve move too in one leap or in several stages to pass through the new intersection point? If the two theories predict not only the same qualitative changes but exactly the same *Y* and *r* combinations, do the *LM* and *BF* curves *coincide* or does a shifting *BF* curve cut the new *LM* curve at each successive stage? Another question: is Grossman's (Herschel I. Grossman, 'Money, interest, and prices in market disequilibrium', *Journal of Political Economy*, vol. 79, no. 5, September–October 1971, pp. 943–61) attempt to isolate *effective* excess demands in various markets readily translatable into *IS-LM-BF* terms?

8 Horwich (*Money, Capital, and Prices*, pp. 434–5) does seem to have grasped this significance, but he accuses Keynes of relying 'on the liquidation of existing securities' despite his citing a passage where Keynes plainly refers to the 'new issue market'. Evaluating Horwich and comparing his views to Leijonhufvud's is not the main purpose of this chapter however.

9 Axel Leijonhufvud, 'The Wicksell connection', in *Information and Coordination*, New York, Oxford University Press, 1981, p. 174, n. 65.

10 Dennis Robertson, *Essays in Monetary Theory*, London, Staples Press, 1940, pp. 72–4, 119.

11 Victoria Chick, *Macroeconomics after Keynes: a reconsideration of the General Theory*, Deddington, Oxford, Philip Allan, 1983, pp. 256–62.

12 The intricacies of the interest rate controversy cannot be examined here, but see S.C. Tsiang, 'Keynes' "finance" demand for liquidity, Robertson's loanable funds theory and Friedman's monetarism', *Quarterly Journal of Economics*, vol. 94, no. 3, May 1980, pp. 467–91 and Jan Snippe, 'Loanable funds theory versus liquidity preference theory', Institut voor Economisch Onderzoek, University of Groningen, Onderzoekmemorandum nr. 134.

13 This assumes that a portion is not hoarded, but this does not materially alter the story.

14 Compare Robertson (*Essays on Monetary Theory*, pp. 118–19) who, for simplicity only, finances continuous investment by new money creation rather than by the re-activation of hoards. Thus he avoids the complications which emerge as *r* rises and *I* falls as Chick (*Macroeconomics after Keynes*, p. 260) notes.

15 Had the transactions structure been different and had workers spent their income *before* investors were given the opportunity to borrow, then the entrepreneurs in the consumption sector would have the 80¢. They would have earmarked that money for payment to the factors of

production to be re-employed the next day and the 80¢ would still be unavailable for borrowing by investors. See Tsiang (op.cit., p. 477, n. 10) for more on this point.

16 Robertson, *Essays on Monetary Theory*, pp. 66–7.

17 Horwich, *Money, Capital, and Prices*, p. 433, is right up to this point.

18 In *IS-LM* terms the first step is a change in *r*, then *Y* changes, then *r* again and so forth. Whether or not the steps cut the *LM* curve or stay on one side depends in part on the responsiveness of *I* to changes in *r* under conditions of confusion and disequilibrium where the elasticity of the *IS* equilibrium locus might tell us little of any use.

19 Leijonhufvud, *On Keynesian Economics*, pp. 182–3.

20 Horwich, *Money, Capital, and Prices*, pp. 430–1, n. 52.

21 Leijonhufvud, 'The Wicksell connection', p. 174, n. 66.

22 F.A Hayek, 'Reflections on the pure theory of money of Mr J.M. Keynes (continued)', *Economica*, vol. 12, February 1932, pp. 22–44. (The argument is also mentioned in 'A rejoinder to Mr Keynes', *Economica*, November 1931, pp. 398–403, at pp. 401, 403.) Note that Hayek (p. 30) considered that losses in the consumption sector were a signal for resources to move into the investment sector, that is, resources are maldistributed. Keynes would label this, rightly, an assumption of full employment, its attainment resulting from the influence of thrift and productivity on the interest rate.

23 G.L.S. Shackle, 'Some notes on monetary theories of the trade cycle', *Review of Economic Studies*, vol. 1, no. 1, October 1933, pp. 27–38, at pp. 27–9.

24 Roy F. Harrod, *The Life of John Maynard Keynes*, London, Macmillan, 1951, p. 408.

25 Joan Robinson, 'A parable on savings and investment', *Economica*, vol. 13, February 1933, pp. 75–84, esp. pp. 83–4.

26 Keynes, *Collected Writings*, vol. xiv, pp. 27, 33–4. See also vol. xiii, p. 280.

27 D.H. Robertson, 'Mr Keynes' theory of money', *Economic Journal*, vol. 41, September 1931, pp. 395–411, esp. pp. 401–3. Only a masochist would study *Collected Writings*, vol. xiii, pp. 271–309 in an attempt to follow through the senses in which 'saving' and 'hoarding' were understood (or misunderstood) by the respective parties.

Robertson also considered that the finance-losses argument recurs in *The General Theory*, though in heavy disguise. See 'Some notes on Mr Keynes' general theory of employment', *Quarterly Journal of Economics*, vol. 51, November 1936, pp. 168–91, at pp. 187–8. Leijonhufvud seems inclined to agree with Robertson (*On Keynesian Economics*, p. 65, n. 13).

28 Keynes, 'A rejoinder', *Economic Journal*, vol. 41, September 1931, pp. 412–23, esp. pp. 416–19 (reproduced in *Collected Writings*, vol. xiii, pp. 219–36, esp. pp. 227–30).

29 At least Keynes presented Robertson's case in this way and Joan Robinson supports Keynes's version ('A parable on savings and investment', pp. 78–9).

30 If consumption employers had only borrowed $1 and were not afflicted by the urge to invest a given autonomous sum, they would have only borrowed the $1 at the existing interest rate needed to pay their workers. Consumption producers would then have invested nothing for they had no retained profits either to spend or to lend to each other. If workers wish to get rid of their remaining barren $9, they would then compete with each other by selling their money at lower interest rates until the quantity demanded of 'loanable funds', 'idle money' or whatever grew a further $9. Those who borrowed the remaining $9 to invest tomorrow may or may not be those very same entrepreneurs in the consumption-sector who suffered losses. The distribution of investment between employers might differ, *but the total does not*. The investment sector invests its $1 of normal profit and the other $9 finds its way to investment at a lower interest rate.

31 Kaldor suggested that borrowings are to maintain the standard of living of the owners of firms (Keynes, *Collected Writings*, vol. xiii, p. 239).

32 Keynes, *Collected Writings*, vol. xiv, p. 214, n. 2.

To accumulate planned inventories one might need to borrow, but why should one need to borrow in the case of unplanned inventories which actually exist and merely attract storage costs? Perhaps Keynes meant that these stocks reduce your liquidity and you need to borrow to effect purchases which would have taken place had those stocks been sold.

It is not clear exactly what authors mean by statements that 'a frustrated producer must finance his intended inventory accumulation' or that 'unintended investment must be financed in one way or another'. See respectively Herschel Grossman, 'Money, interest and prices in market disequilibrium', *Journal of Political Economy*, vol. 79, no. 5, September–October 1971, pp. 943–61, at p. 949; and Chen Fu Chang, 'Liquidity preference and loanable funds theories: a synthesis', *Australian Economic Papers*, vol. 15, December 1976, pp. 302–7 at p. 304.

It is difficult to talk sensibly about dynamics if no 'transactions structure', to use Leijonhufvud's terminology (*On Keynesian Economics*, p. 90), is specified. Otherwise we risk writing equations and drawing arrows on diagrams which represent motion physically impossible for transactors to achieve. Either that or the verbal description of the correctly plotted aggregate motion might sound plausible but be incorrect. This is one reason, incidentally, why Leijonhufvud is rightly cautious about *IS-LM* analysis.

33 Axel Leijonhufvud, 'What was the matter with IS-LM?', in Jean-Paul Fitoussi (ed.), *Modern Macro-economic Theory*, Oxford, Basil Blackwell, 1983.

34 Leijonhufvud, *On Keynesian Economics*, p. 31.

35 When Richard Jackman, 'Keynes and Leijonhufvud', *Oxford Economic Papers*, vol. 26, 1974, p. 259–72, at p. 264, criticizes Leijonhufvud for rejecting *IS-LM*, he seems to miss the very point Leijonhufvud sought to make. He asserts:

What Leijonhufvud appears to be attacking is not the IS-LM model as such, but particular assumptions that some 'Keynesian' economists may have made as to the shape of the underlying behavioural functions.

36 Leijonhufvud, 'What was the matter with IS-LM?', pp. 66–9, 79. For example, the rational expectations approach implies the short-circuiting of Keynesian adjustment paths.

37 Axel Leijonhufvud, 'The varieties of price theory: what microfoundations for macrotheory?', UCLA Discussion Paper, no. 44, January 1974 (unpublished), pp. 45–6, citing Keynes, *The General Theory of Employment Interest and Money*, London, Macmillan, 1936, p. 108.

38 Leijonhufvud, 'The varieties of price theory...', p. 36.

39 Leijonhufvud (ibid., pp. 1–2) notes that, in the US, neoclassical microtheory had attracted great prestige and that for a generation almost everybody had been trained in the Walrasian tradition (ibid., p. 4). The Chicago School defended Marshall on methodological, rather than on microtheoretical, grounds.

40 Joan Robinson, 'Book Review' of *On Keynesian Economics*, in *Economic Journal*, vol. 79, September 1969, pp. 581–3.

41 See Axel Leijonhufvud, 'Schools, "revolutions" and research programmes in economic theory', in *Information and Coordination: essays in macroeconomic theory*, New York, Oxford University Press, 1981, pp. 291–345, at p. 345, n. 67, for the passage quoted and pp. 329, n. 51; 343, n. 62.

42 Robert W. Clower, 'Reflections on the Keynesian perplex', *Zeitschrift für Nationalökonomie*, vol. 35, 1975, pp. 1–24, at p. 10. For Leijonhufvud's view, which is similar, see *On Keynesian Economics*, p. 230.

43 Clower, 'Reflections...', pp. 11–12.

44 Leijonhufvud, 'The Wicksell connection', pp. 140–51. Who would reject supply and demand curves *per se* simply because they do not in themselves embody rules about expectations upon which cobweb dynamics are based?

45 For some evidence of the imprecision of prose relative to arithmetic, see A. Asimakopulos, 'Finance, liquidity, saving, and investment', *Journal of Post Keynesian Economics*, vol. 9, no. 1, Fall 1986, pp. 79–90; Jan A. Kregel, 'A note on finance, liquidity, saving, and investment', *Journal of Post Keynesian Economics*, vol. 9, no. 1, Fall 1986, pp. 91–100; Paul Davidson, 'Finance, funding, saving, and investment', *Journal of Post Keynesian Economics*, vol. 9, no. 1, Fall 1986, pp. 101–10; Peter G. McGregor, 'Professor Shackle and the liquidity preference theory of interest rates', *Journal of Economic Studies*, vol. 12, no. 1/2, 1985, pp. 89–106.

Chapter six

On bootstraps and traps

Introduction

This chapter deals with the theory of interest rates so far as bear speculation plays a part. Whether interest rates can raise themselves by their bootstraps is discussed from both the theoretical and exegetical perspective. Attention is also devoted to the existence and role of the liquidity trap in Keynes's writings.

Fundamentalists tend vehemently to reject the role of thrift and productivity in determining interest rates. If investment is unstable in the real world, then fluctuations of the transactions and finance demands for money persistently agitate the financial sector. Furthermore, regardless of any independent influence thrift might or might not have, fundamentalists consider that speculation over future interest rates causes agents to adjust the composition of their portfolios. There would then be no particular tendency towards any long-run equilibrium. The interest rate would be by nature a restless variable, as would income. In so far as hydraulic Keynesians once accepted that the liquidity trap could emerge on account of bear speculation, then at least some part of Keynes's vision was preserved. Speculation, however, promoted the rigidity of interest rates in the textbook approach. To a fundamentalist, by contrast, speculation and price rigidity can scarcely be reconciled, because the former connotes disorder and volatility if Knightian uncertainty prevails.

Leijonhufvud's views on such matters are clear. He maintained[1] in 1968 that the 'Liquidity Trap notion...[was] explicitly repudiated by Keynes'. Keynes wrote: 'But whilst this limiting case [absolute liquidity preference] might become practically important in future, I know of no example of it hitherto.'[2]

Leijonhufvud accepts the importance of bear speculation[3] because it allows the role of interest rates greater prominence than that accorded it by the Keynesians, but he rejects liquidity preference both as a viable theory of dynamics (as we have seen) and as a coherent theory of the long-run determination of interest rates. Leijonhufvud[4] appeals for 'a viable synthesis of the worthwhile elements of classical theory and Keynes' theory'.

His suggestion is that bear speculation can be confined to the theory of short-run movements while the domain of the classical theory is that of the long-run level of the interest rate. By contrast, it is argued here that it is sensible to consider Keynes to have held that speculation can be a long-run phenomenon and that savings and investment can merely have effects on short-term movements. It is possible that real forces, even in the long run, cannot overcome speculation attaching to the minimum sustainable rate of interest.

Leijonhufvud feels uncomfortable about Keynes's view that the interest rate 'may fluctuate for decades about a level which is chronically too high for full employment'.[5] In 1968, Leijonhufvud felt that this statement should be read in conjunction with views in the *Treatise* where the 'obstinate maintenance of misguided monetary policies' was the cause.[6] Later Leijonhufvud came to realize that perhaps Keynes meant to uphold a radical view on speculation. Ten years later he more confidently asserted that Keynes's views were implausible and false.[7]

Leijonhufvud accepts that Keynes's theory is of a bootstraps kind as it stood.[8] This is because Keynes, somewhat carelessly, did not direct his attention sufficiently to long-run forces at work and tended to treat the long-run rate as given in much the same way as he did the money wage.[9]

By contrast to Leijonhufvud, the approach taken here is to stress the conventional character of the interest rate and to argue that Keynes was prepared, if pressed, to resort to the liquidity trap as a means to defeat classical arguments to the effect that money-wage deflation could have restorative consequences. Against the fundamentalists, a case is made that speculation and stability are conceivably consistent. While the existence of the trap is not essential to Keynes's model, if it does exist in some circumstances, then one aspect of the old hydraulic account can in part be defended.

Because money wages are relatively stable in practice, deflation to increase real balances has never been seriously put to the test. Neither have saturation bond-purchases been attempted with a view to reducing long rates and defeating a depression. Passages in Keynes exist to suggest that the trap could in logic prevent even the theoretical possibility of the automatic restoration of full employment. The success of monetary policy would depend on how experimental the government's easy monetary policy was seen to be. Injudicious expansion in practice is more liable to be defeated by perverse shifts in private sector behaviour rather than by the liquidity trap. It is unlikely that money-wage deflation is, however, likely to be seen as anything other than an extreme and ill-judged policy.

Keynes had doubts about his earlier views[10] on how monetary policy could be implemented:

> Just as a moderate increase in the quantity of money may exert an inadequate influence over the long-term rate of interest, whilst an immoderate increase may offset its other advantages by its disturbing effect on confidence; so a moderate reduction in money-wages may prove inadequate, whilst an immoderate reduction might shatter confidence even if it were practicable.[11]

Keynes apparently envisaged a knife's edge, or, on a literal reading, he could be doubting the very existence of a policy which even *could* be successful. If neither moderate nor immoderate policies could work, what is left? The problem of non-existence seems the more acute for the case of flexible money wages, the mechanism of vital theoretical interest to preserve the long-run, self-adjusting nature of the classical system.[12] In practice, the social unrest induced by strenuous wage-cutting policies could only undermine confidence and increase bearishness. A wage policy can 'shatter' confidence while monetary policy is liable merely to 'disturb' it.

Conventions and interest rates

Keynes emphasizes the durability of the normal rate of interest:

> [I]ts actual value is largely governed by the prevailing view as to what its value is expected to be. *Any* level of interest which is accepted with sufficient conviction as *likely* to be durable *will* be durable...[13]

If the fluctuations caused by changing real activity and therefore the transactions demand for money can be abstracted from, as is reasonable in considering the logical character of a state of long-run equilibrium in which entrepreneurial expectations have long been given and in which the consumption sector has fully adjusted to the impact of the multiplier, then we can examine the behaviour of speculators in isolation to see if there is reason for their views to change.

Leijonhufvud believes that savers will ultimately realize that the interest rates they seek are beyond those which investors are prepared to pay them, and the savers will thus relent. British fundamentalist Keynesians, on the other hand, prefer to argue that the interest rate is, within conventional limits, an inherently restless variable and, for example, bulls and bears who expect a change will be disappointed and adjust their portfolios thereby inducing a change in some direction or other in interest rates. A middle position, stressing conventions, is possible where interest rates are both stable and too high for full employment.

Keynes's emphasis on the conventional foundation of interest rates were not stray remarks:[14]

> It is evident...that the rate of interest is a highly psychological phenomenon.

> It might be more accurate to say that the rate of interest is a highly conventional, rather than a highly psychological phenomenon.

> [I]t may fluctuate for decades about a level which is chronically too high for full employment; – particularly if it is the prevailing opinion that the rate of interest is self-adjusting, so that the level established by convention is thought to be rooted in objective grounds much stronger than convention...

> [It] seldom or never falls below a conventional figure.

Keynes clearly argues that fluctuations about the normal level are, first, due to subtle and unpredictable changes in expectations that alter the balance between the bull and bear camps and are, second, due to changes in real activity which affect the demand for transactions purposes. The normal *level* is governed by convention, real forces partially account for short-run *movements*. In this interpretation, although speculation exists in the *Treatise*, in *The General Theory* it becomes dominant. There is an evolutionary continuity and yet a clear shift in emphasis which indicates a qualitatively different vision.

Keynes, however, does, in a tantalizing titbit, blur what is often a sharp distinction in his more fundamentalist sounding writings between the real and objectively true and the expected and subjectively perceived. In answering a question about what governs the liquidity premium that a saver seeks he remarked, in some rough notes of 1945:

> In practice, of course, what some stockbroker who knows nothing about it advises him, or convention based on old ideas or past irrelevant experience. But assuming enlightened self-interest (which probably influences convention) it is your expectation... and uncertainty about the future changes in the r. of i.[15]

Keynes also described the circumstances necessary to upset the normally durable convention. It is likely that

> the dismay and uncertainty as to the future which accompanies a collapse in the marginal efficiency of capital naturally precipitates a sharp increase in liquidity-preference – and hence a rise in the interest rate.[16]

The interest rate, instead of falling, rises. This possibility is not emphasized by Leijonhufvud as he considers changes in liquidity

191

preference and the MEI schedules outside of the domain of the basic model.[17]

Theoretical foundations of the trap

Does it make sense to have a theory of long-run rates of interest which dismisses thrift and productivity?

The extent to which Keynes's argument raises itself by the bootstraps need not be exaggerated, even if Keynes himself sometimes does. The origin of the interest rate might well lie in thrift and productivity. If money made available to borrowers is scarce, then, because in the first day of Eden there is no past experience upon which to base speculative expectations, real forces are all that remain.[18] If, over a period of time, interest rates are fairly stable,[19] conventions evolve and speculation can historically emerge as the dominant partner.

It might also be that governments have tended to act to prevent undue changes in interest rates and have played an essential role in this evolution. This makes bonds attractive to those who represent the interests of risk-averse widows and orphans. It is worthwhile to contrast the stability of the bond market to that of the share market where the government does not have a history of intervention and which is all the more uncertain by virtue of shares not guaranteeing an income to its owner.[20]

Whatever has accounted for the emergence of conventional valuations, are they so durable that the trap is a possibility? In this connection, mention should be made of an argument of Johnson.[21] He suggests that, if periods of low income persist, then the low interest rate that arises on account of the low transactions demand for money, will ultimately reduce the average observed interest rate and therefore the 'norm' upon which speculation is based.

This is plausible, but it need not defeat a long-run liquidity trap. The value of interest in the trap is not necessarily a function of the *average* level of recorded rates, although bears would be guided by that criterion for interest rates that arise above that value. If interest rates had been consistently low at 2 per cent, this does not disconfirm the belief that there is an absolute floor at $1\frac{1}{2}$ per cent. If people are unanimous on the basis of past behaviour about the *absolute* range within which interest has fluctuated hitherto, prolonged experience at the low end of the spectrum need not affect expectations about the whereabouts of the lower boundary. Consequently, the 'Johnson effect' might cause interest rates to sag to just above $1\frac{1}{2}$ per cent, but if the rate required to restore full employment has a value of less that the value at the trap, nothing can be hoped for. Just because the interest rate is not merely what people expect it to be on account of indirect 'real' influences, this does not imply that it can be a value which nobody expects it can be.

There is no clear reason why the perceived floor should depend upon the average of recorded rates, yet no suggestions are confidently offered here to explain how the floor is determined initially. Perhaps it is a figure 'just below' the lowest value ever recorded during a 'relevant' historical period. It might be that the persistent low levels might affect the size of the gap between the floor and the lowest realized figure, thereby causing the floor to sag, but the point is too hypothetical to warrant further examination.

It is true that speculation ordinarily concerns the differences of opinion about deviations from the safe or normal value for interest rates whereas the trap concerns some absolute figure. The trap, however, is abnormal in that it is a limiting case involving uniformity of bearish sentiment. Quotations stressing the importance of perceived average figures[22] are irrelevant to the issue of the existence of a further constraint on changes in interest rates, namely, an absolute floor.

Leijonhufvud maintains[23] that Keynes suggests an unstable, long-run, demand-for-money function and that this implies that the perceived 'safe' level of interest rates will be revised over time. The passages he cites,[24] however, do not deny the argument in the text that experience can confirm a level as being 'safe' as much as it can cause expectations to change. Even if interest rates 'crumble' in the face of recession this does not deny the logical possibility that there exist absolute values so low that everybody perceives them as diverging significantly from a safe figure.

If one postulates that investors remain pessimistic but that the interest rate is an inherently stable variable by virtue of its history, how can the system plausibly respond? One possibility is that savers are prepared to hoard their accumulations of cash forever in the belief that to buy a bond at a momentarily lower interest rate is virtually equivalent to throwing money away.

Another possible reaction is that, because money is barren as a store of value, savers will change their plans and adopt the second-best strategy of spending some portion of their hoards on consumption. Entrepreneurial pessimism and bearishness could therefore affect the system's growth path. If dishoarding generates full employment the very long-run investment share declines.

In some respects this resembles Leijonhufvud's description of what happens if the Pigou effect bears the full brunt of the adjustment in response to a long-run decline in money wages.[25] As the Pigou effect operates on consumption and leaves the relative price of capital 'too low' for full Walrasian equilibrium, he finds that the size (and structure) of the capital stock will be distorted in the very long run. When savers ultimately decide to deplete their savings they will find to their dismay that the physical capital stock does not exist to meet their demands. The difference between these two cases is that, in the former (when responding to the trap), the savers have dishoarded and have chosen to save less. They do not anymore have the money which they ultimately find has a less than planned command over real resources. They consciously selected a different consumption path. It is only on the Pigou-effect route where savers are ultimately disappointed.

A third possibility is that as time goes on the convention will set rock-solid in the absence of some traumatic shock.[26] Bulls and bears might steadily dwindle in population but this need not set the interest rate adrift. The market might become inhabited by oxen, if the extension of the zoological analogy can be forgiven. Oxen are the stodgy, conservative neuters who only feel comfortable in a predictable and safe environment. Their inertia and refusal to believe that rates will fall stems more from a lack of imagination and drive than from shrewdly planned speculative strategies.

Floors to interest rates therefore can make sense. However, some would have misgivings about the theoretical soundness of the trap having in mind a discussion by Patinkin.[27] In particular, for the financial sector to absorb unlimited quantities of money, unlimited supplies of bonds would need to be given in return. Patinkin rightly notes that a point could arise where the government becomes the sole debt-holder as only the government has no qualms about holding bonds at low interest rates. This outcome indicates that monetary policy could have limitations because in order to 'succeed' the economy's institutional structure is radically altered and government intervention is far from being as subtle and indirect as its advocates claim are its principle advantages over fiscal policy. Curiously, however, Patinkin concludes that this 'is a limitation which originates in political, and not economic factors'.[28] If it is logically possible that the private financial sector can fail to allow interest rates to fall to their optimal level, why label this limitation 'political'? If the bears refuse to yield, this is an entirely 'economic' phenomenon. The trap cannot be dismissed on simply semantic grounds.

Whatever might be felt about the trap at the purely theoretical level, the question still remains whether Keynes indeed relied upon it. This requires textual examination.

The liquidity trap in Keynes

In view of the emphasis given to conventions and to the defence against the bootstraps criticisms, it is probably no surprise that disagreement with Leijonhufvud's denial of the liquidity trap is part of this interpretation of Keynes.

Leijonhufvud has been criticized by Jackman, Brothwell and Friedman,[29] the last of them giving extensive evidence strongly suggestive of the trap. Yet, extraordinarily, Leijonhufvud, in 1978, was prepared to maintain his position.[30]

While it is difficult to be confident that one has understood Leijonhufvud's position, he now seems, fully in accordance with his earlier views, to argue as follows. The trap could plausibly exist but only on Keynes's 'Day of Judgement', that is, in the 'very long-run' context of the secular stagnation hypothesis.[31] It is only in this situation in which full information of the real parameters of thrift and productivity has become known, that full employment can be nevertheless threatened. Leijonhufvud (rightly) reasons that the Pigou effect must take the burden of adjustment because *real* forces have put a floor on interest rates. One is surely entitled to complain that it is strange to refer to such a situation as a 'trap' for the simple reason that rates are 'right' (conforming as they do to the state of time preference, there being, in this world of certainty, no speculation which prevents their adjustment). It is a 'real trap' rather than a liquidity trap, and it is easily escaped (in theory at least) by the Pigou effect. Leijonhufvud is playing with words. There is no reason to follow him and confine Keynes's remark that the trap 'might become practically important in future'[32] to the case where capital saturation is postulated.

If there is a liquidity trap in *The General Theory* Leijonhufvud has problems. Even if Leijonhufvud is taken to argue that in the long run, through the Keynes effect, recovery can in logic occur, though conceding in practice that other forces would swamp the benign effects of lower interest rates, he cannot allow Keynes to have a theory of interest-rate movements which can rule out even the conceptual possibility that endogenous and fully restorative mechanisms must exist.

Furthermore, in denying the trap, Leijonhufvud plays down other phenomena to which Keynes appeared to attach significant weight. Indeed as a possible explanation of a floor to the interest rate, they seem to have a roughly equal footing with speculation. Keynes[33] saw a role for borrower's and lender's risk, and for the cost of bringing both parties together. Risks of failure of an intended project together with the lender's fear of default provide a difficulty 'in the way of bringing the effective rate of interest below a certain figure'.[34]

One can understand Leijonhufvud's aversion. Price rigidities rather than sticky adjustments would then become part of Keynes's message. Perhaps they are *ad hoc* afterthoughts relevant only in the crisis phases of the trade cycle and therefore inessential to the basic model, but perhaps they also indicate that such precautionary motivations are strong and durable in the face of depressed conditions. Furthermore, there is the hint that those expectations about riskiness are fairly volatile and depend not only upon current and past circumstances, but involve extrapolation into the future, which explains why some, unlike Leijonhufvud, would prefer to emphasize these moral risks.

During a boom the popular estimation of the magnitude of both these risks...is apt to become unusually and imprudently low.[35]

Keynes's views on the trap have certainly puzzled many. Differences of opinion about what Keynes said are widespread. Hansen[36] after citing Keynes[37] to substantiate the legitimacy of absolute liquidity preference finds Keynes's retreat in knowing of no example hitherto as 'strange and inconsistent', and goes on to suggest that US experience, especially from 1934 on, provides a good example.

Patinkin, who undertook a close and systematic analysis, considered that Keynes viewed the trap as a theoretical possibility and a phenomenon of possible future, but little contemporary, relevance.[38] He could only find one isolated passage[39] where the trap was discussed as if relevant to current policy-making.

There appear, however, to be several passages which suggest that policy-makers at that time would be well advised to bear in mind the trap. While not believing the trap has been experienced hitherto, its presence is threatened. Keynes even nominates 2 per cent as the figure lying just below the floor.[40]

Some evidence in favour of the trap as a matter of practical concern appears in chapter 23 when he refers to a land with which he was familiar, though at a distance:

The history of India at all times has provided an example of a country impoverished by a preference for liquidity amounting to so strong a passion that even an enormous and chronic influx of the precious metals has been insufficient to bring down the rate of interest to a level which was compatible with the growth of real wealth.[41]

Leijonhufvud's position certainly is open to more criticism than is Patinkin's because the latter accepts that Keynes conceived of the possibility of the trap and repudiated it only as a current practical concern. Keynes expressly refers to the 'certain psychological minimum'.[42] (Indeed, as Jackman[43] has pointed out, Leijonhufvud has a blind spot when it comes to the word 'minimum'.) One must agree with Patinkin that Keynes at the very least considered the trap as a theoretical possibility.[44]

Patinkin also points out that no allusion is made to the trap where it might have been reasonable to expect it.[45] Thus Keynes could not have considered it of much practical importance. While Patinkin does not make the stronger claim that Keynes denies the purely theoretical importance of the trap, nevertheless some comment on his argument can be made. In reply, it could be said that passages which assert that money-wage cuts could result in full employment do not weaken other passages which state that other forces, such as the trap, could nevertheless thwart recovery. Keynes wrote

> [T]here might be no position of stable equilibrium except in conditions of full employment; since the wage-unit might have to fall without limit until it reached a point where the effect of the abundance of money in terms of the wage-unit on the rate of interest was sufficient to restore full employment.[46]

It is true that here, as Patinkin notes, the trap is not mentioned and that only *one* result is described, but the trap is perhaps irrelevant in this context. First, Keynes says 'might' twice, which indicates that not all possibilities (such as the trap) were encompassed. Furthermore, the meaning of 'stable equilibrium' is not clear. Were the trap in existence, there conceivably could in one sense be no 'stable equilibrium'. If interest rates did not fall then, abstracting from other real balance effects, unemployment would persist and money wages would continue to fall. There would therefore be no equilibrium of prices and quantities. Quantities remain constant, but not prices. 'Stable equilibrium' could refer to both prices and quantities being constant.

This sounds contrived but it is fully consistent with Keynes's earlier argument[47] where he refers to two possible long-period 'positions', one of full employment and one of unemployment. The latter 'position' made possible by the trap is not an 'equilibrium'. There was therefore no need for Keynes to mention the trap in the context where Patinkin expected it, and to omit it there does not mean, as Patinkin suggests, that it must therefore play no important role in Keynes's system. Consider the passage in question:

> [T]here will, it is true, be only two possible long-period positions – full employment and the level of employment corresponding to the rate of interest at which liquidity-preference becomes absolute (in the event of this being less than full employment).[48]

This distinction between 'equilibrium', of which there is one, and 'position' of which there are two sounds highly artificial yet apparently Keynes used these terms in this way.[49] He did not use the word 'equilibrium' to describe the two possible 'positions'. That term was reserved for the multitude of price and quantity equilibria which were possible only if money wages were given – a proposition which Keynes took Ricardo to have denied. Keynes held that monetary policy was not nugatory if money wages were given, that is, if the government could actively use monetary policy to change employment as would be possible where no automatic tendency to full employment existed (as Ricardo had held).

Keynes was himself, however, not too dogmatic:

> The point upon which I shall *cast doubt* – though the contrary is generally believed – is whether these 'automatic' forces will, in the absence of deliberate management, tend to bring about not only an equilibrium between saving and investment but also an optimum level of production.[50]

A slightly stronger-sounding statement is:[51]

> On the one side are those who believe that the economic system is, in the long run, a self-adjusting system, though with creaks and groans and jerks, and interrupted by time lags, outside interference and mistakes.... But they do believe that it has an inherent tendency towards self-adjustment, if it is not interfered with and if the action of change and chance is not too rapid.... On the other side of the gulf are those who reject the idea that the existing economic system is in any significant sense, self-adjusting.... There is, I am convinced, a fatal flaw in that part of the orthodox reasoning which deals with the theory of what determines the level of effective demand...; the flaw being largely due to the failure of the classical doctrine to develop a satisfactory theory of the rate of interest.[52]

Note that Keynes finds fault with the *long-run* classical theory of interest rates. Furthermore, the interesting question arises as to the meaning of self-adjustment 'in any significant sense'.[53]

With regard to the latter, it is now generally agreed[54] on pragmatic grounds that automatic recovery is likely to be too bumpy and too slow ('creaks and groans and jerks' as Keynes put it). Pigou never recommended wage-deflation as a policy, advocating instead public works, as did Keynes.

A more penetrative understanding of 'significant sense' stems from Leijonhufvud. Adjustments, possible in theory, are themselves of little value beyond the symbolic. Even if deflation did not destroy the money-using system, then the interest rate sufficient to offset pessimism, and the money wage required to restore full employment by a Keynes effect, would both be 'too low' relative to their ideal Walrasian values. Furthermore, if the Pigou effect were relied upon the system would then be off its ideal growth path. Further dislocation would ensue; the brief restoration of full employment would be a hollow theoretical victory. Leijonhufvud seems content to stop here.

There is, however, a more radical sense in which endogenous adjustments which could occur are 'insignificant'. Even if (to agree with Leijonhufvud) there exists a hypothetical interest rate which could restore full employment, there might be no means of achieving it on the grounds of the trap. The main remedy suggested by Keynes in *The Listener* was to reduce the interest rate, but by 1936 perhaps Keynes's views had changed. The difference of view, according to the interpretation suggested here, was not due entirely to a perception of the practical difficulty of causing interest rates to fall, but rather was due to the fear that it could prove impossible to reduce them because speculation could prevail even in the long run.

Keynes gives equal weight to two theoretical possibilities neither of which has ever been experienced in reality.[55]

[T]here will...be only two *possible* long-period positions – full employment and the level of employment corresponding to the rate of interest at which liquidity preference becomes *absolute*.[56]

Leijonhufvud has been inconsistent. If he rejects the trap as irrelevant because it has never been experienced hitherto, then so too must he reject the Keynes effect as irrelevant. But he emphasizes the Keynes effect.

Some concluding remarks on the trap

The trap is defended as a logical limiting case, hitherto not experienced even in the deepest depression recorded because, in fact, monetary authorities did not then attempt to purchase long bonds with any vigour and because flexible-wage policies were not pursued either. The evidence for the existence of a trap is stronger for the case of flexible money wages. Keynes did not claim that monetary policy was impotent, only that in deep depression it is impracticable – on this point Leijonhufvud's views are confirmed. Under ordinary conditions, and this embraces the case of sluggish real activity, the trap is, in practice, not responsible for the inadequacy of monetary policy.

Drawing *LM* schedules with a significantly large horizontal portion does not accord with Keynes's writings, but at low levels of income one can reasonably represent his position by a curve that is very flat.

In logical time, it is possible to play with such theoretical possibilities as the capture of speculative hoards in a long-run liquidity trap. In historical time, the system however is often jarred and opinion is likely to be divided between bulls and bears. The interest rate is, therefore, liable to a degree of instability around some generally agreed 'normal range'. Some of fundamentalist disposition would consider that placing Keynes's model into a framework of logical time is as absurd as taking a fish from a pond to examine its natural motion. A fish only properly functions in water, just as Keynes's model must live in historical time. Nevertheless, even from the writhings of a fish on dry land we can learn something, and dissection is far more convenient in a more rarefied environment.

The trap does play some role in the logic of *The General Theory*. It makes possible a position of long-run quasi-equilibrium where deflation and unemployment co-exist. The more important argument of *The General Theory* should not be obscured however. If money wages are stable, the trap is irrelevant because real balances do not endogenously expand without limit.

One suspects that the tenacity with which some might be willing to reject or uphold the trap is not due to its theoretical or practical importance *per se* but rather its symbolic value: if at least one way exists to frustrate the classical dynamics of thrift and productivity, then faith in its long-run infallibility as a reference point simply disappears.

Even if the trap is not and never was worthy of emphasis, this does not imply that stressing the conventional nature of interest rates is an out-of-date approach. One can reasonably deny it empirical importance these days in view of inflation carrying (nominal) rates far outside what had been considered conventional limits,[57] but, in the context of a much longer run, the idea might still have appeal to those who are eager to find fault with neoclassical growth theory and who are not patient enough to thread their way through the convoluted re-switching debate.

Although the trap itself is irrelevant today, the ideas which form its basis need not be. The notion of durable conventions overcoming real forces in the long run serves a valuable purpose by forcing us to consider the logical possibility, which may take different forms in different institutional, historic and economic settings, that expectations can live a life of their own. We cannot complacently believe that it makes sense only for 'correct' views to ultimately emerge in the absence of stochastic shocks. Gravitational tendencies need not centre around an equilibrium either with full information, or – assuming the more moderate renditions of the rational expectations hypothesis to be truly representative of the school – with the information that is both the best that is humanly obtainable and devoid of systematic 'objective' error. If 'true' messages are confusing, weak or non-existent, then actions become increasingly dependent on conforming to the actions of others until the convention that emerges appears to have real solidity.

Notes

1 Axel Leijonhufvud, *On Keynesian Economics and the Economics of Keynes: a study in monetary theory*, New York, Oxford University

Press, 1968, p. 158. See also p. 410. On occasions, he relies on the *Treatise* (see pp. 202–3, n. 26).

2 J.M. Keynes, *The General Theory of Employment Interest and Money*, London, Macmillan, 1936, p. 207.

3 Mark Blaug ('Discussion', in Michael Parkin and Aveline Nobay, *Current Economic Problems: the proceedings of the Association of University Teachers of Economics, Manchester, 1974*, Cambridge, Cambridge University Press, 1975, p. 215) considers Leijonhufvud's emphasis 'undue'. Leijonhufvud, by contrast, objects to how Keynesians have gradually pushed the notion into the wings, *On Keynesian Economics*, pp. 213–14, 239–50.

4 Leijonhufvud, *On Keynesian Economics*, p. 393. See also pp. 174–6, 213.

5 Keynes, *The General Theory*, p. 204. A similar statement (pp. 307–8) is quoted by Mark Blaug (*Economic Theory in Retrospect*, London, Cambridge University Press, 3rd edn, 1978, p. 676).

6 Leijonhufvud, *On Keynesian Economics*, p. 383, n. 27.

7 Axel Leijonhufvud, 'The Wicksell connection', in *Information and Coordination: essays in macroeconomic theory*, New York, Oxford University Press, 1981, p. 171, n. 59.

8 Leijonhufvud, 'The Wicksell connection', p. 171. Others, such as Alan Coddington, *Keynesian Economics: the search for first principles*, London, Allen and Unwin, 1983, pp. 81–2, are rather more caustic in their comments on the excesses of liquidity preference theory.

9 Leijonhufvud is consistent here. Compare *On Keynesian Economics*, pp. 213–14 with 'The Wicksell connection', p. 181, n. 84. His arguments are more convincing with regard to the money wage than they are to the interest rate however.

10 Note Leijonhufvud's reliance on the *Treatise* of critical junctures (*On Keynesian Economics*, pp. 383, n. 37, 411–12).

11 Keynes, *The General Theory*, p. 267.

12 ibid., p. 278, n. 2.

13 ibid., p. 202. Note the affinity to arguments in *A Treatise on Probability* where it is rational to act if you have *sufficient* evidence.

14 Keynes, *The General Theory*, pp. 202, 203, 204, 324–5 respectively.

15 Keynes, *Collected Writings*, vol. xxvii, p. 391. Note that objective forces do matter but they influence rather than govern conventions. Keynes, perhaps unlike the radical fundamentalists, saw some connection between objective reality and our perceptions of it. One wonders whether Shackle would speak of *enlightened* self-interest because, in one sense of the term, there is no objective reality for us to even attempt to perceive. It is not clear how 'radical' Shackle is or whether he would find the passage quoted a little disconcerting.

16 Keynes, *The General Theory*, p. 316. This effect is most likely to occur in the turbulence of the trade cycle rather than during the jerky but usually sluggish motion a system normally experiences.

17 As Keynes's views are difficult to ascertain, I shall not criticize Leijonhufvud for failing to consider sufficiently the feedback

relationship between the two schedules. See Keynes, *Collected Writings*, vol. xiii, pp. 148, 160 (para. 33), 235; vol. xiv, pp. 11, 118.

18 Usury laws might have been at least as important, but this is in part a 'political' phenomenon. See Keynes, *The General Theory*, pp. 351–2.

19 Speculative demand has a strong historical justification. Keynes remarked that 'for more than a hundred years past the long-term rate of interest has fluctuated round a stable level'. See *Collected Writings*, vol. xiii, p. 446, n. 1.

20 On *a priori* grounds, therefore, one would be reluctant to aggregate bonds and equities.

21 Harry G. Johnson, 'Some Cambridge controversies in monetary theory', *Review of Economic Studies*, vol. 19, no. 49, 1952, pp. 90–104, at pp. 101–2.

22 For example, 'what matters is not the *absolute* level of r but the degree of its divergence from what is considered a fairly *safe* level of r' is not evidence against a trap as it might at first appear. See Keynes, *The General Theory*, p. 201 (emphasis in original). Compare *On Keynesian Economics*, pp. 202–3 where Leijonhufvud, relying on this passage and (n. 26) the *Treatise*, considers that, in the long run, speculation will fade.

23 Leijonhufvud, *On Keynesian Economics*, p. 360.

24 Keynes, *The General Theory*, pp. 201, 203.

25 Leijonhufvud, *On Keynesian Economics*, p. 281, n. 30.

26 How might such a convention be mathematically examined? The formation of planets from swirling clouds of gas and dust provides one analogy, the setting of blancmange another.

27 Don Patinkin, *Money, Interest, and Prices: an integration of monetary and value theory*, New York, Harper and Row, 2nd edn, 1965, ch. xiv: 3.

28 ibid., p. 354.

29 Richard Jackman, 'Keynes and Leijonhufvud', *Oxford Economic Papers*, vol. 26, 1974, pp. 259–72, at pp. 264–70; John Brothwell, 'A simple Keynesian's response to Leijonhufvud', *Bulletin of Economic Research*, vol. 27, May 1975, pp. 3–21, at pp. 14–15; Milton Friedman in Robert J. Gordon (ed.), *Milton Friedman's Monetary Framework: a debate with his critics*, Chicago, Chicago University Press, 1974, pp. 15, 21 *et seq.*, 173–4.

30 Leijonhufvud, 'The Wicksell connection', p. 190, n. 98.

31 Unfortunately, Leijonhufvud refers to this possibility as a 'long-run' one (ibid., p. 191) meaning perhaps that he considers the trap to be of relevance only in this hypothetical future world. If we imagine that we have leapt to that position in future history, we can examine what happens in 'the long run' from that day onwards given the tastes and expectations then prevailing.

32 Keynes, *The General Theory*, p. 207.

33 ibid., pp. 144–5, 208, 218–19. In the last of these passages cited, Keynes considered the floor to be likely to be quite high and one which 'may soon be realised in actual experience'. See Leijonhufvud, *On Keynesian Economics*, p. 410 where, with no direct exegetical justification, borrower's and lender's risk, together with the cost of financial

intermediation, are shunted onto a branch-line and thereby are deemed to have no importance in Keynes's basic model.

34 ibid., p. 208.

35 ibid., p. 145.

36 A.H. Hansen, *A Guide to Keynes*, New York, McGraw-Hill, 1953, p. 132, n. 1.

37 Keynes, *The General Theory*, pp. 202, 207.

38 Don Patinkin, 'The role of the "liquidity trap" in Keynesian economics', *Banca Nazionale del Lavoro Quarterly Review*, vol. 27, no. 108, March 1974, pp. 3–11, esp. pp. 7–11.

39 Keynes, *The General Theory*, p. 309.

40 ibid., p. 202. Keynes (p. 309, n. 1) refers to Bagehot: 'John Bull can stand many things, but he cannot stand 2 per cent.'

41 ibid., p. 337. See also p. 233 where he refers to 'circumstances such as will *often* occur [which] cause the rate of interest to be insensitive, particularly below a certain figure, even to a substantial increase in the quantity of money...' (emphasis added).

42 ibid., p. 306.

43 Jackman, 'Keynes and Leijonhufvud', p. 270. Leijonhufvud (*On Keynesian Economics*, p. 405) quoting *The General Theory* (p. 309) does not give the passage in full. In Leijonhufvud's defence, he might have felt that the durable minimum existed simply because the monetary authority had never seriously tried to push the rate to any lower figure.

44 Leijonhufvud differs from George Horwich (*Money, Capital, and Prices*, Homewood, Ill., Richard D. Irwin, 1964, p. 429, n. 50), the latter accepting that Keynes viewed the trap as a 'distinct *possibility*' (emphasis in original).

45 Patinkin, 'The role of the "liquidity trap"...', pp. 9–10.

46 ibid., p. 253. Compare p. 172.

47 Keynes, *The General Theory*, p. 191, given below.

48 ibid. Brothwell ('A simple Keynesian's response...', p. 14) considers that this passage clearly indicates the existence of a trap as a theoretical possibility. The passage is however difficult so far as its context, a discussion of Ricardo's views on the non-neutrality of monetary policy, is concerned. Some might say that Keynes was saying no more than did Hume when he referred to the transitional non- neutrality of money. If the monetary authority persists in changing the money supply, *ceteris paribus*, the system is kept in a state where real effects are experienced. Keynes (*The General Theory*, p. 343, n. 3) was clearly aware of Hume's views. The issue of non-neutrality is (marginally) clarified by Keynes (*Collected Writings*, vol. xxix, p. 221).

49 Keynes, *The General Theory*, pp. 253, 269–70, is consistent with this use of terms. In the latter case 'unstable equilibrium' is used to distinguish it from 'equilibrium' as used elsewhere. For Don Patinkin's views on 'equilibrium', 'stable equilibrium', and 'position', see his *Keynes' Monetary Thought: a study of its development*, Durham, North Carolina, Duke University Press, 1976, pp. 116–17.

50 Keynes, *Collected Writings*, vol. xiii, p. 395 (emphasis is added).

51 ibid., pp. 486–7 (from *The Listener*, 21 November 1934).
52 ibid., p. 489.
53 Compare Clower and Leijonhufvud, 'The coordination of economic activities: a Keynesian perspective', *American Economic Review*, vol. 65. no. 2, May 1975, pp. 182–8, at p. 182 (their emphasis): '[W]e have yet to resolve the central question posed by Keynes's assault on received doctrine: Is the *existing* system, in any *significant* sense, self-adjusting?' Evidently the authors had the article from *The Listener* in mind when drafting their paper.
54 There are, however, some extreme versions of rational expectations models which would deny the statement in the text. Whether money wage adjustments *can* restore full employment is not questioned much these days. New classicists seem to have faith in the market-clearing approach even in deflationary regimes.
55 See Patinkin, *Keynes' Monetary Thought*, p. 109, no. 3.
56 Repeating Keynes, *The General Theory*, p. 191 (emphasis added). Note that when Keynes maintains, 'It is not possible to dispute on purely theoretical grounds that this reaction [the Keynes effect] might be capable of allowing an adequate decline in the money-rate of interest', this does not exclude the possibility that the trap *might* also be capable of preventing that decline, *The General Theory*, p. 232. See also p. 233, para. (c).
57 See Victoria Chick, *Macroeconomics after Keynes: a reconsideration of the General Theory*, Deddington, Oxford, Philip Allan, 1983, pp. 228–9.

Chapter seven

Expenditure and the interest rate

An overview

This chapter deals with the interest elasticity of investment. Leijon-hufvud argues that Keynes's analysis is somewhat classical in the sense that investment, contrary to the teachings of the income-expenditure theorists, is interest elastic. The existence of a level of investment that is insufficient to sustain full employment can be largely attributed to bear speculation that prevents the rate of interest falling sufficiently to offset a decline in the marginal efficiency of investment.[1] Fundamentalists, on the other hand, stress the volatility of the investment demand curve and are not particularly interested in the elasticity of a wildly unstable function.

The volume of investment depends upon the difference between the discounted income that is expected to be earned from the marginal capital good (the prospective yield) and its supply price.[2] If the prospective yield of investment increases on account of entrepreneurial optimism, then investment will increase, unless the capital-goods supply curve is perfectly inelastic. Investment also depends upon the rate of interest. If the interest rate falls, the yield of bonds falls relatively to any given prospective yield of capital goods. This induces an upward shift in the demand for capital goods, the size of which depends on the extent to which bonds and capital goods are substitutes. Consequently, if prospective yields are constant in the short run, and if bonds and capital goods are close substitutes, the flow of investment will be sensitive to changes in the rate of interest. Leijonhufvud summarizes Keynes's position as follows:

> The income streams flowing from capital goods are regarded as perfect substitutes for bond-streams of comparable time-profile.
> ... In Keynes' analysis of the short run, the State of Expectation (*alias* the Marginal Efficiency of Capital) is assumed given, so that the price of assets varies simply (inversely) with 'the' interest rate.

In Keynes' language, 'a decline in the interest rate' *means* 'a rise in the market prices of capital goods, equities, and bonds'. Since the representative non-money asset is very long-lived, its interest-elasticity of present value is quite high. The price-elasticity of the output of augmentable income sources is' very high. The interest-elasticity of investment is therefore necessarily significant, as a purely logical matter, in terms of Keynes' model.[3]

To gauge the extent to which Keynes treated bonds and capital goods as substitutes, one needs, in Leijonhufvud's view, to examine Keynes's aggregation procedures. Did Keynes treat bonds and capital goods as a homogeneous lump or did he segregate them into different groups and analyse their separate roles? Leijonhufvud selects the former, fundamentalists tending towards the latter.

The purpose of aggregation is to simplify a model sufficiently to make it useful to the analysis of the complex real world. For example, a vast array of heterogeneous commodities may be lumped together as 'aggregate consumption' in order to highlight the important feature that is common to all components of the group. Consumption as a whole is, for example, a function of income. Macroeconomists are not concerned with substitution effects which occur within a given aggregate, because they are assumed to be unimportant in the explanation of macro-economic change. Aggregation is designed to focus upon important interrelationships between groups as a whole. If one aggregates consumption and capital goods (as do the income-expenditure theorists), then this reflects implicit theorizing to the effect that the relative prices of consumption and capital goods, and any substitution between them, is not at the heart of the macroeconomic process under study. If, on the other hand, one aggregates capital goods and bonds under the heading of 'non-money assets', then one abstracts from changes in the relative prices of bonds and capital goods. The focus then is upon the price of non-money assets relative to the prices of consumption goods and labour.[4] Leijonhufvud argues that Keynes adopted the latter approach.

The adoption of this aggregation procedure is an important link in the chain of Leijonhufvud's reasoning because Keynes is interpreted as accepting that deflation, which causes the rate of interest to fall, can, in logic, restore equilibrium.[5] If, however, the fundamentalists are right to treat capital goods as being poor substitutes for bonds on account of violent fluctuations in the marginal efficiency of capital, neither deflation nor monetary policy can conceivably be relied upon to restore full employment. It will be argued, in support of the fundamentalists, that it is preferable to distinguish between bonds and capital. Nevertheless, Leijonhufvud's case is not fatally weakened, and a reconciliation is possible.

The aggregation question: evaluating Leijonhufvud

The two major contributors to the somewhat arid debate over the legitimacy of Leijonhufvud's suggested aggregative procedure are Richard T. Froyen[6] and Santi K. Chakrabarti.[7] Their views can be briefly summarized prior to an evaluation.

Froyen considers that *The General Theory* clearly diverges from the aggregative structure of the *Treatise* and he maintains that even drafts of 1932 to 1934 can be distinguished from the final 1936 version. There is, in this respect, a 'clean break', because Keynes chose to explain, as have many subsequent Keynesians, the essentials of his revolution in terms of a one-commodity model. Froyen aggregates currently produced capital and consumer goods and distinguishes them from the existing stock of capital goods (and equities). For a given state of long-term expectations, bonds and equities are grouped together, and it is the price of these long-term assets relative to the price of newly produced output that is crucial. Instead of aggregating newly produced capital goods with the stock of existing long-term assets (as does Leijonhufvud), he assigns them to a one-commodity composite.[8] Froyen[9] notes that there is a single aggregate supply curve where there is only one commodity. Froyen proposes that investment is governed by the divergence between the prices of newly produced and existing capital goods, and not, as in Leijonhufvud, by the relative price of the stock-flow capital goods to the flow price of consumer goods. Froyen sees no need to take the interest rate as an inverse measure of the price of newly produced capital goods. He considers that Keynes's arguments, which Leijonhufvud has stressed, that investment is interest elastic and that windfall effects on consumption can occur in response to an increase in private sector wealth, can both be derived from a one-commodity model.[10]

Froyen[11] continues by suggesting that the relative price of newly produced capital and consumption goods is not important in Keynes, ironically, because of short-run price inflexibilities suggested initially by Leijonhufvud. He considers that Keynes had seen large changes in the prices of assets whereas the effect on the prices of newly produced goods was indirect and delayed.[12] One notes immediately that if Keynes, contrary to Leijonhufvud (of 1968) and Froyen, considered flow prices of output to be flexible, then Froyen's argument is weakened. Because Keynes is also happy to treat inventories as investment (so that not much of significance separates fixed and the more liquid forms of capital), Froyen is confident that Keynes's model has only one newly produced commodity.

In response to Froyen's judgement, Chakrabarti maintains that a one-commodity model implies that the consumption function and multiplier have no special role in explaining the equilibrium levels of output and employment. Only the division of output between consumption and investment is specified.[13] Whereas Froyen[14] considers that Keynes distinguished investment only to draw attention to differences between classes of *transactors* who demand the output, Chakrabarti insists that, where necessary to the central argument, Keynes does distinguish between the different kinds of *commodities* that are demanded. For example, Chakrabarti refers to Keynes's distinction[15] between wage goods and non-wage goods when discussing the real wage. He points to the continued adherence[16] to the two-commodity structure of the *Treatise*. He goes on to argue that Froyen's evidence, although conscientiously extracted from Keynes's writings and cogently interpreted, is nevertheless capable of alternative and probably superior interpretation.[17]

Taking the evidence at face value, Froyen's views have much to commend them. However, Chakrabarti does sensibly explain how the apparently dramatic change in Keynes's aggregation procedure is not really so. It appears reasonable to interpret the passages as indicating not, as Froyen argues, a sudden change between 1934 and 1936 – a change to which, incidentally, Keynes felt no reason to draw attention – but rather a shift in emphasis. Supply conditions no longer are considered of equal ranking with the state of demand and are thus allowed to fall away into the background (as, indeed, do many and various details described in the *Treatise*).

Chakrabarti concedes to Froyen that Keynes did speak of his revolution lying in the determination of the level of *output* as a whole. However, this was an alternative way of expressing his concern for the level of *employment* as a whole. Keynes wanted to show that output, money income and employment can generally be regarded as being uniquely related.[18] Keynes did not wish to distinguish between those employed in the two sectors because labour was regarded, in the simplest of his models, as homogeneous.[19] Even in the case where Keynes acknowledged heterogeneity, he did not consider that different types of labour were systematically found in the two sectors. Contrary to Froyen, because Keynes distinguished between the elasticities of employment of the two sectors, and because an employment function is, in effect, an inverse of a supply function, there is evidence to support the two-commodity model.

When Froyen[20] complains that, in a two-commodity model, no unique relationship exists between money income and employment, he appears to have overlooked something important. While, as Froyen reasons,[21] it is true that, if the elasticities of employment differed between the two sectors, we would need to know the composition of demand between consumption and investment in order to be able to determine employment, Keynes does make simplifying assumptions which makes this possible.[22] If confidence affects each industry in the investment sector in a fairly predictable way, a given level of effective demand is associated with a vector of quantities of investment. Given the cost conditions, a given change from a given starting point generates a particular amount of additional employment. Given that workers' tastes between consumption goods remain as stable as the fundamental psychological propensity to consume itself, a reasonably predictable multiplier response in the consumption sector emerges. So long as tastes and costs remain stable, a one-to-one relationship between level of investment, consumption, employment and money income exists.[23] If money income and employment are closely associated it is not because Keynes has a one-commodity model but simply that a reasonably predictable pattern of response in a two- (or even *n*-) sector model is assumed.[24]

One can also reply to Froyen[25] that Keynes tossed unsold consumption goods (inventories) into the investment category not because he felt that such goods had much in common with other investment goods (as Froyen maintains), but simply for convenience so that his terms would have precise meaning and so that – and how wrong Keynes turned out to be on this – the terms 'saving' and 'investment' could be defined as identical to make it easier for others to understand the theory of liquidity preference. If Keynes used 'investment' in *ex ante* and *ex post* senses without due caution, we ought not deduce from this a belief that *ex ante* investment in fixed capital is not singled out.

One does not find too many references to inventories in those passages which talk about animal spirits and the crucial nature of decisions involving large commitments of durable[26] capital. Bravery and a bold pioneering spirit hardly seem essential to decisions to squirrel away some inventories. If for particular formal purposes inventories are called 'investment', this indicates nothing of Keynes's overall vision.

Froyen also considers that new capital goods and equities, which are grouped together by Leijonhufvud, are not perfect substitutes. In support of that view he cites the following:

> Nor does the price of existing securities depend at all closely over short periods either on the cost of production or on the price of new fixed capital. For existing securities largely consist of

properties which cannot be quickly reproduced, of natural resources which cannot be reproduced at all, and of the capitalised value of future income anticipated from the possession of quasi-monopolies of peculiar advantages of one kind or another. The investment boom in the United States in 1929 was a good example of an enormous rise in the price of securities as a whole which was not accompanied by any rise at all in the price of current output of new fixed capital.[27]

By 1936, Keynes continues to decline to lump new capital goods with titles to the old. He distinguishes their prices, but he does appear to accept that their substitutability is growing. This marginally weakens Froyen's case.

But the daily revaluations of the Stock Exchange...inevitably exert a decisive influence on the rate of current investment. For there is no sense in building up a new enterprise at a cost greater than that at which a similar existing enterprise can be purchased. ... Thus *certain classes* of investment are governed by the average expectation of those who deal on the Stock Exchange.... This does not apply, of course, to classes of enterprise which are not readily marketable or to which no negotiable instrument closely corresponds. The categories falling within this exception were *formerly extensive*. But measured as a proportion of the total value of new investment they are *rapidly* declining in importance.[28]

Chakrabarti[29] considers that Keynes does have an adequate explanation of how investment is influenced by share markets and how there is a connection between equity prices and the market prices of investment goods. Whether one would wish to *aggregate* the liquid titles and the illiquid physical assets is, however, a different question. We can conclude that this is yet another illustration of the difficulties involved in trying to ascertain Keynes's aggregation procedure.

Turning now to the grouping of bonds and physical capital, Chakrabarti[30] rejects Leijonhufvud's[31] interpretation of a passage from Keynes[32] in which Keynes expresses dissatisfaction with the aggregation procedure of *The Treatise*:

Whilst liquidity-preference due to the speculative-motive corresponds to what in my *Treatise on Money* I called the 'state of bearishness', it is by no means the same thing. For 'bearishness' is there defined as the functional relationship, not between the rate of interest (or price of debts) and the quantity of money, but between the price of assets and debts, taken together, and the quantity of money. This treatment, however, involved a confusion

between results due to a change in the rate of interest and those
due to a change in the schedule of the marginal efficiency of
capital, which I hope I have here avoided.

Leijonhufvud holds that this passage ought to be read as affirming the
view that the demand for money depends on the given (expected)
income stream of both bonds and other assets (physical capital or
equities). Keynes was simply making a technical point that, in the
Treatise's formulation, changes in the MEI, which change the price of
non-money and non-bond *assets*, were not distinguished from changes
in interest rates which affect the price of the standard income *stream*.
But Leijonhufvud, being prepared to hold that, in the short run, the MEI
is fixed, then calmly proceeds to re-marry all non-money assets.
Chakrabarti, on the other hand, sees this passage as driving a wedge
between bonds and other non-money assets for the reason that the MEI
is *not* fixed in the short run.[33]
It is therefore perhaps wise not to push Keynes confidently into any
mould. While there clearly is a systematic interdependence between
income, investors' confidence and financial bearishness as evidenced in
chapter 22, consider the following written only a month after the
publication of *The General Theory*:

I am unable to see that the changes in the schedule of the marginal
efficiency of capital have any obvious or predictable effect on the
liquidity function.... You [Hawtrey] say that when new investment
declines 'the prices of securities will rise.' Why should they? I
should expect them more likely to fall.[34]

To lump bonds and fixed capital together on the grounds that they are
both long and illiquid, as Leijonhufvud does,[35] is doubtful for surely
fixed capital is significantly more illiquid than securities and carries far
greater risk of changing in value by virtue of changes in the prospective
yield to which bonds are immune.[36] As the fundamentalists insist, the act
of buying a physical and durable investment good is a crucial and
irreversible one. Today's mistakes are prolonged burdens, and, in a
world of uncertainty, speculative expectations about the price of
equities can have an independent bearing on the level of investment
quite apart from the expectations by investors about prospective returns
to enterprise. Thus, shares might deserve separate treatment even in
isolation from newly produced investment goods.
One suspects that to prevent a disintegration into a large number of
groups, an aggregative structure suitable to the purpose at hand and to
the *ceteris paribus* conditions maintained (explicitly or implicitly) by
Keynes at any point needs to be selected. It is only a very basic model

which can be presented in a four-sector model, and it is worth asking what modern theoreticians and historians of thought have to learn from any model which suppresses so much.

On balance, therefore, the interpretation of this work is friendlier to Chakrabarti, who distinguishes bonds, capital goods and consumption goods and prefers a five-good and a two-commodity model. Unfortunately, the exegetical issue is not quite as clear-cut as Chakrabarti holds because passages also exist in *The General Theory* where the two commodities are not contrasted at all.[37] Distinctions are often drawn both between many industries and within the two sectors.[38] They cut across the categories of consumption and investment.[39] It is only occasionally (though often at important junctures) that Keynes chooses to segregate the consumption and investment sectors.[40] On balance, it seems that Keynes considered that a relatively detailed story should probably sharply distinguish the two sectors, but that the reader ought not be unduly burdened.[41] It is far from clear that any significant changes occurred between 1930 and 1936 (or, for that matter, after *The General Theory*).[42]

Furthermore, the relevance of the passages obtained from sources prior to *The General Theory* itself can be questioned.[43] Indeed, this is how Froyen dismisses much of the evidence from Keynes which suggests a two-sector approach. Chakrabarti appears not to have realized that Froyen does not recognize as valid the evidence gleaned even from 1934 drafts of *The General Theory*. Froyen sees the considerable lessening of the distinction between the two sectors as evidence not of simplifying unnecessary details about the supply side which would distract the reader from his theory of demand, but rather a deliberate and clear change of mind on Keynes's part.

Delving into the meaning of the materials written by Keynes during this transitional period is a difficult task indeed and requires a Patinkin-like dedication to detail. Portions need to be interpreted in the light of ideas bubbling through Keynes's mind when he was engaged in the dramatic process of identifying in his own mind how *The General Theory* went beyond the *Treatise*. One might, for example, give considerably more weight to the writings of 1934 than to those of 1932 if one agreed with Patinkin's view that certain theoretical innovations were only made relatively late. An 'evolutionist' would be more willing to supplement his arguments with passages written in the early 1930s. To this extent, subjective interpretation of the textual evidence becomes all the more crucial.

Finally, as is often the case in Leijonhufvud's book, important passages are concealed in the footnotes, and his reviewers do not appear to have appreciated his argument on its own terms:

It has already been indicated that Keynes, in many passages of *The General Theory*, discusses a larger 'menu' of goods. Similarly, not all contributions to the income-expenditure literature confine the analysis to the four goods listed above. Yet, for a coherent comparative analysis it is necessary to keep the 'level of aggregation' the same for the two brands of theory. Possibly, a case could be made for the five goods/four prices level of aggregation as being more appropriate for the comparison than the four goods/three prices level chosen here. The analytical distinctions to be drawn stand out in sharper relief when the present approach is taken. This is desirable *per se*. In my opinion, this does not involve us in significant distortions of the analytical content of the two types of theories nor in substantial exaggeration of the differences between them.[44]

Several points emerge from this paragraph. Primarily, the aggregation procedures chosen by Leijonhufvud as being representative of Keynes and the Keynesians are simply intended to highlight conveniently the differences in substance between the two, even though neither school rigidly employed their respective procedures. This is typical of Leijonhufvud's methodological style which is one of rational reconstruction. Furthermore, if passages are found in which the parties concerned adopted other aggregative procedures, this is by no means a refutation because Leijonhufvud is simply claiming that it is useful to look at things in the way in which he suggests. He deliberately strives to enhance the picture and to present differences 'in sharper relief' and yet without 'substantial exaggeration'. If one accepts that interest rates are important and that there is a Wicksell connection, it is a case perhaps of the ends justifying the means. To categorize separately consumption and investment goods allows the distinction to be clearly made, though the fundamentalist case can be validly put that, by his going on to group bonds and capital together, the importance of interest rates to the latter is thereby exaggerated by Leijonhufvud. Importantly, however, Leijonhufvud is flexible enough to subdivide the categories further and thereby allow bonds and fixed capital to be analysed separately in line with fundamentalist teachings.

Some concluding remarks on the aggregation question can now be made. Primarily, this discussion ends with a note of protest. It is not clear why we would want to impose onto Keynes's writings a single model, even the most basic one which gets, one hopes, to the heart of the matter. Keynes's own view was that an economist should be equipped with an array of models and an appropriate understanding of the theory and the world to which any model is sought to be applied.[45] A detailed knowledge of financial, commodity and other markets is needed by any practitioner. Reading his book would hardly suffice. It is the modern mind which insists upon a precise and consistent model, whereas Keynes was largely concerned with arousing the intuition without undue regard for detail.[46] To relax the hold that 'habitual modes of thought' have had over economists and to dispel their faith in Say's Law, a primitive, comparative-static and formal model was employed in some of the earlier chapters. Qualifications, polemics, poetry and intellectual seduction were left to others. Detailed factual analysis, which would be limited to a particular time and place, but which is also vitally needed by policy-makers, is left to the reader's experience and judgement both to supply and interpret. If *The General Theory* is seen in this light, squabbles about the aggregative structure are of little real importance. If particular assumptions are made to illustrate particular points, then such passages ought to be regarded as having a heuristic purpose and not representing Keynes's exact beliefs about the world. Which interpretation of Keynes is the better should not depend crucially on scholastic details concerning the more convenient and illuminating aggregation procedure. It is better to search for direct evidence about Keynes's beliefs regarding the elasticity and stability of the investment function.

Investment and the rate of interest

Matters relating to the elasticity at points along a given MEI schedule must not be confused with those dealing with shifts of the schedule.[47] The former issue is considered first, the latter in the next section.

On the textual evidence, Leijonhufvud maintains that the interest elasticity of investment is large, but part of his argument is invalid and can be dismissed briefly. He states: 'The notion that Keynes assumed saving and investment to be interest-inelastic is...unfounded. Price incentives are effective.'[48] The income-expenditure model, according to Leijonhufvud, postulates erroneously 'that intertemporal price incentives were almost completely ineffective – neither savers nor investors respond to changes in interest rates'.[49] He cites the following in support of his contention.

> It might be, of course, that individuals were so *tête montée* in their decisions as to how much they themselves would save and invest respectively, that there would be no point of price equilibrium at which transactions could take place. In this case our terms would cease to be applicable,...prices would find no resting-place between zero and infinity. *Experience shows, however, that this, in fact, is not so.*[50]

Leijonhufvud seems to have made two mistakes. First, price inelasticity of demand has nothing to do with the effectiveness of price incentives. The demand for salt may be relatively price inelastic, but this would in no way controvert neoclassical price theory which requires that transactors respond to price incentives and maximize utility. Second, the passage cited from Keynes has no direct bearing on the question of the interest elasticity of investment. Keynes does not exclude the possibility that the demand-for-investment curve is inelastic. All that Keynes meant was that markets generate equilibrium and positive interest rates.[51]

Leijonhufvud, however, presents other, more convincing, arguments in support of his claim that investment is responsive to changes in the rate of interest. He analyses the effects of the four elasticities relevant to the nature of the schedule of the marginal efficiency of capital.[52]

The first elasticity is that 'of the demand price for capital goods, for some given rate of discount, with respect to the rate of growth of the capital stock'.[53] As Leijonhufvud explains,

If the investment under consideration is in equipment of a type for which there is already excess capacity and that excess capacity is not expected to be absorbed for the better part of the short life of the assets, the prospective addition to future revenues net of operating costs will be almost nil. This is the kind of situation envisaged in much of the income-expenditure literature,...[but] Keynes' conception of investment in 'Fixed Capital' is quite different.[54]

Leijonhufvud cites the following to indicate that it was Keynes's view that the elasticity under consideration is quite low.

Willingness to invest more or less in manufacturing plant is not likely to be very sensitive to small changes in bond-rate. *But the quantity of new fixed capital required by industry is relatively trifling even at the best times, and is not a big factor in the situation.* Almost the whole of the fixed capital of the world is represented by buildings, transport and public utilities; and the sensitiveness of these activities even to small changes in the long-term rate of interest, though with an appreciable time-lag, is surely considerable.[55]

Keynes indicates clearly that the rate of interest exercises a strong influence over investment in general, but there is nothing to suggest that the reason for making an exception of industrial fixed capital is that its prospective yield diminishes rapidly when its stock rises. Further evidence is needed to clarify Keynes's position. It is relevant to discuss Keynes's views about the 'Spectre of Secular Stagnation' because it is an extreme instance where the marginal revenue product approaches zero as the stock of capital rises. If Keynes were hostile to the stagnationist arguments, we could infer that he was closer to the opposite end of the spectrum and believed that the elasticity under consideration was close to zero. If, on the other hand, Keynes were sympathetic to such arguments, we could reject Leijonhufvud's interpretation. Unfortunately, Keynes's position on this matter is somewhat ambivalent.

In his *Treatise*, Keynes criticizes N. Johannsen who was a forerunner of the Keynesian stagnationists.

> Mr Johannsen regarded the failure of current savings to be embodied in capital expenditure as a more or less permanent condition in the modern world due to a saturation of the Capital Market, instead of as a result of a temporary but recurrent failure of the banking system to pass on the full amount of the savings to entrepreneurs, and overlooks the fact that a fall in the rate of interest would be the cure for the malady if it were what he diagnoses it to be.[56]

But in his *General Theory*, Keynes speculates on the possibility of the volume of investment being

> so great that it would eventually lead to a state of full investment in the sense that an aggregate gross yield in excess of replacement cost could no longer be expected on a reasonable calculation from a further increment of durable goods of any type whatever. Moreover, this situation might be reached comparatively soon – say within twenty-five years or less.[57]

One is unsure of the reconciliation of these two views. Perhaps a case can be made for the 'clean break' hypothesis.

Leijonhufvud also argues that the fact that Keynes held that the elasticity under consideration is low can be inferred from the following:

> If there is an increased investment in any given type of capital during any period of time, the marginal efficiency of that type of capital will diminish as the investment in it is increased, partly because the prospective yield will fall as the supply of that type of capital is increased, and partly because, as a rule, pressure on the facilities for producing that type of capital will cause its supply price to increase; *the second of these factors being usually the more important in producing equilibrium in the short run*, but the longer the period in view the more does the first factor take its place.[58]

Leijonhufvud reasons that because the second factor is more important, the first must be relatively insignificant. The problem with

Leijonhufvud's argument is that if the short-run supply curve of capital was of very low elasticity, it can render negligible the effect of even a quite low elasticity of the prospective yield with respect to the rate of growth of the capital stock. Consequently, it is important to discover whether Keynes held that the supply curve was of very low elasticity, but again we find that his position is difficult to determine.[59]

Keynes seems to argue that supply curves tend to be inelastic only when full employment is approached and bottlenecks appear.[60] This would support Leijonhufvud's view. On the other hand, however, Keynes criticized Marshall for overlooking the possibility that, because an extensive increase in the demand for capital goods cannot be met immediately by an increase in supply, the supply price would increase sharply.[61] It is difficult to assess the validity of Leijonhufvud's interpretation on this point.

We are now left with Leijonhufvud's final argument that, because Keynes rarely mentions the effect of the rate of investment on the slope of the schedule of the marginal efficiency of capital, he could not have considered this factor to be important.[62] We are set the task of interpreting Keynes's silence. One could suggest that, contrary to Leijonhufvud, Keynes did not stress the importance of this factor in all circumstances because he did not wish to distract the reader, whose attention Keynes wished to focus on specific points of interest. Keynes might have believed that this factor would always be kept at the back of his readers' minds and that it was not necessary to remind them incessantly of its importance. Another explanation of Keynes's lack of complete rigour is that he was more concerned with shifts of the schedule than with matters of detail concerning its slope. This matter will be pursued in the next section.

In conclusion, nothing can be said with great confidence about Keynes's assumptions in relation to the first elasticity.

The second elasticity relevant to the determination of the slope of the schedule of the marginal efficiency of capital is 'the interest-elasticity of the discount rate applied to the evaluation of income-streams accruing to physical capital'.[63] Leijonhufvud explains that this elasticity is unity if bond-streams and capital-streams (adjusted for risk) are perfect substitutes.[64] This depends on the MEI schedule being fixed. However, if agents can be assumed to appreciate the greater volatility of the demand for capital than for bonds, then the substitutability is much less. This matter has been discussed in the aggregation section where bonds and capital are considered to be better treated as separate entities contrary to Leijonhufvud.

The third elasticity is the discount rate elasticity of the present value of the standard capital-stream. Put more simply, if the life of the typical asset is long, then the interest elasticity of the demand price for capital

goods is relatively high. The issue then becomes whether the typical
asset is long-lived or whether, as in Keynesian accounts, it is short-
lived.[65]

That Leijonhufvud's view is sound is evident. Apart from the
evidence he cites,[66] one passage is absolutely clear:

> I should add that I had in mind (e.g.) 'houses' and 'buildings'
> generally, or 'roads' and 'railways', as typical capital goods
> affected by changes in the pure rate of interest, rather than
> 'machines'. Mr Robertson's habitual use of 'machines' as typical
> capital goods, though he may intend to include 'houses' and
> 'roads' under this term, creates, to my mind, rather a false
> suggestion, because 'machines' in the natural sense of the term,
> i.e. 'factory equipment', which are, it is true, somewhat insen-
> sitive to changes in the pure rate of interest, are quantitatively a
> very trifling proportion of the total stock of capital.[67]

On balance it seems preferable to follow Leijonhufvud and hold that
there is, contrary to the textbook Keynesians, a significant degree of
elasticity to the typical demand curve for investment goods. On
elasticity (3) the findings here support Leijonhufvud, but on elasticity
(2) they support the Keynesians. The interpretation offered here is
therefore poised uncomfortably between the two extremes. One
imagines that fundamentalists would derive some satisfaction from
Leijonhufvud's argument that the orthodox Keynesians are wrong.
There is no obvious reason for them to disagree strenuously with
Leijonhufvud. Whether they would regard the question of the interest
elasticity of investment as being so central is doubtful however. It is the
stability of the function which interests them.

The stability of the MEI curve

Attention turns to Keynes's views on the nature and extent of shifts in
entrepreneurial estimates of future prospects over the longer term. It is
here where Leijonhufvud's argument is at its weakest, and the
fundamentalist case requires recognition. Leijonhufvud fails to give
enough weight to the volatility of the confidence and expectations of
investors.[68] In accordance with his earlier arguments, Leijonhufvud
prefers to construe investors as having relatively inelastic expectations,
the past being a reasonable guide to the future. Although a shift in the
MEI curve can be at the source of the disequilibrating shock, the shift is
relatively small and it is the multiplier which causes the system to move
far from full employment.[69] As times goes on, expectations only
gradually become more pessimistic.[70]

Leijonhufvud's beliefs on the inelasticity of expectations stem from his interpretation of passages from Keynes. It is argued here that his interpretation is seriously defective. While he properly notes that Keynes held that there were no means by which correct estimates of distant demand could be known, it does not follow that Keynes held that this must mean that expectations can only change by large amounts at intervals.

It is true that 'there is no mechanism to ensure that incorrect estimates will be quickly discovered'[71] but that does not mean that incorrect estimates will persist and not be rapidly displaced by other estimates which may or may not be correct (in some sense). He[72] cites Keynes:[73] '[I]t is the nature of long-term expectations that they cannot be checked at short intervals in the light of realized results.' This cannot be taken to mean that, if they cannot be checked, they will have no particular cause to be revised. Discontinuous changes need not be infrequent.

Leijonhufvud asserts that the MEI curve is fixed in the short run. He relies heavily on this assumption throughout his book but he supplies no textual support,[74] and even omits words from a passage which he cites[75] that contradict that position. The significant missing words are:

> Moreover, the expectation of future consumption is *so largely based on current experience* of present consumption that a reduction in the latter is likely to depress the former, with the result that the act of saving will not merely depress the price of consumption-goods and leave the marginal efficiency of existing capital unaffected, but *may actually tend to depress the latter also*. In this event *it may reduce present investment-demand* as well as present consumption-demand.[76]

It is perfectly possible for current results to affect long-term expectations.[77] There is no reason to take a given state of expectations, necessary to derive a short-run equilibrium position, as anything other than a simplifying assumption for heuristic purposes.[78]

Leijonhufvud does not distinguish between the producers and the purchasers of investment goods. The expectations of the former are 'more often gradually modified in the light of results than in anticipation of prospective results'.[79] Keynes continues: 'Nevertheless, we must not forget that, in the case of durable goods, the producer's short-term expectations are based on the current long-term expectations of the investor.'

In other words, producers respond passively, but rapidly, to the demand for investment goods. They are not speculators. Their short-term expectations reflect the long-term expectations of investors. It is the investor who is confronted by difficult decisions to make and his or her behaviour is of a far less determinate character. The uncertainty of investors generates instability in the demand for investment goods but there is little uncertainty on the supply side. Supply simply meets demand.

Clearly areas exist where Keynes considers the possibility of elastic expectations of investors. A good example is where money-wage cuts are expected to continue and this discourages current investment.[80] Leijonhufvud, curiously, cites another passage[81] from the same page without realizing the inconsistency. Keynes gave equal weight to the possibilities of investors expecting even lower money wages and the reversal of motion back towards normal levels. Leijonhufvud recognized only the latter.

Keynes's views seem quite different from Leijonhufvud's.

[T]he state of expectation is liable to constant change.... It would be foolish, in forming our expectations, to attach great weight to matters which are very uncertain. It is reasonable, therefore, to be guided to a considerable degree by the facts about which we feel somewhat confident, even though they may be less decisively relevant to the issue than other facts about which our knowledge is vague and scanty. For this reason *the facts of the existing situation enter, in a sense disproportionately*, into the formation of our long-term expectations; our usual practice being to *take the existing situation and to project it into the future*, modified only to the extent that we have more or less definite reasons for expecting a change.

The outstanding fact is the extreme precariousness of the basis of knowledge on which our estimates of prospective yield have to be made. Once doubt begins it spreads rapidly.[82]

These passages have a fundamentalist flavour and suggest both a potential for volatile change and a fairly high elasticity of expectations (although not necessarily of at least unity). How can a model, such as Leijonhufvud's, embodying inelastic expectations embrace both of these properties? In such a model expectations slowly change according to some weighted average of past results. Now, to incorporate volatility, one needs to posit large random shocks to expectations, but in such a world, would rational agents continue to act as if the future were like today and yesterday in the face of clear evidence that considerable variance is possible?

The difficulty with Leijonhufvud's position goes beyond that which rational-expectations theorists could suggest, however. He seems simultaneously to want to accept Knightian uncertainty together with the 'dark forces of time and ignorance which envelop our future'[83] on the one hand as well as accept the theory of real productivity, espoused by the classicists, on the other. It seems that he argues that behind the veil of uncertainty, the shape of concrete truths can vaguely be discerned.

Leijonhufvud goes to extraordinary lengths to tame the MEI. He even claims:

> Stock market prices adjust on the 'market day' – to a level consistent with current expectations which are in turn inelastic on the 'market day' and are, indeed, only revised in the 'long run'; effective excess demands in commodities markets become zero only in the 'short run'. There is ample evidence for the assumption of this ranking of the relative adjustment speeds in Keynes' work.[84]

Such a statement is a stunning contradiction in both letter and spirit of Keynes's famous chapter 12 where the issue of share prices is specifically discussed. Share speculators, who play increasingly important roles in influencing investment by the private sector, do discard old expectations rapidly, and even in the face of flimsy evidence. Their expectations are very elastic:

> Day-to-day fluctuations in the profits of existing investments, which are obviously of an ephemeral and non-significant character, tend to have an altogether excessive, and even absurd, influence on the [share] market.[85]

The reaction of the average (American) speculator is an extreme one, more extreme than that of people of enterprise who attempt to forecast yields over the whole life of an asset. The latter group was comprised in 'former times...of individuals of sanguine temperament' who did not really rely 'on precise calculation of prospective profit'.[86]

By the 1930s, their boldness had subsided and evidence from current experience was given greater weight in the decision to invest. Nevertheless, animal spirits were held by Keynes to persist though the pioneering spirit was dying.

Leijonhufvud, of course, is aware of such passages but he dismisses them as a mixture of flamboyance and otiosity. He notes, validly to a degree: 'The colourful language tends to swamp the more sober counterpoints.'[87] He refers to Keynes's qualifications such as: 'it is by no means always the case that speculation predominates over enterprise.'[88]

But this overlooks that the spirit of enterprise itself is fickle and non-rational. More importantly, however, Leijonhufvud reverses Keynes's emphasis. Sober realism in share markets was to Keynes the exception and not the rule. It is doubtful to argue that these opinions about irrationality merely reflected Keynes's personal (and somewhat biased) opinion and therefore cannot be incorporated into the vision of the basic model.[89]

In referring to the notorious games on the stock market, where the players have little regard for even the attempt to evaluate the potential earnings over the life of the assets, Leijonhufvud remarks, 'Now, this does not seem right.'[90]

Now, as exegetical technique, *this* does not seem right. He then tries to make sense of Keynes by repeating that share market speculation does not matter much anyway in Keynes because the problem in Keynes's mind was a level of interest rate that was too high. Keynes's chapter 12 can simply be read down to refer to infrequent and relatively minor misjudgements about prospective yield. Such an approach is highly dubious, but Leijonhufvud is at least consistent.

Leijonhufvud binds himself to the pervasive nature of inelastic expectations in Keynes and endeavours to render consistent such expectations with the classical economics of thrift and productivity.

Both savers and investors in the long run look to real prospects.[91] Speculation by savers account only for short-term movements in the interest rate.[92] Eventually, they relent and become prepared to lend to investors. The demand for investment goods is not governed by speculation on the share market, but by a more sober judgement about productivity.

What view can be attributed to Keynes is difficult to ascertain. It is true that chapter 22 emphasizes the perverse movements of the MEI schedule, but chapter 18 points to 'the tendency of a fluctuation in one direction to reverse itself in due course' when investment proceeds at unaccustomed levels.[93] There is no suggestion, however, that such a reversal is to some 'true' position consistent with a calm and accurate assessment of the prospects.

It is difficult to follow how Leijonhufvud can argue that productivity rules in the long run after validly emphasizing that savers cannot send accurate messages to investors. Perceptions of productivity are subjective because savers are not sending signals of effective demand for any specific commodities. It is clear that Keynes criticizes classical theory, and it is plain that Leijonhufvud validly stresses this. Pigou was no straw man and in his review of *The General Theory* he wrote that someone saves 'not in order to accumulate money in a stocking or in a bank balance, but in order presently to buy a house or a motor car, or to invest in interest-bearing securities'.[94] Pigou conceded that the act of investment might lag behind saving but considered that equilibrium would tend to be disrupted only in transitional stages if the rate of saving changes. Saving is reliably channelled into appropriate forms of real investment.

Pigou's statement can be contrasted with one of Keynes's emphasized by Leijonhufvud. Pigou wrote: 'A decision to have one's teeth extracted is not in itself a decision to buy false ones. But few people in fact make the first decision without also making the second.'[95]

Pigou's analogy is somewhat misleading. It is not clear that having one's teeth extracted resembles an act of saving because the dentist knows that his patient will return. A better illustration stems from Keynes[96] and plainly Pigou simply did not grasp the point: 'An act of individual saving means – so to speak – a decision not to have dinner today. But it does *not* necessitate a decision to have dinner...or to consume any specified thing at any specified date.'

In pointing out that a communications failure prevents the co-ordination of savings and investment flows at values consistent with full employment, Leijonhufvud certainly seems on the right track. That markets are incomplete and that those for future and contingent deliveries do not generally exist is also emphasized by Tobin.[97]

On this point, oddly enough, Shackle[98] chides Keynes and accuses him of missing the essential idea:

Money...makes it possible for choice to be deferred until knowledge of needs and opportunities has improved.... [W]hy is it convenient to have a store of general purchasing power? Because we are not yet sure of what we want to buy.

But Keynes[99] himself says, as Leijonhufvud is right to point out, that savings represent 'a potentiality of consuming an unspecified article at an unspecified time'. Shackle is perhaps entitled to amplify the point because liquidity was often stressed by Keynes in connection with the speculative demand for money, but it is not true to say that Keynes overlooked the point and, by implication, that Keynes is in need of others to clarify what his fundamental idea really was. Also worth noticing is that Shackle, the fundamentalist, and Leijonhufvud share common ground in that money, if unspent, cannot transmit information, particularly if that information about future consumption patterns simply does not yet exist.[100]

Consequently, even sober and rational agents cannot be relied upon to make decisions that are 'right' in the Walrasian sense. The best feasible outcome is that reasonable investors' subjective perceptions of future demand are verified in the aggregate. This is an important point, and one with which a fundamentalist would be able to agree. Being neither unduly optimistic nor pessimistic does not imply accuracy in one's judgement. In the realms of romance, for example, one can reasonably believe that the creature you worship from afar would spurn your advances. Your prospective partner could well believe the same of you. You can both die and never know. History changes irretrievably and the lost opportunity is never revealed.

Leijonhufvud finds it sensible to argue that we can learn in the long run not to be slaves to speculation on the share market, and yet he wishes to marry that notion with two others which seem to contradict each other. Investors, usually cautious and wait-and-see types, suffer mysterious, sporadic and epileptic bouts of pessimism. He wants us to believe on top of this that, while excessive pessimism can suddenly appear on no objective grounds, pessimism does not rapidly worsen when there is quite a good reason, namely, when today's business worsens. Substantial and infrequent instability, inelastic expectations and long-run learning are concepts difficult to reconcile.[101] One solution is to regard them as alternative possibilities, each of which illustrate the problems of co-ordination under conditions of imperfect information.

While Leijonhufvud's treatment of uncertainty can be seen as somewhat awkward, at least it does play some part in his story. He certainly gives greater weight to the problems of inter-temporal co-ordination than did the textbook Keynesians. He does so by emphasizing the interest rate. This, however, leaves him open to the charge of downgrading shifts in the MEI schedule. While this may be fair criticism, to stress the volatility of the MEI can obscure Keynes's clearly held view that the interest rate was 'the villain of the piece'.[102] It was almost Keynes's obsession to scuttle the classical theory of the automatic adjustment of the interest rate. Why devote so much intellectual effort for a decade or so (since drafting the *Treatise*) to such an issue if it were not a crucially important part of the story?

Perhaps a middle ground between those who emphasize shifts and those who point to the interest elasticity of the MEI schedule can be found. Both the fundamentalists and Leijonhufvud exaggerate. Over longer periods, it can be argued that entrepreneurial moods even out. This does not require perfect knowledge, simply a psychological propensity to prefer undisturbed mental states. Feelings can settle around a sober and quietly calm degree of confidence. In such a state of mind, interest rates are important. This does not imply that there is any systematic or mechanical force at work in so far as moods must assume a wave-like pattern through time. All that is involved is the idea that a business community can over long periods settle upon some level of confidence which it is *reasonable* to hold.

Fundamentalists who insist that shifts in the MEI are paramount can be reminded of Keynes's view that there are 'certain important factors which somewhat mitigate in practice the effects of our ignorance of the future'.[103]

Keynes refers to the risk sharing (uncertainty sharing?) involved in long-term contracts for the occupancy of buildings and to the stability of the perceived social yields accruing to public investment. In view of the likely interest elasticity of the demand for funds for buildings and for public projects, Keynes's position can be taken to be somewhere between that of Leijonhufvud and those who emphasize animal spirits and non-rational urges.

That uncertainty is, however, subject to a systematic influence of sorts is suggested by Keynes himself:

> More probably there will be a cyclical movement round this equilibrium position. For if there is still room for uncertainty about the future, the marginal efficiency of capital will occasionally rise above zero leading to a 'boom', and in the succeeding 'slump'...may fall...below...zero.[104]

Consideration of the nature of a possible synthesis of Leijonhufvud's and a fundamentalist's perspectives is undertaken in further detail in a subsequent chapter on conventional behaviour. It is argued that conventions can help to tame the MEI, but the creature remains at heart a beast of the jungle.

Keynes on monetary policy

If the preceding analysis is correct, Keynes accepted that the investment function was fairly elastic but also prone to sudden and significant shifts. This seems to imply that monetary policy would be weak as a short-term instrument, but, over a longer period, a low interest-rate regime would facilitate a higher average level of investment. One tentative conclusion is that the fundamentalists have the better case for the short run, but Leijonhufvud's evaluation of the role of monetary policy stands for the long run. This is a partial victory for Leijonhufvud, in a sense, because his aim was to point to a role for fiscal policy which was confined to short-term stabilization in the face of severe contractionary disturbances. Leijonhufvud never attributed to *The General Theory* support for the general use of monetary policy as a short-term instrument.

Leijonhufvud's views about the difficulties in changing the interest rate, rather than the lack of response of expenditure to it, being at the heart of Keynes's rejection of counter-cyclical monetary policy do seem borne out in some passages:

> If the long-term rate of interest could be controlled on short-period considerations, it would obviously be a useful weapon for regulating the pace of recovery.... But it is obvious that such a policy is impracticable...[because] the long-term rate at any time can only depart by a strictly limited small amount from the expected average rate over the period in question. For this reason the long-term rate is ineligible for use as a short-period weapon.[105]

This passage was written in 1937 and is no relic prior to any 'clean break' from the *Treatise*. However, it can be counter-argued that a weapon that is 'useful' can still be inadequate to do the job alone, and so it is not clear that the interest elasticity of investment is so great that any likely degree of pessimism is liable to be capable of being offset by low interest rates.

Keynes considered it an open question whether, over a fairly long period of history, lower interest rates can reduce the duration and amplitude of slumps, and it is possible that Leijonhufvud is more confident about the potency of monetary policy than Keynes was himself.[106] The issue is difficult to settle in that Keynes's position was not black and white: 'Only experience, however, can show how far management of the rate of interest is capable of continuously stimulating the appropriate volume of investment.'[107] None of this assists us with the problem of whether a persistent degree of pessimism can be overcome by monetary policy. Quotations directed at the practical matter of recommending low interest-rate policies do not help if it is implicit that investors' expectations change through time in the real world and become more optimistic.

Keynes points to this possibility: 'If the rate of interest were so governed as to maintain continuous full employment, Virtue [that is, thrift] would resume her sway.'[108]

It remains difficult to apportion between low interest rates and buoyant levels of confidence the burden of responsibility for the preservation of full employment. Keynes seemed to make them roughly equal partners without indicating in particular whether a low interest rate was in some sense senior and alone could spur sufficient investment. There is no evidence to suggest that optimism is the dominant partner in that at no stage does Keynes consider the possibility that euphoria can for prolonged periods[109] overcome the depressing influence of high interest rates.

One relatively strong passage indicating the importance of the state of credit – and, to some extent, the interest rate could be taken as a proxy for this – is:

> A collapse in the price of equities, which has had disastrous reactions on the marginal efficiency of capital, may have been due to the weakening either of speculative confidence or of the state of credit. But whereas the weakening of either is enough to cause a collapse, recovery requires the revival of *both*.[110]

Make what you will of the following:

> Thus after giving full weight to the importance of the influence of short-period changes in the state of long-term expectation as distinct from changes in the rate of interest, we are still entitled to

return to the latter as exercising, at any rate, *in normal circumstances, a great, though not a decisive*, influence on the rate of investment.[111]

[The] daily revaluations of the Stock Exchange...inevitably exert a decisive influence on the rate of current investment. For there is no sense in building up a new enterprise at a cost greater than that at which a similar existing enterprise can be purchased.... Thus certain classes of investment are governed by the average expectations of those who deal on the Stock Exchange as revealed in the price of shares, rather than by the genuine expectations of the professional entrepreneur.[112]

A final possibility, this time in favour of monetary policy's prospects, is that a wider understanding of Keynes's own book would itself have beneficial effects in the future. He complains of the mistaken view which overlooks the speculative component in the interest rate and observes that 'the failure of employment to attain an optimum level [is] in no way associated, in the minds either of the public or of authority, with the prevalence of an inappropriate range of rates of interest'.[113] It seems that, when the public and their governments are better educated, the responsiveness of key variables can change. (This resembles the commonly encountered argument that, when fiscal policy is understood by the business sector, it no longer need have perverse effects on private investment.)

One should recall that Leijonhufvud's primary purpose was to indicate that Keynesians had exaggerated the importance of fiscal policy in Keynes. Perhaps he goes a little far in the opposite extreme, but it is true that 'Keynes' position on the issue was a good deal less clear cut than one would gather from standard textbook expositions of the "Keynesian system"'.[114]

Leijonhufvud observes that the many standard arguments against monetary policy are absent from *The General Theory* and that the radicalism of the 'socialisation of investment' can be read down.[115] The arguments are sensible ones, and we can at least confidently attribute to Keynes a very significant degree of reliance on monetary policy as a long-run tool. Leijonhufvud does, however, play down Keynes's doubts about using monetary policy, for example, to defeat a slump, so far as the dismissal of the liquidity trap is concerned.

There is one other major reservation about Leijonhufvud's portrayal of Keynes's views. It relates to the debate between Keynes and Robertson over the use of monetary policy to bring booms under control. Leijonhufvud seems to exaggerate Keynes's confidence in monetary policy.

Keynes versus Robertson on monetary policy

Leijonhufvud considers Keynesians to have failed to recognize the potential for manipulating long interest rates. It is important to note that Leijonhufvud uses the *Treatise* to supply, in part, the rationale for that belief.[116] He also considers Keynes to have entertained seriously Robertson's 'nip-the-boom-in-the-bud' doctrine. He claims that, although Keynes was more pessimistic about the potency of monetary policy pursued exclusively, the shift of his opinion between 1930 and 1936 'was very subtle and far from drastic'.[117]

This section is devoted to the strength of monetary policy in an upswing. In particular, Leijonhufvud emphasizes a passage from Keynes to support the view that Keynes here saw an important role for monetary policy. The context is in the aforementioned debate with Robertson:

> It should be remembered that the *General Theory* castigated as '*dangerously and unnecessarily defeatist*' the notion that even 'the *most enlightened* monetary control might find itself in difficulties...[such that] none of the alternatives within its power might make much difference to the result'.[118]

It is argued that Keynes has been misconstrued. The context of Keynes's remarks needs to be supplied.[119] He is not solely concerned with arguing in favour of the power of monetary policy. Contrary to Leijonhufvud, attacks on monetary policy are not defeatist. This is left an open question. It is the 'austere view' that is 'dangerously and unnecessarily defeatist', and it is the view which (according to Keynes at least) Dennis Robertson has unsuccessfully attempted to justify.

> [I]t is, I think, *arguable* that a more advantageous average state of expectation might result from a banking policy which always nipped in the bud an incipient boom by a rate of interest high enough to deter even the most misguided optimists.[120]

Keynes, however, doubts that this austere argument is sound and points out that the Federal Reserve, especially with the weapons it then possessed, might have little power to curtail investment anyway. He continues:

> However this may be [i.e., whether the Federal Reserve could even achieve this result or not], such an outlook [as Robertson's] seems to me to be dangerously and unnecessarily defeatist. It recommends, or at least assumes, for permanent acceptance too much [in particular, a tendency towards unemployment] that is defective in our existing economic scheme.[121]

The defect is not that monetary authorities have failed to put pressure on the long rate, though obviously Keynes considers this relevant. Rather, Keynes objects to the defeatist assumption that 'full employment is an impracticable ideal and that the best that we can hope for is a level of employment which is more stable than at present and averaging, perhaps, a little higher'.

Keynes, on the contrary, argued that, far from trying to check the oncoming boom, one should lower interest rates to help keep us 'permanently in a quasi-boom'.[122] Leijonhufvud's interpretation gives monetary policy power in checking a boom. Keynes thought this to be possible, but considered a steady low-interest policy preferable.

Note that while Keynes was not prepared to raise interest rates in advance of boom conditions, he willingly advocated high nominal interest rates, of 10 per cent in 1920, to break inflationary expectations under conditions when physical controls were impractical as an alternative after the war. By 1942, Keynes had realized the dangers to employment that dear money raised and envisaged a five-year period of controls.[123] One can advocate the tightening of monetary conditions to break an actual boom without also suggesting the same policy merely to nip some hypothetical one in the bud. The latter would be fine-tuning employing monetary policy, a view difficult to attribute to Keynes.

It appears overall that Leijonhufvud, while validly criticizing the orthodox Keynesian view whereby monetary policy was dismissed as impotent, has strayed to the other extreme. By playing down Keynes's radicalism over policy issues, Leijonhufvud has fuelled suspicions that he is trying to tame Keynes and render him more respectable in the eyes of orthodox macroeconomists. One cannot be surprised, therefore, if fundamentalists are hostile.

Notes

1 Axel Leijonhufvud, *On Keynesian Economics and the Economics of Keynes: a study in monetary theory*, New York, Oxford University Press, 1968, pp. 42, 174, 280.
2 J.M. Keynes, *The General Theory of Employment Interest and Money*, London, Macmillan, 1936, pp. 135–6.
3 Leijonhufvud, *On Keynesian Economics*, pp. 41–2.
4 See ibid., pp. 111 *et seq.*
5 Remember also that Leijonhufvud claims that Keynes 'explicitly repudiated' the notion of the liquidity trap (ibid., p. 158).
6 Richard T. Froyen, 'The aggregative structure of Keynes's *General Theory*', *Quarterly Journal of Economics*, vol. 90, no. 3, August 1976, pp. 369–87.
7 Santi K. Chakrabarti, *The Two-sector General Theory Model*, London, Macmillan, 1979.

8 Recall that 'commodities' refers to consumption and/or capital goods whereas 'goods' have a broader meaning embracing money, labour and so forth.

9 Froyen, 'The aggregative structure...', p. 379.

10 ibid., p. 386. Hines, *On the Reappraisal of Keynesian Economics*, London, Martin Robertson, 1971, p. 27, agrees that the one-commodity version is sufficient to highlight the income-constrained process itself, while it is inadequate to capture other of Keynes's arguments.

11 Froyen, 'The aggregative structure...', pp. 386–7.

12 ibid., p. 374.

13 ibid., p. 2.

14 ibid., p. 373.

15 Keynes, *The General Theory*, pp. 7, 17, 273, 275. William A. Darity and Bobbie L. Horn, 'Involuntary unemployment reconsidered', *Southern Economic Journal*, vol. 49, no. 3, January 1983, pp. 717–33, at p. 720, n. 5, support Leijonhufvud too.

16 Keynes, *The General Theory*, pp. 115–16. See Chakrabarti, *The Two-sector General Theory Model*, pp. 3–4.

17 Chakrabarti, *The Two-sector General Theory Model*, pp. 28–32.

18 Keynes, *The General Theory*, p. 90. Note that Keynes measured aggregates in terms of wage units and that money wages could normally be regarded as being fairly stable.

19 ibid., p. 295.

20 Froyen, 'The aggregative structure...', p. 380.

21 ibid.

22 Chakrabarti, *The Two-sector General Theory Model*, pp. 31–2.

23 See ibid., pp. 3, 22, 26–7 where Chakrabarti cites *The General Theory*, pp. 38, 281–2. To take an analogy, were it to rain and the propensity for people of various kinds to carry umbrellas was known, as well as the composition of these kinds of person venturing into the rain being predictable, one could specify the number of umbrellas taken outside on any rainy day. This does not imply that umbrellas and people (or different kinds of people) are pretty much the same and comprise an aggregate.

24 See Keynes, *The General Theory*, pp. 281–2, 286.

25 Froyen, 'The aggregative structure...', p. 381. Chakrabarti, *The Two-sector General Theory Model*, p. 32 takes a similar view. See also *The Collected Writings of John Maynard Keynes*, London, Macmillan, 1971–, vol. xiii, p. 433.

26 Keynes, *The General Theory*, pp. 146, 149. See also Chakrabarti, *The Two-sector General Theory Model*, p. 32, n.

27 Here, curiously, Froyen ('The aggregative structure...', p. 374) relies on Keynes, *A Treatise on Money*, London, Macmillan, 1930, vol. I, p. 201 (*Collected Writings*, vol. v, p. 222), despite arguing elsewhere that Keynes's views on aggregation changed dramatically during the 1930s, though he goes on to argue that Keynes did the same thing in *The General Theory* with regard to the treatment of shares and new fixed capital.

28 Keynes, *The General Theory*, p. 151 and n. 2 (emphasis added).

29 Chakrabarti, *The Two-sector General Theory Model*, p. 30.

30 ibid., p. 8.

31 Leijonhufvud *On Keynesian Economics*, pp. 137–8.

32 Keynes, *The General Theory*, pp. 173–4.

33 John Brothwell, 'A simple Keynesian's response to Leijonhufvud',
    Bulletin of Economic Research, vol. 27, May 1975, pp. 3–21,
    at p. 11 considers the orthodox aggregation as a lesser evil because
    he reasons, in fundamentalist style, that only in a certain world can
    bonds and real capital be aggregated. He also appears friendly to the
    notion of a five-good aggregative structure, as does Chakrabarti
    (*The Two-sector General Theory Model*, pp. 9–10). Helmut Schuster,
    'Keynes' disequilibrium analysis', *Kyklos*, vol. 26, no. 3, 1973,
    pp. 512–44, at p. 516, also observes that equities and bonds must be
    distinguished if changes in stock market valuations are allowed within
    the short run.

34 Keynes, *Collected Writings*, vol. xiv, pp. 11–12. See also vol. v,
    pp. 222–3 where he clearly states that the prices of bonds and
    shares 'frequently move in *opposite* directions' (Keynes's
    emphasis).

35 Leijonhufvud, *On Keynesian Economics*, pp. 149 *et seq*. A helpful
    summary of some of the differences between Leijonhufvud and
    Davidson is supplied by E. Roy Weintraub, 'Uncertainty and the
    Keynesian revolution', reproduced in John Cunningham Wood, *John
    Maynard Keynes: critical assessments*, London, Croom Helm, 1983, in
    4 vols, vol. 4, pp. 152–68, esp. pp. 166–7, n. 12 and n. 24.

36 John Fender (*Understanding Keynes: an analysis of 'The General
    Theory'*, Brighton, Wheatsheaf Books, 1981, p. 69) has suggested that,
    because the MEI in part is governed by cost conditions in the
    investment-goods sector whereas the LP curve is unaffected by
    bottlenecks in the supply of bonds, this is a further reason to distinguish
    bonds from physical assets.

37 Chakrabarti, *The Two-sector General Theory Model*, p. 12 concedes this.

38 This rather Pigovian preoccupation began prior to *The General Theory*,
    which casts some doubts on Froyen's 'clean break' approach. See
    Keynes, *Collected Writings*, vol. xiii, pp. 399, 451, which allude to
    different kinds of capital goods, and p. 380, which in May 1932 denies
    the use of separating the two sectors for some purposes. See also
    pp. 393, 428–9, 585.

39 Froyen, 'The aggregative structure...', p. 381, prefers to see Keynes as
    occasionally switching from a one-commodity model to an
    n-commodity one. See *The General Theory*, pp. 136, 316.

40 See Keynes, *The General Theory*, pp. 25, n. 2, 187, n. 2, 192, n. 2,
    248, 274 (in addition to those passages already cited).

41 This is clearest from ibid., pp. 115–16.

42 Keynes, *Collected Writings*, vol. xiv, pp. 72, 142, 190 pose similar
    exegetical difficulties.

43 For example, Keynes, *Collected Writings*, vol. xiii, pp. 403, 483–4.

44 Leijonhufvud, *On Keynesian Economics*, p. 136, n. 9. J.S. Fleming, 'Wealth effects in Keynesian models', *Oxford Economic Papers*, vol. 26, no. 2, July 1974, pp. 248–58, esp. p. 257, while not commenting at length on the exegetical accuracy of Leijonhufvud's position, agrees that a preferable procedure is not to oversimplify the model by imposing a four-good structure instead of a five-good one.

45 This is clear from his letters to Harrod. See *Collected Writings*, vol. xiii, pp. 295 *et seq*., and Bruce Littleboy and Ghanshyam Mehta, 'The scientific method of Keynes', *Journal of Economic Studies*, vol. 10, no. 4, 1983, pp. 3–14, at p. 8; and, by the same authors, 'Keynes and scientific methodology: whither and whence', *Indian Economic Journal*, vol. 33, no. 1, July–September 1986, pp. 66–76.

46 Professor Thomas Rymes has compiled the lecture notes of some of Keynes's students, a forthcoming publication. In a lecture (6 November 1933), Keynes criticized scholasticism which strives to formulate abstract, precise generalizations. The world and our thoughts about it are by contrast vague, grey and fluffy.

47 See the *Treatise*, Keynes, *Collected Writings*, vol. v, pp. 180–1; vol. vi, pp. 85–6.

48 ibid., p. 161.

49 ibid.

50 Keynes, *The General Theory*, p. 64, cited by Leijonhufvud (his italics) in *On Keynesian Economics*, p. 161, n. 5.

51 Compare Lawrence Klein, *The Keynesian Revolution*, London, Macmillan, 1952, p. 85.

52 Leijonhufvud, *On Keynesian Economics*, pp. 163 *et seq*. As in Leijonhufvud, a distinction is not made between MEI and MEC curves in the following text.

53 ibid., p. 163.

54 ibid., pp. 164–5.

55 ibid., p. 165 citing the *Treatise*, Keynes, *Collected Writings*, vol. vi, p. 326, with italics added by Leijonhufvud.

56 Keynes, *Collected Writings*, vol. vi, p. 90, n. 2 (also cited in Leijonhufvud, *On Keynesian Economics*, p. 159, n. 3).

57 Keynes, *The General Theory*, p. 324. See also p. 219. Compare Leijonhufvud, *On Keynesian Economics*, pp. 182, n. 2; 410, n. 22; 411. Note that the possibility of capital saturation was merely an *obiter dictum*. Keynes felt no need to pursue the point in detail (*Collected Writings*, vol. xxix, p. 213).

58 Keynes, *The General Theory*, p. 136 cited in Leijonhufvud, *On Keynesian Economics*, p. 165 in abbreviated form. The italics are Leijonhufvud's.

59 Thus attention leaps to elasticity (4).

60 Keynes, *The General Theory*, pp. 187, n. 2, 252, 300–1.

61 ibid., p. 187, n. 2. Compare Paul Davidson, *Money and the Real World*, London, Macmillan, 1978, 2nd edn, p. 229.

62 Leijonhufvud, *On Keynesian Economics*, pp. 165–6, especially n. 14. Compare Keynes, *The General Theory*, p. 147 where express reference

is made to the relevance of changes in the stock of capital.

63 Leijonhufvud, *On Keynesian Economics*, p. 163. Leijonhufvud
   (p. 163, n. 11) points out that the discount rate is referred to as the
   'socially required rate of return to capital' or 'the supply price of
   capital' by other authorities.

64 ibid., p. 166.

65 ibid. Compare Brothwell, 'A simple Keynesian's response to
   Leijonhufvud', p. 12.

66 Leijonhufvud, *On Keynesian Economics*, p. 165.

67 Keynes, *Collected Writings*, vol. xiii, p. 234. He is equally unambiguous
   on pp. 364–5. Lord Kahn, *The Making of Keynes' General Theory*,
   Cambridge, Cambridge University Press, 1983, p. 148, agrees with
   Leijonhufvud too. See also Keynes, *The General Theory*, p. 250.

68 Brothwell ('A simple Keynesian's response to Leijonhufvud',
   pp. 12–13) reaches the same conclusion. One can regard Brothwell as
   being a fundamentalist with sufficient eclecticism to be prepared to use
   IS-LM as a useful teaching tool.

69 Leijonhufvud, *On Keynesian Economics*, p. 340. Indeed, Leijonhufvud
   there blames the *onset* of the depression on unduly high interest rates
   rather than a sudden decline in the MEI. Here again, it seems that his
   views on the *Treatise* have unduly pushed themselves into prominence
   in Leijonhufvud's mind. An extraordinary example of this appears
   (ibid., pp. 192–3) where he interprets a passage from *The General
   Theory* (p. 319) in the light of the *Treatise* without any real justification
   and appears to reply on sheer clairvoyance:

   > The last quotation given suggests a reference to the 'Great Crash' of
   > 1929. Actually, Keynes is thinking of the years following 1930 in
   > which contracting and low incomes did account for a 'serious fall in
   > the marginal efficiency of capital'. He blamed the onset of the Great
   > Depression on a misguided monetary policy.' (p. 192)

   He then (p. 193) cites the *Treatise*. See also pp. 200–1. Contrast
   p. 405, where shifts are 'exaggerated' but, presumably, not wildly
   excessive.

   In 1931, Keynes clearly emphasized the role of interest rates while
   recognizing, as in the *Treatise*, the instability of investment. See
   Collected Writings, vol. xiii, pp. 334, 359. Incidentally, it is not clear
   why Leijonhufvud (*On Keynesian Economics*, p. 407) considers that, for
   the bulk of the *Treatise*, 'entrepreneurial expectations are roughly right'.
   The *Treatise* clearly identifies changes in investment confidence, rather
   than thrift, as the prime source of disequilibrium. Compare Axel
   Leijonhufvud, 'Keynes and the effectiveness of monetary policy',
   Western Economic Journal, vol. 6, March 1968, pp. 97–111, at p. 105;
   On Keynesian Economics, p. 284.

70 'The longer the system wallows in depression,...the farther would the
   dry rot eat into [long-term expectations]' (Leijonhufvud, *On Keynesian
   Economics*, p. 340, n. 11). Compare Slim's adage (p. 375).

71 ibid., p. 279. See also p. 351, esp. n. 28.

72 ibid., p. 279. See also p. 380.
73 Keynes, *The General Theory*, p. 51. Keynes goes on: 'Thus the factor of current long-term expectation cannot be even approximately eliminated or replaced by realised results.' We shall see that no simple rule governs the formation of long-term expectations. 'There is...not much to be said about the state of confidence *a priori*' (p. 149).
74 Leijonhufvud, *On Keynesian Economics*, pp. 42, 44, 124, 137, 141, 152, 156, 173, 174, 191, 197, 206, 342. Likewise Chakrabarti, *The Two-sector General Theory Model*, p. 9, can find no textual support for holding fixed the state of long-term expectations.
75 Leijonhufvud, *On Keynesian Economics*, p. 279, citing Keynes, *The General Theory*, pp. 210–11.
76 Keynes, *The General Theory*, p. 210 (emphasis added).
77 Compare Keynes, *Collected Writings*, vol. xiv, p. 81 for the view that present income has no *predominant* effect however.
78 A similar point can be made in a different context. For analytical convenience money wages are assumed given, but this is not integral to the basic theory, and the effects of flexibility are considered when appropriate. If Leijonhufvud is prepared to allow chapter 19 (which occurs after chapter 18, the re-statement and summary of key elements of *The General Theory* in which the MEI schedule is an independent variable) why not also allow chapters 12 and 22 their full weight too?
79 Keynes, *The General Theory*, p. 51. Note Keynes's acknowledgement of the possibility, though relatively infrequent in practice, of the anticipation of future demand – that is, of an elasticity of expectations exceeding unity. The current interpretation would therefore be hostile to that of Leijonhufvud, *On Keynesian Economics*, pp. 73–4, where Keynes is criticized for failing to fit Leijonhufvud's interpretation. See also Leijonhufvud's (p. 141) criticism of Keynes for allegedly being internally inconsistent whereas a natural alternative is to argue that it is his interpretation that is inconsistent with Keynes.
80 Keynes, *The General Theory*, p. 263, n. 10.
81 Leijonhufvud, *On Keynesian Economics*, p. 340.
82 Keynes, *The General Theory*, pp. 50, 148, 149, 317 (emphasis added). The 'dry rot' analogy is clearly inappropriate.
83 ibid., p. 155 cited in *On Keynesian Economics*, pp. 281, 363.
84 Leijonhufvud, *On Keynesian Economics*, p. 329. Leijonhufvud seems to contradict himself (ibid., p. 285, esp. n. 4) where he refers to how overshooting can occur because of speculating on the trend. If Leijonhufvud simply means to make a general statement that information problems can result both in the under- and over-estimation of prices depending on the circumstances, then his position is less open to criticism. It is his narrow reliance specifically on inelastic price expectations which a fundamentalist can readily challenge.
85 Keynes, *The General Theory*, pp. 153–4.
86 ibid., p. 150.
87 Leijonhufvud, *On Keynesian Economics*, p. 281, n. 31.
88 Keynes, *The General Theory*, pp. 158–9.

89 The exegetical point is a delicate one, it is conceded (see Leijonhufvud, *On Keynesian Economics*, p. 178, n. 29). The complaint is that Leijonhufvud *systematically* reads down Keynes's assault on long-run economics. Of course, in isolation, some of Leijonhufvud's arguments are perfectly plausible.

90 ibid., p. 303.

91 ibid., pp. 202–3, 264–5, 368–77. A similar argument was also made by D.H. Robertson, 'Some notes on Mr Keynes' general theory of employment', *Quarterly Journal of Economics*, vol. 51, November 1936, pp. 168–91, at pp. 189–90. Leijonhufvud's indebtedness to him is once again clear.

92 Leijonhufvud, *On Keynesian Economics*, p. 213.

93 Keynes, *The General Theory*, p. 251.

94 Arthur C. Pigou, 'Mr J.M. Keynes' "General theory of employment, interest and money"', *Economica*, vol. 3, May 1936, pp. 115–32, at p. 126.

95 ibid.

96 Keynes, *The General Theory*, p. 210. Even in the *Treatise*, Keynes recognized this point: 'Not only are the decisions made by different sets of persons; they must also in many cases be made at different times', *Treatise*, vol. I, (*Collected Writings*, vol. v, p. 251).

97 James Tobin, 'Comment', on Kaldor, in David Worswick and James Trevithick, *Keynes and the Modern World*, Cambridge, Cambridge University Press, 1983, p. 31. Leijonhufvud notes that potential gains from trade, stressed by new classicists, cannot happen if intertemporal markets are incomplete. 'Keynesianism, monetarism, and rational expectations: some reflections and conjectures', in Roman Frydman and Edmund S. Phelps, *Individual Forecasting and Aggregate Outcomes: 'rational expectations' examined*, Cambridge, Cambridge University Press, 1983, p. 222, n. 24.

98 G.L.S. Shackle, *Keynesian Kaleidics*, Edinburgh, Edinburgh University Press, 1974, p. 62 (italics removed).

99 Keynes, *The General Theory*, p. 211.

100 One cannot see Leijonhufvud disputing Shackle, *Keynesian Kaleidics*, pp. 72–3.

101 Leijonhufvud even states that revisions of expectations can overshoot the mark (*On Keynesian Economics*, p. 380).

102 Keynes, *Collected Writings*, vol. xxix, p. 16 (March 1932).

103 Keynes, *The General Theory*, p. 163.

104 ibid., p. 218. The remarks are made in the context of secular stagnation and capital saturation where uncertainty could be expected to be at a minimum because of the relative stability of the mature or virtually steady-state system. Residual uncertainty and changes in confidence exist even in a relatively stable objective environment.

In 1931, Keynes was graciously prepared to concede that 'Hayek's methods may be suitable for analysing *some* of the conditions which determine this "long-period" natural rate of interest', *Collected Writings*, vol. xiii, p. 254 (emphasis added).

105 Keynes, *Collected Writings*, vol. xiv, p. 162. In 1944, Keynes held similar views, vol. xxvii, p. 377.
106 John Brothwell, 'A simple Keynesian response to Leijonhufvud', p. 10; 'Rejoinder', *Bulletin of Economic Research*, vol. 28, November 1978, pp. 123–6, at p. 124 argues in like fashion. Note the weight that Leijonhufvud (*On Keynesian Economics*, p. 412) gives to passages from the *Treatise* which are used to tone down the greater radicalism of *The General Theory* and thereby reducing a possible shift in emphasis in Keynes.
107 Keynes, *The General Theory*, p. 164. Note that continuous full employment is a particularly ambitious goal, yet Keynes entertains the notion that monetary policy could achieve it. Leijonhufvud also is careful not to express too extreme a view on the efficacy of monetary policy in Keynes (*On Keynesian Economics*, pp. 412–13). What is clearer is that textbook Keynesians had exaggerated the interest inelasticity of investment and rendered monetary policy largely impotent even without reliance on the trap.

Brothwell, 'Rejoinder', p. 124, sensibly notes that one can agree with Leijonhufvud about the fundamental problem being that the relative price of capital is too low and yet also hold that Leijonhufvud overestimates the ease by which entrepreneurial pessimism can be offset by a lower interest rate. On the other hand, Brothwell appears to exaggerate the difficulty as Keynes clearly saw the interest rate as an important variable.
108 Keynes, *The General Theory*, p. 112. Keynes seemed almost deliberately ambivalent (pp. 250, 375) in that he wished to make known his views on the mere feasibility of such a strategy. One can also mention that, in the open system, where capital outflows result from low domestic interest rates, there is an offset (pp. 335–7) to reduce even the long-run value of having low long rates.

Also notable is Keynes's objection to Tinbergen's finding that the effect of the interest rate on investment was small. Keynes considered that the interest rate had in fact changed very little during the period in question. See Keynes, *Collected Writings*, vol. xiv, pp. 316–17.
109 Keynes, *The General Theory*, pp. 321–2 refers to the temporary illusions associated with genuine booms. For his remarks on the 'later stages of the boom' see pp. 315–16. He does (pp. 317–18) refer to the brief period where negative interest rates would be needed to offset a slump.
110 ibid., p. 158.
111 ibid., p. 164 (emphasis added).
112 ibid., p. 151. Compare p. 153, where share speculation 'creates *no small part* of our *contemporary* problem of securing sufficient investment' (emphasis added). Compare Leijonhufvud, *On Keynesian Economics*, p. 162.
113 Keynes, *The General Theory*, p. 204. This was written with a long-run perspective in mind.

114 Leijonhufvud, 'Keynes and the effectiveness of monetary policy', p. 97. The moderation with which the arguments are made in this paper makes it difficult to criticize him in any confident or aggressive way.

115 Leijonhufvud, 'Keynes and the effectiveness of monetary policy', pp. 100, 102. See also *On Keynesian Economics*, p. 408. For example if most fixed investment is in land, buildings, roads, railways and increasingly in public-sector projects (where interest costs rather than confidence are the more relevant), it is doubtful (especially in view of chapter 24) that Keynes meant stringent and detailed controls or nationalization.

Keynes's mischievous suggestions that burying banknotes and auctioning licences to the private sector to unearth them, or digging holes and re-filling them, would be better than doing nothing have, incidentally, attracted some odd comments. Sheila C. Dow and Peter E. Earl (*Money Matters: a Keynesian approach to monetary economics*, Oxford, Martin Robertson, 1982, p. 251) suggest that such proposals unfortunately fail to focus on how labour could instead be employed more usefully. A.K. Dasgupta (*Epochs of Economic Theory*, Oxford, Basil Blackwell, 1985, p. 139, n. 33) conjectures that Keynes was pointing out that the private sector needs not to feel threatened by the incursion of the state sector. Apparently Keynes's heavy irony (*The General Theory*, ch. 6, part VI) is not generally appreciated. He held in contempt those who saw the legitimate role for public projects being confined to building utterly useless things in which the private sector had no interest.

116 Leijonhufvud, *On Keynesian Economics*, p. 411.

117 ibid., p. 405.

118 ibid., p. 413, citing Keynes, *The General Theory*, p. 327. The emphasis in the passage cited is Leijonhufvud's, as are the insertions and deletions.

119 Keynes, *The General Theory*, pp. 326–9 should be read as a whole.

120 ibid., p. 327 (emphasis added).

121 ibid.

122 ibid., p. 322. For advocacy of the 'austere view' see Henderson in Keynes, *Collected Writings*, vol. xxix, pp. 224–5. For Keynes's reply see p. 235. Pigou also opposed Keynes considering that 'it is desirable to destroy the error of optimism, or, better still, to nip it in the bud', Arthur C. Pigou, *Keynes's 'General Theory': a retrospective view*, London, Macmillan, 1950, p. 38, n. 1. Keynes affirmed his position in *Collected Writings*, vol. xiv, pp. 161–2.

123 For details see Susan Howson, '"A dear money man?" Keynes on monetary policy, 1920', *Economic Journal*, vol. 83, no. 330, June 1973, pp. 456–64, at p. 464. It is doubtful that J. Fleming has correctly maintained that Keynes recommended tight monetary policy in 1942 ('Comment' on Scitovsky in G.D.N. Worswick and J. Trevithick (eds), *Keynes and the Modern World*, p. 245). See also D.E. Moggridge and Susan Howson, 'Keynes on monetary policy, 1910–1946',

Oxford Economic Papers, vol. 26, no. 2, July 1974, pp. 226–47, at pp. 231, 240–1, where Keynes by 1937 was not prepared to employ dear money to quell a boom.

Chapter eight

Recovery in the long run?

Long-run recovery in theory and in practice

Central to the neoclassical synthesis is the argument that real balance effects generate full employment in the long run. Leijonhufvud stressed that Keynes's major contribution lay in the realm of the short run whereby the multiplier amplifies any initial contractionary disturbance. Leijonhufvud's objection to the neoclassical synthesis is that it portrays Keynes's short-run theory in terms of the elasticities of the *IS* and *LM* curves. Leijonhufvud thereby gives the impression that Keynes's theory is best seen as being consistent with long-run classical theory. Fundamentalists challenge any attempt to present Keynes as being in any way in harmony with the neoclassical synthesis.

Neoclassicists tend to place little practical emphasis on real balance effects. Monetary and fiscal policy are more effective short-run means to generate full employment outcomes. Real balance effects work in logic in the long run but are too unreliable. Fundamentalists, by contrast, reject the notion that the full-employment vector can be uniquely specified. The system evolves in historical time and prior disturbances permanently affect its path. Furthermore, real balance effects resulting from rapidly adjusting prices are liable to destabilize the system. Real-world economies begin the adjustment process with inherited currency denominated contracts. Real debt burdens grow if deflation occurs. Bankruptcies are probable. Classical medicine is, therefore, poisonous rather than merely impracticably slow to work.

Leijonhufvud is also hostile to the neoclassical account of the long-run relevance of real balance effects. He stresses different objections, however. He is more prepared to evaluate neoclassicism on its own terms and identify problems internal to it. Rather than dismiss real balance effects as implausible nonsense, he examines the conditions under which they could restore full employment. He concludes that it is conceivable that they could in logic do so, but that money-using economies cannot reasonably be portrayed as being able to self-adjust in any significant sense.

While different from each other, the fundamentalist and reductionist objections to the neoclassical synthesis appear complementary. It is true, however, that Leijonhufvud is prepared to concede more terrain to the classicists than the fundamentalists are. In so far as this is the case, some criticism of Leijonhufvud's interpretation of Keynes does appear valid. Keynes's critique of classical economics does seem to have been read down somewhat. While pointing out means by which full employment could be restored, Leijonhufvud does not adequately present Keynes's reservations about both their hypothetical and practical validity.

Some preliminary issues require consideration. First, the meanings of 'long run' and 'recovery' are not as obvious as would appear. Little attention has been given (except by Leijonhufvud) to the particular matter of the nature of a full-employment 'equilibrium' to which the Pigou and Keynes effects could give rise. The second concern relates to the distinction between a recovery which is a mere logical possibility and one which is claimed to be inevitable in practice. Last, and more importantly, the exegetical aspects need to be attended to.

Several real balance effects could emerge in response to long-run money-wage flexibility. The Pigou effect is one whereby increased real balances, by virtue of proportional deflation, directly affects consumption. The Keynes effect indirectly increases consumption and investment. It results from the decline in interest rates that stems from deflation-induced increases in real balances.[1] In so far as lower interest rates raise asset prices (and thereby private-sector wealth) this induces higher consumption.

Keynes supplies a definition of the long run. It is where 'a state of expectation...has lasted long enough for there to be no hangover from a previous state of expectation'.[2]

For a moment the discussion must turn somewhat metaphysical. One problem is that, in some contexts, the long run is not a theoretical construct in purely logical time. It can sometimes also be used to aid in thought experiments conducted in historical time. In logical time, sequences can be postulated and expectations can be sheltered from exogenous disturbance. Logical time can allow analysis to proceed on the basis that there exists some definite objective reality about which agents can ultimately learn by systematic and endogenous processes. In historical time the objective environment can be in a state of perpetual flux. As time passes, we can learn about the price of copper in the year 2020 by simply waiting until that date, but by that year the now current investment projects require conjectures about the year 2060. Logical time remains a useful concept even though reality evidently exists in historical time. If co-ordination problems can occur even in the former as a matter of logic, our faith in the long-run convergence to optimality would be shaken. The argument that in historical time there are at least tendencies to optimality can be rejected if even in logical time there are no grounds for that conclusion.

Keynes employed both conceptions of time. Fundamentalists emphasize historical time, but Keynes sometimes used logical time for heuristic purposes. In examining the multiplier Keynes was even content to compress logical time into an instant so that two comparative-static states could be compared. This is the instantaneous multiplier where perfect foresight of producers in the consumption sector is assumed. Leijonhufvud attributes to Keynes an explanation of the dynamic multiplier in which the process is slowed down sufficiently to perceive the role played by money as a means of payment. (His account can, as we have earlier seen, be criticized as placing too much emphasis on objective liquidity constraints and not enough on expectations of revenue and the willingness to extend credit.) Leijonhufvud's more prominent innovations point to aspects of Keynes that are readily capable of being couched in terms of logical time. In speculating on likely effects of money-wage flexibility in 'the long run' Keynes likewise chose to suppress historical changes in expectations about the future. If Keynes himself used both conceptions, then fundamentalists and reductionists alike can be regarded as providing partial illumination of Keynes's insights. The alternative, propounded by the fundamentalists, is to regard Keynes as too confused to see the supposed conflict. To reject logical time and the mechanistic models it entails would, it is sometimes claimed,[3] have enabled his real message to have been grasped.

Keynes's views on the long run in logical time as a heuristic concept are somewhat unclear. He wrote:

> I should, I think, be prepared to argue that, in a world ruled by uncertainty with an uncertain future linked to an actual present, a final position of equilibrium, such as one deals with in static economics, does not properly exist.[4]

It is not clear that Keynes meant this in a sense stronger than the innocuous statement, which even Friedman would accept as true, that we could well never in fact reach a long-run full-employment equilibrium though there may be tendencies to send us in that direction. A fundamentalist, however, could interpret that passage as denying the very existence of a long-run position, there being no objective solution and only alternative states which can be imagined.[5]

A middle way, more in line with *A Treatise on Probability*, might be that the general location of the equilibrium state can be taken as known with a sufficient degree of confidence, but that there exists a grey area that contains a set of positions which it is reasonable to believe on the evidence, without undue optimism or pessimism, are candidates. The coexistence of systematic tendencies and free-willed decision-making is then possible. Reality gives us insufficient unambiguous information to narrow down the options to a unique solution, and for some transactors concerned with long-term assets, especially capital goods and shares, there is the Knightian uncertainty of simply having no way of either knowing or confidently guessing, even within a fairly broad domain, at what the future has in store. A narrow band facilitates the use of mechanical models set in the logical time, and, because consumer behaviour is fairly predictable, the multiplier can sensibly be reduced to a simple mathematical expression.

Rather than emphasizing the role of uncertainty, Leijonhufvud is concerned with the following question: 'Is the *existing* [i.e. money-using] economic system, in any *significant* sense, self-adjusting?'[6]

Fundamentalists say no. So does Leijonhufvud, though he stresses different reasons. Leijonhufvud rejects as insignificant any long-run restoration of full employment generated by the Pigou effect. Even if the monetary system did not collapse, the increase in demand for consumption goods at best[7] only cosmetically deals with the excess supply of labour. The 'wrong' rate of interest, which is at the heart of the problem, remains unchanged. An inter-temporal disequilibrium persists. Balanced deflation is not of even theoretical interest.[8]

Required for recovery which is in some sense significant is, according to Leijonhufvud, a decline in interest rates. The fundamental maladjustment is thereby redressed, and attention can be directed to the central importance of interest rates in Keynes's system. Real balance effects can then harmoniously be incorporated in that their possible impact in Keynes is specifically aimed at an appropriate target, unduly low asset prices. Leijonhufvud holds that the Keynes effect is necessary (given entrepreneurial pessimism) for the logical possibility of the restoration, of a significant kind, of full employment.[9]

Leijonhufvud goes on, however, to introduce further complexities which make things more turbid still.[10] Keynes's analysis reflects what, to Leijonhufvud, involves an undue lack of respect for the forces of thrift and productivity. He complains that Keynes's solution involves a multitude of offsetting combinations of pessimism (say, very high) and interest rates (correspondingly very low). The tailoring of the capital stock to fit the consumption stream determined by time preference is overlooked.[11] By involving 'wrong' nominal wages and interest rates, too low in a long-run growth context once confidence eventually is restored, it 'is still a very strange way...for the system to effect the necessary traverse'.[12]

A key issue is whether Keynes held that the Keynes effect *could* or *would* restore full employment. Leijonhufvud does not say that, in

Keynes, deflation restores full employment in the long run. He only says that, in logic it could.[13] He does not say that in practice it would.[14] At best deflation would only help in practice if deflation specifically lowered interest rates. The Pigou effect would be of secondary magnitude empirically and would be of no significance logically because the fundamental defect is not addressed by a proportional fall in all prices.[15]

Leijonhufvud refers to passages which appear to attack directly the very existence of a price vector consistent with full employment which changes in the price level can bring about.[16] Such passages have a fundamentalist flavour and challenge Leijonhufvud's attempt to attribute to Keynes the notion that deflation could restore full employment. Keynes speaks of changes in prices 'without limit' being the result of endogenous processes generated by money-wage deflation. Certainly it is proper for Leijonhufvud to comment that 'Keynes' argument could have been elaborated with more care'.[17] It is not clear whether or how Keynes abstracts from real balance effects when speaking of prices rushing from zero to infinity. One point we can confidently deduce, however, is Keynes's hostility to the mechanism of money-wage cuts. They would increase instability.[18] Leijonhufvud properly indicates that it is difficult to make a plausible case for the view that Keynes had an exclusively inside-money system in mind to defeat the real balance effect.

It is open, however, to offer a fundamentalist interpretation, which does not involve Keynes in the loose use of words and in flamboyant exaggeration as Leijonhufvud suggests is the case. Perhaps Keynes meant exactly what he said. In response to shocks, under a system of flexible money wages, money prices would indeed 'rush violently between zero and infinity'.[19] For deflationary shocks, Keynes arguably had the liquidity trap in mind. One cannot put this view with great conviction, however, because, in an inflationary case one is liable to be beyond the zone of the trap. To have prices rushing to infinity does seem to be abstracting from real balance effects. The issue is a difficult one. Keynes wrote: 'The element of stability would have to be found, *if at all*, in the factors controlling [the impact of the Keynes effect].'[20]

Keynes clearly rejected the Keynes effect as a long-run force, but it is again not clear whether his rejection was on empirical grounds, by virtue of the weakness of the stimulation to investment, or whether he had hypothetical limitations (such as the trap) in mind. He refers to the restorative possibility involving a

> complicated assumption providing for an automatic change in the wage-unit of an amount just sufficient in its effect on liquidity-preference to establish a rate of interest which would just

243

offset the supposed shift, so as to leave output at the same level as before.... In fact, there is no hint to be found in the above writers as to the necessity for any such assumption; at the best it would be plausible only in relation to long-period equilibrium and could not form the basis of short-period theory; and there is *no ground for supposing it to hold even in the long-period.*[21]

Keynes expresses an objection to Haberler in 1938 which must be taken to indicate that Keynes doubted that any degree of nominal-wage reductions could restore full employment even if the classicists did have real balance effects in mind:

> If a decline in employment is associated with an increase in the quantity of money in terms of wage units *ad infinitum* a compensatory factor comes into force: though even so it does not follow that involuntary unemployment can be avoided any more than it can be avoided by increasing the quantity of money indefinitely, keeping money wages unchanged.[22]

It is possible that Keynes was simply doubting the practical use of deflation and even Pigou was with him on that point – and so is Patinkin.[23] While one can question Leijonhufvud's argument that Keynes merely held that practical difficulties prevented deflation having likely restorative effects, the point of view is nevertheless a sensible one and can be used to distinguish Keynes from other economists. Gottfried Haberler[24] and Bertil Ohlin,[25] for example, both saw practical scope for money-wage cuts.

The Keynes effect was certainly taken by Keynes himself as logically meaningful, but certainly useless in practice. Note his sarcastic tone:

> [If wage deflation were relied upon] we should, in effect have monetary management by the Trade Unions...instead of by the banking system.
>
> Nevertheless while a flexible wage policy and a flexible money policy come, analytically, to the same thing,...there is, of course, a world of difference between them.[26]

He was not necessarily directing his sarcasm towards the notion that lower interest rates could work if they could be lowered sufficiently. Keynes's jibe was pointed towards the classicists for implicitly handing over the responsibility to the unions in the hope that wage cuts would be effective.

Because Leijonhufvud considers the MEI schedule to be sufficiently elastic to allow a decline in the MEI to be offset by lower interest rates, he sometimes gives the impression that he argues that the Keynes effect would reliably restore full employment. Were the curve too inelastic, the

Keynes effect 'would indeed be a sham'.[27] The elasticity of the MEI curve is an empirical issue (although, as Richard Jackman complains,[28] Leijonhufvud treated its relative elasticity as knowable a priori). Even if the curve were sufficiently elastic to ensure the existence of a low, but positive, interest rate, Leijonhufvud does not deduce that full employment would be restored. His view does appear to be that, if interest rates were to fall, without the adverse side-effects that stem from substantial deflation, only then would the restoration of full employment ensue.

Leijonhufvud certainly does not attribute to Keynes the idea that wage cuts are a suitable remedy. Not only are nominal wages and prices sent further away from their new Walrasian values,[29] but there is the grave risk that a money-using system would disintegrate. John Brothwell,[30] a fundamentalist, criticizes Leijonhufvud for failing to consider the latter argument so much stressed by Lerner and Davidson.[31] The allegation is unfair as Leijonhufvud definitely concedes that very point.[32] Curiously, however, Leijonhufvud does not emphasize the issue and this has given rise to the mistaken impression that Leijonhufvud attributes to Keynes the notion that, if tried, deflation would work in the long run. In view of Leijonhufvud's rejection of Keynes's theory of liquidity preference in favour of a theory of thrift and productivity, it is little wonder that some reviewers are highly suspicious and consider Leijonhufvud a sort of classical apologist. It is true that Leijonhufvud's views are subtle and his chapter V is difficult to interpret, but it seems better to hold that he was merely indicating Keynes's acceptance of the view that a mechanism exists by which deflation could stimulate the real sector.

Leijonhufvud also fails to emphasize another practical difficulty which again could make a critic suspicious. In the downswing, precautionary demands can plausibly grow and increased bearishness can cause interest rates to rise, further amplifying the initial shock and erasing the Keynes effect. Perhaps this possibility is taken as a refinement of the basic model, this effect being confined to the special case of the sudden reversal of a boom just past the upper turning point of the trade cycle.[33]

It is odd that statements in Keynes suggestive of rather elastic expectations[34] and of doubt, uncertainty and instability are taken as mere refinements of Leijonhufvud. They glaringly contradict the essential property of the system that Leijonhufvud postulates which is one of sluggish price responses and inelastic price expectations. There are too many anomalies in Leijonhufvud's account. What he treats as embellishment and exaggeration can equally plausibly be taken as integral which gives an alternative interpretation of Keynes entirely different characteristics. A richer story is required to try to encompass the diversity and sweep of *The General Theory*.

When reviewing Leijonhufvud's views on long-run recovery in the light of preceding discussion, it is curious that Leijonhufvud stresses forces at work which could induce a recovery and yet consistently overlooks or plays down the importance of forces which could thwart those benign restorative forces. If his aim were simply to show that orthodox Keynesians had overlooked the presence of such things as the Keynes effect, with the result that their one-commodity models failed to capture the importance of the interest rate to Keynes's vision, then his procedure could be justified and the cynics silenced. Yet is not Leijonhufvud's purpose beyond merely pointing out some things that the Keynesians had overlooked? Doesn't he also put forward a positive alternative view considered to be more faithful to the fundamentalists of Keynes's paradigm? Are not his sins of omission therefore nearly as misleading? It is one thing to say (rightly) that Keynes is not guilty of overlooking real balance effects and another to say that Keynes only displaced short-run classical dynamics and left long-run theory essentially intact. If Keynes rejected the Keynes effect on investment, and if he can be taken to have considered lower share prices to nullify the wealth effects on consumption of higher bond prices, why not emphasize this as a refutation of neoclassical long-run theory? Why confine Keynes's revolution to that of discovering new principles of short-run dynamics?

Leijonhufvud has curious blindspots where rising liquidity preference and a violently falling MEI schedule are not considered properties of the basic model even though important policy and theoretical implications emerge. That a loss of detail is the price of simplicity is readily conceded, but too many seemingly untidy complexities have been cast aside by Leijonhufvud.

Leijonhufvud, in order to protect his belief that Keynes need not (and ought not) be taken to have rejected classical long-run theory, is forced into making questionable assertions with which supposedly 'one can hardly quarrel':

> [Keynes]...showed a tendency to generalize in a rather reckless fashion from the results of his short-run analysis to problems of the long run.[35]

Leijonhufvud argues that Keynes preserved an element of long-run classical theory rejecting only its short-run theory. Keynes was prepared to accept that deflation in logic *could* restore full employment in the long run. As evidence for his belief in Keynes's acceptance, despite appearances to the contrary, of long-run classical economics, Leijonhufvud cites the following:

> I do not see...how [the amount of inactive balances can be independent of the rate of interest] *except in conditions of*

long-period equilibrium.... [T]he orthodox theory is particularly applicable to the stationary state.[36]

Two points need to be made against Leijonhufvud.

First, it is probably wise to read this in conjunction with other passages that indicate that although it would be plausible and sensible to confine orthodox teaching to the long run, Keynes was unwilling to do so. You can concede that an argument is reasonable without actually agreeing with it.[37]

The second objection is that Leijonhufvud has misconstrued the passage he cited by failing to consider the significance of its context. Important statements were deleted leaving the impression that Keynes was content with classical economics as a long-run theory.

The passage can be given more fully:

The orthodox theory...*is concerned with a simplified world* where there is always full employment, and where doubt and fluctuations of confidence are ruled out, so that there is no occasion to hold inactive balances.... The orthodox theory is, for example, applicable to the stationary state.[38]

The domain given to orthodox theory is extremely limited and the tone rather patronizing, and, even in a stationary state, Keynes has his secular stagnation hypothesis in reserve. It is clear that the world of certainty, the full-employment stationary state, where nothing dislocative can ever happen, is worth little attention as a practical possibility or even as an interesting hypothetical one.

Another passage from Keynes also merits consideration:

Thus with other commodities left to themselves, 'natural forces', i.e. the ordinary forces of the market, would *tend* to bring their rate of interest down until the emergence of full employment.[39]

The context suggests that, in a fundamentalist vein, there need not even be a tendency towards full employment in a system which uses money as a store of wealth. Only barter systems have this tendency.

In conclusion, the evidence for Keynes supporting classical economics as a valid long-run theory (if rectified by the incorporation of the Keynes effect) is weak. Leijonhufvud's dismissal of Keynes's remarks to the contrary as 'reckless' is an unsatisfactory procedure if one is engaged in textual exegesis.

While Keynes's views on the long-run possibility of the restoration of full employment are not entirely clear, Leijonhufvud's views can be strongly questioned. While Leijonhufvud does legitimately establish a *prima facie* case in favour of Keynes having recognized the theoretical significance of some real balance effects, he unduly attributes to Keynes a degree of support for classical economics as a long-run doctrine.

If one accepts the notion of a long-run liquidity trap, then it is open to interpret Keynes as allowing prices to fall towards zero with no Keynes effect being spurred. To keep the notion of long-run recovery in perspective, however, recall that, in view of the empirical stability of the money wage and the likely destruction of the money-using system if the money wage were rendered flexible by authoritarian policy, the hypothetical effects of money-wage cuts was not an issue upon which Keynes could have been expected to pronounce with precision or confidence.

Wealth effects

This section considers Leijonhufvud's argument that, in Keynes, even consumption can respond to changes in interest rates. If interest rates decline in the long run on account of real balance effects (or the evaporation of bearish sentiment), a restorative influence working on consumption, and not simply investment, exists. Three questions require attention. What did Keynes say? If Keynes did recognize these consumption effects, what empirical significance did they have? How can such effects be legitimately deduced from Keynes's theoretical model? These three matters are discussed in turn, and comparisons with the fundamentalist perspective are made.

Leijonhufvud considers Don Patinkin negligent[40] in overlooking the incorporation in Keynes of windfall effects whereby high consumption is induced by high real value of assets. It seems that Leijonhufvud is arguing that Keynes has anticipated Patinkin's incorporation of real balance effects. Keynes is cited by Leijonhufvud[41] to indicate that the direct substitution effect involving present and future consumption is 'open to a good deal of doubt' whereas the indirect effect that interest rates have on consumption (by increasing the value of assets) causes citizens to feel richer, even if the income from those assets remains fixed.

Patinkin[42] has replied to Leijonhufvud by examining the following passage from Keynes:

Perhaps the most important influence, operating through changes in the rate of interest, on the readiness to spend out of a given income..., depends on the effect of these changes on the appreciation or depreciation in the price of securities and other assets. For if a man is enjoying a windfall increment in the value of his capital, it is natural that his motives towards current spending should be strengthened, even though in terms of income his capital is worth no more than before; and weakened if he is suffering capital losses.[43]

Patinkin doubts that Keynes had grasped the essence of the wealth effect:

I would, however, like to suggest that the evidence from this passage is not as conclusive as it at first sight appears. For let us recapture our pre-Friedmanian innocence and note that the foregoing passage refers to the influence on consumption not of the *level* of wealth but of *changes* in this level.[44]

On this point, Patinkin seems correct but we can put matters into perspective. The point does sound pedantic if, prior to Friedman, the distinction was not clearly made. Keynes clearly had in mind some connection between consumption and asset values; that is, he did not ignore them. Why Keynes should have been expected to draw such fine distinctions is not clear. Besides, whenever Keynes considered the possibility of deflation-induced recovery, he denounced it. It was no practical solution or even one likely to work in practice without generating adverse offsetting influences. So why expect Keynes to go into the question in detail? Both the fundamentalists and Leijonhufvud distrust deflation as a means to restore full employment. (Indeed, so does Patinkin.) The issue is theoretical. Did Keynes conceive of the possibility that lower interest rates induced by deflation could foster a recovery?

Leijonhufvud has been criticized for giving undue emphasis to the empirical magnitude of wealth effects on consumption due to the lower interest rates consequent upon increases in real balances; that is, for taking wealth effects seriously as a real-world phenomenon.[45] In fact, Leijonhufvud is careful not to claim such wealth effects to be of great empirical significance, at least over the short period.[46] Their main relevance is at the theoretical level to indicate that Keynes had indeed considered wealth effects as one means of integrating the real and monetary sectors.[47] Leijonhufvud does perhaps give ammunition to potential critics by not sufficiently emphasizing its merely symbolic worth in indicating that Keynes had understood the possible effect of deflation-induced expansions in real balances. Wealth effects on consumption are embellishments only. They are large enough not to be ignored, but not so large as to nullify the multiplier. The primary empirical force is the effect on investment of declining interest rates.

Brothwell[48] is a fundamentalist commentator who feels that he is attacking Leijonhufvud by pointing out that the magnitude of windfall effects is liable to be relatively small. Brothwell cites Keynes: 'The consumption of the *wealth-owning class* may be extremely susceptible to unforeseen changes in the money value of its wealth.'[49] In other words, only a small minority benefit, and the effect is not liable to be particularly great in the aggregate. Leijonhufvud, however, never said that it would, at least within the short period. Indeed, it would be awkward for him to so hold because Leijonhufvud's rationalization of the multiplier depends on liquidity constraints. If the ordinary worker had buffer savings and wealth to finance consumption during his or her unemployment, the multiplier would not have taken hold of the system.

It is again unfortunate that Leijonhufvud[50] holds the MEI constant in the short run and with it equity prices at given interest rates. This serves to emasculate an effect which would in practice be likely to swamp the weak, but upward, short-run movements in wealth induced by lower interest rates. In Leijonhufvud's scheme, it is only after some time that inelastic expectations bring about a significant further downward revision of sales expectations and therefore a further decline in the MEI, share prices and wealth. If share prices were instead allowed to fall rapidly, a net 'poverty effect' would emerge.

Leijonhufvud does sometimes write in a manner which gives the impression of attaching some empirical significance to positive wealth effects:

> A decline in the marginal efficiency of capital makes the perceived wealth of the owners of that capital decrease; a sufficient reduction in the interest rate would (more or less) offset this negative wealth effect and serve to keep the system on its production possibilities frontier. But speculation, Keynes postulated, will prevent market rate from keeping pace with natural rate.[51]

This passage is difficult to interpret and seems to suggest that, if interest rates fell instantly (or if, in the long run, speculation fades), it is arguable – though 'more or less' is particularly slippery an expression – that wealth effects would outweigh the given poverty effects. Note, however, that the decline in the MEI is merely the initial decline and the passage cited does not consider subsequent pessimistic shifts which would generate further poverty effects. A more important force to return the system to the production frontier is the increase in investment spurred by lower interest rates, but the elasticity of the MEI schedule had already received separate consideration.

Leijonhufvud supplies this representation of his views:

> But the quantitative significance of the wealth effect – as long as moderate variations in the rate [of interest] are considered – should not be exaggerated.... [T]he quantitatively significant effect...is still the effect on investment.... *Theoretically*, Keynes'

wealth effect is at least as interesting as the real balance effect [or Pigou effect].[52]

To elevate wealth effects to at least the same status as the Pigou effect is a modest aim and one fully consistent with giving neither effect any significant empirical weight.

However, Leijonhufvud does suggest that the *long-run* magnitudes are conceivably of empirical significance because large changes in interest rates can become possible once bear speculation recedes (as Leijonhufvud feels it must).[53] Here he is open to fundamentalist criticism in the style of Brothwell. Furthermore, it is not clear that, in Keynes, speculation does fade away and barriers to lower interest rates eventually crumble. Once again, Leijonhufvud presses Keynes into a mould where his major innovations are confined to the short run while leaving long-run classical theory relatively intact. Leijonhufvud prefers to see Keynes as accepting a significant long-run windfall effect.

Leijonhufvud[54] mentions only one passage[55] which could be taken to indicate that lower interest rates might have direct effects powerful enough to maintain full employment and defeat secular stagnation. That passage can, however, be fairly put aside since Keynes was merely entertaining a future possibility and not making a statement about the elasticity relevant for values of the long interest rate then experienced.

If lower interest rates are associated with higher levels of consumption spending, how can Keynes justify it? There is no quarrel here with Leijonhufvud's argument that the direct intertemporal substitution effect plays no significant part in Keynes's model.[56] Keynes found it difficult to generalize about the direct effects on consumption which changes in interest rates would induce.[57]

Leijonhufvud justifies the windfall effect by arguing that the life of the typical capital asset is longer than that of the typical consumer. Owners do not entirely rely on the income flows to finance their consumption. Owners can sell them for money, realizing capital gain, to raise their real consumption profiles while they are still alive to enjoy it.

Jackman has objected that Leijonhufvud's characterization of the behaviour of savers is inconsistent with that of wage earners.[58] Leijonhufvud claims that Keynes held that 'preference functions for alternative time-paths of consumption...exhibit a *considerable degree* of intertemporal complementarity'.[59] In other words, if there is a change in the price of future consumption relative to current consumption, the relative quantities consumed will not change very much. If, for example, the rate of interest rose, then people will not significantly reduce current consumption (that is, save more) in order to enjoy consumption in the future. Jackman claims that Leijonhufvud requires that workers have opposite preferences to savers. Workers readily forego current consumption while searching for the opportunity to enjoy higher future levels of consumption.

Jackman's argument is not as conclusive as it first appears. Leijonhufvud says that household preferences 'exhibit a *considerable* degree of intertemporal complementarity'. He does not say that the rate of interest has *no* effect. If the rate of interest were high enough, then some substitution would occur.[60] In the case of worker preferences, the change in relative prices can be large enough to allow substitution effects. If, for example, in response to a shock an employer insisted on a 10 per cent wage cut, then some workers might prefer to seek employment elsewhere. If they find jobs that pay the old wage after foregoing consumption for one week, then in only ten weeks they will (roughly) have recouped their initial sacrifice. Thereafter they will benefit from a permanent source of income in excess of what they would have received if they had stayed with their former employer. Because the workers (mistakenly) believe that their abstention from consumption will be temporary and amply rewarded, they will be prepared to suffer a relatively small loss while engaged in search activity. By the time the workers realize the need to accept a 10 per cent cut, the multiplier has taken hold and that cut is no longer sufficient and the process therefore goes on. Therefore, in Leijonhufvud, both workers and savers have similar preferences with respect to their time-paths of consumption. In both cases the inducement to defer consumption is large. Jackman's attempt to demonstrate that Leijonhufvud's interpretation is internally inconsistent therefore fails.

We shall now examine Leijonhufvud's arguments which claim that Keynes did appreciate that wealth effects indirectly generated by deflation exist. Leijonhufvud has three strands of reasoning:

(1) he emphasizes the different lifespans of consumer and capital goods – and this topic has attracted the most attention to the exclusion of other themes which Leijonhufvud also relies on, namely

(2) he considers that higher asset prices can encourage consumption on plausible psychological grounds, and

(3) he introduces an idea which one can dub 'effective wealth'.

Leijonhufvud concentrates on the first,[61] but an interpretation with greater affinity to *The General Theory* ought to give more weight to the other possibilities. Although Keynes does not himself provide a theoretical underpinning for the snippets which can be taken to describe wealth effects, these can be supplied in a manner consistent with the tenor of his work as a whole.

Strand (1)

It should be noted that Leijonhufvud only tentatively justifies the wealth effect with the argument that the life of the representative consumer is shorter than that of the typical real asset. Leijonhufvud claims only to have achieved a 'residue of insight'[62] from a 'loose sketch'.[63]

Furthermore, this strand is not the only justification Leijonhufvud suggests. Indeed, it is not even the most interesting. Jackman fairly comments 'that it seems much too sophisticated in terms of Keynes's general discussion of consumer behaviour'.[64]

There is little which can be said about Leijonhufvud's rationalization which is not claimed to be in Keynes but simply consistent with his views. Jackman[65] does rightly point out that other types of capital, apart from long-lived fixed capital, do exist, but we can fairly confidently claim that Keynes did consider the representative asset to be a building, a railway or some other highly durable form of capital. Jackman also observes that agents do bequeath fortunes, but Leijonhufvud is happy to concede that his account abstracts from the richness both of reality and *The General Theory*.[66]

Strand (2)

How plausible is it that agents will perceive themselves to be 'better off' if the value of their bonds and shares increases? This question can be asked prior to another, which is taken up in the closely related discussion of strand (3): are agents really better off if the value of their paper assets grow?

An answer to the former question requires consideration of an omission made when dealing with strand (1). Uncertainty requires explicit incorporation. If the present is known and the future is unfathomable, one's attention might be focused on the present while the future is largely left to sort itself out. You 'feel good' when the bird is currently in your hand and the present is an important proxy for knowledge about the future. Leijonhufvud is openly apologetic about the narrow and highly orthodox explanation offered in strand (1) in which uncertainty is assumed away.[67]

Leijonhufvud, however, says little that suggests positively and exactly how uncertainty can be incorporated to rationalize wealth effects. He does drop a few hints though, and the explanation offered here is likely to blend fairly harmoniously with Leijonhufvud's own thinking as well as being consistent with the fundamentalist concept of Knightian uncertainty.

If the time horizon over which income is anticipated and consumption is planned for with much certainty is relatively short, then higher security prices can give rise to a state of wellbeing so far as assets are held for precautionary purposes (that is, for an imminent, potential rainy day).[68] The sizes of precautionary holdings of cash and relatively liquid securities depend upon the representative saver's degree of *uncertainty aversion*.[69] Little uncertainty attaches to the holding of cash if money wages (and therefore the price level and quantity of real balances) are stable. A certain point can be reached, however, where uncertainty-averse wealth-holders purchase some bonds. If interest rates fall in a slump, bond holdings are to a degree useful in neutralizing real income fluctuations. By contrast, shares have the defect, for someone who is uncertainty averse, of moving in the same direction as income.

If some agents can be described as uncertainty averse, then interesting possibilities emerge. Any news which is difficult to interpret as unambiguously good or bad increases their unease. While calm under stable conditions, any change can put the thought into their minds of an adverse impact on them. For example, any fiscal policy which is judged as experimental, whether it be expansionary or contractionary, finds their disfavour. Some, for example, can see a large devaluation as bad news, as an objective judgement by international capital markets upon a nation. Yet, had a large revaluation occurred instead, the impacts of stiffer foreign competition are singled out to justify despair once again. Perhaps this is why financial 'experts' on one occasion explain upward changes in share prices by virtue of market confidence being enhanced by credible and disciplined monetary policy while, on other occasions, the relaxation of zealously tight monetary policy is credited with the recovery of share prices. Perhaps such explanations are not as *ad hoc* and contradictory as they at first appear. Uncertainty-averse agents like to build around themselves stable and conventional environments. For the 'uncertainty paranoid', the everyday turmoil of life is simply too much and they retire to a monastery where the illusion of certainty cannot be challenged. The merely uncertainty averse, however, find comfort in being in conventional conformity with others in their belief that moderation is good in all things. The reversal of any policy seen to be excessive in plausibly (and possibly even in truth) having adverse side-effects can well promote higher prices for their paper titles to secure living standards.[70]

One suspects that Leijonhufvud would be sympathetic to this style of reasoning because what is perceived by agents here takes on a life of its own. Full information is no longer assumed as it is in meta-static, auctioneer-style models.[71]

In so far as interest rates have fallen, distant and as yet non-specific consumption plans are affected. People realize, however, that interest rates ebb and flow. If wealth is perceived as transitory, it is quickly turned into consumption. Current gains are therefore weighed more heavily. This seems a common-sense explanation and is in accord with the view that consumption is largely governed by current income.[72] The reasoning is in favour of consumption depending also on current wealth.

Strand (3)

Is it rational to feel richer if the stock of physical assets such as land and fixed capital is unchanged? The pure theory of wealth effects is treacherous territory indeed. Nevertheless, some comments in answer to that question seen warranted even if they seem neither original nor profound.

Economics is about choices which depend in part on tastes. If utility is perceived, it is not our task to question whether some 'real' justification exists. If the community *feels* richer and no-one, whose behaviour is capable of being effectively expressed, is identified as feeling poorer, that should be the end of the matter. If the MEI curve shifts upwards, for example, and investors feel that the value of their capital is higher and celebrate with higher consumption, who are we to question the rationality of their conduct?

Let us specifically consider the impact of lower interest rates and higher asset prices. When considering assets such as buildings and land which are fairly readily saleable on account of their versatility, an increase in their prices (in terms of their real command over consumption goods) can to some degree satisfy the precautionary demand for wealth and release holdings of more liquid assets from serving this function. Money can then find its way back into the expenditure stream. Because, at the margin, increased asset values can be converted into cash at the prevailing equilibrium prices, the potential increase in effective demand is as valid an improvement as is the actual receipt of cash. Access to credit is easier too.

That non-money assets as well as money itself can satisfy precautionary needs is clear from *The General Theory*.

> [I]n the absence of an organised market, liquidity-preference due to the precautionary-motive would be greatly increased; whereas the existence of an organised market [dealing with debts] gives an opportunity for wide fluctuations in liquidity-preference due to the speculative-motive.[73]

Holding bonds satisfies precautionary needs if markets are sufficiently developed. Later it appears that Keynes refers to how precautionary needs are met by holding 'an asset of which the value is fixed in terms of money to meet a subsequent liability fixed in terms of money'.[74]

Clearly, securities have two desirable properties: they are saleable and they provide security against unforeseen contingencies by virtue of being fixed claims for sums of money. (To some degree, industrial shares and buildings would enjoy the former property and satisfy precautionary needs to hold wealth during deflationary periods, provided interest rates fall far enough to neutralize the decline in the MEI schedule.)

Let us now put subjective precautionary motivations aside. Although real, or physical, wealth is given in the short run, why should consumption be geared to this? If your Picasso suddenly falls in price on account of the bursting of a speculative bubble, you are worse off although the painting itself is unchanged. Similarly, a machine retains its physical productivity irrespective of its selling price. What changes is not physical wealth but *effective wealth*. A machine that is chronically idle is not wealth in any significant sense because the relevant value of any physical asset is derived from the demand for what it produces. At less than full employment, effective demand is lower and effective wealth falls with it. In so far as deflation increases effective demand – either by reducing interest rates and promoting investment or by raising consumption (by the Pigou effect) – by bringing machines that make consumption goods back to life, effective wealth objectively grows and the consumption function can plausibly shift in response.

Furthermore, if the increase in real balances reduces long rates and if this flows on to short rates, then the variable cost of short loans for input acquisition and for the accumulation of raw-material stocks is lessened. This enhances the prospects for the reactivation of idle equipment in a fully objective way.

There are no grounds for expecting that the current underutilization of machines is temporary and that current and future consumption plans can be based on an assumption that 'permanent wealth' will tend towards that consistent with full employment. To expect the continuation of low effective wealth and to adjust consumption accordingly is perfectly rational. This is true even if machinery, being highly illiquid, is not a component of wealth likely to be held even in part for the precautionary purposes discussed in strand (2).[75] Note also that as machinery is relatively short-lived, the recession is likely to exist for a significant proportion of its life. Currently experienced idleness is not, therefore, something which can be averaged out by transitory booms over the life of the machine.

Even if it is uncertain that wealth effects due to higher real values of paper assets such as money balances and securities are conceptually valid,[76] there is an argument in favour of the objective increase in wealth by virtue of the reactivation of physical capital assets. Therefore, if deflation reduces interest rates without generating greater adverse side-effects on aggregate demand, then, in pure theory, some positive wealth effect ensues due to the higher consumption of the classes owning physical assets. Human capital is reactivated too.

The argument in favour of a net increase in wealth as distinct from a mere redistribution of real wealth is based on the idea that at less than full employment it is possible for somebody to be better off without someone else being made worse off. An increase in the effective wealth of some transactors need not be offset by any losses elsewhere.

This very notion is directly drawn from Leijonhufvud. He observes: 'In a depression, obviously the system is inside the production possibilities frontier so that any event that improves the coordination of current activities and moves it towards the frontier will have a positive "income effect".'[77]

If the notion of effective wealth makes sense and is broadly consistent with fundamentalist teachings, then one further step towards a reconciliation has been taken.

Notes

1 Axel Leijonhufvud, *On Keynesian Economics and the Economics of Keynes: a study in monetary theory*, New York, Oxford University Press, 1968, pp. 324–5, gives the definitions of the sundry effects.

2 *The Collected Writings of John Maynard Keynes*, London, Macmillan, 1971–, vol. xiv, p. 105.

3 G.L.S. Shackle, *Epistemics and Economics: a critique of economic doctrines*, Cambridge, Cambridge University Press, 1972, p. 218.

4 Keynes, *Collected Writings*, vol. xxix, p. 222. Jan Kregel, 'Effective demand: origins and development of the notion', in Jan Kregel (ed.), *Distribution, Effective Demand and International Economic Relations*, New York, St. Martin's Press, 1983, pp. 50–68, at p. 64, validly remarks of this passage that Ricardo, Walras and Clark would have said much the same thing. One can regard Kregel as one of the more eclectic of the scholars of Keynes, but he fits less uneasily into the fundamentalist compartment than any other, despite his charge that Shackle's interpretation is exaggerated and selective.

5 Compare Bjorn Hansson, 'Keynes's notion of equilibrium in the *General Theory*', *Journal of Post Keynesian Economics*, vol. 7, no. 3, Spring 1985, pp. 332–41, at p. 338.

6 Robert W. Clower and Axel Leijonhufvud, 'The coordination of economic activities', *American Economic Review*, vol. 65, no. 2, May 1975, pp. 182–8, at p. 182 (emphasis in original).

7 Leijonhufvud, *On Keynesian Economics*, p. 339.

8 ibid., pp. 327–8, 335–8. Consider the following. 'What Keynes denied was that a *proportional* fall of all money prices could be of significant help' (p. 327). Note the word 'significant'. The word 'significantly' appears again (p. 339) which makes it clear that Leijonhufvud has chosen his terms very carefully. One is entitled to ask, however, if Keynes consciously deleted explicit consideration of the Pigou effect for its 'insignificance'. In reply, it could be said that the significant idea was

stressed while it was only natural that theoretically trifling effects had no cause to enter his head. Certainly, the issues raised are of some subtlety and to say, as did Albert G. Hines (*On the Reappraisal of Keynesian Economics*, London, Martin Robertson, 1971, p. 22) that 'Leijonhufvud's dismissal of the Pigou effect is very neat' involves something of an oversimplification. (Hines can reasonably be regarded as a fundamentalist though one quite friendly, in 1971 at least, towards Leijonhufvud's account.)

The role of the Pigou effect in Keynes is certainly unclear. Don Patinkin suggests ('Money and wealth: a review article', *Journal of Economic Literature*, vol. 7, no. 4, December 1969, p. 1159) that Keynes cannot be taken to have incorporated wealth into the consumption function (by either a Pigou or windfall effect) because at one point (*The General Theory of Employment Interest and Money*, London, Macmillan, 1936, pp. 91–2) Keynes does not mention it at a key juncture. One feels a little uneasy about Patinkin's exegetical technique which places significance on the non-appearance of an idea where one (Patinkin at least) would have expected it to be. He employs a comparable argument in his discussion of the liquidity trap, as we have seen. One does not, however, wish to be seen as defending the alternative technique of asserting that Keynes *would* have understood a certain proposition and then insert that notion into a passage to uncover its hidden meaning.

9 John Fender (*Understanding Keynes: an analysis of 'The General Theory'*, Brighton, Wheatsheaf Books, 1981, p. 108) appears to have missed the subtlety of Leijonhufvud's position, but one can agree with him (p. 110) that the route to recovery could be closed absolutely by the liquidity trap.

One objection to Leijonhufvud on a theoretical, rather than on an exegetical point requires some attention. Christopher J. Bliss ('Discussion', 'The reappraisal of Keynes' economics: an appraisal', in Michael Parkin and Aveline Nobay (eds), *Current Economic Problems: the proceedings of the Association of University Teachers of Economics, Manchester, 1974*, Cambridge, Cambridge University Press, 1975, pp. 209–10, 213) argues that even if interest rates were sticky and inter-temporal disequilibrium were to emerge, its manifestation in the current labour market would vanish if the money wage were to adjust. Bliss doubts that Leijonhufvud has grasped the linkages between chapters II and V of his own book. One suspects that Leijonhufvud would concede that lower money wages could, if the Keynes effect on interest rates (or an increase in the MEI induced by the lower nominal supply price) are assumed away, restore full employment by a pure Pigou effect. This route, however, is of no theoretical significance since the fundamental source of the perturbation remains and because money wages have also moved even further away from their new Walrasian values. Bliss seems simply to have missed Leijonhufvud's point.

10 Leijonhufvud, *On Keynesian Economics*, pp. 281, n. 1, 414; 'The Wicksell connection', in Axel Leijonhufvud, *Information and*

Coordination: essays in macroeconomic theory, New York, Oxford University Press, 1981, pp. 131–202, at pp. 193–4.

11 Leijonhufvud, 'The Wicksell connection', p. 173, n. 62.

12 ibid., p. 193, n. 103.

13 See Leijonhufvud, *On Keynesian Economics*, pp. 323–4, 328, 330, 335, 340 for his carefully worded statements. For example, 'Keynes conceded that, *as a matter of logic, deflation could work*' (p. 324 – emphasis in original). 'The Wicksell connection' also makes reference to 'the Keynes-effect *possibility*' (p. 167: emphasis added).

14 But see Leijonhufvud, *On Keynesian Economics*, p. 317, where he almost states that he does not quarrel with the more extreme neoclassical idea that sufficient deflation *would* restore full employment. Even if he can be taken to have said that, this is a sole blemish in an argument otherwise precisely worded.

15 ibid., pp. 328–9. However the passage (b) on p. 329 is obscure and has been criticized. See Ogden O. Allsbrook Jr and Charles D. De Lorme, 'The Keynes effect and the capital market: a methodological note', *Artha Vijnana*, vol. 191, no. 2, June 1977, pp. 168–72, at p. 170.

16 Leijonhufvud, *On Keynesian Economics*, pp. 319–23.

17 ibid., p. 321. Keynes did, of course, have a penchant for tossing around terms like 'ad infinitum' (and 'without limit') without making clear what assumption lay behind his thought experiments. Leijonhufvud evidently agrees (*On Keynesian Economics*, pp. 321–4).

18 This contrasts with Friedman's view that price flexibility is not the same as price instability. Compare Paul Davidson, *Money and the Real World*, London, Macmillan, 1978, 2nd edn, pp. 392–401 who discusses the effects of contractual indexation.

19 Keynes, *The General Theory*, p. 239.

20 ibid., p. 270 (emphasis added).

21 ibid., p. 180 (emphasis added). There also seems to be a shift in emphasis evident between 1930 and 1936 in that, in some part of the *Treatise*, Keynes could be taken to have been 'sloughing his skin', for example, in *Collected Writings*, vol. v. pp. 165, 185–6. Keynes is friendlier towards the notion that money-wage cuts could have beneficial effects on consumption and investment. In *The General Theory*, he is pessimistic although he accepts as a logical possibility the Keynes effect which would at least make classical theory a *coherent special case*.

   Surprisingly, despite the existence of the passages just cited, Mark Blaug (*Economic Theory in Retrospect*, London, Cambridge University Press, 1978, 3rd edn, p. 686) and Mark Casson (*Unemployment: a disequilibrium approach*, Oxford, Martin Robertson, 1981, p. 13) both remark that Keynes overlooked real balance effects. Perhaps this indicates that Leijonhufvud's chapter II has had a greater impact on the profession's attitudes than has his chapter V. Blaug (p. 677) refers to the Keynes effect as a 'minor qualification' whereas Leijonhufvud would give it considerable symbolic importance.

22 Keynes, *Collected Writings*, vol. xxix, p. 272.

23 Patinkin in *Money, Interest and Prices*, pp. 339, 343, inclines to the view that the 'analytical extremes' where the dynamics are unstable and where, even in the long run, no restoration of full employment is possible, are better put to one side in favour of the view that restorative forces are weak and slow to operate. In *Keynes' Monetary Thought: a study of its development*, Durham, North Carolina, Duke University Press, 1976, Patinkin was prepared to summarize Keynes's view as being that the 'automatic adjustment process is not very efficacious: at best it can bring about only a very slow rate of improvement' (p. 106).

24 Gottfried Haberler, *Prosperity and Depression: a theoretical analysis of cyclical movements*, London, George Allen and Unwin, 1964, 4th edn, pp. 486–7.

25 Bertil Ohlin, in Keynes, *Collected Writings*, vol. xiv, pp. 197–8.

26 Keynes, *The General Theory*, p. 267.

27 Leijonhufvud, *On Keynesian Economics*, p. 330.

28 Richard Jackman, 'Keynes and Leijonhufvud', *Oxford Economic Papers*, vol. 26, 1974, pp. 259–72, at p. 262.

29 Leijonhufvud, 'The Wicksell connection', p. 194.

30 John Brothwell, 'A simple Keynesian's response to Leijonhufvud', *Bulletin of Economic Research*, vol. 27, May 1975, pp. 3–21, at p. 14.

31 Keynes was prepared to accept that 'Marshall was perfectly aware that the existence of debts gives a high degree of practical importance to changes in the value of money. Nevertheless,...fundamental differences between the conclusions of a monetary economy and those of the more simplified real-exchange economy have been greatly underestimated by the exponents of the traditional economics' (*Collected Writings*, vol. xiii, p. 410). See also Pigou's consideration of bankruptcies (Arthur C. Pigou, *The Theory of Unemployment*, London, Frank Cass, 1933, p. 235).

32 Leijonhufvud, *On Keynesian Economics*, pp. 108–9, 332, 353. His views have not changed ('The Wicksell connection', p. 167, n. 50).

33 Keynes, *The General Theory*, p. 316.

34 The reader is reminded of earlier discussions involving the volatility of investors' expectations and their beliefs in continuing falls in the money wage. We have to consider more elaborate theories of expectations where the elasticity of price expectations is perhaps a function of the rate of decline in demand or where it increases the further the distance from the perceived norm.

35 Leijonhufvud, *On Keynesian Economics*, pp. 190–1 (and p. 59, n. 17).

36 ibid., p. 382, n. 36 (with deletions). The added emphasis and the interpolation are Leijonhufvud's. The passage appears in Keynes, *Collected Writings*, vol. xiv, pp. 105–7.

37 For further evidence of Keynes's denial of any long-run restoration of full employment by virtue of the Keynes effect induced by falling prices and wages, see *Collected Writings*, vol. xxix, pp. 55–6. The evidence is not decisive, however.

38 Keynes, *Collected Writings*, vol. xiv, p. 107. In this passage it is taken that 'long run' refers to the mere ticking of logical time while all

parameters (entrepreneurial expectations of prospective yields, the state of bearishness, the capital stock and so forth) are preserved.

39 Keynes, *The General Theory*, p. 235 (emphasis added). This is from chapter 17 where commodity-rates of interest were discussed. The passage takes the case where the money-rate of interest does not 'rule the roost'.

40 Leijonhufvud, *On Keynesian Economics*, p. 326, n. 17. See also pp. 187–205.

41 ibid., pp. 191, 195 citing Keynes, *The General Theory*, pp. 92–3, and pp. 93–4 respectively.

42 Don Patinkin, 'Money and wealth: a review article', *Journal of Economic Literature*, vol. 7, no. 4, December 1969, pp. 1140–60, at p. 1158.

43 Keynes, *The General Theory*, p. 94.

44 Patinkin, 'Money and wealth: a review article', p. 1158. The existence of a Keynes effect on investment cannot be disputed on exegetical grounds in a manner similar to Patinkin's denial of a windfall effect. Here Keynes does speak of higher *levels* of real balances, not merely *changes*, see *The General Theory*, p. 266.

45 For example, John Brothwell, 'A simple Keynesian's response to Leijonhufvud', *Bulletin of Economic Research*, vol. 27, May 1975, pp. 3–21, at p. 13.

46 Leijonhufvud, *On Keynesian Economics*, pp. 328–30. Keynes (*The General Theory*, p. 92) describes windfall changes in capital-values as being 'of much more importance in modifying the propensity to consume' than are some other factors. Richard Jackman ('Keynes and Leijonhufvud', p. 263) deletes the word 'more' which gives rise to the possibility of changing the meaning of the passage from one expressing relative importance to one indicating absolute importance. Keynes (*The General Theory*, p. 93) does go on, however, to refer to such windfalls as 'amongst the major factors' at work. Note that, in a recession, low share prices due to pessimism can at least cancel out windfall gains which can stem from lower interest rates (ibid., p. 319). There can be a net 'poverty effect'.

Boris P. Pesek and Thomas R. Saving, *Money, Wealth and Economic Theory*, New York, Macmillan, 1967, p. 16, take the controversial view that both wealth and Pigou effects are, in Keynes, empirically important. Patinkin soberly evaluates their overall treatment of Keynes in 'Money and wealth: a review article', at pp. 1158–9.

47 *On Keynesian Economics*, p. 325 seeks to defend Keynes from Patinkin's claim that Keynes ignored such effects.

48 Brothwell, 'A simple Keynesian's response to Leijonhufvud', p. 13. Fender, *Understanding Keynes*, p. 72, takes a similar view.

49 Keynes, *The General Theory*, p. 93 (Brothwell's emphasis).

50 Leijonhufvud, *On Keynesian Economics*, p. 192.

51 ibid., pp. 276–7.

52 ibid., p. 204 (emphasis added). Note that 'moderate variations' exist in the short run because bears prevent large changes in interest rates.

53 ibid., p. 366 and n. 12. The argument seems to be that if the *'short-period* influence of changes in the rate of interest...is *often* of secondary importance' that large long-period changes are likely to be of major importance (Leijonhufvud's emphasis). This is not a particularly convincing piece of textual interpretation.

54 ibid., p. 204, n. 30.

55 Keynes, *The General Theory*, p. 377.

56 Leijonhufvud, *On Keynesian Economics*, pp. 196–7.

57 Keynes, *The General Theory*, p. 151; *Collected Writings*, vol. xiv, pp. 247–8, 268–9.

58 Jackman, 'Keynes and Leijonhufvud', p. 267–8.

59 Leijonhufvud, *On Keynesian Economics*, p. 196 (emphasis added).

60 See Keynes, *The General Theory*, p. 94. The 'influence of the rate of interest on individual spending out of a given income is secondary and relatively unimportant, except, perhaps, where unusually large changes are in question'. Compare *Treatise, Collected Writings*, vol. v, pp. 139, 180.

61 Some doubts have been raised about the technical, as distinct from exegetical, validity of this foundation of the wealth effect. See Brian Redhead, 'On Keynesian economics and the economics of Keynes: a suggested interpretation', *Bulletin of Economic Research*, vol. 33, no. 1, May 1981, pp. 48–55, at pp. 53–4; J.S. Fleming, 'Wealth effects in Keynesian models', *Oxford Economic Papers*, vol. 26, no. 2, July 1974, pp. 248–58.

62 Leijonhufvud, *On Keynesian Economics*, p. 258.

63 ibid., p. 207. Similar sentiments appear on p. 299, while on p. 300 he feels that uncertainty about future income and consumption (considered in the next subsection) is so important a part of Keynes's system that a strong case exists for drawing a 'picture significantly different from that of section IV:3'!

64 Jackman, 'Keynes and Leijonhufvud', p. 264.

65 ibid., p. 263.

66 Leijonhufvud, *On Keynesian Economics*, p. 258.

67 Curiously, Leijonhufvud (*On Keynesian Economics*, pp. 216, 228, 257–8) sometimes cites Milton Friedman, but the latter accounts for 'uncertainty' by introducing probability distributions; that is, Friedman's *A Theory of the Consumption Function*, Princeton, Princeton University Press, 1957, pp. 14–15 incorporates quantifiable *risk* which, of course, would not satisfy any fundamentalist who instead stresses unquantifiable Knightian uncertainty.

68 Compare Leijonhufvud, *On Keynesian Economics*, p. 301.

69 Risk aversion is based on probabilistic foundations. It is suggested that agents can plausibly prefer to pay to avoid unpredictable and unfathomable shocks even if there is no reason to expect adverse shocks to tend to be more injurious on average.

70 This paragraph can be read in the light of the chapter devoted later to the role of conventions.

71 Leijonhufvud, *On Keynesian Economics*, pp. 270–1, 275.

72 Jackman ('Keynes and Leijonhufvud', p. 264) cites Keynes, *The General Theory* (p. 95), to indicate that uncertain future income plays little part in governing current consumption. By analogy, one supposes that uncertain future wealth is liable also to play a small part and be discounted in favour of giving weight to current wealth.

73 Keynes, *The General Theory*, pp. 170–1.

74 ibid., p. 196.

75 Similarly, shares (their price being dependent on the MEI which in turn to some degree is a function of income) are inappropriate means to protect against adverse contingencies.

76 In the case of higher bond prices, it might be argued by those of new classical persuasion that agents fully and correctly anticipate higher tax collections to meet the higher real value of the payment of interest and repayment of principal. Compare Leijonhufvud, *On Keynesian Economics*, p. 270 for a remarkable piece of prescience.

77 ibid., p. 272.

Part four

Chapter nine

Conventions

Overview

In this chapter an account will be given which provides an alternative perspective from which Keynes's economics can be viewed. It deals with the role of uncertainty, the nature of conventions and possible ways in which the complexity of dynamic adjustment can be portrayed. Examined is the manner in which transactors in various markets act. It is hoped that lines of thought beginning to find favour in more recently published works can be used to help us understand Keynes better and to broaden our outlook in dealing with current theoretical problems. Much academic attention has been given lately to the rational expectations hypothesis, the chief advantage of which is claimed to be in its refusal to attribute to agents behavioural characteristics of a supposedly irrational kind. We need not be confronted by the bare choice between rational expectations (which are true on average) and those which are not purely rational because they are based on primitive illusion or arbitrary habits. Neither are we forced to follow Leijonhufvud's particular middle-of-the-road approach in which, whether the disturbance is nominal or real, isolated and justifiably confused transactors formulate expectations on the basis of their past experience. An alternative middle way is to recognize that whether or not price expectations are true or false or are elastic or inelastic can depend upon the circumstances of each case. Fundamentalist insights can be drawn upon rather than the somewhat oversimplified rendition suggested by Leijonhufvud. Nevertheless, the two approaches are not incommensurable. Different sectors of the economy can act in different ways, and for good reason. Keynes himself has pointed out such a path, and many in recent times have theorized along similar lines.

Keynes, in his *Treatise on Probability* published in 1921, argued that probability estimates are about degrees of rational belief in the sense that reasonable people can use their judgement on the available evidence to justify their actions. It is not a matter of precise calculation or examining a large number of experimental observations to obtain a purely objective result. There is often a vague and indeterminate character to views about the likelihood of specific future events. To employ the style of Shackle, as the future is unknowable, surprise is always possible and confidence is susceptible to change. Perhaps in harmony with Keynes is the notion that human beings do not possess a perfect, or even highly developed, ability to reason and comprehend even if they were capable of learning of all the things which could be incorporated into an ideal, or true, assessment of risk. While one supposes that Keynes would have welcomed attempts by new classicists to portray agents as grappling with reality to strive to understand it, he would have responded, if the view of the fundamentalists is to be accepted, that probability estimates of events (and of the validity of rival theories of reality) need not be quantifiable even in the abstract. There are grey areas which defy our attempts to make numerical estimates.[1] Keynes, in effect, offered the alternative of *reasonable* expectations,[2] and suggested what sorts of expectations would tend to arise in particular circumstances.

An important possibility stands out. If risk-averse transactors are in an environment of Knightian uncertainty where exact calculation of future gains and losses is not feasible through lack of information, it is possible for gravitation to occur towards a pre-established norm which participants are prepared to adopt as a guide to currently negotiated prices. In the face of small shocks, the elasticity of price expectations could be less than unity. However, if the dislocation is so great that faith in the norm is weakened too much, then uncertainty about the extent and likely reversal of the disturbance can generate an unstable 'follow-the-leader' mentality. This can easily give rise to an elasticity of price expectations exceeding unity, especially in inherently speculative markets. As Alchian notes: 'There is nothing inconsistent in assuming different price-expectation elasticities in different markets; in fact, there is much to be gained in detecting factors that make them different.'[3]

In many ways this can be taken as a refinement of Leijonhufvud's views on the corridor and how he would prefer to go beyond Keynes's basic model. It is argued here that even Keynes's more basic models are rather more complex than Leijonhufvud's simplest (1968) version that price expectations are inelastic and that therefore quantities adjust faster than prices.[4] As has been seen, Leijonhufvud cites with approval G.B. Richardson[5] who argues that information problems occur when the success of my actions depends on yours. Because I do not know what you are doing (nor you I), difficulties will arise in the formulation of sensible strategies. Leijonhufvud also realizes that Keynes emphasized 'the dark forces of time and ignorance which envelop our future', but Shackle considers that this aspect of expectations is inadequately dealt with by Leijonhufvud,[6] the potential for unfathomably complex reactions being so great. Suppose that we hold that Leijonhufvud himself limits the role of uncertainty and misinformation to that of causing predictable and definite multiplier responses which carry the system away from the Walrasian vector in the short run. Surely, however, his views would be capable of extension to accord with a more general approach where ignorance and uncertainty can induce a great variety of responses. One doubts that Leijonhufvud would object to such an extension. His 'corridor hypothesis' points to the possibility that the response of a system depends on the size of the disturbance. Objective factors, such as the size of buffer savings and inventories determine the trigger-point. There is no reason why subjective factors cannot also be enlisted in support.

Indeed, in view of Leijonhufvud's assistance in the preparation of an article by Ronald Heiner,[7] in which the argument is made that the switch from one mental rule of thumb to another can reasonably explain sudden shifts in behaviour, it seems that Leijonhufvud would not be unfriendly to such developments. Curiously, Heiner does not cite Keynes. He does, however, cite Shackle and the Austrians who use subjectivism in order to maintain that expectations and resulting behaviour can be unstable and generally unpredictable. Heiner responds that in an uncertain world, where the capacity of agents to appreciate and digest every relevant aspect of the environment is limited, the resulting reliance on rules of thumb tends to increase the predictability of their actions rather than reduce it. Similarly, I argue that conventions are a response to living in an uncertain world, and they tend to foster stability within reassuringly familiar environments.

Contrary to Heiner, it is not clear that Austrians reject deterministic models entirely. Much of life takes place without conscious decision-making on the basis of routines and on the normally verified assumption that other agents will act much as they have in the past. While Austrians (and the advocates of rational expectations) regard agents as alert, intelligent and flexible, to modify their claims would close the gap somewhat. It is possible to hypothesize that threshold levels exist in that agents cannot assimilate the minutiae. Small pieces of information are perceived only if they loom large in the local circumstances directly experienced by a subset of agents. Entrepreneurship, indeed, reflects an urge to discover an opportunity which is not clearly discernible yet. When to act on the basis of routine and when to strike out in new directions surely is a strongly Austrian theme.[8]

Some key objections to Leijonhufvud's approach can be listed. Leijonhufvud's simplified version could obscure the vision of an economic system which Keynes was trying to convey. Indeed, the dynamics involved are rather more elaborate in that Keynes appears to

269

have several corridors. It is a far more refined attack on classical theories which had paid little attention to the process of short-run adjustments. Furthermore, Keynes's model enables a successful attack in logic to be made against the classical faith in the automatic long-run restoration of full employment. Equilibrium at less than full employment becomes possible. Neither prices nor quantities need show any tendency to change. Leijonhufvud would apparently be unwilling to accept this, even though proceeding along the lines he suggests is the beginning of the journey to this destination. The incorporation of uncertainty cannot merely impose on the system problems of adjustment in the short run. Neither does the problem of uncertainty only require specific attention in an analysis of crisis, the classicists themselves being prepared to concede as much. If uncertainty is persistent, likewise can the conventions which emerge be desirable for long-run stability.

It is not the acknowledgement of uncertainty about the future, however, which distinguishes Keynes from the classicists.[9] Neither is it the recognition of the potential for violent disruption if, under conditions of crisis, panic overcomes the usual state of calmness. Decision-making is 'based on so flimsy a foundation, it is subject to sudden and violent changes',[10] but importantly Keynes states:

> I daresay that a classical economist would readily admit this. But, even so, I think he has overlooked the precise nature of the difference which his abstraction makes between theory and practice, and the character of the fallacies into which he is likely to be led.[11]

It is the influence of uncertainty, and the formation and properties of conventions in various markets, which explain the difference of viewpoint. Uncertainty *per se* is not the disputed issue. It is the effect of uncertainty on economic behaviour at both the theoretical and practical level which classicists had not grasped.

If there are no simple rules governing behaviour, we cannot readily characterize all transactors as mechanically responding to disequilibrating shocks in a similar and predictable manner. People vary regarding their propensity to see the optimistic side of things, their faith in their own judgement as against those of their fellows, their experiences upon which their decisions are based, their capacity to solve complex problems and their degree of risk aversion. Keynes's frequent references to expectations, uncertainty, psychology and conventions reflect his realization that behaviour within any market depends upon the kind of transactor who inhabits it and the nature of the environment within which they operate. The nature of these conventions within which individuals act differ in their stability, but they have essential properties in common.

Knowing that our own individual judgement is worthless, we endeavour to fall back on the judgement of the rest of the world, which is perhaps better informed. That is, we endeavour to conform with the behaviour of the majority or the average. The psychology of a society of individuals each of whom is endeavouring to copy the others leads to what we may strictly term a *conventional* judgement.[12]

When we read *The General Theory* with this in mind, we can detect the existence of many conventions which govern behaviour in various markets. We see that aggregate behaviour depends upon the interactions between different classes of transactors. I argue that these classes differ so considerably that macro-dynamic models may need to adopt a less aggregated form so that the influence of each group can be isolated. These classes can be distinguished by identifying them according to the animals whose behaviour members of each class resemble. It is hoped that what follows captures much of the spirit of Keynes's writings.

Conventions can be distinguished from mere customs or habits. The former emerge from rational or purpose-oriented behaviour[13] under conditions of uncertainty where the actions of others are observed. It is not unthinking behaviour of a kind which only psychologists or sociologists are competent to study (though some economists might argue that customs did emerge on account of purposeful activity in the long distant past and that outmoded customs are simply too costly to change). While customs, animal spirits and various psychological propensities seem non-economic in their essential character, their existence is consistent with Keynes's vision of the world in which uncertainty, rather than calm calculation can be the norm. Conventions arise which give some semblance of coherent behaviour in a world which otherwise would be opaque to the economist.

It is not therefore necessary to follow Tony Lawson or Peter Earl[14] who note that institutional and cultural factors can shape individuals to render conformity. Imitation and faith in the views of others can spontaneously give rise to conventions. It can pay to conform.[15] Naturally, conventions evolve as economies become more complex and as more, and varied, individuals attach themselves to existing clusters. Clearly, similarities exist between conventions and norms both of which give speculators something to cling to and enhance stability by giving atomistic agents some clue about the likely behaviour of the others.[16] Conventions can also, in a sense, form like snowflakes each outcome being unique and difficult, though not impossible, to model. Whether they suddenly melt depends on the hostility of the environment and whether a critical temperature is reached.

Herding is not always instinctive. It can have a semi-rational aspect. The liquidity trap, for example, emerges because agents rightly calculate that others will be bearish at an interest rate just below it. It is not simply a matter of unthinking habit or custom. Agents learn that conformity avoids losses. While not about whim and sentiment, it is, as the bootstraps critics have claimed, about chance.[17] Where the convention happens to settle is not explained within the model but by history. Similar considerations apply to the determination of the money wage.[18]

To point out, as does Lawson, the stabilizing role played by conventions provides a counter-balance to Shackle's extreme subjectivism. Expectations, while mere imagined futures, are not necessarily fragile and foundationless fantasies. Neither is there the stark, dualistic contrast between orthodoxy's rational calculation and irrational animal spirits.[19] A middle way exists.

Conventions short-circuit chains of decisions. To conform reduces marginal transactions and search costs.[20] In a sense, they can be drawn at least into the fringes of the domain of neoclassical logic. For example, in a share market context, conventional valuations are based on individuals' decisions. There is no question of there being any reciprocal, moral obligation of a sociological variety.

Let us consider the role of conventional behaviour in the bond, capital, share, commodities and labour markets so that the kinds of transactor and the nature of the conventions to which they conform can be sharply contrasted.

The wealth holders

Keynes is most explicit about the importance of convention in determining bond market behaviour despite the existence of free individuals who, to some extent, make up their own minds.

> In general...a change in circumstances or expectations will cause some realignment in individual holdings of money; – since, in fact, a change will influence the ideas of different individuals differently by reasons partly of differences in environment and the reason for which money is held and partly of differences in knowledge and interpretation of the new situation.[21]

The convention which establishes the interest rate definitely exists and is usually very stable. 'The interest rate...may fluctuate for decades about a level which is chronically too high for full employment...so that the level established by convention is thought to be rooted in objective grounds much stronger than convention...[22] It is evident, then, that the rate of interest is a highly psychological phenomenon.'[23]

Different animals inhabit the bond market where the price of debts 'will be fixed at the point at which the sales of the "bears" and the purchases of the "bulls" are balanced'.[24] The proportion of bulls and bears that exists at any time is not invariant however. Monetary policy can change the interest rate so that, at the new rate, bulls have become bears, and, in the case of large changes in the money supply, unanimity can arise.[25] The convention, therefore, is not of a kind which prevents change, it merely impedes it, but, on rarer occasions, it can be a cause of deviation *amplification*. It is likely that

> the dismay and uncertainty as to the future which accompanies a collapse in the marginal efficiency of capital naturally precipitates a sharp increase in liquidity-preference – and hence a rise in the rate of interest.[26]

In other words, pessimism in one sector can spill over into the money market causing greater disequilibrium.

To this sketch of the essential properties of the bond market an addition is possible which goes slightly beyond Keynes.[27] The differences between transactors can be shown in greater detail. Bulls might be considered as distinct from oxen, their more docile relatives. A bull acts aggressively according to his beliefs about higher bond (and share) prices. An ox is a conservative advocate of sound finance who, on the basis of past experience, has an unthinking faith in the notion that the interest rate will gravitate towards its traditional level. Bulls charge. Oxen wallow. Bulls bet that tomorrow's price will be better than today's and can over-react in a boom. Oxen merely provide pressure on the market rate to keep it near the norm. The impact of monetary measures depends on whether any particular kind of agent is predominant at any one time. Oxen can account for a long-run liquidity trap.

Two aspects can be distinguished. The existence of a floor can be regarded as conventional. (I believe rates cannot fall because everyone else does too.) Furthermore, under conditions of pessimism and uncertainty, the existence of a substantial risk premium (due to heightened precautionary demand and increased perceptions of borrower's and lender's risk) reflects the general feeling of disquiet, which can also become a conventional belief.

The investors

The demand for investment goods depends, in part, on the state of expectations which, being 'based on shifting and unreliable evidence,...are subject to hidden and violent changes'.[28] Investment is influenced by 'animal spirits – ...a spontaneous urge to action rather than

273

inaction, and not as the outcome of a weighted average of quantitative benefits multiplied by quantitative probabilities'.[29]

Much of large-scale investment was once made by a now disappearing breed of lion-hearted pioneers. These are a rare breed.

> In former times, when enterprises were mainly owned by those who undertook them..., investment depended on a sufficient supply of individuals of sanguine temperament and constructive impulses who embarked on business as a way of iife.[30]

Unfortunately for macroeconomic stability, this kind of investor does not predominate and even the lions lose confidence when surrounded by agents of another kind, the average business man. Stability 'is expansively dependent on the political and social atmosphere which is congenial to the average business man'. Consequently, 'nerves and hysteria' must be taken into account.

Investor confidence, however, is only potentially unstable. Keynes states, 'We should not conclude...that everything depends on waves of irrational psychology. On the contrary, the state of long-term expectation is often steady.'[31] But when confidence gives way, unanimity is likely to result among investors and investment falls suddenly during a period of crisis. In non-crisis conditions, however, investor behaviour is different in that

> the substitution of a downward for an upward tendency often takes place suddenly and violently, whereas there is, as a rule, no such sharp turning-point when an upward is substituted for a downward tendency.[32]

In other words, different circumstances elicit different responses from investors and their behaviour cannot be governed by any simple rule.

The speculators

Share markets also affect the level of investment. Indeed, 'the daily revaluations of the Stock Exchange...inevitably exert a *decisive* influence on the rate of current investment'.[33] Although Keynes's vitriolic attacks on speculation in chapter 12 are well known, certain salient features of his argument deserve stressing.

Keynes describes the game of the share market as 'intolerably boring and over-exacting to anyone who is entirely exempt from the gambling instinct'. It is the long-term investor (such as Keynes was himself!) whose behaviour is 'eccentric, unconventional and rash in the eyes of average opinion'. He complains, with a touch of bitterness, that 'it is better for reputation to fail conventionally than to succeed unconventionally'.[34]

Keynes expressly states that share prices are governed by convention and that this convention is extremely unstable because so many ignorant people participate. The price elasticity of expectations of individuals gripped by mass psychology is equal to, or sometimes even greater than unity.

> Day-to-day fluctuations in the profits of existing investments, which are obviously of an ephemeral and non-significant character, tend to have an altogether excessive, and even absurd, influence on the market.... In abnormal times in particular, when the hypothesis of an indefinite continuance of the existing state of affairs is less plausible than usual even though there are no express grounds to anticipate a definite change, the market will be swept by waves of optimistic and pessimistic sentiment.[35]

Another kind of transactor resides in the share market, the professional speculator who 'is forced to concern himself with the anticipation of impending changes, in the news or in the atmosphere, of the kind by which experience shows that the mass psychology of the market is most influenced'.[36] He can be likened to that despicable scavenger, the *hyena*. The bolder members of the pack, who are also the first to have picked up the scent, are the first to approach the carcass and gorge themselves on the choicest of the pickings. To stretch the analogy, the carcass might be seen as being a sheep, an ignorant member of the general public who simply followed the others and met a gruesome death beside his fellows.

Irving Fisher has made a similar point, though speculation is, in the classical vein, essential only to cyclical excesses rather than built into the very nature of day-to-day practice:

> The chief evils of speculation flow from the participation of the general public, who lack the special knowledge, and enter the market in a purely gambling spirit. In addition to suffering the usual evil consequences of gambling, they produce evil consequences for the non-participating public by causing factitious fluctuations in the values of the products or property in which they speculate. The evils of speculation are particularly acute when, as generally happens with the investing public, the forecasts are not made independently. Were it true that each individual speculator made up his mind independently of every other as to the future course of events, the errors of some would probably be offset by those of others. But as a matter of fact, the

mistakes of the common herd are usually in the same direction. Like sheep, they follow a single leader.[37]

The extent to which speculators are a problem arguably differs between countries. Keynes considered that the United States tended to be afflicted much worse than England.[38]

Before continuing by examining the next category of agent, the producers, a slight digression will be made. It is possible to contrast the attitudes of the investor and the speculator by turning to a psychological phenomenon, drawn recently to the attention of economists by George Akerlof and William Dickens, known as cognitive dissonance.

Some remarks on cognitive dissonance

George A. Akerlof has been at the forefront of attempts to show how actions *perceived* by agents as being in their best interests can lead to stable, but globally suboptimal, results. A recent contribution[39] might have some bearing on the issues raised in this chapter. Emphasis is placed by Akerlof and Dickens on the phenomenon of Cognitive Dissonance, a psychological propensity which is reflected in peoples' desires to interpret events to confirm their chosen beliefs. It is as though there is an inherent desire to avoid the need to re-evaluate and replace views about themselves and their environment. To change one's mind and to admit that one is wrong about a cherished belief is a painful process. Often the greater the hardship suffered and the greater the devotion to a belief that a person has shown, the more deeply entrenched that belief becomes.[40]

Hans and Michael Eysenck[41] supply a colourful example, not as irrelevant to economics as it might at first appear, to reveal that 'man is a rationalizing animal rather than a rational one'.[42] They take the case of religious beliefs and tell the story of how a particular sect believed that a cataclysmic flood was imminent and that the true believers, if assembled in the back garden of one of the members, would be rescued by a flying saucer. Despite the many false alarms and the disappointing non-appearance of either the flood or the extraterrestrials, the group did not decide to try their luck with another religion but rather to minimize their dissonance by the redoubling of their efforts to convert others. Many had quit their jobs and disposed of their possessions and their commitment to their beliefs had been far from merely lukewarm.

A macroeconomic analogy is perhaps found in the treatment of the investment sector and the share market described by Keynes in the fundamentalist gospel contained in chapter 12 of *The General Theory* and the 1937 article in the *Quarterly Journal of Economics*.

The great pioneering investors who devote their lives to the making of those grand investments, which create the wealth and prestige of nations, are those who most fervently advocate that we all should be more like them in their virtue. Their commitment is deep and their faith in the future, and in themselves, is difficult to dislodge. Contrast, at the other extreme, the speculators on the share market whose purchases are far from 'indissoluble, like marriage'.[43] Theirs is a promiscuous life-style, with all the transience, fragility and sheer enjoyment which that implies. The urge of most of them to have the rewards which stem from the ownership of capital and yet to have enough flexibility to avoid responsibility is to a degree offset by a desire that their investments not fluctuate too violently beyond conventional limits. In the face of an uncertain future, people are to a degree willing to rationalize their beliefs and are prepared eagerly to grasp as relevant average opinion to quell their individual doubts. But as the convention is weak, it does not take much of a jolt to induce either the abandonment of hope for a recovery or the arousal of the thrill of the next potential conquest.

The producers

Employers in the consumption and investment sectors are depicted as sensible and calm with regard to their decisions about current output levels. They are not seen as sources of dislocation but as hardworking and uncomplaining *draughthorses*. In Chapter 5 their influence on employment is described.[44] Changes in their short-term expectations are not 'sufficiently violent or rapid...to cause abandonment of work on all productive processes which, in the light of the revised expectation, it was a mistake to have begun'.[45] Shocks tend to be absorbed, taking time to percolate through each industry. Producers respond to changes and they do so with moderation. They do not initiate disturbances through a sudden loss of confidence.

> Accordingly it is sensible for producers to base their expectations on the assumption that the most recently realised results will continue, except in so far as there are definite reasons for expecting a change. Thus in practice there is a large overlap between the effects on employment of the realised sale-proceeds of recent output and those of the sale-proceeds expected from current input; the producers' forecasts are more often gradually modified in the light of results than in anticipation of prospective changes.[46]

Observe that producers' price expectations are quite elastic and approach unity. Their behaviour is utterly different from the ordinary speculator who often acts with an elasticity of greater than unity and

277

from the bears who operate with an elasticity close to zero. There is an occasion, however, when their price expectations are greater than one over a limited range of prices, which is clearly contrary to Leijonhufvud's argument that inelastic expectations are typical in this market. Keynes argued that falling money wages might not increase the MEC and restore full employment, because *further* wage cuts might be expected. Investment would, therefore, be delayed until the wage reached a level beyond which it was not expected to fall.[47]

As a general rule, however, we can say that producers do not imitate others or conform to the behaviour of those around them on that day or in days gone by. No convention linking them to one another exists because they all behave in such a sensible manner that they have no need to fear what their fellows are doing. Individuals are in the best position to judge what they ought best to do in the circumstances in which they find themselves. They have no particular need to imitate others, and have limited information about what the others are doing anyway.

The consumer

The consumption function, which is based upon a 'fundamental psychological law' is a fairly stable function of current income.[48] Sudden changes in saving patterns are not likely to trigger disequilibrium. However, changes in the real value of wealth brought about, for example, by a deflationary recession caused elsewhere, might spill over into this sector. Two secondary effects can result, higher real values of bonds working in one direction to stimulate consumption by increasing the real value of wealth – the wealth effect – and lower equity prices, which reduce wealth, working in the other.[49] Consumers merely respond passively for the most part.

The householder, as suggested previously, can be likened to a *sheep* on account of a strong herd instinct. They do, on occasions, simply follow the leader (to, for example, the doors of a building society which rumour holds to be precariously placed) but, for the most part, they huddle together and do little harm. On the stock market they are easily led by the Judas sheep to the slaughterhouse and, under a system of *laissez-faire*, there is no good shepherd to protect them.[50]

The labourer

Involuntary unemployment occurs when workers are willing to work for a lower real wage but are unable to do so because any efforts to increase employment through reductions in the money wage merely cause commodity stocks to accumulate at their original prices. When prices fall to clear the stocks (at a loss), employment reverts to its initial position where the old real wage is restored. Employers will not expand output the next time that money wages fall (if they are quick learners or have read *The General Theory*).

Under purely competitive conditions and in the complete absence of trade unions, the unemployed would, in theory, try to secure employment by the offer of a lower money wage, if they thought that the possibility of gaining employment (at the expense of those currently employed at a higher rate who are unwilling to match the lower offer) outweighed the costs (in time, effort, transportation and communication) involved in making the offer to any employer. Under these conditions, workers would continue to undercut each other in a desperate attempt to gain or retain employment. A quasi-equilibrium would result (*ceteris paribus*) in which output would remain constant but the price level would fall at, one supposes, an ever-increasing rate as workers become frantic. If the sundry real balance effects or an upward revision of the MEC schedule do not come to the rescue, and Keynes doubted that they would,[51] the economy could not continue to function as a currency-using system.

Fortunately, trade unions ensure that such a disaster would never eventuate. In other words, trade unions are a form of organization of individual workers which serves the interests of the community as a whole – at least in so far as the prevention of wage cuts is concerned. I argue that unions are visible manifestations of conventional behaviour which govern the actions of individual labourers. One reasonable microeconomic justification for their existence, which does not simply involve an attempt to monopolize the supply of labour and to drive the real wage upward, is that each worker realizes the probable futility of eternal wage cuts in an attempt to find a job for himself. Each realizes that other workers will simply match any lower offer. Consequently, conventions arise. Labourers reach a mutual understanding that 'unfair' undercutting should not be allowed. These conventions, however, require institutional enforcement for one simple reason. Individual workers might have an incentive to break the agreement and obtain a short-term gain of employment if the labourer he replaces refuses to retaliate and instead honours his side of the bargain. This is true for each individual. Consequently, it is rational for each perfectly free individual labourer to agree collectively to punish anyone, including himself if necessary, who violates the truce and sends the system hurtling headlong towards monetary collapse.[52]

This argument is by no means novel. Social contract theories (such as those which underlie a Rawlsian conception of justice), James Buchanan's Theory of Clubs and, most relevantly of all, Sen's notion of the Isolation Paradox are examples of how orthodox economics has readily been able to accept arguments based on the idea that individuals each may enter into agreements with large numbers of others so that benefits, impossible for an isolated individual to secure, can be enjoyed by each as a member of a group.[53]

Let us turn to Keynes himself to search for indications that arguments of this kind are indeed recognized.

Conventional behaviour is at the base of worker resistance to changes in the money wage which is of a selective kind and which affects the system of 'fair' relative wages between categories of labourers. Such behaviour does not result from the kind of social contract outlined above.[54] The agreement in this case is motivated by entirely normative considerations of justice and does not reflect the recognition that money-wage flexibility is, in fact, a futile (and, indeed, harmful) in itself. It is, however, sufficient to provide a firm anchorage to the normal wage level.

Keynes, however, seems to be willing to go further than this. He makes comments about the behaviour of workers that raise the possibility that the labour-market convention pertains not only to normative values but also to more purely economic factors. The favourable macroeconomic effects of downward money-wage inflexibility might not have been completely intended or merely incidental to the major purpose of the convention.

> Whilst workers will usually resist a reduction of money-wages, it is not their practice to withdraw labour whenever there is a rise in the price of wage-goods. It is sometimes said that it would be illogical for labour to resist a reduction of money-wages but not resist a reduction of real wages. For reasons given below (p. 14) this might not be so illogical as it appears at first; and, as we shall see later, fortunately so. But, whether logical or illogical, experience shows that this is how labour in fact behaves.[55]

By 'logical' does he mean 'rational' in an economic sense?

Keynes notes that such seemingly bewildering actions by unionists can, in part, be explained by the fact that inflation, with constant money wages, does not alter relativities among labourers.[56] He also seems to argue that administrative difficulties would prevent wage earners being able to demand higher money wages whenever the price of a wage good rose and altered the real wage by an amount which would be impossible to measure precisely.[57] But he teases the reader by leaving a third option open.

> Thus it is fortunate that the workers, though unconsciously, are instinctively more reasonable economists than the classical

school, inasmuch as they resist reductions of money-wages, which are *seldom* or never of an all-round character.[58]

It seems that, even if the reduction in the money-wage rate were across-the-board, the wage cut would still be rejected. Workers would have to be forced to accept even a general reduction in the nominal wage rate even if the administrative machinery were provided.

It is only when a highly authoritarian society, where sudden, substantial, all-round changes could be decreed that a flexible wage-policy could function with success.[59]

Is it not reasonable to argue that Keynes held that workers combine in the interests of them all, and not merely as a classicist would argue, in the interests of those who remain employed at the expense of the unfortunate unemployed? Is there more to a union than an organization which merely serves the part of the labouring class which is able to earn a higher real wage than it would otherwise? Might it not be that, under authoritarian conditions, all workers would agree that the power to suppress the real wage (that is, to reduce it below that possible under collective bargaining with employers) should not be granted to the State?[60] Is it also not conceivable that, under conditions of liberty, a term in the social contract (or mutual understanding) might be that futile reductions in the money wage be prohibited? Conventional equilibria can explain the persistence of false prices which in turn explain multiplier-induced additions to involuntary unemployment. Even if potential multilateral trades were somehow perceived possible between the producers and purchasers of consumption goods, no decline in money wages need be perceived as liable to bring about these potential exchanges. There is the risk of retaliation between workers whereby money-wage cuts are perceived as futile and, so far as producers are concerned, there is the problem that, if the marginal propensity to consume is less than one, expanded output is only feasible if investment grows to fill the gap. Note that the pessimism of investors is undue from the viewpoint of a hypothetical auctioneer, but mere possible futures are not capable of sending signals to the present to spur a suitably temperate degree of entrepreneurial endeavour. Investors have chosen to abstain, but the unemployed workers want to work (if we follow Keynes's 1936 approach where they are off their supply curve). Furthermore, money hoarders have chosen to hoard and producers can be on their supply curves minimizing their losses if unplanned inventories have been run down. A convention in the labour market can therefore keep the system in a position of stable prices and stable quantities, and yet be consistent with a state of involuntary unemployment.

Conventional zones

We have examined the kinds of transactors who trade in particular markets and we have seen that the conventions which shape their conduct are each quite different. The important implication for macrodynamics is that the damage done by a disequilibrating shock depends on which market suffers the initial impact. Knowing this, we can then consider whether or not the convention appropriate to that market has been shattered. Consequently, we can analyse whether mere confusion, largely confined to one market, occurs or whether, going to the opposite extreme, outright panic exists which can spread from one market to another. It is obvious that the bigger the initial shock the more likely any convention will crumble. Even those who might remain calm in the face of a mere disturbance might stampede in an emergency. In the case of speculative markets where conventional stability is the least, large shocks can easily induce a state of frenzy where the elasticity of price expectations is greater than unity. Furthermore, chain reactions are possible where, as we saw earlier, the money market can react, by changes in precautionary demand, to shocks which reduce confidence within the share and investment sectors.

The reader may not be convinced that evidence of this kind of reasoning can be found in *The General Theory*. What follows certainly cannot be given direct textual support. If one accepts that an analysis along the preceding lines might be useful, then it would be appropriate to shape it into something slightly more formal. Let us, therefore, examine how the existence of conventions of different nature and durability can influence the dynamic properties of a macrosystem.

I argue that, while certain conventions remain operative, dynamic motion must be limited to particular zones. If these conventions are subjected to a shock of such violence that they collapse, then the system moves outside these zones.

The symbols are as follows:

P: the optimal price level given the money supply, sound financial institutions and the normal money wage;

N: the full employment level consistent with the 'natural' rate of unemployment;

W: Walrasian optimal equilibrium.

Observe that zones 2–6 are subsets of zone 1 and that 6 is a subset of 5 and so on. Also note that the exact shape and size (both relative and absolute) of each zone is of no significance to the present argument.

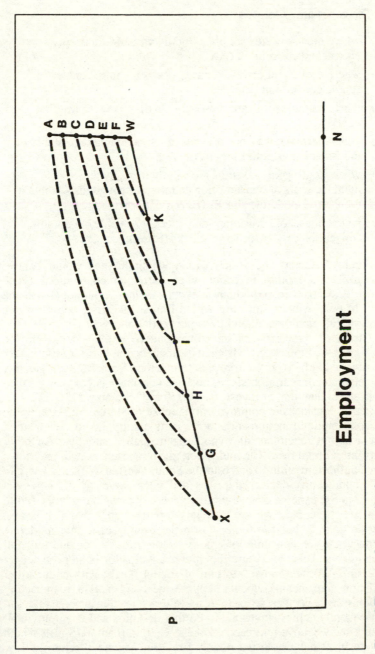

Figure 2 The nest of conventional zones

The zones are as follows:

(1) where money wages are only slightly variable – a deeply entrenched convention (AXW);

(2) where equity and private security prices are fairly stable – a fragile convention (BGW);

(3) where animal spirits are reasonably high – likewise fragile (CHW);

(4) where normal behaviour prevails in the bond market – stable in the face of substantial shocks (DIW);

(5) where contingent decisions are calmly made by the manufacturers of consumption and investment goods – stable in the face of moderate shocks (EJW);

(6) where household consumption patterns are stable – a durable convention except for large shocks (FKW).

Figure 2 depicts the zones within which Keynes would believe disequilibrium motion to occur when particular conventions break down. Pessimism in particular markets can induce reductions in the level of employment, but only within limits. Likewise, optimism can generate full employment and even pure inflation.

The price dimension of the zones can be explained as follows. Starting at W, suppose there is an investment boom. Greater inflationary pressure is likely to ensue from this source than from, for example, any conceivable consumption spree, because consumer behaviour is much more stable than that of investors. Therefore C lies above E.

Let us consider the employment dimension. Starting at W, suppose the consumption function shifts downward slightly, i.e. to such a small extent as not to violate its hypothesized relative stability. All other conventions hold firm. The multiplier, given investment, will result in a new equilibrium within zone 6 to the South-West of W (somewhere in FKW) indicating depressed prices and unemployment. If, however, consumption patterns change violently we will move out of zone 6 into area EJKF. Suppose we are now in the part of zone 5 which is also outside zone 6, but for some reason the usually calm and moderate producers in the consumption-goods sector fear that demand will fall even more and choose to curtail output in anticipation of an even deeper recession. We then move into part of zone 4 (DIJE) with both further deflation and unemployment. Suppose the bond market is unusually nervous and becomes so bearish as to drive up the interest rate and consequently depress investment. Further deflation and unemployment results and we move into part of zone 3 (CHID). If animal spirits which govern investment hold reasonably firm, our new equilibrium will be within this part of zone 3, but, if entrepreneurial confidence gives way, we move into part of zone 2 (BGHC). We remain there unless there is mass panic among speculators which causes share prices to collapse, financial wealth to vaporize and money to be hoarded. This causes even greater dislocation and we enter the part of zone 1 (AXGB) where only one protective convention is left. If the convention holding money wages (and therefore the price level and the real value of contractual commitments) should be breached, utter chaos would result and a monetary economy could not continue to exist. AXW envelops all feasible equilibria. To move outside the zone governed by convention can only lead to a reversion to barter.

Of course, in practice, it is not convention 6 which breaks first, but rather convention 3 (the MEC) which, if shattered too violently, can induce a crisis of confidence in 2. In other words, there can be a domino effect, especially if the initial disequilibrating shock is very large. One convention, stable money wages, is so vital that to remove it will bring the whole system down like a house of cards. The weakest conventions crumble first and the others, which are more difficult to destroy, persist and provide some measure of stability to macro-behaviour. To destroy all conventions and to demand perfect price flexibility could have catastrophic consequences. Money wages, share prices and investor confidence need to be actively rigidified by State intervention whenever their conventional stability is jeopardized. Policies of greater subtlety than mechanical fiscal fine-tuning are required.

Keynes can be interpreted as having realized that controlling an economy is like being a zoo-keeper in charge of an unruly menagerie. Certain species, like the hyena, need to be locked up in dingy little cages so that their speculative activities on the stock market can be kept to a minimum. Lions, on the other hand, are noble creatures who deserve to roam free and, if they have become an extinct breed, governments need to invest in their place. The draughthorses are safe and perfectly tame. They ought not be caged either. On the contrary, the price mechanism ought to be allowed to operate in the commodity markets to serve allocative efficiency. This, incidentally, explains the apparent contradiction in Keynes's writings where, for example, he attacks the market system in chapters 1 to 23 but defends it in chapter 24.[61]

It is hoped that analysis on these lines might be seen to bridge the gap between two rival schools of thought, the neoclassical and the much disparaged psycho-sociological. Although group behaviour has been described, the principle of methodological individualism has not been swept away. Conventions can be understood by examining how individuals of different kinds interact with each other. Indeed the macroeconomic behaviour resulting from interrelationships between the individual and his group might well be capable of formalization using mathematical tools. (Whether such an approach would yield more fruit than the literary and intuitive method is another story.) Different classes could be assigned an appropriate symbol to identify them. The sizes of shock required to destroy each convention could then be ranked. The conditions under which the price elasticity of expectations is greater, less than or equal to unity could be specified for each group. One might then be able to construct a model to portray how shocks of different magnitude can, when applied to different markets at the first instance, cause mild or deep recession or even implosion and reversion to barter.

Although the notion of a corridor located near to the region of full employment is not so easy to explain and is hardly possible confidently to attribute to Keynes, arguments can be made that there exist zones outside of which the system suddenly moves much further away from full employment. Leijonhufvud's own suggestive analogy can be modified to convey the gist of this approach.[62] He likens the economy in a Walrasian equilibrium to a ship floating on an even keel. If the vessel is of classical design, an external force applied to it will cause it to list temporarily, but it will automatically return to its initial position, possibly, however, after a series of violent oscillations. A Keynesian craft behaves rather differently. Unfortunately, its cargo is not securely tied down. If the ship is displaced from its even keel, the cargo slides causing an even greater degree of list that will persist in the absence of further outside disturbances.

It is argued that Keynes himself saw things as being more complicated than this. Different cargoes of different weights are lashed down by ropes of different strength. Some of the cargo is loose. If the ship is tipped by a certain amount, it might be that only the loose portion of the cargo slides and a Keynesian equilibrium would be attained. If the shock is perhaps only slightly greater, some of the lashings could snap and the vessel would tip more steeply still. Should the shock be great enough to cause all the lashings to break, the ship will capsize and sink reaching a new equilibrium on the sea bed with all hands lost. Flexible money wages (where the price of labour is not securely tied down, so to speak) can induce deflation to catastrophic proportions, debtors collapsing into bankruptcy *en masse* being unable to meet the ever-increasing real burden of their contractual obligations.

Catastrophe theory has made sporadic appearances to analyse problems of this kind but has never really gained much support. The problem is not only the conservatism of the profession but also the difficulty of conducting meaningful empirical tests.[63] Naturally the sudden collapse of markets and the associated state of panic can be investigated in this way.[64]

Conventional zones can be regarded as a layered set of corridors. The bigger the initial shock the more likely that the system will be propelled into unexplored zones within which uncertainty is liable to be associated with volatile behaviour. A benign convention, once destroyed, is not easily restored. Hysteresis effects can reasonably be expected as random disturbances can have prolonged, systematic effects. Social policy in the form of money-wage stabilization, government investment and stock market controls were Keynes's suggested means to create greater certainty. Such policies were designed to reform the institutional structure within which capitalism was to operate. Keynes did not advocate nationalization where government officials are faced with the complexity and uncertainty of dealing with the day-to-day microeconomic detail. Certainty is to be promoted by building secure fences and not by the regimentation of market participants.[65] (This accords somewhat with the modern preference to base demand management on rules which strive to create a stable, familiar environment within which agents can make their decisions.)

Perspectives on conventional conduct

A conventional equilibrium is not inconsistent with pervasive uncertainty. Indeed, conventional behaviour can help to resolve a paradox: a stable convention, which can emerge as a response to an uncertain environment, can provide a framework within which an equilibrium construct, such as an *LM* curve, can reasonably be employed. Conventions allow a degree of man-made certainty to displace the uncertainty of the state of nature.

Conventions are a source of stability which prevent violent fluctuations which would occur if individuals were feverishly to follow the policy of price changes in response to any major shift in demand. The benign nature of conventions is especially clear in the labour market where the stability of the price level, and indeed, the money-using system itself, depends on the stability of the money wage.[66]

There is a trinity in which the nominal wage, the demand for money and even its supply by the banking system[67] are seen to be based on conventional behaviour. In discussing the elements of truth in mercantilism Keynes states:

> Now, if the wage-unit is somewhat stable and not liable to spontaneous changes of significant magnitude (a condition which is almost always satisfied), if the state of liquidity-preference is somewhat stable, taken as an average of its short-period fluctuations, and if banking conventions are also stable, the rate of interest will tend to be governed by the quantity of the precious metals, measured in terms of the wage-unit, available to satisfy the community's desire for liquidity.[68]

Furthermore, 'animal spirits' which are too powerful to be constrained by convention – their demise being due to the fundamental change in the structure of capitalism in which the 'captains of industry' are no longer in charge[69] – indicate the importance to Keynes of irrational and passionate urges. Even the working classes are not immune from the lust to gamble[70] although their feelings are milder in degree. Keynes's economy is also based on 'fundamental psychological laws' of consumption.

These are not *ad hoc*, slipshod analytical devices. They all reflect the view that man as an individual[71] is not by nature purely calculative. References to 'psychological propensities' are not just stray remarks, but are surprisingly pervasive.[72]

But we should not leap to the conclusion that the calculating man is entirely eliminated. One class of transactor in particular *is* concerned with equating expected marginal revenue and expected marginal costs. They are the producers of capital and consumption goods. Although their expectations are not based on perfect knowledge, as they tend to assume that the present is a better guide to the future than perhaps it really is,[73] they do strive to maximize profits[74] and therefore give the system greater predictability and allow us to formalize aggregate supply and demand analysis. It is significant that Keynes did not take his theory of conventions to an extreme by making *all* prices conventional.[75] This would have entirely destroyed the calculating man, yet he remains part of man, the composite of many passions. Because producers supplying current markets are not so forward looking,[76] their environment is not 'shrouded by the dark forces of time and ignorance that envelop our future'. They are willing and able to calculate, others are either unwilling, unable or both.

As for those who are unable to calculate by virtue of their uncertain environment, we cannot therefore necessarily say that they possess free will and do not make decisions deterministically but exercise free choice, as Shackle insists. Man instead could be a complex of passions and urges. We might never be able to understand or predict his actions completely or even to any great degree. Reason is there too but it does not govern conduct – and neither does ordinary common sense. If to say that Keynes's transactors are 'imaginative', 'sensible' and 'judicious'[77] can be fairly construed as a subtle rejection of the English conception of man which stems from Hobbes and Locke, perhaps in favour of that of Plato or Aristotle, we should hesitate to take that step. Furthermore, although habits and conventions are a feature of a Greek style of political philosophy and the art of economics, Keynes's use of the concepts might well have Humean origins.

A Hume connection?

Hume stressed that our beliefs about the external world are based not on reason but on custom and our psychological propensities. To attribute causality to events and to give order to the world, we rely on empirical induction.[78] We do not have real knowledge in Hume's sceptical view. Keynes was certainly familiar with Hume's work[79] and this view is central to Hume:

> We are determined by CUSTOM alone to suppose the future conformable to the past.... 'Tis not, therefore, reason, which is the guide of life, but custom.[80]

Leijonhufvud[81] cites Richardson and the latter[82] Hume, but passages exist where Keynes himself draws on Hume. There is quite a strong 'Hume Connection' which gives a degree of consistency not only to Keynes's economic writings but to his overall intellectual position.

Keynes consistently followed an approach laid down in the *Treatise on Probability*. His defence of inductivism from Hume's attack involved a qualified appeal to reason. Keynes felt that he had found the middle ground between Hume's scepticism and the extremes of rationalism.[83] Keynes wrote:

> Yet Hume's scepticism goes too far. The judgments of probability, upon which we depend for almost all our beliefs in matters of experience, undoubtedly depend on a strong psychological propensity in us to consider objects in a particular light. But this is no ground for supposing that they are nothing more than 'lively imaginations'. The same is true of the judgments in virtue of which we assent to other logical arguments; and yet in such cases we believe that there may be present some element of objective validity, transcending the psychological impulsion, with which primarily we are presented. So also in the case of probability we may believe that our judgments can penetrate into the real world, even though their credentials are subjective.[84]

The extent to which 'our judgments can penetrate into the real world' is severely limited, however, in matters economic. The problem confronts equally the policymaker and the economic agent. He identified, in his response to the early econometric work of Tinbergen,

> the central question of methodology – the logic of applying the method of multiple correlation to unanalysed economic material, which we know to be non-homogeneous through time. If we were dealing with the action of numerically measurable, independent forces, adequately analysed so that we knew we were dealing with

independent atomic factors and between them completely comprehensive, acting with fluctuating relative strength on material constant and homogeneous through time, we might be able to use the method of multiple correlation with some confidence.[85]

Compare the view in Keynes's *Treatise on Probability*:

The kind of fundamental assumption about the character of material laws, on which scientists appear commonly to act, seems to me to be much less simple than the bare principle of uniformity. They appear to assume something much more like what mathematicians call the principle of the superposition of small effects, or, as I prefer to call it, in this connection, the *atomic* character of natural law. The system of the material universe must consist, if this kind of assumption is warranted, of bodies which we may term (without any implication as to their size being conveyed thereby) *legal atoms*, such that each of them exercises its own separate, independent, and invariable effect, a change of the total state being compounded of a number of separate changes each of which is solely due to a separate portion of the preceding state.... Perhaps it has not always been realised that this atomic uniformity is in no way implied by the principle of the uniformity of nature. Yet there might well be quite different laws for wholes of different degrees of complexity, and laws of connection between complexes which could not be stated in terms of laws connecting individual parts. In this case natural law would be organic and not, as it is generally supposed, atomic.[86]

The impact on economics is described further, though in a style verging on the mystical, by Keynes in his biography of Edgeworth:

The atomic hypothesis which has worked so splendidly in physics breaks down in psychics. We are faced at every turn with the problems of organic unity, of discreteness, of discontinuity – the whole is not equal to the sum of the parts, comparisons of quantity fail us, small changes produce large effects, the assumptions of a uniform and homogeneous continuum are not satisfied.[87]

Regularities can prove fragile. Behaviour can respond unpredictably. Fundamentalists savour such passages.

Fundamentalism in perspective

Allied to the belief in the existence of uncertainty is the view that, by its very nature, uncertainty must profoundly influence human conduct.

Some fundamentalist comments, however, seem a trifle excessive.[88] Uncertainty may indeed differ from risk, but if it is found that transactors use similar rules of thumb, remembering that in one vital respect the environments are similar, there is no certainty; there may be little *practical* difference and you can therefore sensibly use, as did Keynes, a certainty-equivalent concept.[89] Arrow made a similar point to Davidson[90] who brushes it aside. To illustrate, suppose you are sitting in a cinema which suddenly catches fire. The probability of the fire killing you is unknowable in these historically unique circumstances. Common sense indicates that you should go to the exit rapidly. Would not the rational economic man be right beside you matching you stride for stride? If you are crossing a snow-covered minefield without a detector, a good rule of thumb is to step in the footmarks of others; this is true both for maximizers and for 'judicious' and 'sensible' men.[91] Some decisions indeed create a new environment and we cannot much rely on past experience, but is buying the one-hundredth sausage machine a perilous leap into the future requiring the courage and imagination of Napoleon at Waterloo? The drama of fundamentalism need not capture the spirit of deciding about those everyday banalities which dominate our lives. Perhaps Shackle would not disagree with that.

There are many who consider that fundamentalism sometimes goes too far. Allan Meltzer's view is:

> It is not useful to treat expectations as non-ergodic, since that rules out any serious economic analysis of future states. He [Meltzer] saw no benefits in this suggestion, and did not believe it to be based on a proper reading of *The General Theory* or *The Treatise on Probability*.[92]

Hutchison[93], Solow[94] and Fender[95] can be added to the list.

In view of the Hume Connection, Keynes is hardly going to consign all empirical and econometric research to the dustbin, but one suspects that even Shackle does not take a position as extreme as many appear to think. (If so, prospects of reconciliation are enhanced.)

> In economics, quantitative as opposed to *mere* qualitative thinking is *essential*.... We are bound to applaud the econometrician for seeking to put numbers in place of letters in the formulae supplied to him by the theoretical economist, but we must warn ourselves that numbers are not eternal truths.[96]

Whatever is felt of the validity from both a logical and exegetical viewpoint, is there a concomitant vision at the heart of this distinctive fundamentalist approach? If so, is it that there is no objective data about the future, or is the problem that the subjective reaction of human transactors even to a given present environment is unpredictable? Is it that transactors cannot maximize because of their environment, or is it that they are not by nature maximizers? Fundamentalists seem to accept both possibilities.

Though Keynes described both the investment and the financial markets in a manner rejecting the Benthamite treatment of man as a calculating maximizer, it can be argued that his more dramatic statements were neither meant as all-embracing[97] nor were they suddenly conceived as valid empirical generalizations. Though very important for an understanding of Keynes, the poetry of chapter 12 ought not be over-emphasized. For example, the producers of consumption goods who live in a relatively stable environment do act to equate (expected) marginal revenue and marginal cost.[98] They are not afflicted by crises of confidence and they seem to react fairly mechanically to changes in demand (although it is conceded that estimations of user cost are more difficult to treat as being derived from the current circumstances of which producers are well aware). The demand side might be unpredictable, but supply responses can be captured by movements along a reasonably stable aggregate supply function. Furthermore, perhaps too much is made of Keynes's apparently sudden rejection of Benthamite calculus since he had been hostile to it long before 1936,[99] though, on the other hand, he might have suddenly realized that that rejection was important.

Two main conclusions can be drawn from the argument thus far. First, Keynes is firmly grounded in the empirical school despite superficial appearances to the contrary. Second, there may be a need for some fundamentalist post Keynesians to compare their vision of the economy and their methodology with those of Keynes. If they find real differences and are prepared to go beyond Keynes with open eyes, they are, of course, free to do so, but their claims to represent Keynes's views truly would be weakened.

If some fundamentalists have carried too far their concern with uncertainty, as has been argued above, it might be said that Leijonhufvud has not gone far enough.[100] While uncertainty is difficult or impossible to formalize, its presence could lead to different forms of behaviour – conventional conduct being one kind – and therefore serious attention to it is deserved.[101]

A few words can be said in Leijonhufvud's defence. While it is true that uncertainty is pushed into the wings and he assumes that, in the long run, relatively stable and mutually consistent perceptions of wealth holders and investors can emerge, we are not therefore compelled to reject his analysis of the short-run effects of trading at false prices. 'False' is used in the sense that prices do not reflect the real remunerations transactors would agree on (given their current, mistaken and imaginary perceptions; that is, the tastes upon which notional demands are now based) had an auctioneer existed to enable such a vector to ensue as would have been consistent with the absence of any perceived frustrations of notional demands thus defined. Leijonhufvud's writings on the short-run multiplier should not blind us to his recognition of the initiating impulse, a sudden decline in business optimism.

There are three lines of thought which are mutually consistent. There is imperfect information about the knowable which is currently inaccurately perceived. This is embraced by search literature. There is positively false information generated by the multiplier and by hoarders with which Leijonhufvud is concerned. Finally, there is the fundamentalist belief that key pieces of information about the future are liable to be absent. Each can have their respective domains.

Even if one rejects the notion that a full Walrasian equilibrium can exist, this does not imply that discoordination as an explanation for the lack of effective demand is irrelevant. So long as full employment exists where aggregate supply is perfectly inelastic, there is some benchmark to judge certain states as involving involuntary unemployment whereby if demand were higher so too would be employment. There is a co-ordination failure in that the cause of the trouble, if removed by fiscal stimulation, would generate nominal prices and quantities higher than those which would be generated by an unaided system being impelled by endogenous, fairly predictable, systematic and perverse dynamics. If voluntary exchanges are being thwarted and resources remain unemployed despite a willingness of labour to work, if necessary, at a lower real wage, then co-ordination in some sense is lacking. To say that an 'equilibrium' at full employment logically exists *if* aggregate demand is high enough, does not of itself require that uncertainty, disequilibrium and flux have been assumed away. If perfect co-ordination is impossible because some things are unknowable, this does not imply that much of unemployment – the multiplier-induced component – cannot be explained by a co-ordination failure. The existence of an elastic supply in the face of higher demand is knowable. That workers, if employed, would consume more is also knowable. Workers know they want to work. Much *is* knowable. That some rate of interest could exist which will offset pessimism and drive aggregate investment to levels consistent with full employment in current markets is not nearly the same as saying that a unique, determinate interest rate exists to harmonize specific, well-informed, rational and determinate savings, investment and consumption plans. If Leijonhufvud uses a neoclassical growth model as though, in the long run, it is valid, this of itself does not render invalid his theory of short-run co-ordination failures. One can expunge Leijonhufvud's use of Walrasian equilibrium as the benchmark without entirely rejecting his views on co-ordination failure.

Furthermore, even if uncertainty exists about the present and not only about the more distant future, it is meaningful to reason that a kind of equilibrium can occur if all parties have compatible perceptions about the uncertain environment. Prices and quantities that do emerge are then reflections of discoordination to the extent that superior conjectural or conventional equilibria exist, but there is no way for people to communicate to each other that they can all imagine this alternative state to be a viable equilibrium and that they are prepared to relocate there. This might strike the reader as rather hair-splitting and philosophical, but sometimes it is claimed that Leijonhufvud's perspective is entirely inconsistent with one based on the fundamental insight of the prevalence of Knightian uncertainty.[102] If, given existing expectations, certain prices exist in logic which would encourage action to move the system to some superior position, then the failure for those prices to emerge is a co-ordination failure even if the interest rate, real wage, money wage and so forth are not uniquely ground out by the supposed Walrasian set of simultaneous equations.

Nevertheless, there is evidence of a tension that has always existed in Leijonhufvud's interpretation. In 1968, he apparently considered that, despite our ignorance of the future, the pessimism of investors could eventually recede.[103] More recently, however, he referred to how Keynes might have responded to the rational-expectations school who desire to make even long-term expectations endogenous.

> Keynes would presumably have raised philosophical objections to
> so foolhardy an attempt to harness 'the dark forces of time and
> ignorance' with the actuarial calculus.[104]

Leijonhufvud rejects the notion that expectations can be well behaved in the sense that they 'bear a stable relationship to the observable state variables of a macroeconomic model'. In a fundamentalist style, uncertainty persists in the long run.

It is important to notice that, in Leijonhufvud's scheme, the neoclassical, long-run, full-information growth path is not a useful or appropriate benchmark against which to compare the outcomes generated by alternative theories.[105] He does not condemn Keynes for failing to accept the notion that, in the long run, thrift and productivity must prevail to generate the correct, Walrasian rate of interest. Leijonhufvud's defence of thrift and productivity cannot validly be construed as a defence of arguments supporting an ultimate convergence to the Walrasian vector. His hostility to extreme forms of liquidity preference theory centres on its defects in the dynamic context, as discussed in Chapter 5. In addition, he doubts that savers will forever refuse to hold new securities at an interest rate discouraged investors are prepared to offer. The bears eventually yield if the investors remain pessimistic and the speculative demand for money then fades. However, while the bears and the investors cannot, according to Leijonhufvud, permanently hold inconsistent expectations, there is no reliable mechanism by which investors can, in the long run, discover what the true productivity level is. According to Leijonhufvud, Keynes points to the possibility of multiple long-run equilibria even if the Keynes effect were to restore the full employment of labour. (There is a sense, one supposes, in which a Walrasian model could incorporate the imperfect information reflected in the pessimism of agents. It is as if tastes have changed. Investors now require a larger risk premium and a new Wicksellian natural rate – Keynes called it the 'neutral' or 'optimum' rate[106] – can be computed. Employment in this case is higher than is ground out in the real world if pessimism is not offset by lower interest rates and the multiplier is instead set loose.)

If Leijonhufvud allows subjective factors to influence permanently the position of the MEI schedule, the gap between him and the fundamentalists closes. If the Keynes effect does restore full employment, and if this causes the reversal of the component of pessimistic expectations which had been induced by the earlier period of protracted slump, then the residual pessimism, that which was responsible for the initial deflationary shock, can still remain. There is nothing to say that the latter component exists only if agents are irrational. Reasonable people can be pessimistic and reality need not send signals to warrant any change in attitude.

A conventional equilibrium can be regarded as a special case where agents can learn nothing from realized outcomes which would change their behaviour.[107] It can coalesce at any sustainable employment level.

The absence of excesses of *undue* optimism and pessimism does not therefore imply an ability to calculate prospective yields with accuracy. Once recovery is restored, sufficient pessimism can ultimately fade to leave what might be described as residual Knightian uncertainty which is perceived in a reasonably neutral psychological mood. The ever-present possibility exists that one's perceptions of the future, currently held with an even and sober temperament, can suddenly be transformed when the vague and mysterious future is suddenly reinterpreted. The daemon within us can at any moment spring clear of the constraints of convention and the seemingly equable attitude of the marketplace.

Indeed, the very use of the term *'undue* optimism and pessimism' suggests that *some* standard exists by which attitudes can be rationally judged even if the Walrasian optimum is rejected as an objective long-run standard. An infusion of a form of fundamentalist teaching need not imply nihilism, as Coddington has argued.[108] It is perhaps meaningful to define as a long-run standard whatever interest rate is required to eliminate involuntary unemployment under neutral psychological conditions. In that way, instability in an uncertain environment is allowable as well as the existence of some sort of optimum that can enable a formal analysis to proceed.

Leijonhufvud has, in fact, made statements of a fundamentalist type. There is nothing in his scheme which requires that all economic maladies can be traced to a communication failure in that what is knowable is not made known to all parties. Mirroring his arguments[109] which refer to chapter 16 of *The General Theory*, Leijonhufvud fully accepts that a weakness of Arrow–Debreu stories is that all decisions are made at the first moment in economic time. Actions occur later but in Arrow–Debreu they are governed by contingent contracts decided upon long ago, based on known probability distributions of alternative future states of nature. Leijonhufvud agrees with Hicks that agents are themselves uncertain about their own intentions and may consciously prefer to postpone some decisions.[110]

Accepting the existence of some standard, a reasonable perception of future events, is useful also to evaluate the claims of some fundamentalists. They appear to wish to avoid simultaneously both the claim that the expectations of future events can be predicted by virtue of being governed by systematic laws as well as the claim that they are seemingly random and 'systematic' only in the weak sense that they are normally distributed.[111] Sensible and judicious decisions involving free will and the historical environment within which they are made may well be unique as the fundamentalists insist, but cannot we argue that our *states of mind* could nevertheless be distributed around a mean? Today, a man can be confident because he perceives a unique event in a particular way. Tomorrow, he could be despondent because another unique event appears which again is interpreted in a unique way. On average, however, his state of mind could be 'neutral' and behaviour based on those attitudes could have a systematic aggregate manifestation even in those cases where individuals decide independently and each have different states of mind at any one time.

Furthermore, if interdependent conventional behaviour exists and is such as to allow a stable convergence to an established norm, then average opinion confirms itself and expectations can be systematic and self-fulfilling. States of mind would then converge, but not necessarily to a neutral state. Yet agents acting without what is conventionally regarded as unduly extreme expectations can settle upon any one of a number of possible equilibria, as occurs in Leijonhufvud's account.

This does not imply that a conventional equilibrium is quiescent for they can still emerge out of a balance of conflicting views, such as when the bulls at any moment exactly offset the bears. To employ the analogy[112] of a stew bubbling on the stove, the temperature can be set to ensure a steady simmering, even though, within the stew itself, all is turmoil. To an individual chunk of gristle, the universe is everchanging and every encounter is unique, or even 'kaleidoscopic'. The immutable steel walls of the cooking-pot, however, do constrain it and enable it to rise only by displacing some other morsel. Behaviour in the aggregate remains predictable. Of course, if the heat is turned up beyond some critical point...

Fundamentalism and rational expectations

Fundamentalist arguments originally put forward to counter the 'bastard Keynesians',[113] particularly those textbook writers from the United States, have been thought to apply with equal force to new classical economics and its rational expectations hypothesis.[114]

It is not clear that the difference between the fundamentalists and the advocates of the rational expectations hypothesis is as large as the former believe. One doubts that agents need act, in the models of the latter, as if they had perfect knowledge even in the long run. Agents do not always 'get it right', they only do so on average, and do so without systematic error. Errors can be serious and persistent if the world is not 'ergodic' in that events are unique or are not repeated sufficiently for probability estimates to be sensibly and confidently made. The error term in the regression equation could well be huge if the world is largely noise with little hope for the identification of coherent messages. Of course, it could be that many new classicists see the error term as small and believe that the model, which agents follow as if they were econometricians, is essentially simple (and monetarist). This, however, is a difference of *vision*, not just *theory*. A fundamentalist can agree that agents do not make systematic mistakes while also maintaining that neither are they systematically 'right' in the sense that on average they find the Walrasian vector. A multitude of positions not *perceivably* 'wrong' could exist as conjectural or conventional equilibria. Expectations can be self-fulfilling and we could be 'outside the realm of the formally exact'.[115]

The issue, to repeat, is whether mistakes or unrealized opportunities can be perceived to be systematic. Hahn and Negishi consider conjectural equilibria whereby the market does not send signals to indicate that superior real exchanges are possible. Agents perceive that they face inelastic demand curves, and perhaps, because of search costs, they in fact do. Similarly, Davidson refers to sensible expectations about events which are not liable to be repeated and alternatively about day-to-day events. He seems, however, to make a misplaced criticism of the rational expectations hypothesis.[116]

When crucial choices have to be made, *sensible* agents will reject the information on today's existing probability structure as the basis for their expectations; relying on rational expectations can result in persistent errors when crucial decisions are being made.

Davidson holds that people do not make systematic mistakes, but, to turn his argument around, a rational expectations model must involve sensible behaviour. This is because the central pillar of rational expectations is the absence of systematic error. Mistakes can be very large and persistent in an RE model if exogenous shocks are substantial and persistent and if knowledge about the environment is lacking. All that is denied is perceivably systematic error, not error *per se*.

Leijonhufvud's reaction to RE models seems considerably more appropriate. He doubts that agents are able to solve the communication problems which, in the short run at least, make false trades inevitable in a confused environment. Making nominal adjustments in a decentralized system poses greater problems than the new classical economics school appear to realize. It is not clear that either Leijonhufvud or the new classicists would reject Davidson on the particular point of being 'sensible'.

Some fundamentalist arguments also fail to see parallels between Keynes's theory of expectations[117] and that of rational expectations. If prices are expected to change within limits or according to a pattern, then, at some values, it might be expected that prices, in some circumstances, will rise further and at other values, they might be expected to reverse their trend. There is no simple rule.[118] This is something in common at least with the rational expectations hypothesis.

The significance of the gap between the views of Keynes and the new classicists, so far as the fundamentalists appear to understand the respective theories, can be further diminished. As David Begg[119] points out, it could well be that Keynes treated the *level* of expectations as exogenous in the short run while also holding that *revisions* in expectations cannot be currently foreseen. To explain the level, the rational expectations hypothesis is a possibility to consider. He rejects as 'overly pessimistic'[120] the view that the formation of expectations cannot be made endogenous simply by virtue of Knightian uncertainty. Whether or not economists can explain expectations is an empirical, and not a logical, issue to Begg.

One further point is worth making. To affirm rational expectations and systematic behaviour does not deny the possibility of instability and indeterminacy. If the 'true model' of the world is essentially complex and non-linear, then cannot any number of regression lines fit the known data? If so, the revelation of the true model to the average participant might never occur. Agents could find themselves perpetually confronted by a menu of different models and divergent behaviour between groups could exist if classes of agents happen to select different models. Agents can remain rational and yet determinacy can vanish if many models are equally valid at any time.[121] It is possible that rules by which speculators, for example, try to guess average opinion are liable to differ and, if average opinion follows market trends which themselves can be influenced by the speculators (each of whom acts with no confidently held model about the behaviour of his fellow sportsmen), then many equally rational conventional equilibria could exist. An uncertain world is ambiguous and open to interpretation. People can suddenly choose a new model if sufficient evidence accumulates to call into question the old. Indeed, the notion that learning causes structural breaks in history is central to the Lucas critique.

A concluding remark

An examination of the activities of individual transactors has the advantage that the principle of methodological individualism can be preserved while arguments which tend to find a receptive audience in more institutionalist circles can also be aired.[122] What is rejected is the need to comply with orthodox analysis at its narrowest where the tenet of complete independence of transactors is assumed. While it is fairly commonly accepted that utility functions of consumers are independent in the sense that one unit does not derive utility from perceiving another consume, is it not allowable that agents make decisions on buying, selling and consuming on the basis of what others are doing? What is perceived by A to be desirable for A depends on what A sees B decide as advantageous for B himself. To postulate interdependencies is not really so radical or a kind of regression into sociological styles of argument so out of favour in more orthodox circles. The growth of oligopoly theory,[123] the acceptance of game theory and the prisoners' dilemma, the appearance of critical-mass models[124] and the recognition of the need for collective action in the provision of public goods on account of the free rider all provide evidence that the adherence to strictly independent individualism is often relaxed when convenient.

Even if an individual faces an uncertain external environment, stability can nevertheless emerge at the group level, if conventions hold firm. Aggregate behaviour can be sedate even if isolated individuals possess potentially wayward and unruly expectations. Seeming randomness at the individual level does not imply an absence of systematic effects in the aggregate. Knightian uncertainty therefore does not preclude predictability of itself. Animal spirits, after all, are held by few. Only a minority question conventions and strive to discover new opportunities. Furthermore, there is no necessary conflict between

Knightian uncertainty and reasonable behaviour. Keynes's notion of 'degrees of rational belief' provides a middle way between perfect knowledge and the untrammelled expression of subrational urges to action.

If fundamentalism is about the uncertainty that individuals face, and if Leijonhufvud's emphasis is on the lack of a perfect network of co-ordination between agents, there is good reason to read their works as complementary. If Leijonhufvud stresses the dynamics of the multiplier and its effects on the labour and commodities markets and if the fundamentalists focus on the nature of the forces behind the existence of the initial shock in the investment sector, then again both approaches support each other. If objective factors such as finance and low realized expenditures constrain conduct in the labour and consumption sectors, it is still possible for uncertainty and conventional behaviour to lie behind outcomes experienced in the investment and financial sectors.

If fundamentalism is only one step away from reductionism and if reductionism emerged from an orthodox general-equilibrium perspective, then fundamentalism need not be regarded as so radically different from mainstream analysis. If Edmund Phelps[125] can speak of uncertainty and bootstrap equilibria as being entirely legitimate concepts to raise in the course of evaluating modern developments in the theory of rational expectations, then interpreting Keynes is not irrelevant to the development of modern macrotheory. Some followers of Keynes seem, however, to prefer to stand out in the cold.

Notes

1 See Keynes, *Treatise on Probability* (*The Collected Writings of John Maynard Keynes*, London, Macmillan, 1971–, vol. viii, ch. 3, esp. pp. 32, 34–5, 38–9); Sir John Hicks, *Causality in Economics*, Oxford, Basil Blackwell, 1979, ch. 8, esp. pp. 110–15 and 'IS-LM: an explanation', *Journal of Post Keynesian Economics*, vol. 3, no. 2, Winter 1980–81, pp. 139–54, esp. p. 152 which, rightly or wrongly in the context, acknowledges Shackle. Compare G.L.S. Shackle, 'Sir John Hicks' "IS-LM: an explanation": a comment', *Journal of Post Keynesian Economics*, vol. 4, no. 3, Spring 1982, pp. 435–8, at p. 438.

2 David C. Colander and Robert S. Guthrie, 'Great expectations: what the Dickens do "rational expectations" mean?', *Journal of Post Keynesian Economics*, vol. 3, no. 2, Winter 1980–81, pp. 219–34, esp. pp. 219, 229–30.

3 Armen Alchian, 'Information costs, pricing, and resource unemployment', in Edmund S. Phelps (ed.), *Microeconomic Foundations of Employment and Inflation Theory*, London, Macmillan, 1970, pp. 27–52, at p. 39, n. 21.

4 Axel Leijonhufvud's position (*On Keynesian Economics and the Economics of Keynes: a study in monetary theory*, New York, Oxford University Press, 1968, p. 379) was rather extreme:

> The *General Theory* does not postulate different basic behavior patterns for different markets. The argument that its inelastic expectations are 'limited to one market' we have already controverted above: markets for current output and factor services would indeed clear continuously if sellers were always willing to accept whatever price is acceptable to the buyers with whom they happen to be in contact at the moment.

5 G.B. Richardson, 'Equilibrium, expectations and information', *Economic Journal*, vol. 69, no. 274, June 1959, pp. 223–37, esp. pp. 230–1. See also Roy Radner, 'Competitive equilibrium under uncertainty', *Econometrica*, vol. 36, no. 1, January 1968, pp. 31–58, at p. 35.

6 G.L.S. Shackle,'Keynes and today's establishment in economic theory: a view', *Journal of Economic Literature*, vol. 2, no. 2, June 1973, pp. 516–19.

7 Ronald Heiner, 'The origin of predictable behaviour', *American Economic Review*, vol. 73, no. 4, pp. 560–95.

8 See Gerald P. O'Driscoll Jr and Mario J. Rizzo, *The Economics of Time and Ignorance*, Oxford, Basil Blackwell, 1985.

9 As Frank Knight's review (*Collected Writings*, vol. xxix, pp. 217–18) of Keynes, *The General Theory of Employment Interest and Money*, London, Macmillan, 1936, makes clear.

10 J.M. Keynes, 'The general theory of employment', *Quarterly Journal of Economics*, extracts in Robert W. Clower (ed.), *Monetary Theory: selected readings*, Harmondsworth, Penguin, 1969, p. 217.

11 ibid., p. 218.

12 ibid., p. 217.

13 This accords with the more modern definition of rationality which is becoming more popular than the old-fashioned one based on calculating self-interest. For example, Alan Blinder and William Baumol, *Economics: principles and policy*, New York, Harcourt Brace Jovanovich, 1982, 2nd edn; Richard B. McKenzie and Gordon Tullock, *The New World of Economics: explorations into the human experience*, Homewood, Ill., Richard D. Irwin, 1978, 2nd edn.

14 Tony Lawson, 'Uncertainty and economic analysis', *Economic Journal*, vol. 95, December 1985, pp. 902–27, at pp. 924–5; Peter E. Earl, *The Economic Imagination: towards a behavioural analysis of choice*, Armonk, New York, M. E. Sharpe, 1983.

15 John Haltiwanger and Michael Waldman, 'Rational expectations and the limits of rationality: an analysis of heterogeneity', *American Economic Review*, vol. 75, no. 3, 1985, pp. 326–40.

16 See Nicholas Kaldor, 'Speculation and economic stability', *Review of Economic Studies*, vol. 7 (1939–40), pp. 1–27, esp. pp. 10–12; G.C. Harcourt and T.J. O'Shaughnessy, 'Keynes's unemployment

equilibrium: some insights from Joan Robinson, Piero Sraffa and Richard Kahn', in G.C. Harcourt (ed.), *Keynes and his Contemporaries*, London, Macmillan, 1985, pp. 3–41, at pp. 8–9; Alexander Dow and Sheila Dow, 'Animal spirits and rationality', in Tony Lawson and Hashem Pesaran (eds), *Keynes' Economics: methodological issues*, Beckenham, Croom Helm, 1985, pp. 46–65, at pp. 54–5; Anna Carabelli, 'Keynes on cause, chance and possibility', also in Lawson and Pesaran, *Keynes' Economics*, pp. 151–80, at pp. 172–3 (but a quotation from Keynes is incorrectly referenced).

17 Compare Keynes, *The General Theory*, pp. 162–3.

18 See Victoria Chick, 'Time and the wage-unit in the method of *The General Theory*: history and equilibrium', in Lawson and Pesaran, *Keynes' Economics*, pp. 195–208, at p. 203. Leijonhufvud, *On Keynesian Economics*, pp. 213–14 takes a position similar to the somewhat fundamentalist post Keynesian, Chick.

19 Compare Alexander and Sheila Dow, 'Animal spirits and rationality', p. 55 who cite Earl, *The Economic Imagination*, pp. 65–7, 134, whereas Earl (pp. 121, 157) also refers to how conventions can reduce anxiety about the world and promote coherence and order.

20 Compare Karl Brunner and Alan H. Meltzer, 'The uses of money: money in the theory of an exchange economy', *American Economic Review*, vol. 61, no. 5, December 1971, pp. 784–805, at pp. 788, 799–802. See also the observation of Tobin that money is like language (reported by Frank Hahn, *Money and Inflation*, Oxford, Basil Blackwell, 1982, p. 20).

21 Keynes, *The General Theory*, pp. 198–9.

22 ibid., p. 204.

23 ibid., p. 202.

24 ibid., p. 170.

25 ibid., p. 203.

26 ibid., p. 317. So far as I am aware, Leijonhufvud has not realized that the interest rate not only falls too slowly, but that it can even move upwards perversely.

27 But compare Keynes, *Collected Writings*, vol. ix, p. 63.

28 Keynes, *The General Theory*, p. 315.

29 ibid., p. 161.

30 ibid., p. 150.

31 This and the two preceding quotations are from ibid., p. 162.

32 ibid., p. 314.

33 ibid., p. 151 (emphasis added). Observe that one cannot take the MEC as given for any significant period, contrary to Leijonhufvud's position.

34 See ibid., pp. 157–8, for the three quotations.

35 ibid., pp. 153–4.

36 ibid., p. 155.

37 John Crockett Jr, 'Irving Fisher on the financial economics of uncertainty', *History of Political Economy*, vol. 12, no. 1, Spring 1980, pp. 65–82, at p. 80, quoting Irving Fisher, *The Nature of Capital and Income*, New York, 1906, pp. 295–6.

38 Keynes, *The General Theory*, pp. 158–60, 172, 318–19.
39 George A. Akerlof and William T. Dickens, 'The economic consequences of cognitive dissonance', *American Economic Review*, vol. 72, no. 3, June 1982, pp. 307–19.
40 'This medical treatment is costly and painful. It must be doing me a lot of good.' There is also an obvious analogy in the realm of the methodology of science. Models are seldom discarded but frequently adapted in the face of seemingly disconfirming facts because few can face the awful possibility of having made a costly and humiliating mistake. Scientific schools can themselves be interpreted as having a foundation in a sort of convention.
41 Hans and Michael Eysenck, *Mindwatching*, London, Michael Joseph, 1981, ch. 17, esp. pp. 168–70.
42 ibid., p. 171.
43 Keynes, *The General Theory*, p. 160. Keynes's analogy is less apt now than it once was.
44 Especially ibid., pp. 47–8, 50–1.
45 ibid., p. 48.
46 ibid., p. 51.
47 ibid., pp. 263, 265 and 269.
48 See ibid., ch. 8 and p. 96 for the quotation.
49 Leijonhufvud seems to overlook the latter effect (see *On Keynesian Economics*, p. 319). Consequently, the Keynes Effect is given too much emphasis as a force working to restore long-run equilibrium. To attempt to overcome the 'poverty effect', massive deflation may be required and the risk of monetary collapse is much greater.
50 Compare *A Treatise on Probability*, Keynes, *Collected Writings*, vol. viii, p. 353.
51 Keynes, *The General Theory*, ch. 19.
52 Strictly speaking, the realization that leap-frogging wage cuts are not only futile exercises but also extremely inconvenient for the participants, is sufficient to encourage a collective agreement. Deep concern about the viability of a monetary system need not be imputed to the labourers.
53 See J. Buchanan, 'An economic theory of clubs', *Economica*, vol. 32, February 1965, pp. 1–14; A.K. Sen, 'Isolation, assurance and the social rate of discount', *Quarterly Journal of Economics*, vol. 81, February 1967, p. 112.
54 Reuven Brenner, 'Unemployment, justice, and Keynes's "General Theory"', *Journal of Political Economy*, vol. 12, no. 4, 1980, pp. 582–7.
55 Keynes, *The General Theory*, p. 9.
56 ibid., p. 14.
57 This might be what he means when he uses the word 'impracticable' (ibid., p. 14).
58 ibid., p. 14 (emphasis added).
59 ibid., p. 269. I must point out that if one were to split hairs (e.g. one might say that the word 'substantial' might involve the reduction of the wage to *below* the marginal disutility of labour and that, on this ground

alone, workers would resist, if they were free to do so) one could make counter-arguments. One must acknowledge that pp. 265, 267 and 269 contain subtle differences so far as wage cuts by administrative decree are concerned.

60 The State does have power to reduce the real wage which workers do not. Where the propensity to consume of households is greater than that of employers, money wages can be cut by decree and aggregate demand can be increased (for example by arms expenditure) to prevent an equiproportional decline in the price level and offset the reduction in nominal consumption expenditure.

61 Compare David Laidler, 'Information, money and the macroeconomics of inflation', *Swedish Journal of Economics*, vol. 76, 1974, pp. 26–40; p. 29, n. 2.

62 See Axel Leijonhufvud, 'Schools, "revolutions" and research programmes in economic theory', in Spiro Latsis (ed.), *Method and Appraisal in Economics*, Cambridge, Cambridge University Press, 1976, pp. 65–108. Leijonhufvud's remark (p. 98) bears repetition and applies equally to the modification suggested in the text: 'The crudity of the following metaphor may be objectionable but its use will have the advantage (in addition to brevity) that it is unlikely to be taken too seriously.' The paper can also be found in Leijonhufvud's *Information and Coordination: essays in macroeconomic theory*, New York, Oxford University Press, 1981, pp. 291–345, and the remark at p. 333.

63 Donald George, 'Equilibrium and catastrophes in economics', *Scottish Journal of Political Economy*, vol. 28, no. 1, February 1981, pp. 43–61; Lawrence Harris, 'Catastrophe theory, utility theory and animal spirit expectations', *Australian Economic Papers*, vol. 19, December 1979, pp. 268–82, especially pp. 278–9; Hal R. Varian, 'Catastrophe theory and the business cycle', *Economic Inquiry*, vol. 17, 1979, pp. 14–28; and E. Roy Weintraub, 'Catastrophe theory and intertemporal equilibria', *Economie Appliquée*, vol. 33, 1980, no. 2, pp. 303–15 all see a role for this theory in the macroeconomic sphere. Weintraub (p. 310) expressly refers to Leijonhufvud and how the notion of the corridor could be expressed using such models. So too does Peter Howitt, 'The limits to stability of a full-employment equilibrium', *Scandinavian Journal of Economics*, vol. 80, 1978, pp. 265–82, at pp. 277–8.

64 E.C. Zeeman, 'On the unstable behaviour of stock exchanges', *Journal of Mathematical Economics*, vol. 1, 1974, pp. 39–49.

65 Alan Coddington has argued that it is not clear that government officials face less uncertainty than their capitalist counterparts, but, if Keynes's reforms are institutional and microeconomically non-intrusive, then the criticism loses much of its force. (See Alan Coddington, *Keynesian Economics: the search for first principles*, London, George Allen and Unwin, 1983, pp. 54, 60–1.)

66 Davidson and Lerner are associated with the emphasis of this theme.

67 Customs also play some role in the conduct of the banks in the *Treatise* (Keynes, *Collected Writings*, vol. vi, p. 202) which refers to obligations 'of law or custom'. It is far from clear, however, that banks find

themselves in a conventional equilibrium as distinct from a state of blind inertia.

Keynes, in the *Treatise*, refers to the conventional faith which the public has in the banking system and remarks that a central bank needs to provide liquid reserves for 'ultimate emergencies' and to bolster public confidence. The latter 'object is easily exaggerated, since public opinion is always content with what it is used to' (*Collected Writings*, vol. vi, p. 246). The argument that the Bank of England made do with far smaller reserves than did the Bank of France is, however, not fully convincing because of the stronger tradition of responsible monetary management in England.

68 Keynes, *The General Theory*, p. 336.
69 See ibid., p. 150; Keynes, *Collected Writings*, vol. 28, pp. 33–4.
70 Keynes, *Collected Writings*, vol. 28, p. 413.
71 Compare the 'culture' and 'class' approach of Hans E. Jensen, 'J.M. Keynes as a Marshallian', *Journal of Economic Issues*, vol. 27, no. 1, March 1983, pp. 67–94.
72 To assume 'contrary to all likelihood, that the future will resemble the past' seems almost to be a characteristic of human behaviour generally, for example, about our views on the effects of population growth, Keynes, *Collected Writings*, vol. xiv, p. 125. See especially vol. xxix, p. 294.
73 Keynes, *The General Theory*, ch. 5.
74 ibid., p. 55. Also the real wage equals the marginal (revenue) product (p. 5).
75 See Hugh Townshend, 'Reviews', *Economic Journal*, vol. 47, 1937, pp. 321–6, at pp. 324–5, for this idea which was warmly received by Shackle. That Shackle has, in effect, gone too far is tactfully pointed out by Brian J. Loasby, *Choice, Complexity and Ignorance*, Cambridge, Cambridge University Press, 1976, pp. 161–2, 222. See also J.A. Kregel, 'Money, expectations and relative prices in Keynes' monetary equilibrium', *Economie Appliquée*, vol. 35, 1982, no. 3, pp. 449–65, at pp. 456, 463, n. 1.
76 Mark Stohs, '"Uncertainty" in Keynes' *General Theory*', *History of Political Economy*, vol. 12, no. 3, pp. 372–82, at p. 373, notes this.
77 See Paul Davidson's sneering rejection of orthodox micro-theory, 'Rational expectations: a fallacious foundation for studying crucial decision-making processes', *Journal of Post Keynesian Economics*, vol. 5, Winter 1982–83, pp. 182–98, esp. pp. 183, 190, 196.
78 For a discussion of Keynes as part of the English empirical tradition, see Bruce Littleboy and Ghanshyam Mehta, 'The scientific method of Keynes', *Journal of Economic Studies*, vol. 10, 1983, no. 4, pp. 3–14.
79 See Keynes, *Collected Writings*, vol. xxviii, ch. 4.
80 David Hume, *An Abstract of a Treatise of Human Nature 1740*, Connecticut, Archon Books, 1965, with introduction by J.M. Keynes and P. Sraffa, at p. 16. Hume's writing is full of 'feelings', 'instincts' and 'sentiments'. For Hume's views on free will, see pp. 29–30.
81 Leijonhufvud, *On Keynesian Economics*, pp. 69, n. 4; 60, n. 5.

82 Richardson, 'Equilibrium, expectations and information', p. 233, n. 1. The example from Hume refers to a conventionally established mutual respect for the institution of private property, and I am not aware that Hume sees the stability of prices, which can arise within such a system, as themselves being founded on convention.

83 Similarly, Keynes's theory of convention lies between a theory of custom and one involving a rational and well-informed economic man whose motion towards a Walrasian optimum can be mathematically deduced.

84 Keynes, *Collected Writings*, vol. viii, p. 56.

85 Keynes, *Collected Writings*, vol. xiv, pp. 285–6. He expressly indicates the continuity of his views since the *Treatise on Probability* (see ibid., p. 315).

86 Keynes, *Collected Writings*, vol. viii, pp. 276–7. There are fascinating implications of this long and difficult passage. If economic events are not 'atomic', knowledge will be much harder to acquire and trial and error methods will forever be encountered by unexpected results. There might be no clear nexus between aggregate and micro-behaviour.

87 Keynes, *Collected Writings*, vol. xiv, p. 262. One wonders if this problem in economics appears more in chemistry than in physics, though Keynes (p. 299) groups the latter two together. In a chemical reaction, the properties of the product are often entirely different from its constituents. Actions of catalysts might also have some of the effects described by Keynes. See Thomas Sowell, *Classical Economics Reconsidered*, Princeton, NJ, Princeton University Press, 1974, p. 137 and Mark Lutz, 'Human nature in Gandhian economics: the case of ahisma or "social affection"', *Gandhi Marg*, vol. 4, no. 12, March 1983, pp. 941–55. There is a hint that Keynes was prepared to entertain abandoning methodological individualism, whereas, in *The General Theory*, it is arguable that the aggregate concepts have explicit or implicit microfoundations. Note also the hints of catastrophe theory in the quotation.

88 Davidson ('Rational expectations...', p. 196) gives orthodox microtheory scope in only the most trivial problems.

89 There is a parallel between the crucial investment decision and a chessplayer's way of selecting his move. Note that chess is potentially calculable if you had enough time. Due to the uncertainty caused by the pressure of lack of time bold intuitive leaps are required. Nevertheless, there are rules of thumb and, importantly, the players who win tournaments are those with the best ability to calculate. Stimulating references are Reuben Fine, *The Psychology of the Chess Player*, New York, Dover, 1967, pp. 16–17 and, on the 'heroic sacrifice', Rudolf Spielmann, *The Art of Sacrifice in Chess*, New York, McKay, 1951, pp. 40–1, 82, 121–5, 136.

90 Paul Davidson, 'Book review', *Economica*, vol. 41, November 1974, pp. 452–4.

91 Compare Davidson, 'Rational expectations...', pp. 183, 190. John D. Hey, *Uncertainty in Microeconomics*, Oxford, Martin Robertson, 1979,

ch. 32, considers the sort of model useful in analysing uncertainty. He refers (pp. 233–4) to a lost traveller trying to find his way through a terrain shrouded in fog.

92 As reported in David Worswick and James Trevithick (eds), *Keynes and the Modern World*, London, Cambridge University Press, 1983, p. 84. Compare Heiner's argument, 'The origin of predictable behavior', p. 570, n. 24, n. 27, that uncertainty does not necessarily imply that behaviour is predictable.

93 Terence Wilmot Hutchison, *On Revolutions and Progress in Economic Knowledge*, Cambridge, Cambridge University Press, 1978, p. 211.

94 Robert Solow ('Book reviews', *Journal of Political Economy*, vol. 92, no. 4, August 1984, pp. 784–7, at p. 785) complains that radical fundamentalism seems to deny that the formation of expectations has any coherence at all. Solow takes a similar view in David Worswick and James Trevithick (eds), *Keynes and the Modern World: proceedings of the Keynes Centenary Conference, Kings College Cambridge*, London, Cambridge University Press, 1983, p. 167: '[Keynes] regarded the economy as pretty opaque to most of the participants.... But that is not the same thing as a belief in the arbitrariness of expectations.' One doubts, however, that fundamentalists believe that free will and 'sensible' decisions give rise to arbitrary or random actions, merely that the *potential* for unpredictable behaviour must be kept in mind.

95 Likewise, John Fender, *Understanding Keynes: an analysis of the 'General Theory'*, Brighton, Wheatsheaf Books, 1981, pp. 3, 9, 90–2, has reservations about fundamentalism while considering it a fairly important ingredient in the mix.

96 G.L.S. Shackle, *Uncertainty in Economics*, Cambridge, Cambridge University Press, 1955, pp. 234–5 (emphasis added). See also his 'Book review' of T.W. Hutchison's, *The Politics and Philosophy of Economics*, in *Economic Journal*, vol. 93, March 1983, pp. 223–4, at p. 224. Note that Keynes did not reject econometrics entirely. See *Collected Writings*, vol. xiv, pp. 315–16, where Keynes sees value in breaking the data into sub-periods to test for structural breaks.

97 Compare Brian J. Loasby, *Choice, Complexity and Ignorance*, pp. 161–2, 222.

98 Keynes, *The General Theory*, p. 55.

99 Keynes, *Collected Writings*, vol. x, p. 184, n. 5; vol. vii, ch. 26 and pp. 23–5.

100 For example, Shackle, 'Keynes and today's establishment...'.

101 Solow takes a similar view in 'Mr Hicks and the classics', *Oxford Economic Papers*, vol. 36 (n.s.), supplement, December 1984, pp. 13–25, at pp. 23–4.

102 See John F. Henry, 'On equilibrium', *Journal of Post Keynesian Economics*, vol. 6, no. 2, Winter 1983–84, pp. 214–29, at p. 227, n. 15.

103 This is the impression I obtain from Leijonhufvud, *On Keynesian Economics*, pp. 373–83. If investors have inelastic price expectations, gradually pessimism grows. If or when interest rates fall and the

economy recovers, at least some of the missing optimism will return (p. 353). Revealingly, Leijonhufvud has speculated:

> [T]he 'islands parable..' [of Phelps] to my mind carries more conviction applied to the investment-expectations of individual entrepreneurs than in its original context.

'Book reviews' (on Lucas), *Journal of Economic Literature*, vol. 21, March 1983, pp. 107–10, at p. 108. A fundamentalist might seize this quotation as it appears to indicate that investors are searching for the knowable.

104 Axel Leijonhufvud, 'What would Keynes have thought of rational expectations?', in Worswick and Trevithick, *Keynes and the Modern World*, p. 186, and p. 185 for the next quotation.

105 Axel Leijonhufvud, 'The Wicksell connection', in *Information and Coordination*, New York, Oxford University Press, 1981, p. 136.

106 Keynes, *The General Theory*, p. 243.

107 Gerald P. O'Driscoll Jr and Mario J. Rizzo, *The Economics of Time and Ignorance*, Oxford, Basil Blackwell, 1985, pp. 88–9 regard this as an Austrian theme. Leijonhufvud, 'The Wicksell connection', p. 136 attributes the notion to Hahn, and post Keynesians, such as Davidson, view this notion of equilibrium as Marshallian and as superior to the Walrasian market-clearing variety of equilibrium. There appears to be agreement on the intrinsic merit of the notion.

108 Alan Coddington, *Keynesian Economics*, pp. 57–8 appears to have no difficulty reconciling imperfect knowledge, uncertainty, rational expectations and reasonableness. (Coddington, pp. 58–9, observes that Shackle's nihilistic subjectivism leads only to agents trapped in a life of 'puzzled indecision', but I note that Keynes did speak of animal spirits supplying an urge to *action*.)

109 Leijonhufvud, *On Keynesian Economics*, pp. 276–82.

110 A recent restatement of Leijonhufvud's views appears in 'Hicks on time and money', *Oxford Economic Papers*, vol. 36 (n.s.), supplement, November 1984, pp. 26–46, at pp. 30–1.

111 One could imagine how shocking a fundamentalist would find Sir Karl Popper's *Of Clouds and Clocks: an approach to the problem of rationality and freedom of man*, St Louis, Miss., Washington University, 1966.

112 Shades of Coddington, 'Hicks's contribution to Keynesian economics', in John Cunningham Wood (ed.), *John Maynard Keynes: critical assessments*, London and Canberra, Croom Helm, 1983, in 4 vols, vol. 4, pp. 444–66, at p. 457.

113 Perhaps a less offensive and more modern term, 'love-child Keynesians', could be used instead.

114 Contributors to the *Journal of Post Keynesian Economics* would consider that vital differences still exist between Keynes's and the new classicists' theories of expectations, particularly for 'crucial' decisions. See Paul Davidson, 'Rational expectations: a fallacious foundation for studying crucial decision-making processes', vol. 5, no. 2, Winter

1982–83, pp. 182–98 and 'Reviving Keynes's revolution', vol. 6, no. 4, Summer 1984, pp. 561–75; David C. Colander and Robert S. Guthrie, 'Great expectations: what the Dickens do "rational expectations" mean?', vol. 3, no. 2, Winter 1980–81, pp. 219–36; Malcolm Rutherford, 'Rational expectations and Keynesian uncertainty: a critique', vol. 4, no. 3, Spring 1984, pp. 377–87. Some criticisms appear too extreme in that vulgar forms of the rational expectations hypothesis (REH) are demolished. For example, James R. Wible, 'The rational expectations tautologies', vol. 5, no. 2, Winter 1982–83, pp. 199–207, at pp. 205–6; and Gustavo Maia Gomes, 'Irrationality of "rational expectations"', vol. 5, no. 1, Fall 1982, pp. 51–65, at pp. 58–9.

115 Keynes, *Collected Writings*, vol. xiv, p. 2.

116 Davidson, 'Rational expectations...', p. 183 (emphasis in original).

117 Described as 'sketchy at best' in Leijonhufvud, *On Keynesian Economics*, p. 178.

118 See Keynes, *The General Theory*, ch. 19 and the 'it all depends', though largely pessimistic, attitude of pp. 263 *et seq*. See also *Collected Writings*, vol. xiv, pp. 159, 177. Note also Keynes's refusal to tie perceived investment prospects to *current* income, although he considers it an important element in governing expectations. Keynes often deliberately assumes a non-aligned stance, for example, when stating that 'prices, in so far as they are anticipated, are already reflected in current prices' (*Collected Writings*, vol. xxix, p. 82). This is not inconsistent with rational expectations. Allan Meltzer sees other indications of a rational expectations style in Keynes, but, prudently, he is not too confident in ascribing these beliefs to Keynes, see 'On Keynes and monetarism', in Worswick and Trevithick, *Keynes and the Modern World*, pp. 49–70.

119 David Begg, *The Rational Expectations Revolution in Macroeconomics: theories and evidence*, Oxford, Philip Allan, 1982, pp. 19–20.

120 ibid., p. 18.

121 Compare Christopher Torr, 'Expectations and the new economics', *Australian Economic Papers*, vol. 23, no. 43, December 1984, pp. 197–205, at p. 199, who refers to the debate over the possibility of speculation in an RE world.

122 See Wallace C. Peterson, 'Institutionalism, Keynes, and the real world', *Nebraska Journal of Economics and Business*, vol. 16, no. 3, Summer 1977, p. 27–46, p. 42.

123 See Solow in Worswick and Trevithick, *Keynes and the Modern World*, p. 165. When I was a student, it was considered a defect of kinked-demand-curve oligopoly theory that the outcome seemed indeterminate. Nowadays, this is almost regarded as an advantage because it points to the possibility of multiple equilibria.

124 Thomas C. Schelling, *Micromotives and Macrobehavior*, New York, W.W. Norton, 1978, pp. 102–10.

125 Roman Frydman and Edmund S. Phelps, *Individual Forecasting and Aggregate Outcomes: rational expectations examined*, Cambridge, Cambridge University Press, 1983, chs 1 and 2.

References

Abramovitz, Moses (ed.), *The Allocation of Economic Resources: essays in honour of Bernard Francis Haley*, Stanford, Stanford University Press, 1959.

Addison, John T. and Burton, John, 'Keynes's analysis of wages and unemployment revisited', *Manchester School of Economic and Social Studies*, vol. 50, no. 1, March 1982, pp. 1–23.

Akerlof, George, 'The case against conservative macroeconomics: an inaugural lecture', *Economica*, vol. 46, August 1979, pp. 219–37.

Akerlof, George A. and Dickens, William T., 'The economic consequences of cognitive dissonance', *American Economic Review*, vol. 72, no. 3, June 1982, pp. 307–19.

Alchian, Armen, 'Information costs, pricing and resource unemployment', in Edmund Phelps (ed.), *Microeconomic Foundations of Employment and Inflation Theory*, New York, W.W. Norton, 1970, pp. 27–52.

Allsbrook, Ogden O., Jr and DeLorme, Charles D., 'The Keynes effect and the capital market: a methodological note', *Artha Vijnana*, vol. 191, no. 2, June 1977, pp. 168–72.

Arrow, Kenneth J., 'Toward a theory of price adjustment', in Moses Abramovitz (ed.), *The Allocation of Economic Resources: essays in honour of Bernard Francis Haley*, Stanford, Stanford University Press, 1959, pp. 41–51.

Asimakopulos, Athanasios, 'Finance, liquidity, saving, and investment', *Journal of Post Keynesian Economics*, vol. 9, no. 1, Fall 1986, pp. 79–90.

Asimakopulos, Athanasios, *Investment, Employment and Income Distribution*, Cambridge, Polity Press, 1988.

Baily, Martin Neil, 'Comments', *Brookings Papers on Economic Activity*, 1980, no. 1, pp. 125–32.

Baird, W. *Elements of Macroeconomics*, New York, West Publishing, 1977.

Baird, W. and Cassuto, Alexander E., *Macroeconomics: monetary, search and income theories*, Chicago, Science Research Associates, 1981, 2nd edn.

Barrére, Alain (ed.), *The Foundations of Keynesian Analysis: proceedings of a conference held at the University of Paris I-Panthéon-Sorbonne*, London, Macmillan, 1988.

Barro, Robert J. *Macroeconomics*, New York, John Wiley and Sons, 2nd edn, 1984.

Barro, Robert J., 'Discussion', *American Economic Review, Papers and Proceedings*, vol. 74, no. 2, May 1984, pp. 416–17.

Barro, Robert J. and Grossman, Herschel I., *Money, Employment and Inflation*, Cambridge, Cambridge University Press, 1976.

Barry, Norman P., *Hayek's Social and Economic Philosophy*, London, Macmillan, 1979.

Baumol, William B., 'Say's (at least) eight laws, or what Say and James Mill may really have meant', *Economica*, vol. 44, May 1977, pp. 145–62.

Bean, Charles R., 'Optimal wage bargains', *Economica*, vol. 51, 1984, pp. 141–9.

Becker, G. and Baumol, W., 'The classical monetary theory: the outcome of the discussion', *Economica*, vol. 19, 1952, pp. 355–76.

Begg, David K.H., *The Rational Expectations Revolution in Macroeconomics: theories and evidence*, Oxford, Philip Allan, 1982.

Benjamin, Daniel K. and Kochin, Levis A., 'Searching for an explanation of unemployment in interwar Britain', *Journal of Political Economy*, vol. 87, no. 3, June 1979, pp. 441–78.

Blatt, John, 'Classical economics of involuntary unemployment', *Journal of Post Keynesian Economics*, vol. 3, no. 4, Summer 1981, pp. 552–9.

Blaug, Mark, *Economic Theory in Retrospect*, London, Cambridge University Press, 1978, 3rd edn.

Blinder, Alan and Baumol, William, *Economics: principles and policy*, New York, Harcourt Brace Jovanovich, 1982, 2nd edn.

Bliss, C.J., 'Discussion' of 'The reappraisal of Keynes' economics: an appraisal', in Michael Parkin and Aveline Nobay (eds), *Current Economic Problems: the proceedings of the Association of University Teachers of Economics, Manchester, 1974*, Cambridge, Cambridge University Press, 1975.

Bliss, C.J., 'Two views of macroeconomics', *Oxford Economic Papers*, vol. 35, no. 1, March 1983, pp. 1–12.

Brazelton, W. Robert, 'A survey of some textbook misinterpretations of Keynes', *Journal of Post Keynesian Economics*, vol. 3, no. 2, Winter 1980–81, pp. 256–70.

Brenner, Reuven, 'Unemployment, justice, and Keynes's "General Theory"', *Journal of Political Economy*, vol. 87, no. 4, August 1979, pp. 837–50.

Brenner, Reuven, 'The role of nominal wage contracts in Keynes's *General Theory*', *History of Political Economy*, vol. 12, no. 4, 1980, pp. 582–7.

Bridel, Pascal, 'On Keynes's quotations from Mill: a note', *Economic Journal*, vol. 89, September 1979, pp. 660–2.

Bronowski, Jacob, *The Identity of Man*, Harmondsworth, Penguin, 1965.

Brothwell, John F., 'A simple Keynesian's response to Leijonhufvud', *Bulletin of Economic Research*, vol. 27, May 1975, pp. 3–21.

Brothwell, John, F., 'Rejoinder', *Bulletin of Economic Research*, vol. 28, November 1976, pp. 123–6.

Brothwell, John F., 'The *General Theory* after fifty years: Why are we not all Keynesians now?', *Journal of Post Keynesian Economics*, vol. 8, no. 4,

Summer 1986, pp. 531–47.

Brunner, Karl and Meltzer, Allan H., 'The uses of money: money in the theory of an exchange economy', *American Economic Review*, vol. 61, no. 5, December 1971, pp. 784–805.

Buchanan, James M., 'An economic theory of clubs', *Economica* (N.S.), vol. 32, February 1965, pp. 1–14.

Carabelli, Anna M., 'Keynes on cause, chance and possibility', in Tony Lawson and Hashem Pesaran (eds), *Keynes' Economics: methodological issues*, Beckenham, Croom Helm, 1985, pp. 151–80.

Carabelli, Anna M., *On Keynes's Method*, London, Macmillan, 1988.

Casson, Mark, *Unemployment: a disequilibrium approach*, Oxford, Martin Robertson, 1981.

Chakrabarti, Santi K., *The Two-sector General Theory Model*, London, Macmillan, 1979.

Champernowne, David G., 'Expectations and links between the economic future and the present', in Robert Lekachman (ed.), *Keynes' General Theory: reports of three decades*, New York, St Martin's Press, 1964, pp. 174–202.

Chen Fu Chang, 'Liquidity preference and loanable funds theories: a synthesis', *Australian Economic Papers*, vol. 15, December 1976, pp. 302–7.

Chick, Victoria, 'The nature of the Keynesian revolution: a reassessment', *Australian Economic Papers*, vol. 17, no. 30, June 1978, pp. 1–20.

Chick, Victoria, *Macroeconomics after Keynes: a reconsideration of the General Theory*, Deddington, Oxford, Philip Allan, 1983.

Chick, Victoria, 'Time and the wage-unit in the method of *The General Theory*: history and equilibrium', in Tony Lawson and Hashem Pesaran (eds), *Keynes' Economics: methodological issues*, Beckenham, Croom Helm, 1985, pp. 195–208.

Clower, Robert W., 'A reconsideration of the microfoundations of monetary theory', in Robert W. Clower (ed.), *Monetary Theory: selected readings*, Harmondsworth, Penguin, 1969, pp. 202–11.

Clower, Robert W., 'The Keynesian revolution: a theoretical appraisal', in Robert W. Clower (ed.) *Monetary Theory: selected readings*, Harmondsworth, Penguin, 1969, pp. 270–97.

Clower, Robert W. (ed.), *Monetary Theory: selected readings*, Harmondsworth, Penguin, 1969.

Clower, Robert W., 'Reflections on the Keynesian perplex', *Zeitschrift für Nationalökonomie*, vol. 35, 1975, pp. 1–24.

Clower, Robert W., 'New directions for Keynesian economics', Universita Degli Studi di Siena, Quaderni Dell'istituto di Economia, no. 63, 1987.

Clower, Robert and Leijonhufvud, Axel, 'Say's principle, what it means and doesn't mean: part I', *Intermountain Economic Review*, vol. 4, no. 2, Fall 1973, pp. 1–16.

Clower, Robert and Leijonhufvud, Axel, 'The coordination of economic activities: a Keynesian perspective', *American Economic Review*, vol. 65, no. 2, May 1975, pp. 182–8.

Cochrane, James L. and Graham, John A., 'Cybernetics and macroeconomics', *Economic Inquiry*, vol. 14, June 1976, pp. 241–50.

Coddington, Alan, 'Keynesian economics: the search for first principles', *Journal of Economic Literature*, vol. 14, no. 4, December 1976, pp. 1258–73.

Coddington, Alan, 'Hicks's contribution to Keynesian economics', in John Cunningham Wood (ed.), *John Maynard Keynes: critical assessments*, London and Canberra, Croom Helm, 1983, vol. 4, pp. 444–66.

Coddington, Alan, *Keynesian Economics: the search for first principles*, London, Allen and Unwin, 1983.

Cohen, Jacob, 'Book reviews', *Journal of Economic Literature*, vol. 7, no. 3, September 1969, pp. 841–3.

Colander, David C. and Guthrie, Robert S., 'Great expectations: what the Dickens do "rational expectations" mean?', *Journal of Post Keynesian Economics*, vol. 3, no. 2, Winter 1980–81, pp. 219–34.

Colander, David, 'Was Keynes a Keynesian or a Lernerian?', *Journal of Economic Literature*, vol. 22, December 1984, pp. 1572–5.

Collard, David A., 'Pigou on expectations and the cycle', *Economic Journal*, vol. 93, June 1983, pp. 411–14.

Corden, W.M., 'Keynes and the others: wage and price rigidities in macroeconomic models', *Oxford Economic Papers*, vol. 30, no. 2, July 1978, pp. 159–80.

Crabtree, Derek and Thirlwall, A.P., *Keynes and the Bloomsbury Group: the fourth Keynes Seminar held at the University of Kent at Canterbury 1978*, London, Macmillan, 1980.

Crockett, John, Jr, 'Irving Fisher on the financial economics of uncertainty', *History of Political Economy*, vol. 12, no. 1, Spring 1980, pp. 65–82.

Crouch, Robert L., 'Book review', *Econometrica*, vol. 39, no. 2, March 1971, pp. 407–8.

Crouch, Robert L., *Macroeconomics*, New York, Harcourt Brace Jovanovich, 1972.

Currie, David, 'Effective demand failures: a further comment', *Scandinavian Journal of Economics*, vol. 79, 1977, pp. 350–3.

Darity, William A., Jr and Horn, Bobbie L., 'Involuntary unemployment reconsidered', *Southern Economic Journal*, vol. 49, no. 3, January 1983, pp. 717–33.

Dasgupta, A.K., *Epochs of Economic Theory*, Oxford, Basil Blackwell, 1985.

Davidson, Paul, 'A Keynesian view of Patinkin's theory of employment', *Economic Journal*, vol. 77, September 1967, pp. 559–78.

Davidson, Paul, 'Disequilibrium market adjustment: Marshall revisited', *Economic Inquiry*, vol. 12, no. 2, June 1974, pp. 146–58.

Davidson, Paul, 'Book review', *Economica*, vol. 41, November 1974, pp. 452–4.

Davidson, Paul, 'Money and general equilibrium', *Economie Appliquée*, vol. 30, 1977, pp. 541–63.

Davidson, Paul, 'Why money matters: lessons from a half-century of monetary theory', *Journal of Post Keynesian Economics*, vol. 1, no. 1, Fall 1978, pp. 46–70.

Davidson, Paul, *Money and the Real World*, London, Macmillan, 1978, 2nd edn.

Davidson, Paul, *International Money and the Real World*, London, Macmillan, 1982.

Davidson, Paul, 'Rational expectations: a fallacious foundation for studying crucial decision-making processes', *Journal of Post Keynesian Economics*, vol. 5, no. 2, Winter 1982–83, pp. 182–98.

Davidson, Paul, 'The marginal product curve is not the demand curve for labor and Lucas's labor supply function is not the supply curve for labor in the real world', *Journal of Post Keynesian Economics*, vol. 6, no. 1, Fall 1983, pp. 105–17.

Davidson, Paul, 'Reviving Keynes's revolution', *Journal of Post Keynesian Economics*, vol. 6, no. 4, Summer 1984, pp. 561–75.

Davidson, Paul, 'Liquidity and not increasing returns is the ultimate source of unemployment equilibrium', *Journal of Post Keynesian Economics*, vol. 7, no. 3, Spring 1985, pp. 373–84.

Davidson, Paul, 'Finance, funding, saving, and investment', *Journal of Post Keynesian Economics*, vol. 9, no. 1, Fall 1986, pp. 101–10.

Davidson, Paul and Smolensky, Eugene, *Aggregate Supply and Demand Analysis*, New York, Harper and Row, 1964.

Davidson, Paul and Weintraub, Sidney, 'Jacob and Paul Samuelson, post-Keynesian', *Journal of Post Keynesian Economics*, vol. 3, no. 4, Summer 1981, pp. 602–3.

Davis, J. Ronnie, *The New Economics and the Old Economists*, Ames, Iowa, Iowa State University Press, 1971.

Davis, J. Ronnie, 'Keynes's misquotation of Mill: further comment', *Economic Journal*, vol. 89, September 1979, pp. 658–9.

Davis, J. Ronnie and Casey, Francis J., Jr, 'Keynes' misquotation of Mill', *Economic Journal*, vol. 87, June 1977, pp. 329–30.

Dillard, Dudley, *The Economics of John Maynard Keynes: the theory of a monetary economy*, London, Crosby Lockwood, 1948.

Dillard, Dudley, 'Effective demand and the monetary theory of employment', in Alain Barrére (ed.), *The Foundations of Keynesian Analysis: proceedings of a conference held at the University of Paris I-Panthéon-Sorbonne*, London, Macmillan, 1988, pp. 49–64.

Dow, Alexander and Dow, Sheila C., 'Animal spirits and rationality', in Tony Lawson and Hashem Pesaran (eds), *Keynes' Economics: methodological issues*, Beckenham, Croom Helm, 1985, pp. 46–65.

Dow, Sheila C., *Macroeconomic Thought: a methodological approach*, Oxford, Basil Blackwell, 1985.

Dow, Sheila C. and Earl, Peter E., *Money Matters: a Keynesian approach to monetary economics*, Oxford, Martin Robertson, 1982.

Drazen, Allan, 'Recent developments in macroeconomic disequilibrium theory', *Econometrica*, vol. 48, no. 2, March 1980, pp. 283–306.

Drèze, Jacques H. (ed.), *Allocation Under Uncertainty: equilibrium and optimality*, London, Macmillan, 1974.

Earl, Peter E., *The Economic Imagination: towards a behavioural analysis of choice*, Armonk, New York, M.E. Sharpe, 1983.

Earl, Peter E. and Kay, Neil M., 'How economists can accept Shackle's critique of economic doctrines without arguing themselves out of their jobs', *Journal of Economic Studies*, vol. 12, no. 1/2, 1985, pp. 35–48.

Eatwell, John, Milgate, Murray and Newman, Peter, *The New Palgrave: a dictionary of economics*, London, Macmillan, 1987, 4 vols.

Eshag, Eprime, *From Marshall to Keynes: an essay on the monetary theory of the Cambridge school*, Oxford, Basil Blackwell, 1963.

Eysenck, Hans and Eysenck, Michael, *Mindwatching*, London, Michael Joseph, 1981.

Fender, John, *Understanding Keynes: an analysis of 'The General Theory'*, Brighton, Wheatsheaf Books, 1981.

Fine, Reuben, *The Psychology of the Chess Player*, New York, Dover, 1967.

Fisher, Franklin M., 'Quasi competitive price adjustment by individual firms: a preliminary paper', *Journal of Economic Theory*, vol. 2, 1970, pp. 195–206.

Fitoussi, Jean-Paul (ed.), *Modern Macro-economic Theory*, Oxford, Basil Blackwell, 1983.

Fitzgibbons, Athol, *Keynes's Vision: a new political economy*, Oxford, Oxford University Press, 1988.

Fleming, J., 'Comment', in G.D.N. Worswick and J. Trevithick (eds), *Keynes and the Modern World: proceedings of the Keynes Centenary Conference, King's College, Cambridge*, London, Cambridge University Press, 1983, pp. 244–7.

Fleming, J.S., 'Wealth effects in Keynesian models', *Oxford Economic Papers*, vol. 26, no. 2, July 1974, pp. 248–58.

Fletcher, Gordon A., *The Keynesian Revolution and its Critics: issues of theory and policy for the monetary production economy*, New York, St Martin's Press. 1987.

Fouraker, Lawrence E., 'The Cambridge didactic style', *Journal of Political Economy*, vol. 66, no. 1, February 1958, pp. 65–73.

Friedman, Milton, *The Theory of the Consumption Function*, Princeton, NJ, Princeton University Press, 1957.

Friedman, Milton, 'Comments on the critics', *Journal of Political Economy*, vol. 80, no. 5, September–October 1972, pp. 906–50.

Froyen, Richard T., 'The aggregative structure of Keynes's General Theory', *Quarterly Journal of Economics*, vol. 90, no. 3, August 1976, pp. 369–87.

Frydman, Roman and Phelps, Edmund S., *Individual Forecasting and Aggregate Outcomes: 'rational expectations' examined*, Cambridge, Cambridge University Press, 1983.

Garvy, George, 'Keynes and the economic activists of the pre-Hitler Germany', *Journal of Political Economy*, vol. 83, no. 2, April 1975, pp. 391–405.

George, Donald, 'Equilibrium and catastrophes in economics', *Scottish Journal of Political Economy*, vol. 28, no. 1, February 1981, pp. 43–61.

Gomes, Gustavo Maia, 'Irrationality of "rational expectations"', *Journal of Post Keynesian Economics*, vol. 5, no. 1, Fall 1982, pp. 51–65.

Gordon, Robert J. (ed.), *Milton Friedman's Monetary Framework: a debate with his critics*, Chicago, Chicago University Press, 1974.

Gordon, Robert J., 'Recent developments in the theory of inflation and unemployment', *Journal of Monetary Economics*, vol. 2, 1976, pp. 185–219.

Gordon, Robert J., 'Output fluctuations and gradual price adjustment', *Journal of Economic Literature*, vol. 19, June 1981, pp. 493–530.

Gramm, William P., 'Keynes and the real-balance effect: a note', *Manchester School of Economic and Social Studies*, vol. 36, no. 4, December 1968, pp. 383–7.

Gramm, William P., 'More on Keynes, outside money and the real-balance effect', *The Manchester School of Economic and Social Studies*, vol. 38, no. 3, September 1970, pp. 263–6.

Grossman, Herschel I., 'Money, interest, and prices in market disequilibrium', *Journal of Political Economy*, vol. 79, no. 5, September–October 1971, pp. 943–61.

Grossman, Herschel I., 'Was Keynes a "Keynesian"? A review article', *Journal of Economic Literature*, vol. 10, no. 1, March 1972, pp. 26–30.

Grossman, Herschel I., 'Effective demand failures. A comment', *Swedish Journal of Economics*, vol. 76, 1974, pp. 358–65.

Grossman, Herschel I., 'Why does aggregate demand fluctuate?', *American Economic Review*, vol. 69, no. 2, May 1979, pp. 64–9.

Gylfason, Thorvaldur and Lindbeck, Assar, 'Union rivalry and wages: an oligopolistic approach', *Economica*, vol. 51, no. 202, May 1984, pp. 129–39.

Haberler, Gottfried, 'The general theory after ten years', in Robert Lekachman (ed.), *Keynes' General Theory: reports of three decades*, New York, St Martin's Press, 1964, pp. 269–88.

Haberler, Gottfried, 'Sixteen years later', in Robert Lekachman (ed.), *Keynes' General Theory: reports of three decades*, New York, St Martin's Press, 1964, pp. 289–96.

Haberler, Gottfried, *Prosperity and Depression: a theoretical analysis of cyclical movements*, London, George Allen and Unwin, 1964, 4th edn.

Hahn, Frank, 'Keynesian economics and general equilibrium theory: reflections on some current debates', in Geoffrey C. Harcourt (ed.), *The Microeconomic Foundations of Macroeconomics: proceedings of a conference held by the International Economic Association at S'Agara, Spain*, Boulder, Colo., Westview Press, 1977.

Hahn, Frank, 'Exercises in conjectural equilibria', *Scandinavian Journal of Economics*, vol. 79, no. 2, 1977, pp. 210–26.

Hahn, Frank, 'Monetarism and economic theory', *Economica*, vol. 47, February 1980, pp. 1–17.

Hahn, Frank, 'Comments on McCallum', *Economica*, vol. 47, August 1980, pp. 305–7.

Hahn, Frank, 'Unemployment from a theoretical viewpoint', *Economica*, vol. 47, August 1980, pp. 285–98.

Hahn, Frank, *Money and Inflation*, Oxford, Basil Blackwell, 1982.

Hahn, Frank, 'Comment', in R. Frydman and E. Phelps (eds), *Individual*

Forecasting and Aggregate Outcomes: 'rational expectations' examined, Cambridge, Cambridge University Press, 1983, pp. 223–30.

Hahn, Frank, 'Wages and employment', *Oxford Economic Papers*, vol. 36 (n.s.), supplement, November 1984, pp. 47–58.

Hall, Robert E. and Taylor, John B., *Macroeconomics: theory, performance and policy*, New York, W.W. Norton, 1988, 2nd edn.

Hall, Stephen, 'The cause of non-Walrasian equilibria', Imperial College of Science and Technology, University of London, no. 80/2, Discussion Papers in Economics, 1980.

Haltiwanger, John and Waldman, Michael, 'Rational expectations and the limits of rationality: an analysis of heterogeneity', *American Economic Review*, vol. 75, no. 3, 1985, pp. 326–40.

Hamouda, Omar F. and Smithin, John N. (eds), *Keynes and Public Policy After Fifty Years*, 2 vols, New York, New York University Press, 1988.

Hansen, Alvin H., 'Mr Keynes on underemployment equilibrium', *Journal of Political Economy*, vol. 44, October 1936, pp. 667–86.

Hansen, Alvin H., 'Harrod on the trade cycle', *Quarterly Journal of Economics*, vol. 51, May 1937, pp. 509–31.

Hansen, Alvin H., *Monetary Theory and Fiscal Policy*, New York, McGraw-Hill, 1949.

Hansen, Alvin H., *A Guide to Keynes*, New York, McGraw-Hill, 1953.

Hansen, Alvin H., *Business Cycles and National Income*, London, Allen and Unwin, 1964, exp. edn.

Hansen, Alvin H., Boddy, Francis M. and Langum, John K., 'Recent trends in business-cycle literature', *Review of Economic Statistics*, vol. 18, no. 2, May 1936, pp. 53–61.

Hansen, Alvin H. and Tout, Herbert, 'Annual survey of business cycle theory: investment and saving in business cycle theory', *Econometrica*, vol. 1, 1933, pp. 119–47.

Hansson, Björn, 'Keynes's notion of equilibrium in the *General Theory*', *Journal of Post Keynesian Economics*, vol. 7, no. 3, Spring 1985, pp. 332–41.

Harcourt, Geoffrey C. (ed.), *The Microeconomic Foundations of Macroeconomics: proceedings of a conference held by the International Economic Association at S'Agara, Spain*, Boulder, Colo., Westview Press, 1977.

Harcourt, Geoffrey C. (ed.), *Keynes and his Contemporaries*, London, Macmillan, 1985.

Harcourt, Geoffrey C. and O'Shaughnessy, T.J., 'Keynes's unemployment equilibrium: some insights from Joan Robinson, Pierro Sraffa and Richard Kahn', in Geoffrey C. Harcourt (ed.), *Keynes and his Contemporaries*, London, Macmillan, 1985, pp. 3–41.

Harris, Laurence, 'Catastrophe theory, utility theory and animal spirit expectations', *Australian Economic Papers*, vol. 19, December 1979, pp. 268–82.

Harris, Seymour E. (ed.), *The New Economics: Keynes' influence on theory and public policy*, London, Dennis Dobson, 1948.

Harrod, Roy F., *The Life of John Maynard Keynes*, London, Macmillan, 1951.

Hart, Albert G., 'Keynes' analysis of expectations and uncertainty', in Harris, Seymour E. (ed.), *The New Economics: Keynes' influence on theory and public policy*, London, Dennis Dobson, 1948, pp. 415–24.

Hayek, F.A., 'Reflections on the pure theory of money of Mr J.M. Keynes', *Economica*, vol. 11, August 1931, pp. 270–95 and vol. 12, February 1932, pp. 22–44.

Hayek, F.A., 'A rejoinder to Mr Keynes', *Economica*, November 1931, pp. 398–403.

Hayek, F.A., *1980s Unemployment and the Unions: essays on the impotent price structure of Britain and monopoly in the labour market*, Hobart Paper 87, London, Institute of Economic Affairs, 1980.

Hazlitt, Henry, *The Failure of the 'New Economics': an analysis of Keynesian fallacies*, London, Van Nostrand, 1959.

Hazlitt, Henry, *The Critics of Keynesian Economics*, New Rochelle, NY, Arlington House, 1977.

Heiner, Ronald, 'The origin of predictable behavior', *American Economic Review*, vol. 73, no. 4, September 1983, pp. 560–95.

Hendry, David F., 'Econometrics – alchemy or science?' *Economica*, vol. 47, November 1980, pp. 387–406.

Henneberry, Barbara S. and Witte, James G., 'The unemployment–inflation dilemma in macroeconomics: some contradictory aspects of contemporary theory and policy', *Scottish Journal of Political Economy*, vol. 23, no. 1, February 1976, pp. 17–35.

Henry, John F., 'On equilibrium', *Journal of Post Keynesian Economics*, vol. 6, no. 2, Winter 1983–84, pp. 214–29.

Hey, John D., 'Price adjustment in an atomistic market', *Journal of Economic Theory*, vol. 8, no. 4, August 1974, pp. 483–99.

Hey, John D., *Uncertainty in Microeconomics*, Oxford, Martin Robertson, 1979.

Hicks, John R., 'Mr Keynes' theory of employment', *Economic Journal*, vol. 46, June 1936, pp. 238–53.

Hicks, John R., 'Mr Keynes and the "Classics": a suggested interpretation', *Econometrica*, vol. 5, 1937, pp. 147–59.

Hicks, John R., *Value and Capital: an inquiry into some fundamental principles of economic theory*, Clarendon, Oxford University Press, 1946, 2nd edn.

Hicks, John R., 'Recollections and documents', *Economica*, vol. 40, February 1973, pp. 2–11.

Hicks, John R., *The Crisis in Keynesian Economics*, Oxford, Basil Blackwell, 1974.

Hicks, John R., 'What is wrong with monetarism', *Lloyds Bank Review*, no. 118, October 1975, pp. 1–13.

Hicks, John R., *Causality in Economics*, Oxford, Basil Blackwell, 1979.

Hicks, John R., 'IS-LM: an explanation', *Journal of Post Keynesian Economics*, vol. 3, no. 2, Winter 1980–81, pp. 139–54.

Hines, Albert H., *On the Reappraisal of Keynesian Economics*, London, Martin Robertson, 1971.

Hines, Albert H., 'The "micro-economic foundations of employment and inflation theory": bad old wine in elegant new bottles', in G.D.N. Worswick (ed.), *The Concept and Measurement of Involuntary Unemployment*, London, Allen and Unwin, 1976, pp. 58–79.

Hobson, J.A., *The Science of Wealth*, London, Williams and Norgate, 1911?

Horwich, George, *Money, Capital, and Prices*, Homewood, Ill., Richard D. Irwin, 1964.

Howitt, Peter, 'Wage flexibility and employment', in Omar F. Hamouda and John N. Smithin (eds), *Keynes and Public Policy After Fifty Years*, 2 vols, New York, New York University Press, 1988, vol. II: *Theory and Method*, pp. 61–9.

Howitt, Peter, 'The limits to stability of a full-employment equilibrium', *Scandinavian Journal of Economics*, vol. 80, 1978, pp. 265–82.

Howson, Susan, '"A dear money man"? Keynes on monetary policy, 1920', *Economic Journal*, vol. 83, no. 330, June 1973, pp. 456–64.

Hume, David, *An Abstract of a Treatise of Human Nature 1740*, Connecticut, Archon Books, 1965.

Hutchison, Terence Wilmot, *Keynes versus the 'Keynesians'? An essay in the thinking of J.M. Keynes and the accuracy of its interpretation by his followers*, London, Institute of Economic Affairs, 1977.

Hutchison, Terence Wilmot, *On Revolutions and Progress in Economic Knowledge*, Cambridge, Cambridge University Press, 1978.

Hutchison, Terence Wilmot, *The Politics and Philosophy of Economics: Marxians, Keynesians and Austrians*, Oxford, Basil Blackwell, 1981.

Hutt, W.H., *A Rehabilitation of Say's Law*, Athens, Ohio University Press, 1974.

Hutt, William H., *The Keynesian Episode: a reassessment*, Indianapolis, Liberty Press, 1979.

Jackman, Richard, 'Keynes and Leijonhufvud', *Oxford Economic Papers*, vol. 26, no. 2, July 1974, pp. 259–72.

Jensen, Hans E., 'J.M. Keynes as a Marshallian', *Journal of Economic Issues*, vol. 17, no. 1, March 1983, pp. 67–94.

Jevons, W. Stanley, *Political Economy (Science Primer)*, London, Macmillan, 1898.

Johnson, Elizabeth S. and Johnson, Harry G., *The Shadow of Keynes: understanding Keynes, Cambridge and Keynesian economics*, Oxford, Basil Blackwell, 1978.

Johnson, Harry G., 'Some Cambridge controversies in monetary theory', *Review of Economic Studies*, vol. 19, no. 49, 1952, pp. 90–104.

Johnson, Harry G., 'The general theory after twenty-five years', *American Economic Review*, vol. 51, May 1961, pp. 1–17.

Johnson, Harry G., 'Keynes and the Keynesians: some intellectual legends', *Encounter*, vol. 34, January 1970, pp. 70–2.

Johnson, Harry G., *Macroeconomics and Monetary Theory*, London, Gray-Mills, 1971.

Johnson, Harry G., *On Economics and Society*, Chicago and London, University of Chicago Press, 1975.

Kahn, Richard F., 'Some notes on liquidity preference', *Manchester School of*

Economic and Social Studies, vol. 22, September 1954, pp. 229–57.

Kahn, Richard F., 'Unemployment as seen by the Keynesians', in G.D.N. Worswick (ed.), *The Concept and Measurement of Involuntary Unemployment*, London, Allen and Unwin, 1976, pp. 19–34.

Kahn, Richard F., *The Making of Keynes' General Theory*, Cambridge, Cambridge University Press, 1983.

Kaldor, Nicholas, 'Speculation and economic stability', *Review of Economic Studies*, vol. 7, no. 1, October 1939, pp. 1–27.

Kaldor, Nicholas, 'What is wrong with economic theory', *Quarterly Journal of Economics*, vol. 89, no. 3, August 1975, pp. 347–57.

Kaldor, Nicholas, 'Keynesian economics after fifty years', in G.D.N. Worswick and J. Trevithick (eds), *Keynes and the Modern World: proceedings of the Keynes Centenary Conference, King's College, Cambridge*, London, Cambridge University Press, 1983, pp. 1–28.

Katona, George, *Psychological Economics*, New York, Elsevier Scientific Publishing, 1975.

Keynes, John Maynard, *The General Theory of Employment Interest and Money*, London, Macmillan, 1936.

Keynes, John Maynard, 'The general theory of employment', *Quarterly Journal of Economics*, vol. 51, February 1937, pp. 209–23.

Keynes, John Maynard, 'Relative movements of real wages and output', *Economic Journal*, vol. 49, March 1939, pp. 34–51.

Keynes, John Maynard, *The Collected Writings of John Maynard Keynes*, edited by Donald Moggridge, London, Macmillan, 1971–:

—vol. v: *A Treatise on Money*, vol. 1, 1971

—vol. vi: *A Treatise on Money*, vol. 2, 1971

—vol. vii: *The General Theory of Employment Interest and Money*, 1973

—vol. viii: *A Treatise on Probability*, 1973

—vol. ix: *Essays in Persuasion*, 1972

—vol. x: *Essays in Biography*, 1972

—vol. xiii: *The General Theory and After: Part I: Preparation*, 1973

—vol xiv: *The General Theory and After: Part II: Defence and Development*, 1973

—vol. xx: *Activities 1929–1931 Rethinking Employment and Unemployment Policies*, 1981

—vol. xxvii: *Activities 1940–1946 Shaping the Post-War World: employment and commodities*, 1980

—vol. xxviii: *Social, Political and Literary Writings*, 1982

—vol. xxix: *The General Theory and After: a supplement*, 1979.

Keynes, Milo (ed.), *Essays on John Maynard Keynes*, Cambridge, Cambridge University Press, 1975.

Klamer, Arjo, *The New Classical Macroeconomics: conversations with the new classical economists and their opponents*, Brighton, Wheatsheaf Books, 1984.

Klein, Lawrence, *The Keynesian Revolution*, London, Macmillan, 1952.

Klein, Lawrence, *The Economics of Supply and Demand*, Oxford, Basil Blackwell, 1983.

Kolm, Serge-Christophe, 'Unemployment resulting from preferences on wages or prices', in Omar F. Hamouda and John N. Smithin (eds), *Keynes and Public Policy After Fifty Years*, 2 vols, New York, New York University Press, 1988, vol. II: *Theory and Method*.

Kregel, Jan A., 'Economic methodology in the face of uncertainty: the modelling methods of Keynes and the post-Keynesians', *Economic Journal*, vol. 86, June 1976, pp. 209–25.

Kregel, Jan A. (ed.), *Distribution, Effective Demand and International Economic Relations: proceedings of a conference held by the Centro di Studi Economici Avanzati, Trieste, at Villa Manindi Passariano, Udine*, New York, St Martin's Press, 1983.

Kregel, Jan A., 'Money, expectations and relative prices in Keynes' monetary equilibrium', *Economie Appliquée*, vol. 35, no. 3, 1983, pp. 449–65.

Kregel, Jan A., 'A note of finance, liquidity, saving, and investment', *Journal of Post Keynesian Economics*, vol. 9, no. 1, Fall 1986, pp. 91–100.

Laidler, David, 'Information, money and the macroeconomics of inflation', *Swedish Journal of Economics*, vol. 76, 1974, pp. 26–40.

Laidler, David, 'The "buffer stock" notion in monetary economics', *Economic Journal*, 1984, supplement, pp. 17–34.

Latsis, Spiro (ed.), *Method and Appraisal in Economics*, Cambridge, Cambridge University Press, 1976.

Lawson, Tony, 'Uncertainty and economic analysis', *Economic Journal*, vol. 95, December 1985, pp. 902–27.

Lawson, Tony, 'Realism and instrumentalism in the development of econometrics', *Oxford Economic Papers*, vol. 41, no. 1, January 1989, pp. 236–58.

Lawson, Tony and Pesaran, Hashem (eds), *Keynes' Economics: methodological issues*, Beckenham, Croom Helm, 1985.

Leijonhufvud, Axel, 'Keynes and the Keynesians: a suggested interpretation', *American Economic Review*, vol. 57, May 1967, pp. 401–10.

Leijonhufvud, Axel, *On Keynesian Economics and the Economics of Keynes: a study in monetary theory*, New York, Oxford University Press, 1968.

Leijonhufvud, Axel, 'Keynes and the effectiveness of monetary policy', *Western Economic Journal*, vol. 6, March 1968, pp. 97–111.

Leijonhufvud, Axel, 'Comment: Is there a meaningful trade-off between inflation and unemployment?', *Journal of Political Economy*, vol. 76, no. 4, July–August 1968, pp. 738–43.

Leijonhufvud, Axel, 'Keynes and the classics: two lectures on Keynes' contribution to economic theory', London, Institute of Economic Affairs, 1969, Occasional Paper 30, reproduced in A. Leijonhufvud, *Information and Coordination*, 1981, pp. 39–78.

Leijonhufvud, Axel, 'Effective demand failures', *Swedish Journal of Economics*, vol. 75, 1973, pp. 27–48, reprinted in A. Leijonhufvud, *Information and Coordination*, 1981, pp. 103–29.

Leijonhufvud, Axel, 'The varieties of price theory: what microfoundations for macrotheory?', UCLA, Discussion Paper no. 44, January 1974, unpublished.

Leijonhufvud, Axel, 'Keynes' employment function. Comment', *History of Political Economy*, vol. 6, no. 2, Summer 1974, pp. 164–70.

Leijonhufvud, Axel, 'Schools, "revolutions" and research programmes in economic theory', in A. Leijonhufvud, *Information and Coordination: essays in macroeconomic theory*, New York, Oxford University Press, 1981, pp. 291–345.

Leijonhufvud, Axel, *Information and Coordination: essays in macroeconomic theory*, New York, Oxford University Press, 1981.

Leijonhufvud, Axel, 'Book review, *Studies in Business-Cycle Theory*', *Journal of Economic Literature*, vol. 21, March 1983, pp. 107–10.

Leijonhufvud, Axel, 'Constitutional constraints on the monetary powers of government', *Economia delle Scelte Pubbliche*, vol. 2, 1983, pp. 87–100.

Leijonhufvud, Axel, 'Keynesianism, monetarism, and rational expectations: some reflections and conjectures', in Roman Frydman and Edmund S. Phelps (eds), *Individual Forecasting and Aggregate Outcomes: 'rational expectations' examined*, Cambridge, Cambridge University Press, 1983, pp. 203–23.

Leijonhufvud, Axel, 'Rational expectations and monetary institutions', Working Paper no. 302, UCLA, Department of Economics, September 1983, unpublished.

Leijonhufvud, Axel, 'What was the matter with IS-LM?', in Jean-Paul Fitoussi (ed.), *Modern Macro-economic Theory*, Oxford, Basil Blackwell, 1983, pp. 64–90.

Leijonhufvud, Axel, 'What would Keynes have thought of rational expectations?', in G.D.N. Worswick and J. Trevithick (eds), *Keynes and the Modern World: proceedings of the Keynes Centenary Conference, King's College, Cambridge*, London, Cambridge University Press, 1983, pp. 179–205.

Leijonhufvud, Axel, 'Hicks on time and money', *Oxford Economic Papers*, vol. 36 (n.s.), supplement, November 1984, pp. 26–46.

Leijonhufvud, Axel and Aoki, Masanao, 'Cybernetics and macroeconomics: a comment', *Economic Inquiry*, vol. 14, June 1976, pp. 251–8.

Lekachman, Robert (ed.), *Keynes' General Theory: reports of three decades*, New York, St Martin's Press, 1964.

Lerner, Abba, 'The essential properties of interest and money', *Quarterly Journal Economics*, vol. 66, no. 2, May 1952, pp. 172–93.

Lindbeck, Assar and Snower, Dennis, 'Involuntary unemployment as an insider-outsider dilemma', Institute for International Economic Studies, Stockholm, Seminar Paper no. 282, July 1984.

Littleboy, Bruce, 'Keynes and economic man', Twelfth Conference of Economists, Hobart, 1983, University of Tasmania, unpublished.

Littleboy, Bruce and Mehta, Ghanshyam, 'The scientific method of Keynes', *Journal of Economic Studies*, vol. 10, no. 4, 1983, pp. 3–14.

Littleboy, Bruce and Mehta, Ghanshyam, 'Keynes and scientific methodology: whither and whence', *Indian Economic Journal*, vol. 33, no. 1, July–September 1986, pp. 66–76.

Littleboy, Bruce and Mehta Ghanshyam, 'Patinkin on Keynes' theory of effective demand', *History of Political Economy*, vol. 19, no. 2, 1987, pp. 311–28.

Littleboy, Bruce and Mehta, Ghanshyam, 'Patinkin on Keynes's theory of effective demand: a rejoinder', *History of Political Economy*, vol. 21, no. 4, pp. 711–21.

Littlechild, S.C., 'Comment: radical subjectivism or radical subversion?', in Mario J. Rizzo (ed.), *Time, Uncertainty, and Disequilibrium: exploration of Austrian themes*, Lexington, Mass., Lexington Books, D.C. Heath and Company, 1979, pp. 32–49.

Loasby, Brian J., *Choice, Complexity and Ignorance: an enquiry into economic theory and the practice of decision-making*, Cambridge, Cambridge University Press, 1976.

Lucas, Robert E., 'Unemployment policy', *American Economic Review*, vol. 68, May 1978, pp. 353–7.

Lucas, Robert E., 'Tobin and monetarism: a review article', *Journal of Economic Literature*, vol. 19, June 1981, pp. 558–67.

Lutz, Mark A., 'Human nature in Ghandian economics: the case of ahisma or "social affection"' *Gandhi Marg*, vol. 4, no. 12, March 1983, pp. 941–55.

McCain, Katherine, 'Longitudinal author cocitation mapping: the changing structure of macroeconomics', *Journal of the American Society for Information Science*, January 1984, pp. 351–9.

McCloskey, Donald N., 'The rhetoric of economics', *Journal of Economic Literature*, vol. 21, no. 2, June 1983, pp. 481–517.

McGregor, Peter G., 'Professor Shackle and the liquidity preference theory of interest rates', *Journal of Economic Studies*, vol. 12, no. 1/2, 1985, pp. 89–106.

McKenzie, Richard B. and Tullock, Gordon, *The New World of Economics: explorations into the human experience*, Homewood, Ill., Richard D. Irwin, 1978, revised edn.

Malinvaud, Edmond, *The Theory of Unemployment Reconsidered*, Oxford, Basil Blackwell, 1977.

Marget, Arthur W., *The Theory of Prices: a re-examination of the central problems of monetary theory*, 2 vols, New York, Prentice-Hall, 1938–42.

Marshall, Alfred, *The Economics of Industry*, London, Macmillan, 1885, 3rd edn.

Mason, Will E., 'Some negative thoughts on Friedman's positive economics', *Journal of Post Keynesian Economics*, vol. 3, no. 2, Winter 1980–81, pp. 235–55.

Mehta, Ghanshyam, *The Structure of the Keynesian Revolution*, London, Martin Robertson, 1977.

Mehta, Ghanshyam, 'Keynesian mathematics', Eighth Conference of Economists, La Trobe University, Melbourne, August 1979, unpublished.

Meltzer, Allan H., 'Keynes's *General Theory*: a different perspective', *Journal of Economic Literature*, vol. 19, March 1981, pp. 34–64.

Meltzer, Allan H., 'On Keynes and monetarism', in G.D.N. Worswick and J. Trevithick (eds), *Keynes and the Modern World: proceedings of the Keynes Centenary Conference, King's College, Cambridge*, London, Cambridge University Press, 1983, pp. 49–72.

Meltzer, Allan H., 'Keynes's labor market: a reply', *Journal of Post Keynesian Economics*, vol. 6, no. 4, Summer 1984, pp. 532–9.

323

Milgate, Murray, 'John Maynard Keynes: a centenary estimate', *The History of Economic Thought Society of Australia Newsletter*, no. 5, Autumn 1985, pp. 1–18.

Mill, John Stuart, *Principles of Political Economy: with their applications to social philosophy*, edited by Sir William Askley, Fairfield, NJ, Augustus M. Kelley, 1976.

Mill, John Stuart, 'On the influence of consumption on production', in Henry Hazlitt (ed.), *The Critics of Keynesian Economics*, New Rochelle, NY, Arlington House, 1977, pp. 24–45.

Minsky, Hyman P., *John Maynard Keynes*, New York, Columbia University Press, 1975.

Minsky, Hyman P., 'Frank Hahn's *Money and Inflation*: a review article', *Journal of Post Keynesian Economics*, vol. 6, no. 3, Spring 1984, pp. 449–57.

Mishan, E.J., 'The demand for labor in a classical and Keynesian framework', *Journal of Political Economy*, vol. 72, December 1964, pp. 610–16.

Modigliani, Franco, 'Liquidity preference and the theory of interest and money', *Econometrica*, vol. 12, January 1944, pp. 45–88.

Moggridge, Donald E., *Keynes: Aspects of the Man and His Work: the first Keynes seminar held at the University of Kent at Canterbury 1972*, London, Macmillan, 1974.

Moggridge, Donald E., *John Maynard Keynes*, Harmondsworth, Penguin, 1976.

Moggridge, Donald E. and Howson, Susan, 'Keynes on monetary policy, 1910–1946', *Oxford Economic Papers*, vol. 26, no. 2, July 1974, pp. 226–47.

Morishima, Michio, *The Economic Theory of Modern Society*, Cambridge, Cambridge University Press, 1976.

Mummery, A.F. and Hobson, J.A., *The Physiology of Industry: being an exposure of certain fallacies in existing theories of economics*, New York, Kelley S. Millman, 1956.

Mundell, Robert A., *Man and Economics*, New York, McGraw-Hill, 1968.

Negishi, Takashi, 'Involuntary unemployment and market imperfection', *Economic Studies Quarterly*, vol. 25, no. 1, April 1974, pp. 32–41.

Negishi, Takashi, *Microeconomic Foundations of Keynesian Macroeconomics*, Amsterdam, North-Holland, 1979.

Nell, Edward J., 'Keynes after Sraffa: the essential properties of Keynes's theory of interest and money: comment on Kregel', in Jan A. Kregel (ed.), *Distribution, Effective Demand and International Economic Relations: proceedings of a conference held by the Centro di Studi Economici Avanzati, Trieste, at Villa Manindi Passariano, Udine*, New York, St Martin's Press, 1983, pp. 85–103.

O'Driscoll, Gerald P., Jr, and Rizzo, Mario J., *The Economics of Time and Ignorance*, Oxford, Basil Blackwell, 1985.

Padoan, Pietro Carlo, 'Interpretations of Keynes, monetary economy and price theories', *Rivistadi Politica Economica: Selected Papers*, vol. 69, December 1979, pp. 73–118.

Parkin, Michael, *Modern Macroeconomics*, Scarborough, Ontario, Prentice-Hall, 1982.

Parkin, Michael and Nobay, Aveline, *Current Economic Problems: the proceedings of the Association of University Teachers of Economics, Manchester, 1974*, Cambridge, Cambridge University Press, 1975.

Patinkin, Don, *Money, Interest, and Prices: an integration of monetary and value theory*, New York, Harper and Row, 1965, 2nd edn.

Patinkin, Don, 'The Chicago tradition, the quantity theory and Friedman', *Journal of Money Credit and Banking*, vol. 1, no. 1, February 1969, pp. 46–70.

Patinkin, Don, 'Money and wealth: a review article', *Journal of Economic Literature*, vol. 7, no. 4, December 1969, pp. 1140–60.

Patinkin, Don, 'The role of the "liquidity trap" in Keynesian economics', *Banca Nazionale del Lavoro Quarterly Review*, vol. 27, no. 108, March 1974, pp. 3–11.

Patinkin, Don, *Keynes' Monetary Thought: a study of its development*, Durham, North Carolina, Duke University Press, 1976.

Patinkin, Don, 'Keynes' aggregate supply function: a plea for common sense', *History of Political Economy*, vol. 10, no. 4, 1978, pp. 577–96.

Patinkin, Don, 'Keynes' misquotation of Mill: comment', *Economic Journal*, vol. 88, June 1978, pp. 341–2.

Patinkin, Don, 'New materials on the development of Keynes' monetary thought', *History of Political Economy*, vol. 12, no. 1, 1980, pp. 1–28.

Patinkin, Don, *Anticipations of the General Theory? And other essays on Keynes*, Oxford, Basil Blackwell, 1982.

Patinkin, Don, 'Keynes' theory of effective demand: a reply', *History of Political Economy*, vol. 19, no. 4, 1987, pp. 647–58.

Patinkin, Don and Leith, J. Clark (eds), *Keynes, Cambridge and the General Theory: the process of criticism and discussion connected with the development of the General Theory*, London, Macmillan, 1977.

Pearce, I.F., 'The pathology of Keynes' General Theory', Seventh Conference of Economists, Sydney, Macquarie University, 1978, unpublished.

Pesek, Boris P., 'Book reviews', *Journal of Political Economy*, vol. 77, no. 4, pt 1, 1969, pp. 559–61.

Pesek, Boris P. and Saving, Thomas R., *Money, Wealth, and Economic Theory*, New York, Macmillan, 1967.

Peterson, Wallace C., 'Institutionalism, Keynes, and the real world', *Nebraska Journal of Economics and Business*, vol. 16, no. 3, Summer 1977, pp. 27–46.

Phelps, Edmund S. (ed.), *Microeconomic Foundations of Employment and Inflation Theory*, New York, W.W. Norton, 1970.

Phelps, Edmund S., *Inflation Policy and Unemployment Theory: the cost-benefit approach to monetary planning*, New York, W.W. Norton, 1972.

Phelps, Michael G., 'A simple Keynesian's response to Leijonhufvud: a comment', *Bulletin of Economic Research*, vol. 28, November 1976, pp. 117–20.

Phelps, Michael G., 'Laments, ancient and modern: Keynes on mathematical and econometric methodology', *Journal of Post Keynesian Economics*, vol. 2, no. 4, Summer 1980, pp. 482–93.

Pigou, Arthur C., *Industrial Fluctuations*, London, Macmillan, 1927.

Pigou, Arthur C., *The Theory of Unemployment*, London, Frank Cass, 1933.

Pigou, Arthur C., 'Mr J.M. Keynes' general theory of employment, interest and money', *Economica*, vol. 3, May 1936, pp. 115–32.

Pigou, Arthur C., *Lapses from Full Employment*, London, Macmillan, 1945.

Pigou, Arthur C., *Employment and Equilibrium: a theoretical discussion*, London, Macmillan, 1949, 2nd edn.

Pigou, Arthur C., *The Veil of Money*, London, Macmillan, 1949.

Pigou, Arthur C., *Keynes's 'General Theory': a retrospective view*, London, Macmillan, 1950.

Popper, Sir Karl, *Of Clouds and Clocks: an approach to the problem of rationality and freedom of man*, St Louis, Miss., Washington University, 1966.

Porter, Michael E., 'Interbrand choice, media mix and market performance', *American Economic Review*, vol. 66, no. 2, May 1976, pp. 398–406.

Presley, John R., *Robertsonian Economics: an examination of the work of Sir D.H. Robertson on industrial fluctuation*, London, Macmillan, 1978.

Radner, Roy, 'Competitive equilibrium under uncertainty', *Econometrica*, vol. 36, no. 1, January 1968, pp. 31–58.

Redhead, Brian, 'On Keynesian economics and the economics of Keynes: a suggested interpretation', *Bulletin of Economic Research*, vol. 33, no. 1, May 1981, pp. 48–55.

Rees, Albert, 'Wage determination and involuntary unemployment', *Journal of Political Economy*, vol. 59, no. 2, April 1951, pp. 143–53.

Richardson, G.B., 'Equilibrium, expectations and information', *Economic Journal*, vol. 69, no. 274, June 1959, pp. 223–37.

Rima, Ingrid, 'Whatever happened to the concept of involuntary unemployment', *International Journal of Social Economics*, vol. 11, no. 3/4, 1984, pp. 62–71.

Rima, Ingrid H., 'Involuntary unemployment and the respecified labor supply curve', *Journal of Post Keynesian Economics*, vol. 6, no. 2, Summer 1984, pp. 540–50.

Ritter, Lawrence S., 'Book reviews', *Journal of Finance*, vol. 25, no. 1, March 1970, pp. 188–90.

Rizzo, Mario J. (ed.), *Time, Uncertainty and Disequilibrium: exploration of Austrian themes*, Lexington, Mass., Lexington Books, D.C. Heath and Company, 1979.

Roberts, David L., 'Patinkin, Keynes and aggregate supply and demand analysis', *History of Political Economy*, vol. 10, no. 4, Winter 1978, pp. 549–76.

Robertson, D.H., 'Mr Keynes' theory of money', *Economic Journal*, vol. 41, September 1931, pp. 395–411.

Robertson, D.H., 'Some notes on Mr Keynes' general theory of employment', *Quarterly Journal of Economics*, vol. 51, November 1936, pp. 168–91.

Robertson, D.H., 'Alternative theories of the rate of interest', *Economic Journal*, vol. 47, September 1937, pp. 428–36.

Robertson, D.H., *Essays in Monetary Theory*, London, Staples Press, 1940.

Robinson, Joan, 'A parable on savings and investment', *Economica*, vol. 13, February 1933, pp. 75–84.

Robinson, Joan, 'The theory of money and the analysis of output', *Review of Economic Studies*, vol. 1, no. 1, October 1933, pp. 22–6.

Robinson, Joan, 'The concept of hoarding', *Economic Journal*, vol. 48, June 1938, pp. 230–6.

Robinson, Joan, 'The rate of interest', *Econometrica*, vol. 19, no. 2, April 1951, pp. 92–110.

Robinson, Joan, *Collected Economic Papers*, Oxford, Basil Blackwell, 1951, vol. 1.

Robinson, Joan, 'Book review', *Economic Journal*, vol. 79, September 1969, pp. 581–3.

Robinson, Joan, 'What has become of the Keynesian revolution?', in Milo Keynes (ed.), *Essays on John Maynard Keynes*, Cambridge, Cambridge University Press, 1975, pp. 123–31.

Rotheim, Roy J., 'On the nature of production and contracts in an Arrow–Debreu economy', *Journal of Post Keynesian Economics*, vol. 1, no. 4, Summer 1979, pp. 120–6.

Rotheim, Roy J., 'Keynes' monetary theory of value (1933)', *Journal of Post Keynesian Economics*, vol. 3, no. 4, Summer 1981, pp. 568–85.

Rueff, Jacques, 'The fallacies of Lord Keynes' general theory', *Quarterly Journal of Economics*, vol. 61, May 1947, pp. 343–67.

Rueff, Jacques, 'Reply', *Quarterly Journal of Economics*, vol. 62, November 1948, pp. 771–82.

Rutherford, Malcolm, 'Rational expectations and Keynesian uncertainty: a critique', vol. 6, no. 3, Spring 1984, pp. 377–87.

Salop, Steve, 'Information and monopolistic competition', *American Economic Review Papers and Proceedings*, vol. 66, no. 2, May 1976, pp. 240–5.

Schelling, Thomas C., *Micromotives and Macrobehavior*, New York, W.W. Norton, 1978.

Schlesinger, James R., 'After twenty years: the general theory', *Quarterly Journal of Economics*, vol. 70, no. 4, November 1956, pp. 581–602.

Schumpeter, Joseph, 'Keynes, the economist', in Seymour E. Harris (ed.), *The New Economics: Keynes' influence on theory and public policy*, London, Dennis Dobson, 1948, pp. 73–101.

Schuster, Helmut, 'Keynes' disequilibrium analysis', *Kyklos*, vol. 26, no. 3, 1973, pp. 512–44.

Scitovsky, Tibor, 'The demand-side economics of inflation', in G.D.N. Worswick and J. Trevithick (eds), *Keynes and the Modern World: proceedings of the Keynes Centenary Conference, King's College, Cambridge*, London, Cambridge University Press, 1983, pp. 223–38.

Sen, Amartya K., 'Isolation, assurance and the social rate of discount', *Quarterly Journal of Economics*, vol. 81, February 1967, pp. 112–24.

Shackle, G.L.S., 'Some notes on the monetary theories of the trade cycle', *Review of Economic Studies*, vol. 1, no. 1, October 1933, pp. 27–38.

Shackle, G.L.S., *Uncertainty in Economics*, Cambridge, Cambridge University Press, 1955.

Shackle, G.L.S., *The Years of High Theory: invention and tradition in economic thought 1926–1939*, Cambridge, Cambridge University Press, 1967.

Shackle, G.L.S., *Epistemics and Economics: a critique of economic doctrines*, Cambridge, Cambridge University Press, 1972.

Shackle, G.L.S. 'Keynes and today's establishment in economic theory: a view', *Journal of Economic Literature*, vol. 11, no. 2, June 1973, pp. 516–19.

Shackle, G.L.S., *Keynesian Kaleidics*, Edinburgh, Edinburgh University Press, 1974.

Shackle, G.L.S., 'Sir John Hicks' "IS-LM: an explanation": a comment', *Journal of Post Keynesian Economics*, vol. 4, no. 3, Spring 1982, pp. 435–8.

Shackle, G.L.S., 'Book review', *Economic Journal*, vol. 93, March 1983, pp. 223–4.

Shackle, G.L.S., 'A student's pilgrimage', *Banca Nazionale del Lavoro Quarterly Review*, no. 145, June 1983, pp. 107–16.

Shapiro, Edward, *Macroeconomic Analysis*, New York, Harcourt Brace and World, 1966.

Shatto, Gloria, 'Was Keynes a "Keynesian"?', *Journal of Economics and Business*, vol. 27, no. 1, Fall 1974, pp. 86–8.

Simon, Herbert A., 'Behavioural economics', in John Eatwell, Murray Milgate and Peter Newman (eds), *The New Palgrave: a dictionary of economics*, 4 vols, London, Macmillan, 1987, vol. 1, pp. 221–5.

Siven, Claes-Henric, 'Book review', *Swedish Journal of Economics*, vol. 72, 1970, pp. 93–6.

Skidelsky, R., *The End of the Keynesian Era: essays on the disintegration of the Keynesian political economy*, London, Macmillan, 1977.

Skidelsky, Robert, *John Maynard Keynes Volume One: hopes betrayed 1883–1920, a biography*, London, Macmillan, 1983.

Skidelsky, Robert, 'Keynes' political legacy', in Omar F. Hamouda and John N. Smithin (eds), *Keynes and Public Policy After Fifty Years*, 2 vols, New York, New York University Press, 1988, vol. 1, pp. 3–28.

Snippe, Jan, 'Loanable funds theory versus liquidity preference theory', Institut voor Economisch Onderzoek, University of Groningen, Onderzoek memorandum, no. 134.

Solow, Robert, 'Comment' (on Robert E. Hall), *Brookings Papers on Economic Activity*, 1975, pp. 339–42.

Solow, Robert, 'On theories of unemployment', *American Economic Review*, vol. 70, no. 1, March 1980, pp. 1–11.

Solow, Robert, 'Book reviews', *Journal of Political Economy*, vol. 92, no. 4, August 1984, pp. 784–7.

Solow, Robert, 'Mr Hicks and the classics', *Oxford Economic Papers*, vol. 36 (n.s.), supplement, December 1984, pp. 13–25.

Sowell, Thomas, *Say's Law: an historical analysis*, Princeton, NJ, Princeton University Press, 1972.

Sowell, Thomas, *Classical Economics Reconsidered*, Princeton, NJ, Princeton University Press, 1974.

Spielmann, Rudolf, *The Art of Sacrifice in Chess*, (edited and revised by Fred Reinfeld and I. Horowitz), New York, McKay, 1951.

Stein, Herbert, *The Fiscal Revolution in America*, Chicago, University of Chicago Press, 1969.

Stiglitz, Joseph E., 'Equilibrium in product markets with imperfect information', *American Economic Review Papers and Proceedings*, vol. 69, no. 2, May 1979, pp. 339–45.

Stohs, Mark, 'Uncertainty in Keynes' *General Theory*', *History of Political Economy*, vol. 12, no. 3, pp. 372–82.

Stove, D.C., 'Karl Popper and the jazz age', *Encounter*, vol. 65, June 1985, pp. 65–74.

Struik, Dirk J. (ed.), *Economic and Philosophic Manuscripts of 1844 by Karl Marx*, trans. Martin Mulligan, New York, International Publishers, 1964.

Sutherland, James, *Defoe*, London, Methuen, 1950, 2nd edn.

Thirlwall, A.P. (ed.), *Keynes and Laissez-Faire: the third Keynes seminar held at the University of Kent at Canterbury 1976*, London, Macmillan, 1978.

Thirlwall, A.P., 'Reviews', *Economic Journal*, vol. 98, December 1988, pp. 1256–8.

Tobin, James, 'Money wage rates and employment', in Seymour E. Harris (ed.), *The New Economics: Keynes' influence on theory and public policy*, London, Dennis Dobson, 1948, pp. 572–87.

Tobin, James, 'The fallacies of Lord Keynes' general theory: comment', *Quarterly Journal of Economics*, vol. 62, November 1948, pp. 763–70.

Tobin, James, 'Inflation and unemployment', *American Economic Review*, vol. 62, no. 1, March 1972, pp. 1–18.

Tobin, James, 'How dead is Keynes?', *Economic Inquiry*, vol. 15, October 1977, pp. 459–68.

Torr, Christopher, 'Expectations and the new economics', *Australian Economic Papers*, vol. 23, no. 43, December 1984, pp. 197–205.

Torr, Christopher, *Equilibrium, Expectations, and Information: a study of the General Theory and modern classical economics*, Cambridge, Polity Press, 1988.

Townshend, Hugh, 'Liquidity-premium and the theory of value', *Economic Journal*, vol. 47, March 1937, pp. 157–69.

Townshend, Hugh, 'Reviews', *Economic Journal*, vol. 47, June 1937, pp. 321–6.

Trevithick, James A., 'Keynes, inflation and money illusion', *Economic Journal*, vol. 85, March 1975, pp. 101–13.

Trevithick, James A., 'Money wage inflexibility and the Keynesian labour supply function', *Economic Journal*, vol. 86, June 1976, pp. 327–32.

Trevithick, James A., 'Recent developments in the theory of employment', *Scottish Journal of Political Economy*, vol. 25, no. 1, February 1978, pp. 107–18.

Tsiang, S.C., 'Keynes "finance" demand for liquidity, Robertson's loanable funds theory, and Friedman's monetarism', *Quarterly Journal of Economics*, vol. 94, no. 3, May 1980, pp. 467–91.

Tuchscherer, Thomas, 'Meltzer on Keynes's labor market theory: a review of the *General Theory*'s second chapter', *Journal of Post Keynesian Economics*, vol. 6, no. 4, Summer 1984, pp. 523–31.

Upton, Charles and Miller, Merton, *Macroeconomics: a neoclassical introduction*, Homewood, Ill., Richard D. Irwin, 1974.

Varian, Hal R., 'Catastrophe theory and the business cycle', *Economic Inquiry*, vol. 17, 1979, pp. 14–28.

Viner, Jacob, 'Mr Keynes on the causes of unemployment', *Quarterly Journal of Economics*, vol. 51, November 1936, pp. 147–67.

Wan, Henry Y., Jr, *Economic Growth*, New York, Harcourt Brace Jovanovich, 1971.

Weintraub, E. Roy, *Microfoundations: the compatibility of microeconomics and macroeconomics*, Cambridge, Cambridge University Press, 1979.

Weintraub, E. Roy, 'Catastrophe theory and intertemporal equilibria', *Economie Appliquée*, vol. 33, no. 2, 1980, pp. 303–15.

Weintraub, E. Roy, 'Uncertainty and the Keynesian Revolution', reproduced in John Cunningham Wood (ed.), *John Maynard Keynes: critical assessments*, 4 vols, London and Canberra, Croom Helm, 1983, vol. 4, pp. 152–68.

Weitzman, Martin L., 'Increasing returns and the foundations of unemployment theory', *Economic Journal*, vol. 92, December 1982, pp. 787–804.

Wells, Paul, 'Modigliani on flexible wages and prices', *Journal of Post Keynesian Economics*, vol. 2, no. 1, Fall 1979, pp. 82–93.

Wible, James R., 'The rational expectations tautologies', *Journal of Post Keynesian Economics*, vol. 5, no. 2, Winter 1982–83, pp. 199–207.

Wonnacott, Paul, *Macroeconomics*, Homewood, Ill., 1978, rev. edn.

Wood, John Cunningham, *John Maynard Keynes: critical assessments*, 4 vols, London and Canberra, Croom Helm, 1983.

Worswick, George David Norman (ed.), *The Concept and Measurement of Involuntary Unemployment*, London, Allen and Unwin, 1976.

Worswick, George David Norman and Trevithick, James (eds), *Keynes and the Modern World: proceedings of the Keynes Centenary Conference, King's College, Cambridge*, London, Cambridge University Press, 1983.

Yeager, Leland B., 'The Keynesian diversion', *Western Economic Journal*, vol. 11, 1973, pp. 150–63.

Young, Warren, *Interpreting Mr Keynes: the IS-LM enigma*, Cambridge, Polity Press, 1987.

Zeeman, E.C., 'On the unstable behaviour of stock exchanges', *Journal of Mathematical Economics*, vol. 1, 1974, pp. 39–49.

Author index

Subject index